'A fitting testimony to three brave women . . . powerful, disturbing, yet full of hope. Read it to share their strength.'
Norah Gibbons, Barnardos

'A most graphic insight into the evil and horrors of child sex abuse. The story of the Kavanagh sisters is sad, shocking, traumatic and at times almost unbelievable. That they survived and are now willing and able to publicly share their experiences is a most wonderful achievement. This book is inspirational and uplifting.'
John Lonergan

D1417872

Publisher's Statement

In order to protect the privacy of numerous individuals,
names and identifying details have been changed
throughout this book.

Click, Click

Three Irish Sisters.
A True Story of Abuse.

**Joyce, June and Paula Kavanagh
with Marian Quinn**

HACHETTE
BOOKS
IRELAND

First published in 2011 by Hachette Books Ireland
First published in paperback in 2012 by Hachette Books Ireland
Copyright © 2011 Joyce, June and Paula Kavanagh with Marian Quinn
Copyright Foreword © 2011 Moya Doherty

1

The rights of the individual contributors to be identified as the Authors of the Work have been asserted by them in accordance with the Copyright, Designs and Patents Act 1988.

All rights reserved. No part of this publication may be reproduced, stored in a retrieval system, or transmitted, in any form or by any means without the prior written permission of the publisher, nor be otherwise circulated in any form of binding or cover other than that in which it is published and without a similar condition being imposed on the subsequent purchaser.

A CIP catalogue record for this title is available from the British Library.

ISBN 978-1-444-72540-7
UK ISBN 978-1-409-10107-9

Typeset in Caslon by redrattledesign.com

Printed and bound in Great Britain by Clays Ltd, St Ives plc

Hachette Books Ireland policy is to use papers that are natural, renewable and recyclable products and made from wood grown in sustainable forests. The logging and manufacturing processes are expected to conform to the environmental regulations of the country of origin.

Hachette Books Ireland
8 Castlecourt Centre
Castleknock
Dublin 15
Ireland

A division of Hachette UK Ltd, 338 Euston Road, London NW1 3BH
www.hachette.ie

This book is dedicated to Laura Laffen.
Her strength and courage in telling the truth set us
on our own journey of self-discovery.

Contents

Narrator's Role

When Joyce, June and Paula asked me to help them with their book, they had already spent many years writing, putting their thoughts together and finding ways to tell their story. They had worked with other people over the years but, for various reasons, the book telling their story was never completed. They felt they needed someone to give them direction, keep them focused and help them stay on track. And because I love them all dearly, I can say they were right!

We worked together for over two years and, during this time, we became more clear about what was needed to bring the book to fruition, and what role I could play in supporting this.

Much of what I brought to the process was related to editing and proofreading. After the three sisters had written a chapter or section, they would meet to discuss it. Then I would read their work, and the four of us would meet to agree any changes and what section should be focused on next. We met almost every month for two years to review our work and identify gaps in the story and, on two occasions, we took short residential breaks. The first of these trips gave us an intensity and focus which had been missing previously, and the writing became more emotional as a consequence of this trip.

It became apparent early on that a chronological approach to telling this painful yet inspiring story wouldn't work, and so the structure of using retrospective memories alongside current dialogue emerged. You will be brought back to the sisters' childhood and then sat with them as they discussed what you have just read. The book enables the women to explore their memories with you, to analyse their emotions, explain their behaviours and, ultimately, to heal. The dialogue chapters were written following many hours of discussion with the sisters, and they are verbatim accounts of these long evenings spent together, the only change being that in writing up the sessions, we omitted a lot of the swearing!

Perhaps the most important function I fulfilled was as a facilitator for these discussions. When we first began working together, each of the sisters had been through various therapeutic processes, and had spent a great deal of time writing, so the themes and content of the book were very clear to them. However, they each struggled with elements of their memories, and found it difficult to stay in the past and immerse themselves in their abusive experiences. For very obvious reasons, they were anxious to return to the present. The emotion and power of this book comes from the fact that, with support, encouragement and incredible courage, they each took themselves back there, relived the pain and hurt, and delved deeply into the past.

Helping them with this process by asking probing questions, returning to memories which they had skipped over or dismissed, and challenging them to go to uncomfortable places was my function. At times, it was incredibly difficult as I watched three women I admire and hold dear in such terrible pain, yet I needed to stay focused on my task of extracting the emotions, framing the experience. There were, of course, also times when we laughed from the pit of our bellies and until our cheeks ached. We also drank too much!

Ultimately, my participation in bringing this book to completion has given me far more than I could ever have brought to the process. I have witnessed three amazing women find each other and themselves; I have been part of a journey which most of us cannot begin to imagine, and am so thankful to be part of the destination. I have been embraced by a family of honest, funny, generous people, and have the friendship of three women whom I admire and love. And I have played a part, albeit peripheral, in bringing a story to life which we all believe will bring hope and solace to others who have experienced abuse and pain.

I am deeply grateful to have had the opportunity to know Joyce, June and Paula at such an intimate level, and to have been part of their story.

Marian Quinn

Foreword

The three sisters, Joyce, June and Paula, three exceptional sisters, three extraordinary women, came into my life in the late summer of 1992.

I was then working as a Producer/Director in RTÉ Current Affairs on a documentary series entitled *Tuesday File*. Up to that point, RTÉ programmes on child abuse always had the interviewee's face hidden, voice distorted. The shame of telling the story, the power of the pain, the reluctance to reveal pierced hearts, kept the reality distant, hidden through a hazy lens.

I wanted to make a truthful, powerful programme on the horrors of child abuse. I hoped to persuade someone to reveal themselves to camera, to look directly into the lens, to make eye contact with the viewer so as to shine a light on their face, their story, their life and their pain. In the Ireland of the early 1990s this was a big ask but I set about the search with reporter Miriam Fitzsimons. It was then we met the three sisters, Joyce, June and Paula.

There is little that would prepare you for the whirlwind of energy that is the Kavanagh sisters. Laughter, language (mostly bad), cigarette smoke, camaraderie, care, humour, honesty. We instantly connected. I was overwhelmed by their straightforwardness, their absence of agenda, their strong yet simple desire to help others, their clarity of purpose. And yet, at odds with my hope for the series, I found myself attempting to dissuade them from stepping forward into full scrutiny. They had suffered enough and I needed to be sure they understood the implications of their brave decision.

The three sisters were not for turning. They had made their decision, were apprehensive but clear-headed in their commitment.

The lights were switched on, the camera rolled and the sound recorded as they unfolded the most horrendous catalogue of abuse carried out by a father on his three daughters. That abuse ripped into their childhood, their adolescence, their young adulthood, across twenty long years, two terrible decades.

Despite the attempted injunction by their imprisoned father, the documentary was aired on RTÉ in October 1992, with the support of Peter Feeney, Editor of Current Affairs, and John Masterson, Series Producer, *Tuesday File*.

The sisters were lauded, the programme won a Jacob's Award early the following year and Joyce, June and Paula were nominated as Women of the Year.

We went our separate ways until seventeen years later an email pops up on my computer screen from Joyce Kavanagh. The book was being written. We meet again. Age and time has but enriched the three sisters. Laughter, language (mostly bad) cigarette smoke, camaraderie, care, humour, honesty . . . once more and with feeling.

The first draft of the book – without a title – lands with me in March 2010. It sits on my desktop for weeks, yet I am reluctant to read those words again, those sentences which, when strung together in a certain way, bring you to a sickening place. I am home alone on St Patrick's Day and I face the challenge.

Once again I am punch-drunk with the putrid pain, their putrid pain. Childhood memories. Paula on the day of her First Communion brutally raped in her white Communion dress by her father. Joyce at six years of age, the promise of a new bike, ripped apart and raped. June at the age of eight buggered by her father. June at age eleven raped by her father as her friend lay sleeping beside her during a summer holiday trip. And the childhood memories go on, and on, and on.

Yet through the shadow-image of the child the woman emerges.

Those three strong sisters challenged their father, took him to the High Court and imprisoned him for life.

Those three strong sisters bucked the system and went public on television with their stories.

Those three strong sisters took up full-time studies in alternative medicine, June and Joyce going on to do BA Degrees in Community Development and Leadership and Paula a BSc Degree in Leisure Management.

Those three sisters every day give back to the community and to the system. A community and a system that failed them.

The potent personalities of the Kavanagh sisters are a heady mix; as daughters, sisters, mothers, friends they cut an incredible swathe through life. They are deeply bonded together in pain and in joy. They laugh easily, deeply, loudly. They slag each other mercilessly. Their savage black humour sneaks through *Click, Click* as they describe their search for a 'cure' while engaging in group counselling.

Their commitment to writing their book took them together back to those days in that labyrinthine, dismal dwelling in Ballyfermot, to the misery of those childhood memories, where they shared so much together, knowing they had to protect each other but also knowing they had to protect themselves.

For the three sisters there was no fairy godmother; the system failed them utterly – home, school, hospital, church. Yet they have overcome, they have taught us so much about survival, hope, joy, love, friendship, sisterhood.

Three remarkable women; three remarkable sisters, Joyce, June and Paula.

Moya Doherty, June 2011

Why Now?

March 2011

'It's been a long time coming, hasn't it?'

June thumbs her copy of the publishing contract which arrived this morning. Sitting around Joyce's kitchen table, the three sisters have been scrutinising the document for the past couple of hours, and their initial euphoria has subsided into reflection, as they each consider how they finally managed to get here.

'I did that creative writing course in 1998,' says Paula, lighting a new cigarette. 'That's what got us started on the book, so it's been almost fifteen years. That's hard to believe isn't it?'

'Jaysus, I won't be admitting that to too many people,' exclaims Joyce, as she places a fresh pot of tea on the table. 'That's incredible. What have we been doing all that time?'

'Ah come on, in fairness, we've been busy,' Paula says defensively. 'You two had children, and we all started various education courses and new jobs, and I wasn't able to write the book and go to college, so it was just about timing for me.'

'I remember the day of the court case,' says Joyce, 'when we were all celebrating in the pub after Da was convicted. It was like something you'd see on the TV except it was happening to us; the excitement, the *feeling that we had done something really important, and I knew what a special moment it was. I thought then we should write our story, try and capture the feeling of the day. So the intention was there from the outset. It just took us a while to get here!'*

'*I don't think it was just about finding the time though,' says June. 'We needed the time and space to reflect on each piece we worked on, and feel the impact it had on our lives. Writing about our memories forced us to really acknowledge how devastated and disconnected we were from the feelings about what we had experienced. We needed to think about it, heal. All those breaks we took from writing the book, the times we put it away for months on end – that was necessary, that was survival. And initially, we focused on the technical aspects, the grammar, not the content of what we were writing. That wasn't by mistake, was it? There's been a big shift for all of us, especially in recent years. We have all healed; we know each other better, and ourselves. Look,' she laughs as Joyce places a plate of sandwiches on the table, 'we even eat when we're working on the book now. Remember how for years we weren't able to eat when we were writing?'*

'*No, we just ate the smokes!' comments Paula.*

'*Well some things don't change,' Joyce laughs, as she lights up a cigarette.*

'*I think our involvement in education has been a huge part of the way we've written, and what it's meant to us,' June continues. 'It's given us a big-picture perspective, a world view, and an ability to process things differently, to understand things differently. I feel like all that counselling and holistic healing and talking has all started to integrate; it is a part of who I am now. And isn't that part of why we started this whole thing anyway? To improve how we live with the abuse.' She taps the contract lightly, sending a scurry of ash flickering across the table. 'When we did that RTÉ documentary,' she continues, 'and were nominated for Women of the Year, the awards ceremony was a huge awakening for me. I will never forget*

Moya Doherty when they announced that the first female helicopter pilot had won. I obviously looked at her blankly – you know me!' Her siblings laugh, imagining the innocence of June's smile. 'I was just thinking about the fact that we'd been picked up in a limo, and had had our hair and nails done, and that I loved my new dress! How fuckin stupid am I? I was so embarrassed that I hadn't thought about winning or losing. that I had been concerned with such superficial things. That's the first time I remember feeling like a child in a grown-up world, with no understanding of how things work, and I really wanted to fix that. So getting a better perspective, understanding the big picture, that's been really important to me.'

'And do you think you have that now?' asks Joyce.

'I'm getting better, but I'm not there yet. I reckon that's a long journey for me.'

'You're right about the process, though, June,' says Paula. 'We probably did need to give it that time. I mean, when we started writing, it was very different from the way it's been in the past couple of years, wasn't it? It was shocking actually, so upsetting, having to listen to what each of you went through. There seemed to always be something worse in one of your stories. No matter how bad I thought it was for me, I could never fully comprehend the extent of what Da did.'

'Well, we had never talked in any detail about our experiences, had we?' says Joyce. 'So it was bound to be a shock. I know June and I had admitted to each other ages before that he had abused us, but we only ever discussed it when we were pissed, and it was always in very vague terms. So sharing the kind of detail we have, that was new for all of us.'

'It's funny,' says Paula, 'how we always saw something worse in each other's stories. We are so ready to undermine ourselves; we even look for someone to outdo us in the abuse!'

'But I always felt we were doing something really important. I

felt good when we were writing, even though I spent half the time crying,' says June.

'I know part of the motivation for the book was about ourselves and our healing,' says Joyce. 'We all knew counselling hadn't done what we had expected or hoped, but it was also about highlighting the justice system, and how we had been treated by it. I know I really wanted to make it better for anyone coming after us.'

'When RTÉ made that documentary about us, when was that, Paula?' asks June.

'1992.'

'Yeah, well do you remember how we thought that would change the world? We thought, once that came out, things would never be the same again, that abusers would be named and shamed, that people would come forward in their droves to share their experiences. But it didn't do what it was meant to, and I was so disappointed by the impact it had, or rather the fact that it didn't influence anything. So writing the book seemed like an obvious next step.'

'I thought it would stop people abusing, because they would know they could be prosecuted years after the abuse had happened,' says Paula. 'That's what was so important about our case. They accepted that you could still speak up about child abuse as an adult and have your story heard. Our court case set a precedent about the statute of limitations, you know, how long after the abuse you can take a case, so I really believed it opened doors for people to prosecute when they were ready.'

'Joyce, what are you doing?'

The two women stop and watch their older sister rummaging about in the corner of the kitchen. Joyce empties out a large cardboard box which she pulls out from under the CD player, and is scattering sheets of paper around, clearly looking for something.

'Looking for our mission statement!' she declares.

'Jaysus, I forgot about that,' laughs June. 'That was a long time ago.'

'Here it is.' She waves a typed sheet over her head, visibly delighted. '"August 2007", it says here. So that's recent enough. Ah, Christ, listen to this.' She takes a moment to control her giggles. 'The book will be published when we're somebodies.'

The three sisters roar laughing.

'Well that's a load of rubbish anyway. You'd better not let the publishers see that or they might change their minds about the contract!'

'Go on,' says Paula. 'What other gems did we have in there?'

'Actually, it's not bad,' says Joyce, looking up over her glasses. She holds up the sheet and reads out the sisters' aspirations. '"It will demonstrate that we have come out of the shit, that the abuse doesn't define who you are. We want to help people by:

- *Recognising there is life after abuse*
- *Describing how the counselling gets integrated into how we live our lives*
- *Reassuring people that who they really are, that the qualities they have, can still emerge, despite the abuse*
- *Understanding that the process is the important thing, not the goal*
- *Seeing the importance of the journey, not the outcome*
- *Knowing that it's not a quick fix, it's a process*
- *Not allowing the experience to limit you."'*

The room is silent as the women reflect on their work, their lives, a possible future of change.

'Wow,' says Paula. 'That's not bad. Well, girls, if we give any small part of that to anybody out there, we'll have done a great job. I think we should all be very proud.'

Introduction

We are three of ten children born to Kevin Kavanagh and Joyce Upcott. We were reared in Ballyfermot, Dublin, in the 1960s and 1970s. Ballyfermot at that time was a strange mix of poverty alongside an incredible sense of community.

We all remember the shame of going to the soup kitchen, despite the fact that, or perhaps because, we knew everyone else there. At least once a week, we would take turns pushing a buggy down to the 'gur house' as it was known, with a big pot and a rattly lid, because the pot would be too heavy to carry home. Even though we had more than others, our family had days when the shillings and the pennies simply ran out. With ten children to feed, there was no option but to shoulder the shame.

The weekly bath on a Saturday night was the only time we received a change of clothes, and it was of course timed for us to be clean and presentable going to mass the next day. Three of us at a time would squeeze into the bath, fighting to avoid being the last group into what would have become dirty, lukewarm water.

Monday mornings would see a trail of women at the bus stop taking their husbands' suits to the pawn shop in town, offering them a way to get through the week until the wages were brought home on Friday, and the suit could be retrieved for another weekend.

Despite this, our memories of growing up are largely happy. We spent hours playing on the wide, empty streets – there were so few cars that road safety was never a worry. Games were simple: hopscotch and skipping for the girls; red rover, kick the can and rounders if the boys joined in, and all of us taking turns to swing off a huge rope thrown over the top of the lamppost, yelling at the tops of our voices as we flew across the road, with not a care in the world, unless a garda car drove by, then we would all run away, squealing with laughter and feigned fear.

There was very little crime at that time. Doors were left open, or a key would hang on a piece of string inside the letter box. There was a sense of community parenting, where any adult would feel it completely appropriate to give us a clatter over the head for being cheeky or stepping out of line. You'd never dream of complaining about it, knowing this would only draw attention to the bad behaviour, probably resulting in another wallop!

Despite the age difference between the three of us, we spent a lot of time together outside the house. Of course, the older ones bossed the younger ones, but they looked out for them too. Teenagers played with little ones, and there wasn't the kind of age segregation you see now. Joyce was always in the thick of organising activities for everyone, so June and Paula were included in these events: picnics in the field at the back of the house; putting on a play; building a house by making bricks from old sweet packets stuffed with mud, or holding a massive rounders game. Being outside the house allowed us all the space to breathe and relax, so we relished and extended every moment we could.

They were very hard times on women – although we didn't realise it until we ourselves experienced the deadening of spirit that comes with an expectation that we would aspire to nothing beyond the home and children – where men made the decisions and women managed the consequences; where women donned slippers and headscarves as soon as they were married, no longer having the motivation or energy to take an interest in themselves.

We had a grocery shop, and later a small textile workshop, so there was always money coming in, which was very unusual in that community. We were the first in our neighbourhood to have a car, a TV, a phone, and we got the first of every new toy that came out, but there was only ever one between the ten of us – one bike, one pogo stick, one pair of stilts, one space hopper. What money came into the house didn't last long because our father spent it on mad stuff: drum kits, a fur coat for our mother who never left the house, a piano. He would get these grand ideas which never went anywhere. He spent a fortune every week buying comics for us all. We were the only ones in school to get *Bunty*, *Twinkle* and *Mandy* regularly, and the boys received theirs when our father had read them.

Everyone thought we were loaded, but we were struggling just the same as everyone else. Most of our clothes were bought from the market lady who called round each week with a pram loaded with dresses. Occasionally, we were treated to a shopping trip to Thomas Street, where one of Da's friends had a market shop. We always got a green hair ribbon for St Patricks' Day and a yellow one for Easter. We rarely had matching socks or nice underwear, since these were shared and handed down until they were yellow and threadbare.

The shop was obviously a huge temptation for children, but we were never allowed to have the good stuff. We could only have margarine on our bread, not butter, and corned beef instead of ham.

Da bought the house in the early 1960s, because of the garage space at the side which he renovated and made into the shop (and later extended for the factory). It cost £1,100, an astronomical price at the time, and he borrowed money from the bank to buy it, which would have been unusual at the time. He always had big ideas, and saw the house as an opportunity to make money. In fairness, he was right, although the house was in a terrible state when he bought it and we heard after we had moved in that it was haunted.

Initially, Da bought a van and drove around Ballyfermot, selling cut-price groceries from it. Bags of four or six spuds, individual cigarettes, a dozen tea bags – small units of the staples were the most popular. No one could afford to buy in bulk and Da capitalised on that. Like many other communities, Ballyfermot was built and populated with few facilities for the thousands of residents. There were few local shops, no public transport and very few people had access to a car, so the mobile shop was a great idea. Da got bored with it after a while though, and, for some time, it was just left parked outside the house. That's when Ma took it over, selling from the back of the immobile van, and, in time, the garage was converted into a proper shop. It kept her busy from early morning until dinnertime, when she would take over in the house, cooking, cleaning and looking after us all. The shop was open from nine until eight, and at one stage even stayed open until midnight, so our mother worked hard and long and physically wasn't very available to us. Emotionally, she was also incredibly distant, possibly even cold, and we have few memories of warmth or affection from her, although we have in recent years come to have some understanding of this. We all worked in the shop, before and after school, and, despite the hard work, we were always glad of an opportunity to be with her.

As the shop became less of a responsibility for Da, he developed a factory at the back of the house to make soft toys. It was more of a large shed really, and the three of us worked in it for many years. It was a thriving business in the 1970s, and gave employment to almost all our siblings, so that even the older ones, having moved out of the family home, were around as we grew up.

Swearing was a natural and integral part of how we communicated from a very young age. Everyone swore, all the time. Christian names were rarely used, but rather you would be called by any number of insults: cunt, gee bag, bollox. Of course, we didn't know these words were offensive then. Our mother, who was born and reared in England, never swore, apart from a couple of very significant occasions, which you will hear about. Strangely, though, she never told us off for swearing, or tried to discourage it in any way. She had bigger fish to deal with.

Our father sexually abused all three of us. It started when we were aged around four or five and stopped at different times and in different circumstances for each of us. The experience of abuse continues to shape and influence us, but through talking, sharing and writing, we have found the strength and courage to live our lives with love, enthusiasm and energy.

Given the number of people in the house, and the size of the house, it is incredible, even to us, that this abuse went undiscovered. The layout of the house in some ways allowed for this complicity. It was an old house that was added onto over the years, resulting in something of a maze of rooms which provided plenty of opportunity for concealment. Entering the house, straight from the footpath, you went down two steps to a long narrow hallway. It was dark and unwelcoming; the first door on your left was a bedroom, which was originally the older boys' bedroom. Farther along the hall, on the right-hand side, was a small sitting room, which we called the parlour. That's a very grand name for a small room with a fire, where Ma used to sit and do her knitting. At the end of the hallway was the door into a small, rectangular room about twelve feet by eight, which we called the dead room, because it never had any purpose except to get from one end of the house to the other. You had to walk through it to get to the bedrooms, kitchen or factory, and despite the fact that there were chairs and a table in it, none of us ever used it. When we were very young, we used to eat there, but, as we got older, we stopped using it. It had a glass door which was regularly broken on Sunday afternoons when Da fought with the boys about whose turn it was to mind the shop, so eventually we all felt there was a better place to have meals.

As you went through the dead room, there was a door on the right-hand side that took you into the shop. This was where Ma spent most of her time, and while all of us took turns helping her or minding the shop, it was always her space.

Another door from the dead room led into the kitchen, which was small and, although it never had any seating, it was where we always seemed to congregate, over copious pots of tea. The bathroom was off the kitchen, and the sitting room behind it was a large, square room, with plenty of space and lots of furniture. Armchairs were strewn around the edges of the room, and a large dining table took central place. The TV, a hugely important feature of our childhood, sat in the corner, directly opposite Da's chair. The rest of us would argue about getting the seat closest to the TV, or sitting near the gas fire, but everyone knew which was Da's place. Despite attempts to make it warm and welcoming, this was always a depressing, cold room.

Back in the dead room, stairs led to three upstairs bedrooms. The staircase was narrow and steep, and was some distance from the sitting room, factory and shop. Ma and Da's bedroom was at the top of the stairs. Unusually, the staircase led directly into their room, with no door for privacy, though, as children, this never struck us as strange. There was a high dresser against the wall at the end of the bed, a wardrobe in a corner and very little else. On the right was the girls' bedroom, and the younger boys' bedroom was on the left, both doorways leading directly from our parents' room, meaning that access to our rooms required going through theirs. The rooms were sparse and cold, each furnished with only two wardrobes, a large cardboard box for shoes, and two beds, so sharing was always required.

There were unwritten rules in this house, unstated expectations of us, which supported the abuse, made us complicit in it and protected its discovery. From an early age, we understood that you made noise when you left or entered a room and you never went up the stairs without being heard. Of course these 'rules' were never discussed, they were just known, implicitly. It never occurred to us to discuss them with each other or any of our friends. For many years, we struggled to understand this acceptance of ours, our compliance with the dynamic our father created. Now we know this was how we survived.

Ours is a strange and painful story to tell. It is a hard one to read, but we hope that, ultimately, it will prove to be uplifting. Our siblings have their own story to tell and we hope they find their voices in time.

This is our story.

Chapter 1: Ma Knows

Paula

Tuesday, 10 January 1989

Bang, bang, bang, on the bedroom door.

'It's eight o'clock. Get the fuck up. You'd better be in work in ten minutes or I'll fuckin come in there and kill ya.'

God, he's off again, it's still dark outside. I hate getting up. Imagine, at twenty-five I'm still living at home and working in the factory making soft toys for Da. Just five more minutes I think as I pull the covers up over my head.

Bang, bang, bang.

'Get up now or I'll break down the fuckin door!'

I'd better get up. If I don't, he'll kick the door in again. I put on a tracksuit and jumper. It's freezing this morning. I go to the bathroom and barely throw water on my face when I hear bang, bang, bang.

'That's it, it's gone half eight. I'm docking twenty pounds out of your wages. If you're not out here in one minute, you're fuckin sacked, you lazy cunt.'

He only docked me a tenner yesterday. I'll have to really watch the bastard today. I sit on the edge of the bath for another five minutes, knowing this really annoys him. I hate him. What a way to start every day. Another day of clock-watching, waiting for 5 p.m.

'So you decided to fuckin come in, did you?'

I ignore him and walk into the factory, keeping my head down, focusing on the floor which is barely visible because of the off-cuttings, loose threads and bits of filling, cigarette ash, and pieces of cardboard.

I get the usual smells of damp, stale cigarette smoke and body odour. The last belongs to Da – the dirty, smelly bastard. The noise in the room is very loud as the clatter from the sewing machines tries to outdo the sound of Gay Byrne on the badly tuned-in radio.

I take up my usual position at the cutting table for the morning, knowing that after lunch I have to go on to the finishing, which requires hand-sewing the hole at the back of the teddy and brushing off the loose filling. I begin checking the order list to see what's on for today, before I start to cut. I don't mind cutting because the machine I use is even louder than the sewing machines, which means I don't have to talk to anyone and no one talks to me.

I hate this place. I'm working with Ma, Da and two of my brothers, David and Leonard. David still lives at home and is the youngest of the family. Leonard is four years older than me and still works in the factory, despite having moved fifteen miles away to Kilcock when he got married. Leonard is very creative and a brilliant artist, but Da is always shouting at him and calling him a lazy bollox, so he doesn't do any more than he has to; he's as miserable as me. I suppose it could be worse, the whole ten of us could be here, and that would be some nightmare. The work is boring and he's on my back all the time. I can't relax around him because I never know when he'll explode or what will trigger him off. There is constant fear and uncertainty as we all struggle to avoid being at the receiving end of his latest outburst.

I stand with my back to the others, which means I don't have to look at Da. I'm aware of his presence because I can smell him. I breathe through my mouth to avoid smelling the sweat and urine that permeates the room. The fat fucker never changes his clothes, which are permanently stained, because the lazy bastard won't even shake himself when he goes to the loo. He has constant stubble, hair growing out of his ears and is gummy because his teeth usually remain on the dresser beside his bed.

It's three o'clock and I'm desperate for a cup of tea, but I'm afraid that if he sees me, he'll dock me more money and I can't afford to lose any more this week. I chance it while I'm waiting for work.

'What do you think you're doing? Do you think I should pay you for standing around all day doing nothing, you lazy cunt? Get back out to work, and you needn't think you're going anywhere tonight.'

The only thing keeping me going is knowing that I'm coaching the girls tonight for our basketball match at the weekend. What am I going to do now? I can't let the girls down. How can I say I'm grounded at age twenty-five? Fuck him anyway. I storm back out to the factory and begin working again as I think through my ever-increasing list of ways to kill the fucker.

'What the fuck are you doing? I said brush the fuckin thing, not tiddle it. At this rate the order will never be finished.'

Fuck you!, I shout. But only in my head, only ever in my head. I want to spit in his face as I scream Fuck You to the bastard. But I can't. He'd kill me. I keep my head down and spend the rest of the afternoon plotting how I can get out tonight.

Basketball is all I have to keep me sane, a place outside the madness of this house. I love basketball so much that I would risk him hitting me rather than miss the training session. It's a place where I'm in control. I'm respected for the work I do. The love I have for the sport absorbs my energy and allows me to forget about home. In basketball, no one criticises me, and people call me by my name. It wasn't until I started school at four years of age that I realised my name was Paula, not 'cunt' or 'maggot'.

Five o'clock on the dot, I take great pleasure in spotting the veins throbbing on his neck as I walk past him into the house, knowing that there is nothing he can do. I head for the kitchen to start dinner. The kitchen is one of the many ad hoc extensions that Da has added to the house over the years which produced a warren of small dysfunctional rooms. I begin dinner whilst Ma drops my brother Leonard home.

I'm fed up cooking the same crap each night, so I'm trying a new recipe this evening. An hour and a half later, I place a bubbling golden brown lasagne with a fresh crispy salad on the table, chuffed with myself as I put his plate in front of him because I know how mad he gets if he's not served first.

'What's this foreign muck? You expect me to eat this shit in my own house?' He swipes the plate with the back of his hand and it and several cups smash to the floor. He stands up, throwing back his chair, his stomach bouncing off the table as he leaps up shouting 'I'm only the fuckin boy here.'

As he plonks himself on the couch, in front of the TV, I clean up his mess and take my dinner to my room, as I always do.

I've learned to avoid watching him eat because he chews his food with his mouth open like a cow chewing cud, wipes his greasy hands on the tablecloth, drips food down his front and forgets to put his teeth in. He farts, belches and picks his nose throughout every meal.

When all the washing up is done and the house is clean, I'm ready to make my escape. I sneak to the front door and gently open the latch. I can hear him typing his memoirs or children's fantasy stories, which will never get finished as he will lose interest halfway through, as he always does. I close the door behind me and breathe a sigh of relief as I hurry down the road before he realises I'm gone.

The two hours of coaching go too quickly. Here, I am unrecognisable from the coward who lives in that house. Here, I feel free, I have a voice. I'm good at something. I laugh, have fun. I know I shouldn't but I go for a drink with the girls after the session, but after one drink panic is setting in and I'm anxious to get home. My friend Margaret offers me a lift which I gladly accept, but as we pull up outside the house, I'm mortified to see him standing at the door. The fear of him embarrassing me in front of Margaret has me sweating and desperate to get out of the car.

'Are you all right? Do you want me to come in with you? He won't do anything in front of me.' Margaret knows how difficult he can be. I need her to go before he does anything.

'No. I'm fine. See you tomorrow.' I wave her off and my thoughts begin to race. I shouldn't have gone for a drink; then he wouldn't have noticed I was out. I'll put on a brave face and walk past him.

I cross the road and notice that Ma's car is not in the driveway. I wonder where she is. That's it! I'll ask where Ma is. That'll throw him off guard. He'll expect me to be afraid. He won't expect me to ask him anything. I notice he's wearing his dirty green anorak and has my good leather weekend bag resting on the step beside him.

'Where's Ma? Are you waiting for Ma?'

Why isn't he shouting at me? This is worse than getting a wallop. What's he up to?

'Your Ma knows.'

My stomach churns and my legs go numb. They tremble as I run my sweaty palms over my tracksuit. My head pounds as I try to move my paralysed legs to get away, to find a place to think. I know instinctively what he means. I'm confused. He's standing in the doorway, so even if I *could* move, where would I go? He steps aside, making way for me and, as I pass him, I wonder if I'll reach the kitchen. My legs are trembling, my heart is racing, my head is thumping. What will I do? What happened?

I go from one room to another to find someone to tell me what's going on, but can find no one. Where is everyone? I'm convinced someone must be here – this house is never empty. I don't want to accept that I'm here alone.

Joyce! That's it. I'll ring Joyce. She's bound to know what's going on. She's always calm and level-headed. It feels like a lifetime before anyone answers the phone.

'Hello.'

'Hello, Joyce. What's going on?'

'Is he there?'

Just then, I hear the phone downstairs click.

'Yes.'

'I'll have to ring you back in a while.'

The phone goes dead. I know she couldn't talk to me with him listening. What will I do now? I go downstairs and he's back at the front door. I'm desperate to know what's going on.

I'm panicking and my hands are shaking. I don't know what to do. I go back to the sitting room. The television is turned off, a dead silence hangs in the air. Silence is not a luxury this house has ever known. I need to get out but I can't. He's at the door. I can't use the phone, he'll just pick it up again. I'm trapped.

I light a cigarette and sit on the couch. I need to think. I'm brought back to reality as he enters the room, waving an envelope in his hand. I jump to my feet.

'Tell Leonard to put that cheque in the bank or you'll have no money this week. I'm just waiting for a taxi, so you'll never see me again.'

He leaves the room. Alongside the panic, there's a sense of relief and even excitement at the possibility of him leaving, but I'm concerned that it may not really happen. He has threatened to leave so many times before, usually following one of his temper tantrums, but this time something is different. He's calm, but worried. I wish someone else was here. Where's Ma?

Thinking back, I recall that she had gone out shortly before me and didn't say where she was going. I was so wrapped up in my own escape that I didn't pay any attention, even though it was very unusual.

I hear the front door closing. I want to get up and see if he's gone, but I'm terrified. I wait a few moments then go and check. The door is closed. I run upstairs and look out the window. The taxi is making a U-turn and I can see him sitting in the back. I feel relief as I run down the stairs to finally ring Joyce.

'Hello.'

'Hi, Joyce. What's going on?'

'Is he gone?'

'Yes, he just left in a taxi. Will you just tell me what's going on?'

I sit on the stairs pulling on a cigarette as Joyce quickly fills me in on the events of the day. I hang up the receiver slowly when she finishes and light another cigarette. I don't move for ages, but sit pondering what's happened, and where it will take us. My mind is filled with so many questions, and I am aware of the mixed emotions racing through me – fear, anger, resentment, sadness. And, in spite of all the uncertainty, I know deep in my heart that things will never be the same again.

June

It's seven o'clock in the evening when I finally arrive home from work. I'm tired and fed up as I drag myself up the stairs. I work the day shift in a fast-food restaurant in Baggot Street. My boyfriend Eamonn and I moved in together about five months ago to a one-bedroom flat over a veterinary surgeon's in Malahide. I hear the television on, so Eamonn must be in. He works as a doorman in a nearby nightclub.

We split up for a while and I couldn't believe how devastated I felt, so when he asked me to move in with him, I agreed, unsure of what I was doing but determined not to spend the rest of my life regretting not taking the chance. Leaving Joyce was terribly hard though. I left home to move in with her when she separated from her husband George, and we had the best of times despite not having a bean and her having three kids to rear, but we laughed all day long and made things work for us. So moving in with Eamonn left me torn and guilty about leaving Joyce, but mad to be with him. Even though I'm twenty-seven, this is my first serious relationship, and I'm cautious about committing myself to it, in case I get hurt. Five months on, I know I love him to bits, but he's a lazy bollox and it's driving me mad.

Eamonn is lying on the couch watching *Star Trek*.

'Hello, honey, would you like something to eat? I was just about to start dinner.'

I want to scream at him. Why don't you have dinner ready? I always have it ready for you. Why isn't the flat clean? Why are you sitting on your arse? But we have had so many arguments lately over the same thing that I just don't have the energy.

'Yes, I'm just going to lie down for a while.'

My latest ploy is to not clean up and see how he likes coming home to a filthy flat. I walk by the kitchen and notice dishes piled in the sink. I get another flash of temper. You'd think he would at least clean the dishes in the sink. The bed isn't made and his clothes are all over the floor. I make the bed and lie down. My plan with the cleaning isn't working. He doesn't seem to notice, so the only person affected is me. I feel people look at the place and think it's my job to keep it clean, which drives me mad. I'm right, and I'm not giving in, I tell myself. How will he cook dinner in that kitchen? At least he'll have to wash the dishes.

I doze off and am woken by Eamonn calling me for dinner. The sink is still piled high with dishes. I go into the sitting room where Eamonn is back in front of the TV with his dinner on his lap, so I sit disconsolately at the kitchen table eating my meal, staring at the mound of washing up. I console myself by thinking that at least he cooked the dinner. I've had enough of looking at the mess and know I won't be able to stick it much longer. I decide to have a relaxing bath, but even that requires me giving it a good clean first. I mutter to myself as I scrub off the tide marks.

I am just about to run the bath when there's a knock on the door and, as I walk down the stairs, the familiar smell of animals from the surgery hits me. I must get an air freshener. I open the door and am shocked to find Ma standing there. She never visits anyone.

'Ma, how are you? What are you doing here?' Shit, the place is in bits. Why doesn't anyone call when I've cleaned up? She stands there silently and, as I look at her more closely, I realise she's upset.

'What's wrong, Ma? What is it?'

'I didn't know where else to go. I just have to talk to someone. Is Eamonn in?'

'Yes, but don't worry. We can talk in the kitchen.'

We walk up the stairs. I don't know what to think. The state of the place. What's wrong with her? Why is she here? What does she want to talk to me about? I'm no good at sorting out problems. What if I say the wrong thing? Why didn't she go to Joyce? Everyone always goes to Joyce: she's better at handling problems than I am.

'Sorry about the mess.' I clear a space at the kitchen table for us to sit. 'Would you like a cup of tea?'

'Yes.'

I'm feeling a mixture of fear and panic. What's she going to tell me? She's been crying, her eyes are all puffy. It's rare to see her upset. Eamonn enters the room to see who the visitor is.

'Hi, Mrs Kavanagh.' He looks at her face. 'I'll leave you to talk,' he says, as he heads back to the sitting room.

'Ma, what's wrong?'

She sips her tea, lights a fag and begins to tell me what happened.

'Laura rang me earlier and asked to see me; she told me not to tell anyone. I had no idea what she wanted or why it had to be a secret. I haven't seen her in ages.'

'You mean my cousin Laura? What did she want?' We have so little contact with Da's family lately, I can't understand why his niece would phone Ma. The tears well up in Ma's eyes and she's visibly shaking.

'Laura told me about young Deirdre.' She hesitates. 'Do you remember her?'

'Yes, she's Laura's niece.'

'She's been causing problems at home and has been in trouble with the gardaí. She has her parents' hearts broken. They couldn't understand what the problem was until she confided in her mother.'

Tears are rolling down her face and her voice is quivering. My heart is breaking. I want to hug her, but I can't. I have never hugged her. It would feel too strange and awkward.

'Deirdre tried to kill herself twice!'

Ma is struggling to keep composed. I'm confused. As shocking as this news is, I still don't understand how it's reduced her to an emotional wreck.

'Deirdre's finally told her mother it was because of your father.'

She's now sobbing uncontrollably. My heart is racing and my head thumping. What else does she know?

'What did she come to *you* for? Why did she not talk to Da?'

'Your father's family discussed the situation and Laura was nominated to talk to me. She said, out of respect for me, they have held off acting on this for over a year.'

'Ma, I still don't understand why they came to you.'

'They don't want to press charges. They want him to get help. My God, if he did that to her, who else did he get to? I hope he never went near you girls.' There is a pause as she pulls out a tissue from her sleeve to wipe her eyes. She looks straight at me and asks, 'Did he?'

'Yes.'

The word slips past my lips and hangs in the air. As soon as I have spoken it, fear grips me. I want to take it back, but it's too late. I feel a wall has fallen on my chest. Oh, God, what have I done? The secret I've kept for over twenty years has just been exposed because of my big gob. Joyce will kill me. God will strike me down. What will I do now? I feel panic and terror, and yet there's a huge relief. I didn't know until this moment how much I wanted Ma to know.

Ma is muttering but my head is frantically trying to work out what to do now.

'The bastard! The fuckin bastard!'

I need to be alone to figure out what I've done. How can I get rid of her before I do any more damage? I need space, time to think, to be alone. Most of all I need Joyce; Joyce will know what to do; she'll help me. Joyce has always been the one to fix things, to know what to do, ever since we were children. She's been my best friend all my life, even though she's five years older than me, and I rely on her for so many things, and, right now, I know I can't possibly deal with this.

'Ma, go over to Joyce. I don't think you should go home right now. I don't know what to say to you.'

'Joyce is in work, or I would have gone to her earlier.'

'No, she finishes at seven. She'll be home now.'

'OK, maybe you're right. I can't go home now. I don't know what I'll do if I see the sick bastard.'

We walk to the door.

'I'll phone you in Joyce's later,' I say, as she gets into the car. She looks broken, shrunken somehow. It's only as she pulls away that I realise I shouldn't have let her drive in that state. The tears begin to flow as soon as I close the front door. I want to lock myself away and die. I sit on the bed sobbing and Eamonn comes in.

'What's wrong? What happened?'

I tell him everything.

'Don't worry, honey, it'll be all right. Everything will be OK.'

Eamonn puts his arms around me and I feel huge relief at

not having to explain everything. Thankfully I told him shortly after we met.

'God, I'd better ring Joyce and warn her that Ma's on her way. Do you think I should tell her what I said?'

'Look, I don't think it's important who told her what. Just let her know your Ma is on her way.'

Eamonn hands me change for the pay phone in the hall and, as I walk to it, my legs are shaking. I'm not sure what to say. Joyce will go mad when she knows I told Ma. I bet she wouldn't have been so stupid; she always knows what to say and do in any situation.

'Hello?'

'Paul, it's Auntie June. Will you get your mammy?'

'OK.'

I shift from foot to foot, waiting, desperate to pass this whole mess on to someone else.

'She says she'll ring you back in a few minutes.'

'Paul, will you tell her it's urgent? I have to talk to her now.' Joyce comes on the line.

'Hello, June, what's up?' As soon as I hear Joyce, I begin to cry.

'Joyce, Ma is on her way over to you and she's very upset.'

'Why?'

'Laura told her Da's been at Deirdre.'

There is a pause before either of us speaks.

'Jaysus, what a mess. Ma must be in a terrible state.'

'Shite, Joyce, I'm sorry. I didn't know what to do, so I sent her over to you. She only came over to me because she thought you were in work.'

'How is she?'

'She's in bits.'

'And you let her get in a car on her own?'

'I know. I'm so stupid. I wasn't thinking.' I feel so guilty. If anything happens to her, I'll never forgive myself for letting her drive off like that.

'It's all right, June, don't worry,' Joyce reassures me; her voice is calming. 'Just get over here as quick as you can. I'll ring Laura.'

The phone goes dead. I feel relieved knowing that Joyce is going to look after things. I wish I had the courage to tell her that I've told Ma about us, but I don't think I can handle her disapproval. Apart from that one time when I was about fourteen, when Joyce spoke to our GP about the abuse, we've only ever talked about it when we were pissed, and even then it's been very superficial, not going into any real details. I can't have that conversation with her now. I'm not ready. I feel terrible. I fill Eamonn in and he hugs me.

'You go and get ready and I'll ring a taxi. Would you like me to come with you?'

'No, I think it should be just family for now. I've no idea what's going to happen. I can ring you if I need you.'

I'm so glad that Eamonn is here – he'd normally be in work by now. I need him more than ever, especially now that I've made the biggest mistake of my life. I'm not ready to have this out there, to talk about it. I have no idea how I'll cope with the inevitable questions, maybe even blame. Oh, Christ, what have I done? I didn't mean to tell her, and I know this is going to have repercussions for all of us.

'The taxi's on its way. It's going to be all right. I'll stay up all night. If you need me, no matter what time, call me.'

The phone rings. I charge down the stairs and grab the receiver, assuming it's Joyce.

'Hello.'

'June?'

Oh, my God, it's him. What the hell is he ringing *me* for?

'Yes.'

'Is your Ma there?'

'No. She's gone.' How does he know she was here?

'What did she say to you?'

'Why?' He's looking for information from me. I feel sick! 'Does she know everything?'

I don't want to answer him. He has no right to put me in this position. This is so wrong.

'Yeah.'

'Even about us?'

I feel repulsed. I think I'm going to vomit. I can feel the bile at the back of my throat. How can he include me in that statement? How can he say 'us', as if we were having an affair? As if I was a willing participant. The bastard. He's making me responsible for this. I won't let him. I could beat him to a pulp with my bare hands, but instead I put all my anger into my reply.

'She knows everything.'

I have to let him know I'm not responsible for this. I won't let him blame me.

'OK. I just want to say goodbye. You won't be seeing me again.' He says it in the saddest tone I have ever heard. This is how he ensures I know how upset he is, to make me feel sorry for him.

There's a pause. He's waiting for me to say something but I can't speak. My heart sinks and I hate him for having this effect on me. I'm devastated he can still do this to me, make me feel sorry for him when all I really want is to be angry, furious with him. I hear the receiver go down. I stand in shock with the phone in my hand. Eamonn arrives in time to catch me as my legs go from under me. He holds me as I sob like a baby. I can't believe the mixed emotions I'm feeling. I feel such pity for the man who fucked up my life. I want to hate him but, right now, I can't. I'm worried about him and can't bear to think of him lonely, on his own. I'm confused by what's going on, how he can affect me like this. I could have stabbed him to death on so many occasions in the past. I hate this man with every bone in my body and yet he has the power to reduce me to this.

The taxi arrives and it's a strange journey. Normally, I would chat away to the driver, but tonight I feel as if I'm on my way to a funeral, except I'm not sure who I'm mourning. The silence is deafening, but unusually comfortable. I have a lot to think about.

Joyce

It's 7.15 p.m. and I'm glad to be home. Audrey, my youngest, runs up and pounces on me as I get out of the car.

'Ma, please can I go to Jennifer's house? Her ma's having a party for her and she said I could go. Ma, please, please can I go?'

'All right, love. Just make sure that you're home by half eight.'

'Ah, Ma, can I stay until nine? Please, Ma, please?'

'OK, go on.' I have just completed a double shift at work at the kebab shop, and I'm due in again at ten. I'm exhausted. I've no energy, so I am glad Audrey has something to do. I turn the key in the door and bump into the child minder.

'Sorry, Joyce, I'm in a rush. See you tomorrow.'

I barely say goodbye as I close the door behind her. I'm delighted to find the place tidy. Derek and Paul are watching television and barely look up as I enter the sitting room.

'Hi, Ma.'

'Have you had dinner?'

'Yeah.'

'What are you watching?'

'*Star Trek*.'

'Have you done your homework?'

'Yeah.'

'Good boys.' Derek is ten years old and very responsible for his age. He really loves being given things to do and takes his jobs seriously. 'Derek, would you mind if I lie down for a while? I'm really tired and I have to go back into work later.'

'No problem.'

'I won't stay long. Just a half hour.'

'Go on, Ma. I'll mind Paul.'

I hate leaving them, but I'll never last until nine, which is their bedtime. I drag myself up the stairs and make for the bed. All I can think of is the pain in my body from standing all day at the hot fryer. I don't bother to undress, just kick my shoes off and lie on the bed. It only feels like minutes later when I wake to Paul shouting up the stairs.

'Ma, June's on the phone.'

I glance at the clock and realise it's 8.30. I didn't mean to sleep this long. It's dark outside. I stumble over clothes on the floor. I really must tidy this room.

'Tell her I'll ring her back in a few minutes.'

'Ma, she says it's urgent.'

God, I just can't handle another conversation about how unsure she is about her relationship right now.

'Hello, June, what's up?'

I hear her crying and feel guilty. She fills me in on what's happened and, as I listen through her sobs and snivels, I instantly go into my fixer mode. No time to feel anything: I just have to sort this out. I hang up. What'll I do? Ma is on the way and I don't know how much time I have. What the hell can I do? Maybe when I talk to Laura, I'll have a better idea. Don't panic, at least not until I know what I have to deal with. Imagine Laura and June letting Ma drive in that condition. I'm furious as I dial Laura's number.

'Laura, it's Joyce. What's going on?'

'Where's your ma?'

'She's on her way over to me. What have you told her?'

Laura tells me about Deirdre, and how she eventually told my mother what Da had been doing. She goes on to say that they won't press charges if Da gets help.

'How was Ma when she left you? What did she say?'

'Joyce, she's very upset. I wanted to go with her, but she wouldn't let me. She said you were in work and she was going to June.' That makes me feel better, knowing Laura did at least consider Ma's condition, but this doesn't look good; it's not going to be easy to fix.

'What'll I do? What'll I say to her when she gets here?'

'Joyce, your ma's in shock. She's very upset. Just give her a hug.'

'OK, Laura, I'd better go.'

I'm so annoyed at her advice that I have to get off the phone. Imagine suggesting that a hug is the answer to this. She breaks Ma's heart and wants me to hug her!

I dial Ma's house number, hoping the phone will be picked up in the shop; I need to speak to Ronnie. My mind is working very fast now. I already have a great plan that will sort this out, temporarily at least. Now, all I have to worry about is Da answering the phone. I hold my breath as the phone rings several times. I'm glad to hear Ronnie's voice. Ronnie is the second oldest, coming soon after Pamela. Pamela is the oldest, born in 1946. She left the house when she was around twenty, so we were ten, five and three at that stage. Pamela was a goddess to the rest of us girls. She appeared so confident and we thought she was like someone who had just stepped off a movie set. Ronnie used to work driving trucks for Da, but they fought the whole time and he got other work, so for a long time we didn't see much of him. He never got on with the old fella, maybe because Ronnie was the oldest boy. He took over the shop a while ago and converted it into a video shop, so we've seen more of him lately. He keeps his distance though, always wary of Da, and you couldn't blame him. I take a deep breath.

'Ronnie, Ma knows about Da. You have to get him out of the house before she goes home.'

'What am I supposed to do?'

'Tell him Ma knows, and he has to leave.'

'I can't do that. If I talk to him, God knows what I might do to him. Get Kevin, he's the only one able to talk to him.'

'How can I get Kevin? He has no phone and I can't get over to Clondalkin to ask him.'

Kevin is the fourth of the ten of us, born in 1951, and we had great fun with him as children. He played cowboys and indians, and hide and seek with us, even though he was older. Unlike most of us, he didn't work in the family business, but in a bakery instead. When he married Anne, though, she ended up working with us as a machinist, so we saw a lot of her and sometimes babysat for them.

'I don't know, Joyce. Phone Tony; he lives near enough to you and should be home from work by now. He could get Kevin for you.'

'All right, see you.'

I'm furious. My plan is messed up now. What if I get the same response from Tony? I dial Tony's number. Tony lives around the corner from me, so I see a lot of him. He is the next oldest after Ronnie and I have a good relationship with him. He used to pay me to clean his shoes and iron his shirts when I was younger. I thought I was so grown up!

I pray he'll do something. My heart beats faster as I wait for him to pick up the phone. Things are going so fast, I can't absorb it all. Tony picks up the phone.

'Tony, I need you to do something quickly.'

'What?'

'Ma knows about Da. She's on her way up to me. I need you to get Kevin and make sure Da leaves the house before Ma goes home.'

'What will I say?'

'I don't know. Tell him Ma knows. I asked Ronnie but he won't do it. He suggested Kevin.'

'OK. Ronnie's right, Kevin is the only one who can talk to Da.'

'So, you'll do it? Kevin can do all the talking.' I know I can rely on Kevin because he operates like me: act first, think later.

'Certainly, chicken. I'm on my way.'

'Thanks, Tony, you're a life saver. Ma's on her way up to me. I have to go.'

As I charge up the stairs to the boys, I thank God for Kevin: he is the only one of the boys who could handle this situation.

If Da's gone, Ma will have some space while we work this out. I can't think any further than that for now. I have to move quickly. I barge into the boys' room.

'Paul, quickly, get ready for bed.'

He must have picked up on the urgency in my voice because I've never seen him respond so quickly.

'Where's Audrey?'

'She's in Jennifer's. Quick as you can, go and get her for me.'

Derek is oblivious to the world, he's so engrossed in his game of He-Man. He has all the little figures lined up on his bed ready for action. He's startled as he looks up at me, sensing something's wrong.

'What's up, Ma?'

'Derek, this is very important. Nanny is on her way up to me. She has a bit of a problem and I need to help her. It's very important that you all go to bed and don't come down the stairs, no matter what.'

'Is she OK? What's wrong with Nanny?'

'I don't really know, son. I just want your help. Nanny won't talk if you're downstairs, so I need you to be quiet as mice.'

'All right, Ma, no problem.'

I know I can rely on him. I run downstairs as Paul and Audrey come into the house.

'Ma, can I stay for another little while?' Audrey asks.

'No, you have school tomorrow. It's time for bed.'

'Ah, Ma, you said that I could stay until nine.'

'I'm sorry, but it's bedtime now. Go up and get ready.'

She stomps up the stairs in a huff. The tears well up in her eyes as she looks back at me from the top of the stairs, hoping I'll give in. I haven't got time to worry about her now, but I feel guilty for going back on my word. I call up after her, promising that Jennifer can sleep over at the weekend. She looks at me and my expression must say it all, because she doesn't ask any more, just turns on her heels and goes to bed.

I'm quickly brought back by a knock on the door. Shit, it's Ma. I take another deep breath and open the front door. Nothing could prepare me for what I see. She looks hollow, empty, standing in the light from the hallway, tears rolling down her swollen, blotchy face. She doesn't even look up, just sighs and reaches for the doorframe.

'Are you all right, Ma?' It's a stupid question. I put my arms around her. I feel like someone has reached into my chest and ripped out my heart. I've only ever seen Ma cry twice before, but nothing like this. She stands frail and weak. The woman I think of as a mainstay suddenly feels so fragile. I wish I could take away her pain and make it all right for her. She is not normally emotional. She has been hurt so many times by Da dominating her and constantly undermining her that she can just switch off. She asks me if I'm all right.

I'm puzzled by her question. She raises her head from my shoulder and looks at me so sorrowfully, waiting for a reply.

'I'm fine, Ma.'

I wonder why she's asking me how I am. It seems like a silly question. What has any of this to do with me? She must feel like she's imposing.

'I'm shattered. I don't know what to think. The fuckin bastard, that's all I know, what a bastard.' She's shrieking now and it's scary seeing her like this. I've never heard her swear before.

'Sit down, Ma, while I make some tea.'

I put on the kettle, keep focused on what I'm doing. It's not easy seeing her in this condition. I struggle to keep it together. I join her in the sitting room with the mugs of tea. Tea and fags have always been the way we deal with any crisis in my family. The room is filled with a deadening silence, which makes me nervous and uncomfortable. I want to put on the radio just to have some noise in the room, but decide not to. Ma sits on the edge of the couch.

'There's no way I can face him now. I'll stab him. I don't think it's easy to stab someone, not like it is in the movies. Knowing my luck, I'd miss.'

'Look, Ma, it's sorted. He won't be there when you go home.'

'Why? How?'

'Kevin has gone down to get him to leave before you get home.'

'Oh, Joyce, you're great. You poor thing. You always get stuck with sorting out the mess. I still want him dead.'

There's an edge to her voice that I've never heard before. I don't know how to respond to her, what to say. Thankfully there's another knock on the door.

'Oh, who's that? I should go,' she says, as always thinking she's in the way.

'Don't be silly. It's probably June.' I pray it's June because she always has something to say; she'll break this awkwardness.

'Are you OK, June?'

I ask it on instinct as I open the door to the sister I feel closest to, but, as I look at her face, I realise she's as bad as Ma. June can keep Ma company while I gather my thoughts.

'Is she all right?' June whispers.

'Not really.'

June goes over to Ma and puts her arms around her. They both cry and I can feel the emotion burning the back of my throat as I watch them. I leave them alone, go into the kitchen and put on the kettle again. I desperately want to join them but I feel someone has to keep a clear head. I don't know who the hell I think I'm kidding because my head is anything but clear, but I suppose I look more in control than them. I make more tea and wonder why everyone thinks I can sort this out. I'm not as strong as they think. As a matter of fact, I feel weak at the moment. I can't even think straight. I don't know how I feel or what I'm supposed to do. I'm not going to think about where this might take us. I'll just stay focused on holding it together. That's what gets me through. Everyone needs me. I wipe away the tears, take a deep breath and go into the room, which by now is filled with smoke.

I sit down and we light one cigarette after the other. June looks dreadful. Her eyes are red and swollen. I wonder how

Kevin's getting on. The phone rings and startles us all. It's Paula and I'm disappointed it's not Kevin.

'Hello.'

'Hello, Joyce. What's going on?'

We don't get a chance to speak as Da picks up the extension. That means he's still there. What is going on? Where is Kevin? I'm worried now. Maybe this won't be sorted out after all; maybe he's refused to go. I tell June and Ma it's a wrong number. Poor Paula, she's dying to know what's going on but I can't tell her while he's listening in.

There's another knock on the door. Thank God, it's Kevin and Tony. Kevin's shocked when he sees Ma, and even though he tries not to show it, it's obvious.

'Are you OK, Ma?'

She shrugs and sighs.

I'm dying to hear what happened with Da. I need to know it's sorted.

'Well, I've spoken to him and he's leaving.'

'Where'll he go?' Ma asks.

'I don't know. We didn't get into that.'

Tony jumps in, saying, 'You don't worry about that. You just look after yourself for a change.'

'I'm not worried about that dirty bollox. What about my girls? He got to June, Joyce and Paula too. Did he go near you two?'

'No,' they both answer quickly.

I can't believe what I've just heard! I want the ground to open up and swallow me. My head is spinning. Laura never mentioned anything about us. How does Ma know about us? I make the excuse of getting more tea and leave the room. My legs are trembling, the tears well up in my eyes and I feel a knot in my stomach. I don't know if I'm going to be sick or faint. I do neither, just take a deep breath, wipe my eyes and put on the kettle. Questions are flying round my head. How does Ma know? Who told her? Was it Laura? How come Laura didn't mention it when we spoke? And how would she know anyhow? What does she know? I'm so confused, I don't understand what's going on here. I push the thoughts to the back of my mind, a thing I learned to do many years ago. I go into the room with mugs in hand. I can hardly see for the smoke in the room, so I open the window.

Kevin is trying hard to console Ma, but she's not having any of it.

'Where can I get my hands on a gun? No one will blame me. I can say I was in shock. I'll get away with it.'

Kevin laughs. It breaks the tension.

'It wouldn't be worth it even if you could get away with it.'

'I'd get off. Everyone would understand.'

I feel her frustration because she knows no one is taking her seriously.

'Well, do any one of you know someone who'd do it for me?'

Kevin laughs even harder than before, and we all join in.

'Don't be silly, woman, we'll sort this out,' Kevin says.

She looks relieved as she lets out a deep sigh, but still the tears roll down her face. Kevin looks worried and we are all uncomfortable with this level of emotion. June puts her arms around Ma again and they both sob. I am crying too, but this time I don't try to wipe away the tears. I can't hold myself together much longer and the strain is showing on the boys' faces. What must it have been like for them growing up, never feeling they had the freedom to make choices for themselves or the courage to challenge Da? Worst of all, it's clear from this evening that they knew more than we thought they did and have to be feeling complete failures as men because they believed it was their role to protect us. It's a lot to live with.

I can tell they would do anything to fix this situation. Then again, *I* would too. Seeing Ma in this condition is unbearable.

There's a silence in the room for what seems like the longest time. I glance at my watch and jump. It's 10.45. I'm supposed to be in work, preparing for the pub rush. I'll have to phone Nick, the boss. June and I both work in Abrakebabra for him, in two different stores. I need to let him know I won't be in.

'I'll go with you. I'm not going in tomorrow either,' June says.

I have a splitting headache and my eyes are sore. June turns to me and asks, 'What'll we say?'

'I don't really know. I'll think of something,' I say as I pick up the phone.

'Hello, Nick, it's Joyce. I can't come back to work tonight.'

'Why, is there something wrong?' He asks loads of questions, trying to find out what's going on that's so terrible that I have to miss work. I never skip a shift, so he knows it's something serious.

'Joyce, is your mother all right?' He's guessing at what the problem might be.

With that I break into uncontrollable sobs, and hand the phone to June. She isn't much better.

'Thanks, Nick, but honestly there's nothing you can do.'

She hangs up.

'He'll ring you tomorrow. God love him, he's so concerned.' June gulps back another sob and looks at me.

'It was me, Joyce. I told Ma about us,' June says anxiously.

We throw our arms around each other and cry. We have had several conversations about the abuse lately but I never would have told Ma, not in a million years. Still, I'm relieved to know where she got the information; at least that helps me to make some sense of what's happening.

I can hear the muffled voices coming from the other room but

I can't focus on what's being said because my head is spinning. I take two painkillers and go back into the sitting room to collect the cups. The phone rings again and I run to pick it up.

It's Paula. She tells me that Da has left the house and I briefly fill her in, telling her to wait for David to come home as Ronnie has taken him out for a drink to get him out of the house. David is the youngest of the family, and very close to Da. Himself and Paula are the only ones left living at home now. We adored him as a baby, with those big brown eyes of his. David is great fun and has this wonderful sense of humour. He would do anything for any of us, and would happily give you his last penny and never think of asking for it back. God love him, he hasn't been told anything about this yet, and it'll be hard on him. We'll have to think about how we mind him.

There's another knock on the door. I don't know what to expect any more. It's Ronnie. I point him towards the sitting room, saying they're all in there. He looks ashen and I can smell drink off him.

'I've just dropped David home. We've been playing snooker, but I couldn't explain what's gone on. I'm sorry, I know I should have done.'

'It's all right, Ronnie, don't worry. It's all out now.'

He walks into the room and stands in silence, looking awkward. My heart goes out to him. Of all the boys, Ronnie feels the worst; after all, he's the oldest. Physically he is much bigger and stronger than Da, yet emotionally he's weaker and he had a particularly hard time from Da. He looks much older than forty, and that's nothing to do with tonight. I love him with all my heart at this moment and I'm really sorry for not being more understanding earlier on the phone. The phone rings again. It's David this time.

'What the hell is going on?'

I have to be careful because David is very sensitive. 'David, it's hard to explain on the phone. Everyone will be leaving here shortly. It may be better to wait until they get home.'

'Paula says Da is gone but she won't tell me what's going on. Where's Da going?'

'Look, try not to worry. There was an incident with young Deirdre which has caused a bit of a mess. Just wait and June will tell you when she gets there.'

'Is Ma there?'

'Yes, but she's going home soon. She's just finishing a cup of tea. Don't worry. June'll be back with her and will fill you in.'

Ma gets up to go.

'I think we should go home now. There's no point in sitting here all night. Besides, you must be exhausted, Joyce.'

I don't argue. I'm glad they're leaving. I close the door behind them all, light another fag, and sit in silence. It's almost two in the morning and I'm physically and emotionally drained. I close the window, turn off the lights and go to bed. There are so many thoughts going through my head that I'm convinced it's going to explode. The tears begin to flow as I lie on the pillow. I can feel them in my ears and on my hair, but I don't care. I haven't the energy to wipe them away. I cry myself to sleep.

Chapter 2: Click, Click

Paula: 1970

I'm so excited, I can't eat or sleep. Only a week to go till I make my First Holy Communion. I'm seven years old and it's the first time I've ever been shopping on my own with Ma. She got me all new clothes and they're the most beautiful clothes I've ever had.

When I put them on, my ma says, 'You'll be the prettiest girl there.' I'm so happy. I can't wait for Communion day. I'm raging that Ma is working in the shop. I wish Da would work in the shop. It means Joyce has to bring me down to the church. She's only fourteen. I want Ma to take me.

The day finally arrives and I'm the first one to wake. I can't stop looking at my new dress hanging on the wardrobe door. I want to put it on now. It's white satin with a big bow at the back. I have a beautiful white cardigan with small white pearl buttons, and frilly white lace stockings with pearl drops to match my cardigan. My shoes are white soft shiny leather with a strap across the top and silver buckles at the side. My handbag is white and shiny and matches my shoes, with a strap that I can make long or short. My tiara headpiece glitters when the light catches it and it sits lovely on top of my veil that also has sparkling diamonds all around the edge. I even have a new vest with a little bow in the front and new pants with frills on the back. I've never had new underwear before. I open my bag to look at my medal, mother of pearl rosary beads and prayer book. My prayer book is the nicest book I've ever seen. The cover looks like shiny white marble with a picture of Mary and the baby Jesus on the front. There's a place on the inside for me to write my name, address and age. I feel like the luckiest girl in the world.

I wish I could put my dress on, but it's too early and Ma'll kill me if I get it dirty. I'm so happy, my belly feels all funny. After a long time, I hear Ma going downstairs, so I run down after her.

'Is it time to get dressed now, Ma?'

'No. It's far too early. You've ages to go yet.'

'Ah, Ma, please, let me put on my dress.'

'It's too early. I don't want you to get it dirty.'

'I won't, Ma, I promise. Please, please, Ma, can I just put on my new dress?'

'No, it's too early. Sit down there and I'll do your hair.'

I sit down in the kitchen while she takes the rags out of my hair to make it all curly. They really hurt when she put them in last night and my head is sore from lying on them all night, but I'm so happy when I look in the mirror to see my hair looking lovely and shiny.

'Go upstairs and colour in a picture or play with your dolls. I'll be up shortly to dress you. Just give me time to clean up first.'

'Ah, Ma, can I not dress myself? I won't get anything dirty, I promise.'

'It's too early. I won't be long. Now go on. I'll be there in a minute.'

I don't care. I'm going up to look at my dress and put my name in my prayer book. I run up the stairs to look at my new clothes again. June and Joyce are awake and sitting up in their bed. I walk over to my dress and lift the plastic cover to feel it. It's lovely and soft.

'If you don't leave that alone, you'll have it black before you even put it on,' June says.

'Shut up you!'

June and Joyce get dressed and go downstairs, leaving me all alone to look at my new holy dress. I take up my new bag and look at my sparkling rosary beads. Then I pick up my shoes and smell them. They smell so new, I want to jump all round the room.

Ma finally comes in and says, 'Right, let's get you dressed.' I'm so happy, I can't stay still. She helps me put on my new underwear first and then my new white socks and shoes. Next I hold my arms over my head while she slides on my dress and tells me to turn round so she can zip up the back. Then my cardigan. It feels so soft, I love it. I look up at my ma's face. She's smiling.

'There, go look in the mirror and see how pretty you look.'

I walk into Ma's room, looking down at my new shoes, trying to walk properly so I don't get them creased or dirty. I look into the mirror and I feel gorgeous. My new dress is shining and my hair looks lovely.

'Ma, can you put on my veil now?'

'Not yet. I'll put it on when you're leaving.'

I don't make a fuss, because I'm happy just looking at myself in the mirror.

'Come on downstairs and show everyone how pretty you look.'

'OK.'

When I get downstairs, Joyce, June and Leonard stare at me and tell me I look lovely. David tries to feel my dress, so I have to tell him to leave me alone in case he gets it dirty.

'Ma, can I go back upstairs until I have to leave?' I don't want anyone touching my dress and I want to see my veil again.

'OK, but be careful not to dirty yourself.'

I'm standing in Da and Ma's bedroom, looking at myself and how pretty I am when Da comes up the stairs.

'Are you not ready yet?'

I swirl around to show him my new clothes.

'Well are you fuckin ready or not?'

'Yes.'

I don't want anything to spoil my day, so I answer really quickly, 'But Ma still has to put on my veil.'

He hasn't told me I look lovely. Why hasn't he told me? Then he looks at me with his funny look. He raises his hand and snaps his fingers. Click, click.

'Get over here and take your knickers off.'

I feel like getting sick. The sick is in my head too. My head hurts. Oh, God, please not now. My head is gone all fuzzy. There's no way out of this. I'm trapped. Inside my head I'm screaming, Please God, don't let Da do this. Not now, not today, not in my holy dress.

'Ah, Da, please don't. Not today, Da, please.'

'Take your knickers off now!'

I start to cry. 'Please, Da, not now. Please, not today. Please, Da, don't.'

'Shut up, you fuckin whinging maggot, or I'll give you something to cry about.'

I sob as I take off my knickers. He smacks me across the head, real hard and I nearly fall over.

'Lie down on the fuckin floor now or I'll fuckin kill ya.'

'My dress'll get dirty, Da.'

'Get on the floor now. I won't tell you again.'

I get down on the floor and he gets on top of me, trying to put his thing inside me. He doesn't even use the Vaseline. He's hurting me something awful but all I can think of is my new dress. I want to die. Now my lovely dress is ruined. It's not lovely any more. It's ugly and bad, not holy, just bad like me. This is my holy day but God knows I'm bad or he wouldn't let Da do this, not today.

I lie as still as I can while he's doing it. He really hurts me but I'm not crying any more. I don't care about my dress. I'm an ugly, evil little bitch. I hate Da and I hate God too.

He finishes and fixes his trousers.

'Get into your room.'

I pick up my new knickers and bring them into my room. I'm not crying. I'll never cry again, I'll never beg for anything ever again. God doesn't care and I don't fuckin care either. I'm not excited any more. I don't even want to go out now. I want to take off my dress and get into bed. Fuck him, I hope he dies. I hope he dies in a car crash when he goes out. I hate him, the fuckin bastard.

I lie on the bed and don't care if my dress gets crumpled. I see my veil and tiara sitting really carefully on top of the chest of drawers. The diamonds don't seem so sparkly now.

Paula: 1972

I feel sick. My stomach and head hurt. I'm cold but sweating. I cry and head down to see Ma. I spent all last night doing my homework to make sure all my words were right and tidy like the teacher says, but, because I can't spell, I have to use my rubber so much that my pages are all dirty. I rubbed so hard, I put holes on the page and the teacher will go mad again. No matter how I try to learn my words, I can't remember them in school. Da says I'm a gobshite and thick as shit. He's right: nothing stays in my head. I must be stupid. I'm nine years old now but I can't seem to learn anything.

I have to find Ma to ask if I can stay home because I'm sick. She's standing in the kitchen putting on her apron for work.

'Ma, I'm not well, my stomach is hurting. I'm going to get sick.'

'Make her go to school,' June says. 'There's nothing wrong with her, she's only pretending.'

I hate her. She's a cow. Ma feels my head.

'You're not hot; you have to go to school. If you're sick, the teacher will send you home. Go have your breakfast. You're probably just hungry. Go on, Joyce has the breakfast ready for you. Quick or you'll be late.'

I know she's serious, so I go inside crying. Why won't she let me stay home? I'm really sick. I hate school. If June wasn't here, she'd let me stay. June's laughing and making faces behind Ma's back. I want to kill her, the bitch. I sit at the kitchen table and Joyce plonks a bowl of lumpy porridge in front of me. I try to eat fast because I don't like the taste of porridge. Joyce won't let me put more sugar on it and I know she'll make me eat it all.

I eat quickly and start the long walk to school. I'll be in trouble because I'm late again. I always get ready slowly, hoping Ma will say it's too late and let me go back to bed. Sometimes I sneak upstairs when everyone has gone and hide behind my bed all day colouring my book or reading *Twinkle* until I hear the others come in. Then I go downstairs, pretending I just came home.

When I reach the school, the gates are still open. Sometimes they're closed by the time I get there because I'm so late. I feel sick in my stomach and my head is banging when I see the gates open. When they're closed, I sometimes sneak off to the back of the church where I found a hiding place that no one else knows. I don't like it there, because it's cold and I'm starving and scared that I'm going to get caught and sent to jail by the school inspector, but anything is better than getting into class late and being made a show of.

There's loads of girls in my class, but I don't speak to them cause all they talk about is boys and *Top of the Pops* bands, like the Osmonds. I like The Stylistics and Dr Hook and the other girls think my music is crap. I know I stink because I still sometimes dirty myself, so I only talk to Amanda. She's my only friend. All the other girls call her 'snotty nose' and 'crusty' because she always has a runny nose and wipes her snot on her sleeve until it goes all hard.

I stay quiet so the teacher won't ask me anything, but she calls my name and tells me to stand up and answer a question. I try to stop the poo coming out of my bum, squeezing my bum real tight, but the poo comes out anyway. I can't hear the question and all the girls laugh. I'm sweating and the teacher is waiting for an answer, and she shouts at me, 'Well, Miss Kavanagh, are you going to answer me?'

I don't know the answer, so she makes me stand at the back of the class with my back to the girls until lunchtime. I'm worried that my poo will run down my leg. All the girls can smell me. I want to run home, but I'm too scared to move.

I go to the toilets at lunchtime and take off my pants. They're not too bad, so I wrap them in toilet paper and put them in my pocket till I get home. Sometimes I have to leave them in the bin, if they're really bad, but I'm always afraid of someone catching me doing it.

The lunch bell rings and we all sit waiting for the teacher's pet to hand out our bottle of milk and corned beef sandwich.

The only lunch I like is Friday's when we get the buns; they're lovely and even have currants. After that, we go out into the yard. It's freezing cold.

I see Michelle running around with her gang. She's real cheeky and always answers the teacher back. I think she's very brave, but I stay out of her way as she calls other girls names and pushes them in the yard, so I'm a bit scared of her. Some days, when I rob a packet of chocolate biscuits out of Ma's shop, all the girls come around and ask for one. I give them all away so that they'll like me. Sometimes I rob a fifty pence piece and give it to Amanda to buy everyone crisps and a bar. I don't buy them myself because I don't know how to count. When I give them sweets, they leave me alone, and for a little while they like me.

Paula: 1973

The children from the local playground are going away for a week to County Wicklow because it's the summer holidays, and they asked me to go too. I'm ten years old and I really want to go so I beg Ma to let me and to ask Da's permission.

After lots of pleading, Da finally gives in and says I can go. I'm so happy, I can't wait. I'm upstairs packing for the hundredth time because we're going tomorrow and I'm so excited.

Click, click.

I keep my eyes on my bag and pretend I don't hear him clicking his fingers.

Click, click.

'Are you fuckin deaf?'

Please, please go away. Please not today.

'Get your knickers off and get in to my room.'

I begin to undress. Oh, God, why me? Why today? I wish he

hated the others the way he hates me, so he would do this to them and leave me alone.

'Get on the bed.'

He drops his trousers. The smell. Oh, God, the horrible smell of his wee and sweat! I'm going to get sick.

'Hold it,' he says pointing at his thing.

I do as I'm told. It's soft and floppy and the smell gets stronger.

'Hold it harder.'

I clench my teeth, grab it as hard as I can. I want to hurt him, but it's too big for my hands.

'Pull it in and out the way I showed you, you stupid cunt.'

I pull harder and harder until my hands hurt. Wallop across the head. 'Do it right, fuckin maggot.'

I squeeze as hard as I can, holding my breath, so I can't smell him. My hands feel sticky and are getting really tired. I can't go any faster.

'You stupid cunt, lie back.'

He pushes me down on my back real hard and jams his legs in between mine to open them.

'Open your fuckin legs wide, you stupid cunt.'

He's so heavy, I can't breathe. I try to move my head to the side to get some air. I look at the ceiling, not making a sound.

'Open up.'

I tighten myself down there, as much as I can. I don't care if he hurts me. I want to hurt him. He pushes my legs farther apart.

'Keep them there.'

I put my hands under my knees to try to hold my legs up because they are so tired and I can feel pain in my hips.

'Put it in the fuckin right hole for me.'

I wish I could throw up all over him, I hate him so much. I

move his thing to where he wants it and he pushes hard into me, much harder than he usually does. Jesus, it hurts!

'This'll make you remember me while you're away off having a good time. Put your legs around my waist and hold on to my neck.'

Yuck, even thinking about putting my arms around his neck makes me sick, but I do as I'm told while he lifts me up from the bed and moves to the floor. His thing falls out just as he reaches the floor.

'You stupid cunt. Put it back in.'

He hits me across the face. I put his thing back where he wants it and he pushes inside me harder and harder. His breathing is getting faster. He's pushing so hard that my bum is rubbing on the carpet and stinging me.

'Keep your legs open.'

The pain is so bad, I feel as if my insides are ripping open. It has to be over soon. He never usually takes this long.

'This will keep you going. You won't forget this.'

I squeeze my lips together and bite my tongue to stop from crying, but I can't help it, he's really hurting me. I hate myself for being weak. He goes faster and then stops.

'Get into your room, and you make sure no boys go near you while you're on holiday.'

I try to stand up but fall over because my legs feel all funny. He shoves me and I fall on my knees. He kicks me in the back and sends me flying forward.

'Get in that room now, or I'll fuckin kill you.'

I crawl into my room because I can't stand. Between my legs is hot and stingy. Tomorrow I'll be free for a whole week. I just have to hang on until then. I pull myself up slowly. My hips hurt and down there is all sticky. I can still smell him, so I go to the bathroom to wash him off me. I'm burning and itchy. I put a cold cloth between my legs to try to stop the burning, but something is hanging down.

For the next few hours I keep cold cloths between my legs to try to make it better, but nothing works. I'm really scared; I have to tell someone, but who? Ma's out in the shop and, anyway, I'd be mortified. What'll I do?

'Who's in there? I'm bursting to go. Will you hurry up?' I hear Ma outside the bathroom as I am replacing the cold cloths.

I open the door and she looks at me.

'What's wrong?'

I can't help it. I start to cry.

'There's something wrong with me down there.' I point between my legs.

'What's wrong? What do you mean?'

'I don't know. I'm all sore and there is something hanging down.'

I pull down my knickers to let her see and the look on her face makes me even more frightened.

'How did this happen? Did you fall or something?'

'No, it just happened.'

I'm so ashamed as Ma is looking between my legs.

'What's wrong with me?'

'I don't know.'

'Your da needs to have a look. He'll have to bring you down to the hospital.'

'Ah, Ma, no. Don't tell Da.' But it's too late. She's already on her way to get him. He'll kill me. I have to stand here and show him. I wish I was dead. Ma and Da walk into the bathroom.

Ma turns to Da and says, 'Kevin, look. What'd you think?'

He bends down on one knee facing me and goes white in the face. He looks more scared than me. I have never seen him look like this before.

'I don't think it's anything to worry about.'

'I don't know, Kevin. It looks sore. Don't you think we should bring her down to the hospital to get it checked?'

His face goes grey and he's sweating. I want to pull up my knickers and get out of there. I don't want to go to any hospital and have anyone else look at me.

'Ma, I don't want to go to hospital.'

'There's no need for that,' Da says. I'm not sitting in the hospital for hours for them to tell me it's just a bit of swelling. I'll put her to bed and see how she is in a while.'

'Are you sure, Kevin? Would it not be better to bring her and get someone to have a look?'

'She'll be fine. I'll put her to bed and keep an eye on her. She wants to go away tomorrow. You don't want to spoil that for her, do you?'

'If she's not better in the morning, I'll bring her down to hospital myself. Holiday or no holiday,' Ma says.

'You go back out to work and leave her to me.'

Now I'm really scared. He'll go mad.

'You go up and get into bed and I'll be up in a few minutes,' he tells me.

I do as he says, waiting to be killed. He comes into my room holding a bandage in his hand. He looks worried.

'Stand out on the floor.'

He wraps a bandage around my waist and in between my legs.

'There, that should make you better.'

He's being nice to me. Why? Why's he not slapping me? There must be something really wrong.

'You be a good girl and keep your mouth shut and I'll make sure that you go on your little holiday tomorrow. I'll be back in a while. You just stay in bed and don't move.'

He's never like this. He looks worried; he even looks scared. This must be serious. He said I can still go on my holidays, so I don't care what's wrong with me. Half an hour later, he checks under the bandage, to see if the swelling is gone.

'Tell your ma that you want to go away and that you don't want to go to the hospital or she'll stop you going and you wouldn't like that, would you? If she wants you to go to the hospital, you'd better start to cry or you'll be going nowhere.'

Joyce and June are working in the factory. I pretend to be asleep when they come upstairs after tea. They ignore me as they hurriedly brush their hair before going out to play. Da comes in again to check on me as soon as they are gone.

This continues all night, with Da looking more and more worried because the swelling isn't going down. I'm sore and itchy but I don't care, I just want to go away.

In the morning, Da comes into the room and hands me a tenner.

'Get dressed for your holiday. If your mother asks if you're all right say yes, or she won't let you go anywhere.'

I get dressed and go downstairs. Ma asks me, 'Are you all right?'

'Yes, Ma, I'm fine.'

'Is the swelling gone down?'

'Yes.'

'Come into the bathroom and let me see.'

'Ma, I'm fine. Really I am.' I don't want to show her because she mightn't let me go.

'Come on, it won't take long.'

I walk as slowly as I can. I know she's going to stop me because I'm still all swollen and really sore, but I want to go on my holidays. I have to take down my knickers and show her.

'Sorry, love, I'll have to bring you down to the hospital, so someone can check you out. I can't let you go away in that condition.'

'Ah, Ma, I'll be all right. I don't want to miss the bus. I want to go to Wicklow.'

'No, you can go after the hospital checks you out. I'm not letting you go anywhere like this. I'll just go and get someone to look after the shop and tell your father.'

I'm in big trouble now. Da's going to go mad. He'll kill me. I did everything he told me but Ma wouldn't listen.

Da storms into the bathroom.

'What did you do, you stupid cunt? I told you to tell her you were all right. Go and sit in the car, and don't say a word or you're fuckin dead.'

My legs begin to shake. I don't want to do this. Please, God, don't make me do this. I get into the car and Da sits in the front, slamming the car door.

'Tell the doctor that you were playing with a stick.'

I say nothing. No way I'm saying that to a doctor. I don't care if he kills me. Ma gets into the car and for the entire trip to hospital we sit in silence. I can't tell who's more worried. When we get there, Ma explains to the woman at the desk what my problem is and I'm brought into a small room where a nurse asks me to take off my trousers and pants and lie on the bed. Ma and Da stay outside.

I'm frightened. Now I wish my ma was with me. The doctor comes in and examines me. I feel so ashamed and naked; my legs are shaking and my heart is beating like crazy. He asks me questions.

'How old are you?'

'Ten.'

'Do you have a boyfriend?'

'No.' Why's he asking me that?

'Did anyone go near you?'

'No.'

I can hear Ma and Da outside talking. I can't hear what they're saying, but I know my da'll kill me if I say anything. He's going to be mad because I won't tell the doctor I was playing with a stick, but I don't care.

'Why are you so worried?' the doctor asks me.

'I want to go away on my holidays today and I'm afraid that you'll stop me.'

'I don't think I can let you go,' he says and leaves the cubicle.

I cry. I want to get away for a whole week. He doesn't understand how important this is to me. Outside I can hear Da saying, 'It's her age, she's just curious. She was probably playing with a stick or something.'

Ma comes in and tells me to get dressed. She tells me, 'The doctor says you can go on your holidays.'

When we get to the car, Da looks very happy and gives me more money for my holidays.

June: 1969

Paula, David and me are playing snakes and ladders on the floor of the sitting room. For the first time ever, I'm winning! At eight, I should be able to beat Paula, who is only six, but she usually beats me and David doesn't often play with us, so I'm really delighted with myself for getting so far ahead.

Click, click.

Oh, no, I hope he doesn't want me.

Click, click.

If I don't look, he might leave me alone. Maybe he's looking for a cup of tea or the TV channel changed. He might not want 'that'. I'm not turning around, just in case.

Click, click.

Oh, God, he's still there. What'll I do?

Click, click.

It's in my ear, so I have to look at him. He nods for me to go upstairs. I feel sick in my stomach. Why does he have to ruin everything? I'm having fun; it's not fair. I'd love to punch him, but he'd kill me. I look into his face, hoping he can see how I feel and that he'll tell me it's OK that I can stay and beat the other two, but he doesn't. I have to go. Maybe he'll be quick and I can get back and finish the game.

I'm at the top of the stairs, but he's not following me. I'm supposed to get ready but I've got trousers on. If I take them off, someone might come up and see me, but if I'm not ready he'll go mad. What'll I do? I could run into my room and put on a skirt but then what if I'm not in his room when he gets upstairs? I'm supposed to take off my knickers and hide them. Oh, shit, here he is. What'll I do? It's too late. I'll have to pretend I forgot.

'Why aren't you ready? Get your fuckin knickers off.'

Can't he see I have trousers on? If I take them off, I'll only have my jumper on.

'What the fuck are you doing? Get them off I said.'

I open my trousers slowly.

'Come on, come on, for fuck's sake.'

I pull down my trousers but he looks mad. I have to take off my knickers as well. I hate my knickers, they're always smelly and dirty because of him. All that stuff that comes out of his thing keeps coming out of me, making me red and sore down there. I try to pull my jumper down to cover myself, but it's too short and goes back up. I hate not being able to cover my bum. I look round the room, but there's nothing I can use. What if someone comes, how will I hide myself? What if I'm caught? What'll I do?

'Come over here.'

He lifts me up on the dressing table. I hate it. It's cold and my bum sticks to it. He pulls me to the edge and I feel like I'm going to fall off. He takes out his thing and puts my hand on it.

'Pull it.'

The smell goes right up my nose. I turn my head away. It's awful. I hate this part. I can never do it right and he always gets mad.

'Tighter.'

My hand is hurting and I can't hold it any tighter, it's all wet and gooey. I wish he'd take it and do it himself. I'm doing it as hard as I can. I'm even squeezing my face, so he knows I'm really trying. He pushes my hand away and does it himself.

'Look, this is how you do it.'

It's horrible, it's all purple and sore-looking. Yuck! My hand is all sticky now; it feels like snots. I look for something to wipe it on, but there's nothing. He pulls out a blob of Vaseline and rubs it on me. I jump back because his nails are sharp and really hurt and the Vaseline is freezing. I know I've done something wrong, so I move my bum back. He puts his fingers inside me but I don't move because I don't want him to get angry. His hands are dirty and I want to tell him to get away from me, but I'm afraid.

'Ouch.' His nails are hurting me.

'Hold it. Put it in the right hole.'

I do it, and pull my hand away quickly, but it's all wet now. I've nowhere to wipe it. I'm listening very hard in case anyone comes up and catches me. He's breathing funny, like a dog. I don't like it. My legs are sore. I stare at the corner of the room. He stops moving.

'Wrap your arms and legs around me.'

He wants to move to the bed. I hate putting my arms round him. It feels horrible. I wipe my hand on his T-shirt; at least I got rid of that awful stuff.

He puts me on the bed and gets on top of me. He's too heavy and I can't breathe. I make a sound to let him know, but he ignores me. He's annoyed and then his thing falls out.

'Fuck it. Put it back in.'

I put my hand down, it's all gooey again, but I get his thing back in. It's taking a long time today. I wish he'd hurry up; I want to get back to the snakes and ladders. When I think he's nearly finished, he stops. I try to get up, but he pushes me back down.

'Turn over.'

'What?' He's never asked me to do that before.

'Turn fuckin over.'

'Turn over where?'

'On your belly.'

What's he talking about?

'Lie on your fuckin belly.'

I lie on my belly and he touches my bum with his thing. I don't like this. I can't see what he's doing. He's putting it in wrong. Doesn't he know he's putting it in wrong? He mustn't. He's trying to push it into my bum and he's hurting me. I feel something sharp in my bum, like glass.

'Da, you're putting it in the wrong hole!'

He mustn't hear me. It's hurting really bad and I start to cry.

'Da, you're putting it in the wrong hole.'

'I fuckin know. Now shut the fuck up.'

'Da, it's hurting me. Please, Da.'

I'm roaring and crying. I can't help it. He's really annoyed and he stops and shoves me off the bed.

'Get inside, you whinging little cunt.'

I grab my clothes and run into my room. I put my smelly knickers and trousers back on, so I'm covered up. I hate myself and my body. I'll never wear trousers again. My bum is stinging me. I think there's something still up there. I can't go to the toilet because my eyes are too red and everyone'll know I've been crying.

The bastard! I hate him. Why did he do that? How could he

hurt me like that? I hope he drops dead. How could God let him do that to me? Maybe I'm bold and God is trying to hurt me. Maybe Da doesn't really mean to hurt me. He couldn't know it hurts so much. He couldn't be that bad. Am I that bad? I must be.

I bet they've finished the game of snakes and ladders by now. Shit, I would've won.

I'm late again. I open the door as quietly as I can. I let out a deep breath as there is no one in the cloakroom. I hang up my coat but all the other coat hooks are empty. Maybe the teacher isn't in and all the girls have gone to other classrooms. If there's no one in my class, I can slip out again and tell Ma that we were sent home because our teacher didn't turn up.

I hope there's no one in my classroom. I hate going into someone else's class unless Martina is with me. I hope Martina is in. She's my best friend in school and I feel OK if I'm with her. I open the door to my classroom and I'm disappointed to find that everyone is in.

The teacher doesn't even notice me, but I wonder why everyone has their coats on.

'We're going over to confession. You'd better get your coat,' Susan Duffy says.

'Is that today?' I ask in shock.

'Yes. You were told weeks ago. Remember the letter you brought home to your ma?' says Mary Maguire, the class busybody.

I've forgotten all about it. I'm making my First Holy Communion in a couple of weeks and we have to go to confession. We have to make more promises to God, and tell him our sins so that we don't go to hell if we die. If you tell the priest your sins in confession, you go to heaven, even if you did sins, so most of my class think it's a good deal, but I feel sick. I don't want to tell anyone my sins, but if I don't tell the priest, he'll know I'm hiding something. How can I get out of this? I'm terrified the priest will see how awful I am. I feel everyone can see that there's something really bad in me. I feel they know I'm black on the inside and soon the priest will see it too when I'm in the confession box. I look around the classroom.

'Where's Martina?' I ask.

'She's not in today.' Mary Maguire knows everything.

I feel like crying. I really need Martina here today. How could she not come in today of all days?

We walk in twos over to the church and I feel scared. My hands are all sweaty. Everyone else seems fine but they don't have the secret I have. They all have friends and my friend isn't here. I feel alone. Nobody else even likes me. Who can I talk to? I just want to be the same as everyone else, but I'm not. What am I doing here?

Even God hates me. I'm sure he thinks I'm just a dirty smelly bitch. I sit in the church waiting for my turn to go into the confession box. I think about telling the priest about my da. Maybe he can help me. Maybe he can stop Da doing it to me. If I tell him and he forgives me, I won't feel so horrible all the time and then he can tell God and God won't hate me any more either. Then maybe it will stop.

I'm last in the queue. I hope when it gets to my turn, the priest will be called away, but the queue is moving fast and it's getting near. I start to panic.

Oh, God, what will I say? I turn to Sandra O'Neill, who is sitting beside me. 'What are you going to say?'

'I'm just going to say that I told a lie once, I was disobedient twice and said a bold word once.'

'That sounds good to me. I think I'll do the same.'

I go over it in my head, but I can't concentrate. My heart is beating so fast that I look down at my chest to see if the others can notice it. I'm sure everyone can see it banging so hard against my ribs. Sandra is talking to me, but I'm so nervous I can't hear a word. All I can think of is how many girls are in front of me and how much time I have before my life is over.

The voice inside my head is saying, 'Tell the priest, tell him,' but the rest of me is saying, 'I can't.'

It's my turn. I go into the confession box and close the door behind me. I'm trembling. I kneel down in the dark, and can't see a thing. It is pitch black and I know I won't be able to see until the priest pulls the sliding door across. Now I'm here, it's like a coffin. I can feel myself panic, so I try to calm myself by listening to what he is saying to the person on the other side. I know the priest is talking to someone else because I can hear mumbles. Even though I can't make out a word, I'm convinced that people will be able to hear me. I'll whisper I promise myself. I hope the other person has loads of sins and takes ages but I also wish they would hurry up and let me get this over with.

The little sliding door opens and I quickly spurt out my list of sins. I told a lie once, I was disobedient twice and I said a bold word once. There, I did it. I can breathe again. I won't say anything else. I'll wait for the priest to tell me what prayers to say.

'Is there anything else you would like to tell me?'

I wasn't expecting that. Did I forget something? I panic and, before I know it, the words fly out of my mouth. 'Eh, my Da does things to me.'

There's a pause before he answers, 'What kind of things?' Maybe he can help me.

'Umm, he touches me,' I say nervously.

'Where exactly does he touch you?'

'Down there,' I say, wondering whether or not I should say anything else.

'And when he touches you, does he use his finger or his thing?'

I'm frightened, but I say nothing.

'Well, my child, does he use his finger or his thing?'

I'm afraid but I have to answer him.

'His thing.'

My mind is racing and I wonder if there is any way the priest can get to me? I want to get out of the confession box. Oh, Mammy, help me. I'm sorry I opened my mouth. I'm in here too long. I hope my teacher hasn't forgotten me. Oh, God, it's very quiet outside. I look for the handle of the door. He doesn't ask me anything else, he just says, 'I want you to do something for me. Will you tell your father I want to see him? Will you do that for me? You can tell him that I said that I would like to speak to him.'

'Yes, Father.'

It's been a stupid mistake. I hope he doesn't ask me anything else.

'Three Hail Marys, five Our Fathers and a decade of the rosary.' He makes the sign of the cross and closes the door.

I open the door of the confession box and am delighted to see that all my class are still there. They are staring at me. I realise I am the last one for confession and they are all waiting for me. I want to hide my face. I can feel it turning red with the shame and embarrassment.

'You must have lots of sins,' Mary Maguire says to me.

I look over my shoulder and see the priest pulling back the curtain. He knows who I am now. Maybe he knows where I live. I try to calm down by telling myself that he can't do anything to me here but I'm not happy until we get out of the church.

'How come you were so long? What did you say in there?' Annette Daly asks me.

'Nothing. I just said that I told a lie once, I was disobedient twice and I said a bold word once.' I know she doesn't believe me, but I can't think of anything else to say.

That night it takes me ages to get to sleep. I keep getting the thumping in my chest and it's hard to breathe. I want to tell Joyce about it but I can't because it's meant to be a secret. I dream the priest is chasing me through the church grounds with nothing on only a white shirt and a pair of socks and his thing is dangling as he runs after me. I'm terrified even after I wake up. He had no face, but he was dressed like Da.

June: 1971

Da says, 'We're going to visit Pam in England. I'm bringing Joyce, Leonard and you, and you can bring your friend.'

'Really, Da, can I?'

'Yes, but you'll have to ask her ma if she'll let her go.'

I can't wait to tell Martina the news. I'm so excited, I can't believe it.

'We're going to England to see my sister Pam. She moved to England when I was only a baby and I only see her now when she comes to visit. Me da said you can come, isn't it great? Ask your ma. It'll be brilliant. We're going on the boat. Joyce and Leonard are coming too.'

It takes ages before Martina gets permission. Her ma thinks that, at eleven years old, she's too young to travel without her parents, but she keeps on and on until they let her go. We're thrilled and, for days, we sit and make lists of the things we'll bring. Finally, it's the night before we leave and I know I won't be able to sleep because I'm so excited. This is the best thing that has ever happened to me. I'm only ten and I'm going on holidays. I've never been away before, and I don't know anyone who's been to England apart from my biggest sister.

I'm delighted Martina's coming, but I wish Leonard wasn't. He's my older brother and we're always fighting. He punches me in the stomach and when I tell Ma, she gives out to me for telling tales. I'm glad Joyce is going, though, because I feel better when she's there.

It's still dark when Da calls us. It feels like Christmas. I climb onto the mattress in the back of the van. Da put it there in case we get tired. We all sing songs on the way to the boat. I can't believe how many cars are driving on to this huge boat. I hope we don't sink. Everything feels special. In the canteen, they have the tiniest boxes of cornflakes and the biggest sausages I've ever seen and Da says we can have anything we want. It's so funny watching everyone trying to stand straight while the boat is rocking. Even the plates and cups are sliding along the table.

When the boat stops, it's really dark. Da drives for a little while and stops at the side of the road to let us all get some sleep. We're all giggling as we pull the blankets up. Da and Leonard sleep at one end of the mattress and us three girls at the other. We all fall asleep.

I can feel something between my legs. I can't believe it! It's him; he's trying to get his hand between my legs. Not here, I didn't think he'd do anything here. He's breathing in my ear. But I have trousers on. I'll pretend to be asleep. What can he do? How did he get beside me? Oh, Jesus, I hope no one can hear him. I hope everyone's asleep. Get away, not here. He's behind me, and Joyce and Julie are on the other side. I hope they can't hear anything. What's he doing? Can't he see Joyce and Julie are right beside me?

'Psst.'

Oh, God, just go away, I'm not helping you.

'Psst, psst, June. Wake up.'

He won't leave me alone until I wake up and I don't want to. What if Martina hears? I'd better wake up and get it over with. I'd love to punch him, the big fat bastard.

'Psst, June, wake up.'

I hate him. Why can't he leave me alone? Why can't he let me have this holiday without having to do this?

'Take your trousers off.'

I try to take my trousers off under the blankets, so no one will hear. I move really slow, hoping he'll change his mind. What if someone wakes up? What if Julie sees me? What'll she think? She'll never talk to me again. She'll think I'm a dirty bitch. Can he not see that? Tears are falling into my hair. I can't make a sound. I don't want anyone to wake up. There's nothing I can do. I give up. I start to turn around. He grabs my arm.

'Stay there.'

Why does he want me to stay this way? I hope he doesn't try to put it in my bum because it's horrible and hurts so bad, and I'll cry and make too much noise.

He puts his thing in me from behind. At least he didn't put it in the wrong hole. He's breathing too loud. He's going to wake Julie. What if she's only pretending to be asleep? Oh, I'll die if she knows about this. How can I face her again? His zip is digging into me. It's really hurting me but I have to be quiet. How can he do this to me, here? How can he not know how awful this is? He sounds like a dog, but I have to listen for anyone waking up. I hate him. Oh, Jesus, I think I hear something. I think someone's awake.

It's over.

I feel dirty and wet and I have nothing to clean myself with. He's a big smelly bollox. I put my hands under the blankets and try to find my trousers without waking anyone. I hate this holiday. I want to go home.

It's lashing rain outside. I know I'm going to be really late for school, but I hope that maybe I won't have to go. Ma shouts up the stairs again, and I go down really slow, hoping she'll tell me it's too late to go now, but Da says, 'Get fuckin moving and get out to school.'

I hate school. I have a sick feeling in my stomach and I'm going to be in trouble for being late again.

The Glassy Lane is a shortcut, but I heard that a big hand comes after people when they go through that lane, so I think I'll take the long way to school. When I get there, a girl is closing the door. She won't open it for me but points, letting me know that I have to go in the main door beside the head nun's office. I don't want to because the nun will give out to me. I beg the girl to please let me in, but she won't, the bitch.

I walk in the main door shaking, trying to think of a good excuse to tell the nun. I sneak in, hoping no one will hear me but the nun isn't there. I walk real fast to my class, feeling afraid all the time in case I'm caught. My heart is pounding and now I have to think what I'm going to say to the teacher.

The hallways are empty, but when I go into my classroom everyone stops and stares at me.

'Sorry, Teacher. My Ma didn't call me till late.'

They all giggle.

'You're ten years old, Miss Kavanagh. Can you not get yourself out of bed?'

I feel stupid and don't know what to say, so I just stand there.

'Sit down,' she says.

I rush to my seat at the back of the class. The girls are in the middle of copying something from the blackboard, so I get my pen and paper and try to focus on what's written up for us. It's all blurry but if I half-close my eyes, that way I can make out most of the words. The teacher lets out a roar.

'June Kavanagh!'

I jump and my heart pounds.

'Can you not see the board? Sit up the front here.'

Oh, God, she saw me squinting. I have to move, but I don't want to. What can I do?

'OK, Teacher,' I answer as I gather my things.

I move to the top of the class where all the clever girls sit. I don't like this. She can see everything. What if she asks me something and I can't answer it. What'll I do? She'll be able to see my horrible writing, and what about Martina? I don't want to sit anywhere without my best friend.

I look at the other girls. They are better than me. They look clean with nice hair and always have pencil cases and new crayons and copybooks. I never have nice stuff with me; pencils never last in our house. And, anyway, I'm stupid. I never get my homework right.

I notice Ann Burn sitting across from me. None of the class wants to sit beside her because she has long hair with knots in it and they say she has nits. At least I'm not that bad. I can really see the board from here, so at least that's something.

It's jam and bread today for lunch and I hate it because there's only a tiny bit of jam in the middle of the bread, but I'm starving, so I eat it. I don't like going out to the yard at lunchtime because it's cold. Me and Martina sit in the shed waiting to go back in to class.

After lunch, the teacher takes out the Buntús board. It's a big black velvet board that you stick little pictures and Irish words on. I hate that board. I don't understand what she's saying, and, the more I try, the worse I get.

After Irish, we do the weather chart. Teacher usually picks the clever girls to do it. They fill in the weather forecast. I don't know how they do it.

'June Kavanagh, you haven't done the weather chart yet. You can fill in the wind direction today.'

I pretend I can't hear her. She says it again.

'What?'

'You fill in the wind direction today.'

I look at her. I'm sure she can see I haven't got a clue what she's talking about, so she speaks loudly and says, 'Go outside and find out what direction the wind is blowing in today.'

I look around for someone to help me. One girl looks at me and says, 'You have to go outside and find out which way the wind is blowing.'

'How?'

But before she can answer, the teacher shouts at me to get on with it.

I stand outside the class for a minute and decide I'd better go outside and see what happens. I'm in the yard feeling like an idiot, hoping the answer will come to me. I'm wondering what I'll say when I go back. I haven't a clue how to find out about the wind. I want to cry. A girl passes and I ask her if she knows how to tell the wind direction and she tells me to hold up a blade of grass and that will tell me. Then she runs off.

I pull up a blade of grass and hold it up, but nothing happens. The wind is blowing, but I don't know where north or south are. I feel stupid and sick at the idea of going back in to the class. What can I say? What will I tell the teacher? I don't know what to do but a long time has passed and I think I'd better head back.

My heart is pounding as I walk back to the corridor. I walk up and down a bit, scared of another teacher seeing me out here, till I finally get the courage to go into class. The teacher is busy with a group of girls, so I go over to the weather chart and try and look like I know what I'm doing. I copy what was put in the book yesterday and then get back to my seat. I want to run and hide behind my desk, but I walk slowly, like I'm really confident. All the time my tummy is doing loops and I keep wiping my hands on my skirt to get rid of the sweat. A few minutes later, the teacher asks me, 'Have you filled in the weather chart?'

'Yes, Teacher,' I answer, as calmly as I can. She doesn't check. I look down at my book, pretending to read; my heart is still jumping. I wait for her to ask me how I know and keep my eyes down, looking at the blur on the page.

June: 1973

'Lie down and I'll tell you a story,' says Joyce. Paula jumps into her single bed, and me and Joyce pull the blankets up over us. Joyce is seventeen and should have her own bed, but Paula got it because she's always sick, even though she's only ten. Ma's gone to Spain with Pamela and her husband and we're all missing her, so Joyce tries to make us all feel better by telling us a story. She tells us great stories, using all different voices and funny sounds, and Paula and I lie quietly, listening to every word. I don't remember falling asleep but I wake up to someone calling me.

'Psst, June, come over here.'

I sit up in the bed, thinking it's Paula and I stare over at her bed. It's dark but it doesn't look like her and then I realise she's crawled over to me and Joyce, and is in our bed. They are both fast asleep. I rub my eyes and see it's him; he's in her bed! I'm raging. If I'd known it was him, I wouldn't have sat up. Now he knows I'm awake, so I pretend I don't understand what's happening.

Click, click.

'Come over here.'

I'm caught; I have to go over. I walk slowly, rubbing my eyes, pretending I'm sleepy. He pulls back the blankets and moves over to make room for me. Oh, God, what's he doing? Why does he want me in Paula's bed with him? Why is he in here? Ma never goes to bed till really late, so he usually calls me into his room while she is finishing her jobs downstairs. I don't like him being in here. This is our room, and, anyway, the girls might wake up.

'Get the fuck in.'

I climb into the bed. It feels awful. What does he want? He puts my hand on his thing.

'Squeeze it tight, and pull it up and down.'

I hold his thing as tight as I can. It's terrible, and the smell is making me feel sick.

'Put it in your mouth.'

'What?'

'Go on, put it in your mouth.' He lifts up the blankets and pushes me down to his thing. Oh, God, the smell. I'm going to be sick.

'No, Da, I can't.'

'You can. Go on, just put it in your mouth.'

I can't put that thing in my mouth. I can't do it. I'll be sick. I start to cry.

'Please, Da, don't make me. I can't.'

'Go on, just put it in your mouth.'

He puts his hand on the back of my neck and pushes my head down.

'No, no, no, Da, I can't.'

He's pushing my head close to his thing. I can't stop crying and I know I have to be quiet because I don't want to wake up the girls. My head is right on top of it now. I'm gagging; I can feel the hot sick in my throat. His hand is hurting my neck and he won't let me go.

'Just fuckin do it.'

There's no way I can put that in my mouth; it's too big. I'll choke and the smell is really bad.

'Open your fuckin mouth.'

I try to open my mouth but when I get near, I close it again. I can't. He's going to kill me, but I really can't. I nearly get sick. He's pushing my neck too hard and I can't hold my head back any longer.

'Put the fuckin thing in, you stupid cunt!'

I put it in my mouth. I choke and have to take it out. Yuck, it's disgusting. What will I do? He's still pushing my head so I try again, but I can't. I'm trying to take it back out of my mouth but he won't let me. He's holding my head tight, so I can't move and I start choking. He kicks me out of the bed.

'You useless cunt.'

He's right. I *am* useless. I can't do anything. He's so mad, I'll pay for this. I don't stand up, just crawl over to my bed, sobbing.

It's near the end of my first year at secondary school. I'm twelve years old and have spent the year trying to imitate the loud confident girls in my class. The school is scary, the way you have so much freedom, and how easy it is to mitch. I feel completely out of control, and I don't like it. Being one of the popular girls, being funny and cheeky, gives me some sense of being important, a bit of status, but I can only do that in one class with Mr Tebitt, because he's so soft, and never gives out. Poor bastard. With the rest of them I am quiet as a mouse because I know they won't let me get away with it.

The one day I went on the mitch with some of the girls, we spent the morning in my friend Aileen's house, but my heart never stopped racing, and I was terrified of being caught. Any time they asked me after that, I had to pretend I wasn't interested because I just hated every minute of it.

I am fat and self-conscious, and think I must be so ugly, not normal, like other girls who look pretty and have small feet and neat hands. My huge size-eight feet are laughed at by everyone. The day they took my runners and threw them around the classroom, I thought I would die. Why can't I be like everyone else?

Near the end of the summer term we get given a note to bring home. I read it slowly as I walk home and begin to feel excited. I can feel butterflies in my stomach. When I get home I read it to Ma.

'Ma, it says here if you want your child to return next year, I need to bring in three pounds to school. Does this mean that I don't have to go back?'

'You'll have to talk to your father about that,' she says.

I march into Da, nervous and excited at the same time. This is my escape plan and I'm determined to get my own way.

'Da, Ma said it was OK with her if it was OK with you that I leave school because this note says that if you want your child to attend school next year you have to send money.'

'If it's OK with your ma, then it's OK, but you'll have to get a job.' He doesn't even look up from the newspaper when he answers me. I can hardly get out of the room quick enough.

And that's it. I'm out of school! All my suffering is over. I can't believe it was so easy. I won't have to go back to that awful place ever again, but where am I going to get a job?

I run over to tell Christine how lucky I am and she tells me that her sister is going job hunting the following morning and that I can go with her.

The next morning, Noleen knocks for me and we begin our search. There are a load of clothes factories just over the bridge in Ballyfermot, so we take the short walk to them first but have no luck. Most of them say that I look too young and I think Noleen is regretting having me along. She has worked before but the place she was working in closed down the week before.

'We'd better head into town,' she says.

I'm so glad I'm not on my own because Noleen knows where to go and if we get a job together at least I won't have to get the bus on my own in the mornings. We get off the bus in Thomas Street and begin knocking on doors. Still no luck, but one man looks at me and asks me how old I am.

'Thirteen,' I lie.

'If you come back with a letter from your school saying you've left, I'll give you a job.'

I can't believe it. I can easily do that and then I'll have a job, great!

We try a few more places and decide to go home. I am trying not to look too happy because I'll have a job as soon as I get my letter but poor Noleen won't.

The next morning at about ten o'clock I go down to the school and it feels strange. The hallways are all empty but I don't feel scared any more because I don't have to come back here. I spot the head nun and walk over to her.

'Hi,' I say, all chatty and full of beans. I never spoke to the woman in my life, but what can she do to me now? 'My name is June Kavanagh and I need a letter to say I've left school.'

She's looking at me funny.

'I'm looking for a job,' I explain patiently, thinking maybe she's a bit touched in the head, 'but the man I spoke to said that I need a letter from the school to say I have left.' She looks hard at me and it feels like something is wrong here.

'How old are you?' she snaps.

'Eh, just thirteen.' I'm sorry I came in here now! I didn't figure on this. She'll probably make me come back and she doesn't look happy. How can I get out of this?

'You're only twelve! You shouldn't even have left school.'

'Eh, my ma and da said it's OK and I'm looking for a job.'

'Get out of my sight now or I'll have the inspector on to you.'

My face is red and I turn around and walk out of there as fast as I can. I run all the way home and tell Ma what the nun said, and she says, 'Don't worry, Da says you can work in the shop with me.'

Wait till I tell Paula – she'll be sick! Not only do I not have to go back to that shithole, but I get to spend the whole day with Ma! No more feeling stupid, no more break-times with no friends to play with, no more eating that crap they give you, or worrying over homework and tests. I might even get paid for working in the shop! I start thinking about what I'll do with my first week's wages and run upstairs to make Paula jealous, humming 'Welcome Home', the new Peters and Lee song, loudly to myself.

Joyce: 1961

Da's taking me into town and I feel so special. He's grabbing my leg while he's driving and it tickles so much, I laugh till my stomach hurts. I love it when he talks to me because I am only six, and he's so clever. He explains why I cry when he does it to me.

'You have a skin. It stops me getting my thing into you, and that's why you cry. When I break the skin, it won't hurt any more. Tonight I'll give you a tablet; it'll put you to sleep. And when I break the skin, I'll buy you a new bike.'

He's great for explaining it all to me. I'm so excited about my bike, I can't wait for bedtime.

He is tickling me. I can't stop laughing.

'I can't wait to tell everyone about my bike, Da.'

'No, don't tell anyone yet. It's our little secret.'

'Ah, Da, can I just tell Leonard?'

'No, then he'll want one.'

He keeps putting his hand up my skirt.

His nails are scraping me, but I don't cry because I really want a bike. I keep looking out the window to make sure no one sees me. I'm trying to close my legs because a man in a lorry beside us is looking out of his window, but Da tells me to keep them open. I'm looking for something to cover me but Da has my skirt up high and there is nothing to put over me. I'm scared. What'll I do if someone sees what he's doing? They'll think I'm dirty.

When we get home, it's six o'clock. I'm dying to tell someone about my bike but I can't, so I sit waiting for bedtime.

'What time have we to go to bed, Da?'

Leonard and June think I'm mad because they don't want to go to bed. I wait and wait until he finally says, 'Chop chop, time for bed.'

'Ah, Da, please, can we stay up for a little while?' Leonard begs.

I jump up real quick and go straight to bed. I'm so excited. Da shouts at Leonard and he stomps up the stairs crying. Da follows us up and checks to see if I have taken off my knickers. I pull up my nightie and show him. He gives me a tablet and a drink of water. I nearly choke because the tablet's too big.

'Take a drink and swallow real quickly.'

June and Leonard want a tablet too but Da tells them that I've a pain in my leg. I can't sleep, all I can think about is my bike. I can't wait to get it. I'm the only one awake when Da comes up.

'It didn't work, Da.'

'It's OK if you're not asleep. You'll still be relaxed and it'll make it easier for me. Come in here.'

I climb out of bed and go in to his room. He opens his trousers and takes out his thing.

'Here, hold it tight and pull it up and down, like this.' His thing is all soft and stinky. I squeeze really hard and pull it up and down like he says. It's purple with a slit on top. I try my best but my hand's hurting. He's angry and takes it off me to do it himself.

'Lie down and open your legs.'

I get on the bed and pull up my nightie so I can't see what he's doing. He puts Vaseline down there and I jump because it's freezing. He lies on top of me. I'm squashed and I can't breathe. What's wrong? I can feel it, he's hurting me. He said it wouldn't hurt. I put my hand in my mouth so I won't make noise. I don't want him to be angry. He'll hit me if I make a noise. I look at the ceiling and think of my bike. It's really hurting. I can't think of my bike any more because my legs are killing me. He's digging his thing into me. I try to be brave, but I can't stop crying.

'Open your legs wider.'

I try to stretch my legs but they're open as wide as I can make them, and he's breathing all heavy and right in my ear. The squishy sound is horrible. I want to put my fingers in my ears but if I take them out of my mouth, I'll make too much noise.

'Shush. You'll wake the others and you won't get your bike.'

I can't be quiet, it hurts too much. He pulls me up off the bed and slaps me across the cheek. My face is stinging.

'You sniffling little cunt, fuck off back to bed and you can forget about that bike.'

'I'm sorry, Da. I won't cry any more. Don't be mad, please, Da.'

He picks me up and throws me across the room. I hit my back off the wall and slide onto the bed. He's gone, he hates me and I won't get my bike. I pray to God to make me good for Da.

Joyce: 1964

It's so exciting; Da is making the shop bigger. It means we won't have to stand out in the cold when we are weighing the potatoes. It looks huge. Ronnie, Tony and Kevin are helping him and he is letting me help out too, even though I am only eight.

The wall is getting really high now as they put one brick on top of the other. I can barely see the field outside. Da tells me he is going to put shelves along this wall and we can make more money because we will have more room for things. He says we will be rich when this is done, and I believe him because he's great.

Ronnie and Tony are working on the other wall and Kevin is mixing cement. The boys are laughing and joking and I am so happy because they are all having fun and there is no fighting. A man looks over the wall and asks Da what he's doing; he's from the Corporation he says, and I stand on my tippy toes to see him and I notice he's holding a board in his hand and writing down something.

'I'm extending the shop,' Da says.

'Who is the owner?'

'I am,' says Da, not even looking at the man.

'You need permission to build an extension. You can't build without it.'

'Watch me.'

'I am sorry, Mr Kavanagh, but this building has to come down.'

'You can't tell me what to do on my own land. Now get the fuck off my property.'

'I will have to send the authorities out to see you, Mr Kavanagh.' The man stands back a bit from the wall and I can see he is scared. Da is so brave talking to this man with his clipboard.

'Send whoever you fuckin like. This is my property and you won't tell me what to do with it.'

The man looks afraid. The paper in his hand is shaking and he won't look at Da. He turns and walks away.

Ronnie asks, 'Will we stop, Da?'

'No you fuckin won't. Get building and don't mind that bollox. No one will tell me what I can and can't do with my own fuckin house.'

'What if he gets the police, Da?'

'I don't give a bollox. This is my land. Now get back to work. Fuck them, this is my house. Now give me the hammer. Did you see the little fucker running away?' Da asks the boys.

'No, but I'd have run away if I was him!' Ronnie says, and they all laugh.

Da is so brave, no one can hurt him. He's too strong and he's not even afraid of the police. No one can mess with him; he'd kill them.

Joyce: 1968

Oh shit, he caught me again. I quickly pull down my nightdress, feeling naked. Da does this every morning. I feel dirty and want to smack him as he glares at me. I hear him give his usual orders to get up, but I'm annoyed, so I ignore him.

'Did you wet the bed again? You dirty little bitch. You can clean them fuckin sheets when you come home from school.'

I feel sick. Why am I the only one to wet the bed? I'm twelve, and too old to wet the bed. He's right – I am a dirty bitch. No matter how hard I try, it keeps happening. I dream I'm sitting on the toilet. That's how it happens. June looks at me but says nothing, she's annoyed because she is smelly because of me, and Paula has a smirk on her face. I want to kill her. Why me? What's wrong with me?

I pick my clothes up off the floor and put them on. They're crumpled and dirty. I wish I could look like Sharon Butler. She's always so clean, with her white pleated skirt and her spotless white socks and the ringlets in her shiny hair. She looks lovely all the time. I've no clean socks or knickers again, so I have to wear the ones I had on yesterday.

I go down and start breakfast. Ma tells me to make porridge because the milkman's not here yet. I pour the porridge in the pot, stir and watch it bubble and I whisper the poem I had to learn for homework. I know I'll get it wrong again.

'June, Paula, breakfast is ready. Come now or we'll be late again,' I roar up the stairs as I sit down to eat mine.

They saunter into the kitchen, June with her big smile which annoys the hell out of me, and Paula with her whinging, trying to get off school again. Ma falls for this all the time, sitting Paula on her lap, stroking her hair like she's a little baby. I'd have to drop dead before she'd sit me on her lap. I hate the two of them. I do all the work here and no one ever notices me.

'Can I have more sugar?' June asks.

'No, just eat and shut up,' I reply as I shout up the stairs, 'I'm going to school now, Ma.'

I slam the door behind me as I head to school. I don't like school. I knock for my friend Barbara. Like me, she's always late. We talk about how we hate Sharon for being the teacher's pet. Barbara starts singing 'I Got You, Babe' and 'Help Me, Rhonda', the rest of the way to school, laughing when we forget the words.

I sit at my desk near the back of the class. My pencil is worn right down, but I put it in the little groove of the desk and hope no one notices.

'Get out your catechisms and open at page 23,' the teacher says.

Shit, not this. I can remember all the Latin when I'm in mass but not in class. I open the page and read to myself. It's like double Dutch, but I move my lips with everyone else as we recite the prayer. I watch Kate's lips carefully, so no one will notice that I don't have a clue what I'm saying.

'OK, girls, English books and recite "Daffodils",' she says.

Oh God, I've learned the wrong one. What'll I do? My hands are shaking and sweaty as I take out my English book. My throat is dry. I need a drink of water.

'Right. All together, girls, the poem please.' The teacher pushes her glasses up onto her nose.

My heart is pounding. I pray she won't call me. I'd better move my lips so she doesn't notice. 'I wandered lonely as a cloud' the class is chanting. I can't even find it in my book.

'Miss Kavanagh what's the next line?' the teacher asks me.

I stumble to my feet, trying to spot the answer in the English book. I look around, hoping someone will give me the answer, but all I hear is my heart pounding.

'Well, Miss Kavanagh, are you going to tell me or is it a secret?'

'Ehh, ehh.' I'm stalling, hoping the floor will swallow me.

'Give me the next line!' she roars at me.

I'm frightened now. 'I don't know,' I say. I try to hold back the tears but they flow down my face.

'What are you crying about?'

The room is quiet and everyone stares at me.

'I don't know, Teacher. I learned the wrong poem last night,' I say, wiping my tears with my sleeve.

'Come up here, Miss Kavanagh.'

I walk up to her slowly, my legs shaking. I can feel every eye on me. I have to use my sleeve again to wipe my nose and tears as I get closer to her.

'I'm sorry, Teacher, I learned the wrong poem. I made a mistake, Teacher.'

'I only asked you a question. What are you so upset about?' she asks, her voice softer.

I sob and can't get any words out of my mouth. My sleeve is really wet as I stand in front of her.

'I want you all to go over your poem, girls. Sharon, you're in charge,' she instructs the class as she takes me by the arm and leads me to the door.

Oh shit, I'm in big trouble now. She must be taking me to the principal's room. I'm afraid.

'Teacher, I'm sorry. I learned the wrong poem.' I keep saying it over and over as she takes me into the hallway. I can hear the class giggling as the door closes behind us and Sharon shouts at them to be quiet. Teacher brings me to the big window outside our classroom and stands in front of me.

'Joyce, is there something wrong?' she asks in her nice voice.

I'm crying so much now, I can't talk.

'I learned the wrong poem.'

'Is everything OK at home?'

I don't get it. What's home got to do with me not knowing my poem? I wish she'd let me go back to my desk. She asks me again if everything is OK at home. I'm sobbing, so it's hard to answer.

'Yes.'

'Are you sure, Joyce?' she asks, stroking my hair.

'Yes, Teacher.'

What's she on about? What does she want me to say? I can't think of anything to tell her.

'Why are you crying?'

'I learned the wrong poem, Teacher.'

'Pull yourself together. Go clean yourself up, then come back to class and learn your poem for tomorrow,' she says.

I walk down the corridor to the toilet, still sobbing. I wet my face in the sink, hoping it will hide my big red eyes, but it doesn't. I look for something to wipe my face on but there's nothing, so I use my jumper again. I can't stop crying and every time I wipe my face more tears come down. I don't want to walk back into the class because I know they'll all stare at me but the teacher will be mad because I've been so long. I can hear them all saying their tables as I stand outside the door. I take a few deep breaths before I open the door and walk in. They go quiet as I go to my desk and I can feel their eyes staring.

'Did I tell you to stop?' The teacher says to the class, banging her ruler on the desk.

I jump with fright and slip into my seat. I want to go home.

It seems like forever until the bell rings and it's time to go home. I rush out to the gate to see Barbara waiting for me. We laugh all the way home and she never mentions what happened in class.

As I turn the corner to my street, I notice Da's car isn't there. I run through the shop, knowing I can get my housework done and go and play before he gets back. I finish really quickly, and look around to check everything before I rush out the door.

I skip up to the little field at the top of the road to meet the girls. It's nearly six o'clock when Da stands at the door and shouts at me to come in. I hope he doesn't hit me in front of everyone because I go real red.

'Where's that bollox, Leonard?'

'Don't know, Da.'

Everyone is kneeling in front of the telly waiting for the Angelus to begin. The bells start and we begin saying the Our Father. There's still no sign of Leonard. He'll get it when he turns up. When we finish our prayers, I start the dinner.

'Cunt, get me a cuppa,' he says, handing me a filthy cup with stains down the side and a big crack in it.

I pull a clean cup out of the press and pour the tea out of our army teapot which smells of burned tea bags. I hand him the tea and head back to the kitchen to get the dinner. He shouts at me, 'Where's my fuckin cup? What kind of a fuckin idiot are you? Get me my own cup, gee bag.'

I empty the tea into his dirty chipped cup. I want to spit in it before I give it back, but I don't. My hands are shaking with temper. I wish I could tell him to fuck off.

Ma's still in the shop, so I prepare the spuds, steak and kidney pies and peas. When it's ready, I signal by shouting 'Dinner' to no one in particular, as I place his dinner on the table.

'Who do you think you're feedin, a fuckin mouse? Give me more fuckin spuds. I'm only the bleedin boy in this house.'

I pick up the plate, top up the spuds and give it back to him. Everyone sits in silence at the table except him. He laughs at the telly with his mouth full and dribbles down his shirt. After dinner, Da tells Paula to help me with the washing up. I wash and she dries, not a word between us. I put Ma's dinner in the oven and check the sheet for my bed to see if it's dry. It's still a little wet but I sneak upstairs to make my bed and give the room a quick tidy. I throw the shoes in the big cardboard box in the corner and quickly make the bed with the horrible smelly blankets that itch my skin. I really want to see *Get Smart,* which starts in a minute. I rush down in time for the start and sit on the floor in front of the TV.

Click, click.

I hear it in the background but I pretend not to notice.

Click, click.

'Oi! You lot, feet.' He points at me, Paula and June.

I run in to get the basin and June grabs the powder and a towel. I really want to see *Get Smart,* so I hurry and put the basin down in front of him. The lazy sod won't even move his feet, so Paula lifts them and takes off the smelly socks, which are making her sick as she plonks his feet in the water.

'It's too fuckin hot! Are you trying to scald me?' he shouts as he hits me on the back of the head.

I lift the basin to add cold water. I'm missing my programme. We each do our job on his feet while we watch *Get Smart.* When it's over, he tells us to go to bed. I have to learn my spellings and my tables, so I jump up. It's like a speed test as we all want to be in bed when Da comes up to do the knicker test, checking to see that we're not wearing our pants. He says they're dirty, and we're not allowed to wear them in bed. When he's gone, I learn my tables and do the rest of my homework until I am too tired.

'Will you tell us a story please, Joyce?' June asks.

'OK, give me a minute.'

I make up a story of how brave I am in school, telling my sisters lies about how everyone likes me and I have loads of friends.

'I have to go to the loo, June.'

'Yeah, I have to go too,' June replies.

We both get out of bed, pull up our nightdresses and slide

72

our bums under the bed, listening to the hissing sound as we pee. We wait until it seeps into the carpet and get back into the bed again.

We always pee under the bed because we don't have a bucket in our room like the boys. To use the toilet downstairs, we have to pass through Da's room and I'm afraid he'll call me to do something. It's a wonder no one ever says a word about the smell.

'Paula, turn off the light,' I shout over. We cuddle in and go to sleep.

Joyce: 1971

It's bedtime. The other two have already gone but I was allowed to stay up and watch *Dad's Army* cos I'm older. When it's finished, I run up and get undressed before he comes up to do the knicker test.

'Have you got your knickers off?'

'Yes, Da.'

'Let me see then.'

He pulls back the blankets and we lift our nightdresses quickly and pull them straight down again.

'Good, now straight to sleep.'

He turns out the light and closes the door behind him.

'I miss Ma. Do you, Joyce?'

'Yes.'

'Me too,' shouts Paula from her bed across the room.

'When is she coming home, Joyce?'

'I don't know. She's at a funeral in England; she could be gone for a week.'

June is ten now and Paula eight, and they miss Ma. I do too, but I am enjoying playing Mammy while she's away. I feel very grown up. After all, I'm fifteen now, and I do all the dinners and get the girls ready for school anyway.

I wake up feeling Da's hand under the blankets. He's trying to get between my legs. It's very dark, so I turn around and pretend to be asleep.

'Psstt, psstt?'

If I stay asleep, he'll go away.

'Psstt, Joyce?'

Why won't he leave me alone? It's dead quiet, his hand is gone. He must think I'm asleep. He's lifting me up. I keep my eyes closed. Where is he bringing me? What's he doing? He's putting me down. Where am I? I'll have to wake up. I sit up rubbing my eyes and yawning, so he'll think I'm only waking now.

'Where am I?'

'Shush, it's all right, you're here with me.'

Oh, God, I'm in his bed! I should've woken up when I was in my own bed. What's he going to do?

'Can I go into my own bed, Da?'

'No, I want you to sleep with me tonight.'

'What, all night?'

'Yes, won't that be nice?'

'But, Da, I want to sleep in my own bed.'

He laughs. 'That's only because you never slept with me before.'

I don't want to be with him all night. What can I do? What can I say?

'When you do it, Da, can I go back to my own bed?'

'Shush, be quiet. Take off your nightdress.'

'What? But, Da, I've nothing on underneath.'

'Take it off.'

'Will I just pull it up out of your way, Da?'

'No, take it fuckin off.'

Oh, Mammy, oh God, help me.

'Come on, take it off.'

I pull up my nightie slowly, hoping he'll change his mind. Oh, Jesus, what'll I do? He grabs my nightie and reefs it off me. I'm freezing. He pulls me down beside him and puts his arm round me, rubbing me all over to make me warm. He rubs my belly and moves up to my tits. I haven't even got tits. They're just little lumps. He's never touched me there before.

Oh Mammy, Mammy, Mammy, someone help me. I close my eyes real tight, and try to think of something nice. Think of Christmas. Oh, Jaysus, I can't. I can't because Da's hand is between my legs. He's putting his finger inside me and his nail is killing me. His other hand is on my tits and it feels really horrible. Please help me, please, anyone. I close my eyes tighter and think of the fun we had at Christmas with Kevin.

God, what's he doing? He's kissing me on my mouth. I'm going to be sick. I try to turn my head to get away, but he turns too. His face is rough and it's hurting me. The smell is terrible. I can't believe he's doing this; he never did this before. Does he think I'm Ma? She's not here. I'm trapped. There's no one to stop him. He sits up. What's wrong? Is he going to hit me over the kissing thing? He gets on top of me. He's too heavy. I can't breathe.

'Open your legs.'

They are open, you eejit. I can't get them any wider.

'Open your fuckin legs I said.'

I stretch my legs as wide as I can and he leans on me again. His knuckles are digging into my legs because he's trying to put his thing into me and I think my legs are going to break. He has it in, so he'll be moving his hand away now and maybe it won't hurt as much. I look at my usual spot on the ceiling.

It's dark and I can't really see it but I don't care, I know where it is. He's making that funny sound; he must be nearly finished. I hope I can go back to my own bed now.

Something's wrong. He stops and gets off me. He's breathing funny. I hope he doesn't hit me. I must've done something wrong.

'Can I go back to my own bed now, Da?'

'No, I'm not finished.'

Why did he stop if he wasn't finished? I'm cold, the blanket is at the bottom of the bed and I have nothing on. I want to cover myself but I'm afraid to move. He rubs me down there and keeps putting his hand on my tits. What's he doing? Why did he stop?

'Turn around.'

'What? Around where?'

'On your belly.'

'Why? For what?'

'Just do what you're fuckin told!'

I lie on my belly and he gets on top of me. He slaps me on the back of the head and tells me to be quiet. His knee is between my legs. He's putting his thing in from behind. I wish he'd hurry up and finish. He pulls my bum in the air and touches my tits. He's on his knees pushing my head into the pillow. I can't breathe. I try to lift my head but he pushes it back.

'Oh, yes, yes.'

'Can I go back to my own bed now, Da?'

'Don't move. I'm not finished.'

Why does he keep stopping? He's rubbing my bum again with his thing and he keeps putting it in and taking it out again.

'Almost there.'

My legs are killing me, so I move a little.

'Ah, yes, that's my girl. You're enjoying this now.'

Oh, God, how does he think that? I'll never move again. I feel a pain in my bum like a knife. I let out a scream. I can't help it, he's putting it in the wrong hole.

'Da, you're putting it in the wrong hole.'

He pushes my head into the pillow. The pain, oh, God, make him stop.

'Da, you're putting it in the wrong hole. It's hurting me.'

He puts his hand on my neck and pushes my head into the pillow. I can't breathe. I try to move but I can't. I can see a white light.

'Yes, yes.'

I can hear him, but the light is getting brighter. I can't feel anything. No more pain. It feels lovely. I must be dead.

I hear someone calling me and my face is stinging me. It's Da, he's smacking me on the face. I don't want to wake up; it's nice here. He's smacking me again, so I have to open my eyes.

'You silly girl. That's what happens when you don't do what you're told.'

'Can I go back to my own bed now?'

'Yes.'

I pick up my nightie and go to the toilet. I sit in the corner and rock myself until I stop crying.

Joyce's Kitchen 2010

It's 2010, and the women have been working on their book for several years now, albeit with lengthy and frequent breaks. This is the most intensive period of writing so far, though, and whilst they can feel something shift, a letting go taking place, it's tough, painful and exhausting.

The room is silent as Paula tidies Joyce's kitchen table, moves papers, empties ashtrays and damp tissues into the bin and clears away half-drunk cups of tea. The sisters are emotional, tearful, wrung out.

'Reading that, you realise the innocence,' says Joyce. 'It's a reminder that we were just children. You forget that sometimes. Remembering how young we were really helps me to believe that it wasn't my fault.'

The cold, dull Saturday afternoon has been spent sitting in Joyce's kitchen, reading each other's childhood memories. It's been a struggle for all three sisters, and their red puffy eyes and the overflowing ashtray are testimony to the emotion of the day.

'Me too,' says June, wiping her nose and sniffing. 'It's the first time I can really see it had nothing to do with me. That it was done to me. Jaysus, that's been a long time coming.'

June bows her head and sobs, this time long and hard.

'I know what you mean, about accepting that it wasn't our fault,' says Joyce gently. She is eager to talk, analyse and interpret what they have shared in their writing. 'It was difficult to accept I was innocent because he made us have an active role in the abuse. We had to take it out for him, get it ready for him, put it in the right hole for him.'

'I know,' says Paula, between deep drags of her cigarette. 'He was never ready, never turned on. It wasn't about the sex for him, or needing the release. It was about power and control.'

'And apart from the physical stuff,' Joyce continues, 'and being complicit in the abuse, I also had this huge need to be loved, to be needed, to please him. Did he make you go to confession? He made me go, and I did it! Imagine the stupidity, given what was going on. You'd think he would have been worried.'

'No, I never had to do that, but he obviously had a fetish for

Communion dresses,' says Paula. 'I'm pretty sure that's the first time he went the whole way with me.'

'Me too,' June says. 'At least I think so. I know there was definitely full sex on my Communion day and I don't think he had done that before then. The abuse had started long before that though. I remember my feet would dangle off the side of the bed when he was at me. They didn't reach the ground, that's how young I was. But full sex, yeah, I'm pretty sure that was in my white Communion dress.'

'I never had any of those feelings,' says Paula angrily. 'You know, wanting to please him, the way you did, Joyce. There was no part of what I did that was about him. I had given up trying to make him like me, even at that young age.'

'That's a lie!' explodes Joyce. 'You were constantly disappointed when he didn't acknowledge you or when he excluded you. You're the only one who went to his funeral, for God's sake!'

'Yeah, come on, Paula,' says June; 'that's just not true that you stopped wanting to please him. Looking for his approval was a huge thing for you.'

Paula shakes her head, a wry smile on her face. 'You fuckers,' she laughs. 'Jaysus, you get away with nothing with you two! I know, I know, I've really struggled to acknowledge that actually I spent years trying to get his approval. To be honest, it's only now I'm joining up the dots. The coaching sessions at work and the focus on taking responsibility, they made me realise that I can't blame everyone else, which is what I did for years. If I was in a bad mood, it wasn't my fault; it was other people upsetting me. Anything that went wrong, any difficulties at all, I was always able to find someone else to blame, rather than take any responsibility for it myself. Before I went to counselling, I was convinced it was all my fault, that the abuse was my fault. Then in counselling, I didn't engage, but I kept hearing that I'm not responsible, this was done to you. So I took that on, but lived my life believing I had no responsibility for anything. I didn't separate out that the abuse was one thing, my life another.'

'I was really worried that this writing process would somehow justify you not taking any responsibility,' says Joyce. 'I knew that revisiting the abuse, and beginning to understand our innocence in it, might leave you thinking that you could live your life as the victim, taking no ownership. That would have been really hard on all of us, so it's great, finally, that you're starting to separate those things out.'

There is gentle laughter as the sisters enjoy the teasing, and the comfort that comes with knowing each other so intimately. The deep sense of each other is hugely reassuring for them.

'It's only in writing this book that I realised I've been angry for years,' says Paula. 'I know it started with him, but I took that anger everywhere with me. I used to get such pleasure from annoying him in small ways where I had some control. I couldn't stop the abuse, but I could irritate him with things like moving his stuff on the table, or coming in ten minutes late, so that's where I put my energy.'

'I think you were really brave doing that,' says June.

'But that was how I got my daily conquest! I knew I couldn't stop him, so you take control where you can, don't you?'

'What strikes me most is our willingness and passion to protect him, how we took on responsibility for everything,' says June. 'We were the ones who would have assumed the blame if we got caught, so we watched in case someone came up the stairs. That's the hardest thing to hear, and even in counselling that was the most difficult thing to accept, that I had taken responsibility for the abuse, because then I had to stop doing that and start blaming him.'

'I don't remember trying to protect him,' says Paula. 'I didn't tell anybody about the abuse because I was convinced it was my fault. I know I protected people and him by not telling anybody but I *thought I was protecting me, and stopping Mammy leaving. It wasn't because I wanted to protect him.'*

'I can't believe how stupid I was,' June laughs, but her expression immediately turns to one of sadness, regret. 'I couldn't feel sorry for myself because I thought I was to blame. I wasn't able to relinquish the hurt and pain, because I believed I had to take some responsibility for what happened. I always suffered under the delusion that he couldn't possibly understand what he was doing, because he couldn't have done it if he did. I couldn't cope with the idea that he had made choices. Even in counselling, I couldn't take it when they said he was evil. I was ever the optimist. When the abuse came out, I said to Joyce, "Da wasn't always bad. Remember he took us to Butlin's?" And she said, "Yeah and what did you have to do for that?" I never put those things together. Thick, eh?'

'We all so quickly call ourselves stupid,' says Joyce, stubbing out her cigarette. 'And think of ourselves as dense. But now, discussing this, I realise that actually it was innocence. It makes sense that we didn't understand things. There is something very freeing in that for me, understanding I wasn't stupid; that I was just a naïve child. That's a powerful realisation.'

The room is calm now, and for a moment the sisters look out at the darkening sky, each remembering their own innocence.

'I was oblivious of the possibility that the same thing was happening to others in the house,' says Paula, 'so we were all naïve or innocent or stupid, in our own way. I firmly believed it was only me, because he hated me. I was convinced that what was happening was only happening to me and to nobody else. It didn't cross my mind for a second that the same thing had happened to you.' Paula avoids her sisters' eye contact as she fidgets with the sheets of writing strewn across the table.

'There have been so many secrets, haven't there? It's not just the abuse itself,' says Joyce, 'but even when this all came out, and people talked about it, they just referred to him as "your father". It was a taboo subject, and he was powerful, wasn't he?

'He certainly didn't suffer fools lightly,' laughs June.

'I used to get very upset when people criticised him. I took it really personally when people on the road called him "jug-head"!' Joyce laughs at herself as she thinks about the many occasions when young people on the road would have shouted abuse at their father. 'But they only ever did it from a safe distance. They weren't eejits!'

'I thought they were great because none of us had the guts to do that. I really admired people for criticising him, especially June when she did it,' says Paula.

'I don't remember anyone criticising him!' June stares wide-eyed and laughing at her sisters. 'Honestly, I don't. Did they?'

'Jaysus, June, you were the worst! Even Paula felt sorry for him when you gave out to him. You had a wicked tongue.'

'June, you were great at slagging people,' Paula says. 'We all loved how you amused us so much.'

'I slagged myself because it was easier than waiting for them to slag me! It was a good defence mechanism I guess. I always anticipated being called names, so I tried to get in there first, and being funny is part of that protection too, isn't it? You can't be hurt if you're laughing.'

Paula picks up some of the papers and flicks her finger against a sheet. 'The thing I found the most disgusting reading this, what really made me feel sick, was him trying to kiss you, Joyce. It's like a prostitute saying she'll do anything but don't kiss me.'

'Oh no,' says June. 'The worst thing was yours, Paula, and your insides coming out.'

'Girls,' says Joyce impatiently, 'we're not going to compete over what was the worst experience! They were all terrible. None of it should have happened.'

Paula and June nod, eyes down, chastened by Joyce's uncharacteristic outburst.

'Do you know what I hated most?' continues Joyce. 'When he'd try and touch you up, grab your chest, or your arse.'

'He never touched my chest. I hadn't got one!' says June.

'He didn't just grab your arse,' says Paula, 'He'd go right up your shift! He did it to everyone: women who came into the shop, anyone. But everybody passed it off as a joke. He'd convince you that if you had a problem with it, there was something wrong with you.'

Joyce adds, 'He'd be at you the whole time. You'd be making a sandwich and he'd be in at your nipples. It made my skin crawl, but it was just the norm.'

'"Gis a look", do you remember that?' asks June. 'He'd say, "Gis a look" and you'd have to open your legs so he could see your fanny.'

'I remember one night he was in bed and called me in,' says Joyce, 'and there he was reading a book, not the Bible for a change. It was obviously an erotic book, and he was fiddling with himself, and feeling me, and he says, "Do you like that?"'

'"No," I say. "Really?" he says, all disappointed. "No," I say. "Well, it says here, that's good. It says here if I touch your clitoris, that you'll really like it." Jaysus, I was eight! I hadn't even heard of a clitoris! Come to think of it, I haven't fuckin heard much about one since!' Joyce roars laughing. They all do, deep belly laughs. 'But really, I was disgusted. The idea that he thought I might like it,' she adds, more sombrely. 'I remember one time asking him if I could have tights. I must have been about sixteen,' says Joyce, lighting another cigarette. 'D'you know what the dirty fucker did? He went and bought me stockings, and, girls, wait till I tell you, it gets worse … he put them on me!'

'He what? Ah, Jaysus.'

The three sisters collapse with laughter. Between gasps of breath, June manages to add, 'I'll go one better, girls. He bought me a see-

through black negligee. I think he thought I'd parade around the house in it!'

'Well, I didn't get anything like that,' says Paula. 'The only thing he ever bought me was that silver catsuit thing. I looked like someone had pissed on me! I couldn't walk down the road in it without everyone laughing at me.'

'Yeah, it was a one-off, wasn't it?' says June.

'Ah, Jaysus, Paula, it was desperate,' says June, struggling to speak through her giggles.

The laughter gives way to the sadness again, as the three women look at the written pages covering the table, shuffling painful memories into neat piles as they begin to finish their work for the evening. The room is dark now, but, despite the tiredness, they are elated by the sense of their lives coming together, both on paper and around the kitchen table.

'I had such anxiety about going to school, being noticed, everyone knowing how thick I was,' says June, lighting another cigarette. 'I would have done anything to be invisible, to avoid my name being called.'

'Yes, that was the worst, having your name called out and everyone looking at you,' agrees Joyce. 'I just went blank, I fell apart. I'd start crying, blubbing, trembling from head to toe. I remember feeling my heart pounding in my chest. It was terrible, just from the teacher calling my name. It's only recently made sense to me, that what I really wanted was to be invisible.'

'I only realised that too as we've been writing this book,' says June. 'It was the being seen that was so difficult, so being called out of class, being asked to do something, or something being expected of you, was so exposing, really frightening.'

'Knowing I was stupid, it was obviously only a matter of time before everyone else would know it, so you'd try and avoid the attention. I'd see white and go blind if the teacher called my name.

I couldn't see anything,' adds June, dragging on her cigarette.

'That's interesting you went blind,' says Paula. 'I went deaf! As soon as my name was said, I couldn't hear another word. I was so scared that I would either shit or wet myself. I used to spend the whole day clenching my butt cheeks. The whole day! I couldn't focus on what was happening in the classroom.'

'You always got out of school; we hated you for that,' June says, looking at Paula.

'I couldn't breathe! In hindsight, my bronchitis was probably psychological. It was instant. As soon as I was called for school, I felt the panic and then the struggle to breathe. I'm not saying that all the time I cried off school it was because of my bronchitis, but as soon as I made the connection between being sick and getting Ma's attention and then being allowed to go back to bed, I used it to my best advantage and as often as I could. I used to cry in Ma's face and ask if I could get into her bed with her. I knew Ma didn't want me there – she would turn her back and I knew I wasn't to touch her – but it was the only safe place in the house.'

'We didn't understand that. We didn't believe you were sick at all; we thought you were just a weasel. I remember being so annoyed. I'd be really irritated by you. I know now it was jealousy. You got off school, whereas we were always just sent off, it didn't matter what was wrong with us,' says June.

'The fear and terror of being at school was so disproportionate, for all of us,' Joyce says. 'And yet, it never dawned on me that there was any connection between how I felt at school and the abuse at home. That time the teacher asked me if there was anything wrong at home, it never occurred to me that I could tell her about Da. I didn't see the link.'

'Do you remember sewing class? My hands would sweat so much, I couldn't hold the needle. The material would end up being damp and the stitches would be all over the place,' Joyce continues.

'You'd be mortified handing up this scabby bit of material, or the knitting with all the holes,' says June. 'I hated it so much, not being able to take some pride in my work. And yet we could sew and knit with our eyes shut at home. There was just constant fear at school. No wonder we all thought we were thick. We were never able to answer a question in school, so of course we assumed it was because we were stupid. Plus the fact that at home nobody ever said well done for anything. We were told all the time how dense we were, how we couldn't do anything right. And we never knew that we were all going through the same thing. I thought I was the only one who panicked that way.'

'I used to sweat so much out of nerves that the page would be wet. School was a disaster, the copybook would look like I'd walked on it, or spilled something on it. You'd be so embarrassed,' says Paula.

'There was a real innocence in us though, even when we were teenagers,' says Joyce. 'I was still playing skipping and games on the road when I was seventeen and eighteen, and I was happy doing that. Mentally, we were much younger than our age. Things were different then, children were children for longer, but we were very sheltered too. In a strange way, we were brought up in a cocoon.'

'I think you're right, Joyce. None of us got our periods until we were in our late teens, and we didn't even develop boobs until we were old, much older that our friends, and in my case not until I got pregnant!' June laughs. 'In some ways, our bodies were refusing to grow up, weren't they? It's like we were in denial that we were becoming adults.'

Joyce's daughter knocks on the door and puts her head into the kitchen. A routine has emerged as the sisters' writing has developed, and the families know not to disturb them when they are working.

'Ma, I'm hungry. Is it time for tea yet?'

'Yes, love. I'll get it now.'

Joyce gets up from the table, puts on the kettle, and pulls out a bag of potatoes from under the sink. 'I'd better get these guys sorted,' she *says, emptying the spuds into the sink. 'But, listen, I think we're doing great. It's really coming together, isn't it?'*

'Abso-fuckin-lutely,' confirms June, emptying the ashtrays. 'That's been a good day's work.'

Chapter 3: Decision Time

2 February 1989

The days following the disclosure of the abuse are filled with confusion and fear for all the family, but especially for the three sisters. No one is clear about what will happen next, or what they should do, and they all worry about how their mother is coping. She reverts to her usual quietness and is withdrawn and remote. Whilst the distance is typical of her, it worries the women as they struggle to interpret what she's thinking or feeling. Occasionally, she has an outburst of anger, calling her husband a bastard and saying that she wants him dead, but mostly she keeps herself busy working in the factory, the rhythm of the sewing machine giving some sense of normality to the day. She needs routine.

The sisters are surprised to find they are relieved that the secret is finally out, and, over the days, they tentatively begin to share their experiences and talk through their common hurt. They welcome the opportunity to talk openly about their abuse, and although it is gradual and slow, the conversations are filled with emotion.

There is, however, a constant fear in the house that their father will come back and act as if nothing has happened or deny the allegations, and that no one will be able to do anything about it. Their brothers are ever present, an unspoken understanding that they need to be around, to offer reassurance, possibly even protection, in the event that they are needed. The murmur of hushed conversations, whispered debate, is an incessant backdrop to the apparent normality of the house.

Kevin is the only one in contact with their father, who is staying in a B&B in town, and he comes to the house each day, always with another list of demands from him.

'What the fuck does he want this time?' Paula fumes, snatching the list from Kevin's hand. 'His sweets? His fuckin Vicks sweets? Can you believe the neck of the bastard?'

'He just wants us worrying that he's sick,' says Joyce calmly.

'He *is* fuckin sick, but it's nothin a packet of Vicks will sort!' Paula says.

A few days later, Kevin comes for the typewriter, and, the next day, the request is for their father's binoculars.

Kevin gets verbal abuse from his siblings with every request he brings, and he keeps reminding them that he is only the messenger. He is genuinely worried that his father may harm himself and, on one visit, he tells his sisters that he has agreed to let their father move in with him for a while. 'Just till we know what we're going to do. At least this way we know where he is and he can't get up to anything,' he adds.

'How can you let that man into your house? What exactly do you think is going to happen here? Do you think he's going to wake up some day and be better?' Paula screams.

But June and Joyce are relieved to know someone will be watching over their father and that he will have a decent place to stay. They understand Paula's anger, but avoid eye contact with her and remain quiet. The contradictions within them feel like a growth in their lungs, putting pressure on their breathing, making it difficult to swallow. They know this man has committed terrible hurts, dreadful betrayals of trust, yet they can't bear to think of him cold or not being looked after.

A few weeks after their father moved in with his son, Kevin catches Joyce, June and Paula in the kitchen over lunch. He takes a cup of tea and a deep breath and the sisters wait quietly, knowing he has something important to say.

'So, Da and me had a chat last night, you know, about what he did, you know …' his voice trails off, embarrassed, awkward. 'He admitted he's done wrong, and realises he has a sickness, but he said he hasn't done anything for over six years. He says that's all in the past now.'

'So what about Deirdre?' June asks, thinking about how this whole exposure came about. 'That only happened in the last couple of years, didn't it?'

'Da says, and don't go mad, I'm only telling you what he said, but he says it was Deirdre who tried to seduce him and that he only touched her dickey.'

'He thinks an eight year old can seduce a grown man? That it's nothing to touch a child's vagina?' Joyce spits with contempt. 'How dare he, the sick bastard!'

'He says he's battling with it. He's been getting confession at least three times a week and going to mass every day,' Kevin says.

'Does he think going to confession makes it all right?' Paula asks.

'Look, I know it sounds pathetic but this is the crap he's coming out with. At least it gives us an indication of what's going on in his sick head.'

The sisters shout over one another, angry, furious, reminded sharply of the sense of injustice, powerlessness.

'How could he say such a thing?'

'How could he think we would believe such rubbish?'

'How can he justify what he's done?'

Kevin tries his best not to get involved in the women's reaction – he knows they understand how uncomfortable his position is – but it's still incredibly hard, being the go-between.

The conversation goes on for hours as the kitchen fills with cigarette smoke and frustration. The main concern is the possibility of their father committing more abuse, since he clearly doesn't accept responsibility for his most recent actions. Kevin patiently explains how carefully he is monitoring their father's movements, how he is practically under house arrest, not being allowed out of his room without permission, not even being permitted to change the TV channel unless he says so – but the women cannot be pacified. Eventually, it is decided to phone the family GP and ask for advice. Kevin agrees to speak to the doctor, who has treated their father for years and knows him well. It's decided to also phone Joyce's doctor to get a second opinion.

Joyce's doctor arrives that evening, and their mother joins them for the discussion. The family sits around the table and relates the events of the past few days to the GP.

'Joyce, I've been treating you for depression for years and, I must say, I did suspect sexual abuse, but never for a moment did I suspect your father. Why did you never tell me?'

Joyce shrugs. Now that it's out, it's hard to explain why it was such a closely held secret for so long.

'That doesn't matter now,' Joyce says, dismissing the question. 'What's important is that he doesn't hurt anyone else. What can we do to stop him?'

'I'm not sure there is anything.'

'Could we have him committed?' Joyce asks. 'At least that way he would be away from any children and he could get the help he needs.'

'I'm sorry, but he wouldn't fit the category. He's not a danger to himself, nor is he a danger to society.'

'But he *is* a danger to society,' they all answer together.

'You can't prove that. It's just your word against his. You can't get a committal unless you have solid proof, and they are always suspicious when there is an attempt to commit an elderly person, because they believe it is a ruse to get rid of them.'

'There must be something we can do to make sure that he doesn't abuse anyone else,' says June.

'I'm afraid your sole option is to prosecute him. That's the only thing I can tell you.'

No one says anything as the doctor stands to leave.

'I'm sorry I couldn't be of more help. You know where I am if you need me.'

Their mother walks the doctor to the front door, and when she returns to her daughters, she is visibly shaking.

'Are you OK, Ma?' June asks. 'Here, sit down, I'll make fresh tea.' She gets up from the table and puts on the kettle. Their mother sits down wearily.

'He asked if I was sure that I could manage without your father,' she says.

'What did you say?' asks Joyce.

'Of course I can manage without him. Sure he never lifted a finger anyway, so he'll be no great loss.'

'Is that all he said?' June asks, suspicious that her mother isn't telling them everything.

'He told me not to be influenced by you lot, that you were more than likely exaggerating. He asked if I wanted your da back because it's not too late if I do. I told him if I had a gun I would shoot him myself for all the pain he's caused, and then he gave me these.'

She tosses four Valium tablets on the table.

It's late the following evening when Kevin gets back to tell the women about his conversation with the doctor. Their eldest sister Pamela arrived home from England that morning and he's surprised to see her sitting at the table with her sisters.

'We thought it would be good for Ma to have Pam around,' explains Joyce quietly. 'It'll distract her, if nothing else. Anyway, she needs to be here.'

Kevin hesitates to start when he realises his mother is going to stay in the sitting room, but she evenly returns his gaze, saying, 'Will you all stop trying to protect me? No more secrets. Secrets have destroyed this family.'

'The doctor gave us a referral to the psychiatric institution in St Loman's,' Kevin explains. 'Da and I went over there this morning and saw a doctor, but she said she can't make a decision on whether to commit Da or not until next week, when the head of her department gets back from leave.'

'Does that mean he's still with you?' Joyce asks.

'No, I had to threaten her. I told her that she would be responsible if Da did anything to another child, that she didn't realise just how dangerous a man she was dealing with.'

'So what happened?'

'Eventually she agreed to get Da to sign himself in.'

'How did Da react?' June asks.

'He looked slightly confused and surprised by it all. You know him. I'm sure he was calculating what the right thing to do was. He wasn't about to refuse to go because he knows I'm his only contact, and he needs to keep in my good books. But he did do his best to look sad and broken.'

'Can he be helped?' June asks. She tries but is unable to stop the concern showing in her voice.

'I don't really know. I guess we just have to wait and see what happens. The psychiatrist wants to speak to you girls and hear your side of the story. She said it would give her an indication of what she's dealing with.'

'Does that include me?' Pam asks.

'Yes, why wouldn't it?' Joyce responds quickly.

Pam shifts awkwardly. She has a lot of catching up to do. Her sisters have been sharing their stories for several weeks now, and she is unsure how to step into this new dialogue.

The following day, Kevin drives the four sisters to see the psychiatrist.

'Do you think there's any chance we might run into him?' asks June nervously.

'Who, Da? No way, they'll have him locked up somewhere safe, or he'll be busy writing his memoirs,' laughs Joyce. 'Don't worry, he'll be as anxious to stay out of our path as we are his.'

The car is silent as they drive through the traffic, the wipers making a screeching sound on the windscreen every so often.

'Put the radio on, will you?' Paula asks, keen to dissipate the tension.

Kevin puts on the radio and the sound of Rick Astley blasts through the car.

The loud, upbeat tempo is incongruous with the atmosphere in the car and, after a couple of moments, Joyce leans over and switches it off. No one complains and they finish the journey in silence.

They enter the old psychiatric building and Kevin leads the way down a long, narrow, white-washed corridor. The women are nervous, walking slowly and trying not to look at the strange patients walking by, singing or talking to themselves.

They do their best to avoid any eye contact, but June has a fit of giggles as her nerves get the better of her, and the mood lifts.

'Which one's Nurse Ratched, girls?' laughs Joyce.

'I wouldn't mind stumbling on Jack Nicholson, mind you!' Pam joins in the giggles but they are careful not to make too much noise.

The nerves quickly return as they sit waiting for their appointment outside a heavy brown door, feeling intimidated and very small. A middle-aged woman, smartly dressed, directs them inside, saying she wants to speak only to the girls. Kevin sits back down on the uncomfortable chair to wait. The room is small and has just three chairs, so Pam, June and Joyce take a seat and Paula stands at the back against a filing cabinet. The psychiatrist introduces herself and invites the women to do the same.

'If there is anything you'd like to know, please don't hesitate to ask,' she says. 'If anything I ask is uncomfortable for you and you prefer not to answer, I'll understand.'

The room is silent except for her voice.

'Could you tell me what kind of man your father is in general?' she asks.

'He's an obnoxious man; he has to be in control all the time and he's very aggressive,' Joyce answers quickly.

'He's a dirty, smelly, useless bastard who orders everyone around,' June adds.

'The reason I ask is because he told me that you would not be able to cope without him.'

They all snigger at the idea of this.

'He told me that you could not even get out of bed in the morning if he wasn't there to make you.'

'How can he justify that statement when half of us don't even live in the same house?' June says. 'Don't mind him, the lazy bastard. He's never done a day's work in his life. He's so lazy he wouldn't scratch himself. The only thing he does is tell everyone else what to do.'

'He said that you couldn't survive without him, so he doesn't seem to be worried at all about the possible consequences of his actions. He clearly believes you will take him back,' the psychiatrist adds.

'Survive without him? It's surviving *with* him that's the problem!' says Joyce.

Joyce, June and Paula begin to give some vivid detailed descriptions of their abuse, determined not to leave anything out. Pam is quieter but adds her support every so often, and some details of her own story. Occasionally, the psychiatrist intervenes with a question, but mostly she sits back, listening intently. 'Did he ever use bribery with any of you?' she asks after some time.

'He used to give me money sometimes,' Paula answers.

June turns to Joyce, 'Did he ever pay you?'

'No. Did he ever pay you, Pam?'

'No.'

'He gave you money!' Joyce says loudly as the three sisters all turn to look at Paula, confusion on their faces. Simultaneously, they collapse in laughter at the expression of shock and embarrassment on Paula's face. Gradually, they calm down, conscious at some level of the inappropriateness of their response, and wanting to make a good impression on the psychiatrist, but also hugely relieved at the impact of the laughter on the atmosphere and energy in the room.

'Do you think you can help him?' Joyce asks.

'He is a strange man. He is outside at this very moment typing another short fairy tale for me I suspect, trying to prove his intelligence and his love for children. Every time I try to talk about his reason for being here, he tells me about his latest fairy tale or the teddy he has made, or all the jobs he has worked at in the past. In my opinion, he is feeling no remorse. He doesn't appear to feel any responsibility and has no conscience at all about what he has done,' the doctor replies.

'Isn't there anything that can be done?' June asks her. 'What about those drugs that suppress sexual urges?'

'Arsenic,' Paula says, and they all laugh again.

'As you already know, abuse is not about sex, so that wouldn't really help and, anyway, you can't be sure that he would even take the tablets.'

'Can you keep him in here?' Paula asks.

'Not really. He voluntarily signed himself in, so by law he is free to leave any time he wishes.'

'Is there any advice you can give us? He's a dangerous man and we don't know where to go from here,' Joyce asks.

'I know this is very hard for all of you, but my hands are tied. I will continue to work with him and I promise that I'll do all I can. But if he doesn't want to be helped, then there really isn't a lot that I can do. I'm sorry I can't be of more help.'

With nothing left to say, the women stand up to leave.

'Again I'm sorry that I can't give you more answers. But if any of you ever need to talk, I am always available.'

'Thanks,' Joyce says as they walk out of the room feeling utter confusion and despair.

Joyce briefly fills Kevin in.

'It's hard to believe there's nothing to be done, isn't it?' he says. 'He's a clever bastard; you have to give him that.'

The siblings drive home in silence. They dread having to explain to their mother that no one has been able to offer reassurance, a way out.

'I'm going to tell him he can't come back with me,' says

Kevin. 'I'll go see him tomorrow. It might help him to stay in the hospital, but we can't take him back, I can't listen to any more of his crap.'

The response is a combination of relief and concern.

'What will he do? Where will he go?' June asks.

'I don't give a bollox,' says Paula. 'Just as long as he doesn't come near us again.'

The next few weeks are difficult for everyone, as the family tries to resume some semblance of normality, by returning to work. Joyce and June agree to return to Abrakebabra, while Paula says she will prepare some work from the factory for her and Ma to get on with. Pamela stays on, making weekly calls to her job in England to explain her ongoing absence. The days are a strange contradiction of normality and routine, within a fog of uncertainty and doubt. The sisters talk and wait, defer and avoid, hoping that the decision will be taken out of their hands, knowing that whatever choices they make, they need to be able to live with them.

'Don't worry, girls,' Joyce reassures them. 'The answer will come; we just need to give it time.'

They continue to gather every evening in their mother's, an unspoken acceptance that they all need support and to be together.

A couple of weeks later, their father signs himself out of St Loman's, but no one knows where he has gone. He had gone to Kevin's when he'd first got out, but they only let him stay one night. He left the next morning, looking very sorry for himself, and none of them have seen or heard from him since. It's a welcome respite, yet an unnerving absence.

The daily rounds of tea and chat, possible solutions and likely barriers get thrashed out, and inconclusive conversations ended. They go around and around the limited possibilities, but the conflicting needs within the family stop them being able to agree about what to do next. At times, they argue with each other, are frustrated and stressed, but mostly, they are tired. So very tired.

June arrives one afternoon to find her three sisters and their mother settled at the table, with tea and fags in hand.

'Wait till you hear this, June,' Joyce says, pouring the tea.

'Ma had a visit from a priest,' says Paula. 'Apparently Da is living in an apartment in Clondalkin. The priest reckons he's filled with remorse and is haunted by what he's done,' she spits out sarcastically.

'Yeah, sure he is,' June smirks.

'Shush,' Joyce says. 'Let her speak.'

'He wants me to take him back,' Ma interrupts. 'I was livid and told him all the things Da has done and the people he's damaged.'

'He was so rude too, wasn't he, Ma?' adds Paula. 'He completely dismissed me and spoke over me. He obviously didn't want me there; it was Ma he wanted to influence. The priest claimed he knew it all already, and that Da has confessed everything to him.'

'And he said he's an old man and that his behaviour is in the past and that I should forgive him.' Their mother sounds tired, but she is clearly not taken in by the priest.

'I asked what made him think this behaviour was in the past, but he refused to make eye contact with me and continued to talk over me.' Paula is furious. 'Honestly, girls, I felt sick listening to him; this "man of God" telling us that we should let him back. I couldn't believe the tripe coming out of his mouth. Thank God I was here, I wouldn't have liked Ma to have had to deal with him on her own. Anyway, I sent him packing and told him that I hope the fucker rots in hell. I think he got the message he's not wanted here, but I wouldn't be sure he's given up yet.'

'The cheek of him, what would *he* know?' June says.

'We have to tell Kevin,' Joyce says. 'He'll find out more details about where exactly Da is.'

'Kevin is on his way. I spoke to him just before I left home,' June tells them.

When Kevin arrives, he's filled in. Neither Paula nor her mother can remember the name of the priest but Kevin agrees to investigate because there aren't many churches in Clondalkin. He leaves immediately and agrees to come back if he finds out any more.

The women take up their usual positions at the table with tea and fags, waiting for his return. They discuss how long it will take him to drive there, how long to find out which priest it is, find someone he can talk to, drive back …

'He'll be back before the nine o'clock news,' Joyce concludes confidently.

Anger and frustration fill the air as the family discuss the fact that their father has been able to manipulate yet another person. His ability to convince people of his story is worrying – it leaves them all doubting themselves, wondering how they can compete with this seemingly invincible man.

It is getting dark and the hope of Kevin returning is slowly dying.

'He mustn't have been able to find out anything or he'd be back by now,' June says.

'Give him another half an hour and then we'll call it a night,' Paula replies. Everyone readily agrees. It's clear none of them will be able to sleep without some information about their father's whereabouts. Joyce gets up to refill the cups and, as she places the tea on the table, they hear someone at the front door.

Kevin walks into the room; his face is ashen. No one says a word, but wait in anticipation of what is clearly bad news.

'Da's apartment overlooks the school grounds, and I think he has a job in the school teaching children arts and crafts,' he says.

'What! Who got him the job?' Joyce asks.

'Which school, how did he get the apartment?' June says.

Questions are fired at Kevin.

For once, Paula sits quietly, too angry to speak. She shakes her head every so often, trying to dispel the image of her father watching, with his old binoculars, over the school playground.

Kevin agrees to call into the school the next day and ensure that they are aware of whom they have hired. The conversation continues going around and around but they are all exhausted and struggle to make sense of what is happening.

'One thing is for sure,' says Joyce determinedly. 'We have to make a decision about how we manage Da long term. We can't let him have this hold over us forever.'

They call it a night and each shuffles off for a restless, fitful sleep.

The next morning they take up their positions at the table, tea pot brewing, ashtrays strategically placed and fags always nearby. There is a silence as they know a decision must be made, yet they are all afraid to state the obvious. Paula clears her throat and prepares to say what needs to be said. After all, someone has to.

'We've got to prosecute. We have to. That bastard has his eye on other children. We can't stand by and let him hurt anyone else.'

She can't look her sisters in the eye. She knows her real motivation is about ensuring that he never returns to the family home. She knows that June and Joyce know that too, and she is ashamed of herself.

Joyce is rational, calm, as she says, 'Paula, it's all right to have selfish reasons for doing this. None of us could live with ourselves if we thought he was doing it to anyone else, but the truth is, I'm just as concerned about being blamed by others as I am of the actual potential for abuse. It's not very brave of me, but it's the truth.'

'Hang on a minute,' says June, clearly agitated. 'This is our da we're talking about. I know he's done bad things, and he hasn't been much of a father, but he is our da and he's nearly seventy. You know what they do to people like him in prison? I couldn't live with knowing we're sending him somewhere where he'll be beaten up or picked on. I don't want to be a part of that.'

The tension in the room mounts as the sisters argue about what to do next. Emotions are high, loyalties are called into question and, eventually, Paula stands up so sharply, her chair falls back from the table, banging against the wall with an almighty clatter. The noise brings quiet to the room.

'I can't believe we're even having this conversation. I just can't fuckin believe it! That bastard ruined our lives. He abused us, buggered us, turned us against each other. God knows how many others he did the same to, but we know there are plenty. And you're worried that he might be *bullied*? I don't give a fuck about the bastard. Let him die screaming!'

She slams the door and can be heard closing the front door with equal force. Joyce and June look at each other, shocked and pale.

'I have to say, June, I agree with Paula. We have no choice. I know you're not happy with that, but sleep on it and we'll talk tomorrow.'

June's head is thumping when she gets home, so she lies down on her bed, trying to clear her thoughts. She's scared. It's all moving so fast. If only it could all slow down. All she can see are images of her father behind bars, alone and afraid. She is torn. She can't do this to him, but the alternative is to do nothing, and she knows that's not an option either.

Resting her head against the pillows, she recalls the evening she took Joyce's kids to her mother's house where she minded them while Joyce worked nights. Herself and her mother had work to do, so they went out to the factory while the kids watched television in the sitting room. They were well settled into the sewing when Audrey ran out.

'Granda said he's going to give us all a bath,' she said excitedly.

June recalls her horror at the suggestion, and how she quickly jumped up and went into the house, to find the bath running but no sign of her father. She put the three kids into the bath, washed them, and got them into their pyjamas. Her father walked into the bathroom at one point, but nothing was said. Putting Audrey's nightdress on, June made sure she also put on her knickers, 'to keep warm', and the children went back to the sitting room to watch a cartoon. A little while later, Audrey came back out to the factory, asking for help to go to the toilet. June shivers as she remembers her annoyance at being disrupted again, but how rapidly that disappeared when she realised in the bathroom that Audrey had no knickers on.

'Where are your knickers?'

'Granda told me to take them off because they're dirty.'

Lying on the bed now, her head pounding, June feels her stomach lurch, just as it did that evening. She thought they would be OK, all of them watching TV together. Her naïveté led her to believe they were safe with her and her mother there, but he was so manipulative, no child would ever be safe around him.

June sits up determinedly and goes down to the phone.

'Joyce, you're right. Let's do the bastard.'

7 February 1989

The house feels as if someone has died. The atmosphere is solemn. The sisters and their mother are waiting for Inspector Mick Carolan to arrive with a ban garda to take statements. Kevin went down to the police station yesterday and spoke to the inspector about how to prosecute their father. It turns out the inspector knows the family well, having had several unsuccessful attempts at catching their da breaking the law. Kevin reassured his sisters that the inspector is a good guy and will treat them respectfully but they are on tenterhooks.

June and Pamela are sitting in the kitchen drinking tea and chain-smoking when Paula enters, looking pale and shaken.

'Are you OK?' June asks.

'No, I didn't sleep too good, thinking about this. I just took one of the Valium the doctor left us.'

'You mean one of the four tablets he left? Just how upset does he think we are? I mean four tablets, between all of us!' June snorts with derision at the GP's inadequate response.

'Is the Valium working?' Pamela asks.

'No. I'm still shaking. I don't know if I can do this.'

'You can do it.' Ma is assured and calm, and the sisters are surprised by her apparent confidence in them.

'I don't know what they expect from me,' Pamela says. 'I don't remember anything. He didn't do the same things to me as he did to you three.'

'I'm sure you'll be fine. Just tell them what you remember,' June says.

The door bell rings and Ma brings the inspector and Gabby, the ban garda, into the sitting room. Gabby informs them she would like to see them one at a time. The inspector then leaves, saying he will return for Gabby later.

'I'll go in first,' says June.

'No, let me. I want to get it over with.' Paula is white and her hands are trembling.

'I'm dying to get in!' says June. 'I remember everything, and if it's details they want, then that's what they'll get. It's OK, you go ahead, Paula, but I'm next.'

Paula enters the sitting room, visibly shaking, and closes the door. The kitchen is quiet as the women all sit deep in thought, going over their own stories in their heads.

'Where's Joyce?' Ma asks.

'She's on her way. I was just talking to her on the phone,' June says.

'Do I have to give a statement?' Ma asks.

'Yes, Ma. You're a victim too,' says Pamela.

Paula's with Gabby for almost an hour and when she opens the door, she is still pale and shaking. June doesn't say a word, but just gets up and goes into the room. Joyce has arrived and she and Pam ask is unison, 'How was it?'

'OK.' Paula looks down at the floor and hunches her shoulders as she lights a cigarette. It is apparent that there will be no further conversation from Paula at this point.

An hour passes and June comes out.

'Who's next?'

'I'll go,' says Pamela, eager to get it over and done with, as Joyce sits patiently in the kitchen.

'What did she ask you, June?' Joyce asks as she fills the

kettle, and starts cleaning away the used cups and overflowing ashtrays.

'She really wanted the details. It wasn't as easy as I thought. I'm raging. I didn't say enough. I don't think what I said was bad enough,' June says, taking the freshly brewed pot of tea and pouring a cup for her mother.

'Yes, it was hard, but she looked as nervous as me, and she seems nice,' Paula says.

'It was really embarrassing; she wanted the exact words to write down. When I said "willie" she corrected me with "penis" and when I said "gee", she said "vagina". I felt so stupid,' says June.

'And she asks you what age it started and ended,' Paula adds. 'God, I was mortified. I really wanted to lie but I didn't. I was so ashamed to tell her how old I was when it ended. I told her I was in my Communion dress when it started, but I know I was younger.'

The kitchen is filled with a gentle murmuring when Pamela returns, almost half an hour later.

'I told you I couldn't remember anything.' Pamela sits dejected in the chair, and takes the cup and cigarette offered to her by a sister on either side.

'You must have said something. You were in there for a while,' June says.

'Not much. I don't even know what I said; it was all a blur. I know I told her he made me wank him, but wouldn't let me look. He used to lie on the floor and make me take off my pants and stand over him as he looked at me. He often lay with paper and a pencil and drew pictures of my vagina. I told her I can't remember how old I was when he first tried to enter me but I do know I cried because it hurt so much and he stopped. He didn't try that again but he continued with looking and touching me, and used to sneak into my room when I was asleep and put his hands under the covers. I know that went on until I left home at nineteen.'

'Jaysus, Pam, I thought you said you didn't tell them anything! That's plenty,' said June.

'Well I'm glad you were here to tell her that. That's the important thing,' says Joyce.

Gabby puts her head around the door and indicates to Joyce to go into the sitting room. The other sisters are more relaxed now, relieved that their interview is over, but Ma's confidence in her daughters has given way to her own agitation, and she is visibly on edge now.

'Why do they want a statement from me?' she asks. 'It was you he abused, not me.'

There are uncertain offers of reassurance, as the sisters glance cautiously at each other, not knowing what to do, and wishing Joyce was there to say the right thing. The kitchen fills with smoke, despite the sporadic opening of windows to clear the air. The afternoon drags on through endless pots of tea and cigarettes, the only movement being when one of the women has to go to the bathroom, everyone afraid of missing something. Joyce seems to be gone for ages and when she eventually returns, she immediately whisks their mother in to Gabby, with a firm and supportive arm around her shoulder. Each of the sisters rubs her arm or back as she passes them, letting her know they will be waiting for her, that it will be OK.

'How was it, Joyce?' Pam asks.

'Well, to be honest, I felt I had to mind her. She seemed more affected by what I was saying than I was!' There is laughter for the first time, a tentative, nervous laughter. But there is also caution in the giggling, informed by a fear that letting go of the emotion in the room might unleash more than any of them is able to handle.

'Seriously, though, it was difficult. You know, giving the details, that was tough.'

The room is quiet when their mother comes back into the kitchen. There is a collective sigh of relief when she asks for a cup of tea, and, although she's pale, she appears equally glad that the interview is over.

They don't ask any questions, recognising that their mother needs to calm down after the interview. When the inspector returns to collect Gabby, she looks as if she can't get away quickly enough. He thanks the women for their help and tells them they just have to wait now. Slowly the cups are cleaned and ashtrays emptied as the women reluctantly tear themselves away from the kitchen table. At some level, they are all conscious of wanting to stay there, in the security of each other's company.

April 1989

By the middle of April, there is no word about a hearing or information about the possible trial. Every so often, one of the sisters brings it up in conversation, wondering how long it will be before the case is brought to court, and, occasionally, there is even a suggestion that someone should enquire about it. Generally, though, the women welcome the opportunity to avoid thinking about their statements, or the possibility of a court appearance, and the discussions always end rapidly, with a shudder of relief. Pamela has returned to England, and old routines and responsibilities have been picked up again.

One warm Thursday afternoon June is sitting at Joyce's

kitchen table when the doorbell rings and Derek, Joyce's oldest son, lets Paula in.

'You're not going to believe it!' Paula fumes. Her face is red and she is shaking with anger. 'We went looking for justice. We must be fucking mad!'

The children are ushered into the front room to watch TV as Joyce puts the kettle on while Paula recounts her conversation with a cousin she has met that morning.

'He was up in court on Tuesday,' she says.

'Who was? What are you talking about?' June is confused and upset by Paula's anger.

'Da! He was in the District Court, charged with abusing us, based on our statements! And nobody fucking told us. Can you believe it?'

Joyce phones Inspector Mick Carolan. They are all furious at not having been informed of this significant development.

'Hi, Mick,' says Joyce, when the call is eventually put through. 'It's Joyce Kavanagh. We're just wondering what's going on. It's just we heard something about a court appearance this week.'

Joyce listens intently. Paula and June are afraid to move in case they distract her from the conversation.

'I see,' says Joyce, nodding slowly, but avoiding looking at her sisters. 'Well, I guess that's all good, but the thing is, Mick, this is our lives we're talking about. We need to be a part of it. We need to know what's going on.'

Again, silence as Joyce listens to the inspector's response.

'Is that it?' Joyce says, turning her back on June and Paula. She doesn't want them to see how angry she is, not while she's on the phone. 'I see, OK, well thanks for that.' She hangs up the phone, and turns to her sisters. 'Bastards!' she says, reaching a trembling hand across the table and lighting up a cigarette. She is shaking with fury and it takes her a moment to collect her thoughts. Paula and June stay quiet, watching her and waiting for the explanation.

'Well, you're right,' says Joyce, exhaling deeply. 'He was in the District Court this week. Mick said that Da corroborated our statements by pleading guilty, so there was no need for us to be there. The DPP agreed that the state should take our case, but Da is denying he did anything to Pam and says she's just jumping on the bandwagon. Her statement isn't going to be included.'

'She'll be devastated,' says June, immediately concerned for her older sister, knowing how hard this will be for her, and the potential for it to drive a wedge between them all, with some of them being believed and Pamela having her story doubted.

'It's terrible, but she knew that might happen. We have each other supporting our stories, but because she's so much older, she doesn't have anyone to give that back-up.'

'And what about informing us?' Paula asks. In her agitation, she is hardly able to sit down. 'What are they going to do about that? Did he explain why we weren't told?'

'Apparently, we don't need to be there. The DPP is handling everything,' Joyce says with as little emotion as she can. She doesn't want to heighten the upset, so she tries to play down the hurt they are all feeling. 'The case will be reported in the papers, but his name won't appear to protect the family. That's how it works, he says.'

The room is quiet, as each sister sits back, considering her position, her role in the drama that is now becoming a reality.

'This isn't how it was meant to be,' says Paula quietly, the anger gone now, replaced by a sense of defeat. 'It was supposed to be different from this; we should be there, in the middle of it. We're not even on the sidelines. We're just not part of the picture. This is so wrong.'

June is sobbing gently, shaking her head in disbelief. The

feeling of having no control is flooding back to her, and it's terrifying. She thought she had moved on from all that.

Joyce stubs out her cigarette determinedly and puts a hand on each sister's arm.

'This is our fight and we're going to be part of it, whatever those fuckers think is the right way to do it. If we have to track the case ourselves, so be it. We've been through a whole lot worse than that!'

Joyce constantly phones the police to find out when the next court appearance will be, and when they find out that their father is due to appear at Kilmainham Court, Joyce and Paula are there to hear the proceedings. It is the first time either of them has been in a courtroom. They find the tightly packed space cold and intimidating, and yet are shocked by the informality of the process. People talk throughout the cases being heard, demonstrate no shame at being there and have no apparent interest in what is taking place. Everyone appearing before the judge is given another date to return. It seems that nothing is actually getting resolved.

Standing at the back, the sisters try to stay hidden, because they realise that everyone will hear the charges against their father when he is called and they don't want to be associated with him or the abuse. They constantly worry about bumping into him. But here, in the court, they know that they will see him, so staying at the back might give them some distance. Suddenly, Joyce hears their father whispering in her ear, 'It's fuckin freezing out, isn't it?'

Joyce's legs go to jelly and she can't move for several minutes. She feels dizzy and looks around to grab Paula's arm for support, but her sister has gone. Her stomach churns, and she can still feel his breath on her neck as she pushes her way through the crowd, trying to reach fresh air. She gets outside and sees Paula puffing intently on a cigarette, also clearly shaken. Joining her sister, Joyce takes out a cigarette and Paula lights it, neither saying anything and both avoiding eye contact. They are ashamed of the impact he has on them still, even in a court house crowded with gardaí and prison officers. They stand smoking until their heartbeats calm and the feeling returns to their legs. Eventually, they look at each other, and burst out laughing.

'The fucker. How did that fat bastard sneak up on us like that?' Paula is amused at their da's stealth, and shakes her head with reluctant admiration.

'Well, whatever he's got, it runs in the family. Jaysus, talk about the invisible woman! You were gone like a bat out of hell. And me, like the feckin eejit, standing there looking for you to help me, and my knees gone all weak. Remind me not to rely on you in an emergency!'

'Should we go back in?'

'Ah, Jaysus, no. I couldn't take any more excitement today,' Joyce says, and the two head off down the road to the bus stop, arms linked, testing out different ways to tell and exaggerate their story to the others later.

It is several months before there is news of another hearing. They agree that they need strength in numbers the next time, so when they eventually get a court date, June, Joyce, Paula, David, Kevin and their mother all attend.

The family arrives early and finds seats at the back of the court. Each sits quietly, watching the door for his arrival. It's not long before he appears, in his scruffy old anorak, looking dishevelled.

'Ah, Jaysus, I can't believe he's wearing his shagging overcoat here,' June whispers, horrified at her da's lack of respect for the court.

'Shush,' their mother says, unnerved by the fact that her husband has moved to the other side of the court to sit exactly opposite the family, so that it is difficult for them to avoid looking at him.

'What's he up to, rubbing his arm like that?' Joyce asks. They all try not to be obvious about watching him, but he is definitely rubbing his arm self-consciously. He returns their gaze, with a sad, familiar, self-pitying look.

Suddenly, he lets out a cry, and there is a scuffle of bodies, as a group gathers around him. There is confusion, and people lean out of their seats trying to see what's going on, when someone from the circle shouts, 'Call an ambulance.'

'Oh, for God's sake.' Paula is disgusted by this performance. 'Can you believe he'd pull a fast one like that here?'

Inspector Mick Carolan rushes over to the family. 'I think your father is having a heart attack.'

'He hasn't got a fuckin heart,' their mother says loudly.

The family adjourns to the pub across the road while they wait to see what's going to happen. Watching out of the pub window, they see him walk into the ambulance as it pulls away with the siren on.

'He can't be that bad if he's able to walk to the ambulance,' Kevin points out. 'They've taken him to St James's, so we'll wait for a while and then ring to check on him.'

'Do you think he's faking it?' June asks, deflated by the way the day has turned out.

'Of course he is, the chancer,' Kevin says. 'He wasn't even rubbing the right arm, the fuckin idiot. Surely you're not falling for that crap?'

One by one, the siblings recount memories of times when their father claimed illness in order to get sympathy, and in no time the bar is filled with laughter. But it's not real and the strain is tangible on their tense faces. There is a mixture of anger and uncertainty because the sisters are unsure about what to feel, relief or disappointment, while the two brothers simply focus on keeping everyone's spirits high. Their mother sits quietly, smiling at their stories but not engaging in them. After a while, Kevin gathers some change and rings the hospital. There is silence, as everyone waits for his return.

'He's fine and has already been released,' he announces a few minutes later.

'Bastard! I told you so,' Paula says with venom. She's furious that he still has the ability to control their day.

Everyone makes feeble jokes as they reassure each other that they weren't fooled for a minute, and gather themselves for the journey home.

Weeks later, the sisters find out they have missed another court appearance, and Joyce phones Mick Carolan again, this time holding back none of her fury.

'Let me tell you, Inspector Carolan, we are not every other Joe Soap. This case is about our lives, our childhoods. That bastard robbed us of so much, and now you are all doing the same thing. Waiting for some form of justice is all that's keeping us going right now. You have a duty to help us to be part of this case.'

Joyce is shouting now, and Paula and June sit watching her, admiring her ability to say exactly what it is they want to say, but also nervous of annoying the gardaí and it backfiring on them somehow. June gestures with her hands for Joyce to calm down, and Joyce takes a deep breath before saying any more.

'Mick, please, we just want to be told when there's going to be another court appearance. Please will you do that!'

Eventually she comes off the phone, her anger largely

dissipated, and sits at the table, letting out a deep sigh.

'Well?'

'Apparently nothing will happen until the case is transferred to the Circuit Court, so he reckons there's no need for us to be bothered at this stage. I told him ... well you heard what I told him!'

'The whole feckin street heard what you told him, Joyce!' June laughs, so proud of her sister, so grateful to have someone managing all these unanticipated complexities.

'Anyway, he said once it moves to the Circuit Court, he'll keep us informed of what's happening. It'll be a while before that happens though.'

'God, how long is this going to take? I never thought it would be like this.' Paula speaks for them all as they sigh, light up new cigarettes and look out of the window in wistful anticipation of a time when it will all be over.

Chapter 4: Growing Up and Moving Out

Paula: 1977

It's always the same: Christmas, Halloween, birthdays, he takes any chance he can get to let me know I'm different. Even though I'm fourteen, I still can't help hoping it will be different this time. I hate myself for being so weak. He arrives home with three of the biggest Easter eggs I've ever seen, for his precious girls, Ma, Joyce and June. As usual, there is nothing for me.

'Only the biggest and the best for my girls,' he says, and it takes three trips to the car to carry them into the house.

They're covered in bright shiny plastic, with big colourful ribbons flowing down the sides. Inside the wrapping are little chicks sitting on top of the big eggs, and larger chicks placed on either side of the basket. Joyce and June jump around, protecting them as if they're made of gold. I feel so envious and yet at the same time guilty. In the Bible envy is a sin and God punishes those who commit sin. Da says that even bad thoughts are a sin.

As usual, Ma feels sorry for me and buys me an egg, but it's too late, and it's not the same as theirs. Ma doesn't believe in wasting money, so it's a small egg and, anyway, it's him I want to buy the egg, not her. I hate that it matters. Why do I care so much? Why do I want him to care?

Paula: 1978

Da arrives home from town and comes into the factory where we're all working away on the machines. June's friend Emily started working with us a couple of months ago. He has a big smile on his face. He stands beside the cutting table and says 'Joyce, June and Emily come inside. I have a surprise for you.'

They jump up and run inside. Turning to me, he says, 'If they leave anything, you can have it.'

It isn't uncommon for Da to buy stuff for June and Joyce and not for me but now he is putting June's friend in front of me too. I try not to show that I'm interested. But I'm curious. What did he buy this time?

I can hear the girls' screams of excitement. I hate him so much, but, at fifteen, I hate myself more, because no matter how many times he does this, it still hurts. I never learn. I still hope he'll remember I'm here, that he'll pay me some attention and treat me the same as the others. I know I'm expected to be grateful for the leftovers, but fuck him.

After a few minutes the girls run out, showing off their new wrapover skirts.

'What do you think of mine?' they ask one another.

No one even notices what he's done. Again. Don't they give a bollox? It's not that I care about the skirts because I don't – in fact, I wouldn't be caught dead in one – but I feel left out and unimportant. I feel hurt and unwanted. The fuckin bastard.

'Well, what do you think? Lovely, aren't they?' June asks me. I smile and agree. She adds as an afterthought, 'There's two left inside. Have a look at them.'

At this stage I don't care, but not wanting them to know how hurt I am, I go inside to have a look. There are two skirts left, a white one with big black flowers plastered all over it, and a hideous green one, with brown squiggly lines running through it. I feel like crying.

Da walks into the room as I'm holding the skirt in my hand. The deadpan expression on my face, which has taken me years to perfect, ensures that he doesn't know how deeply affected I am. He huffs, turns on his heels and leaves the room.

Paula: 1979

I'm lying on the bed, looking at the posters I have plastered round the room. Unlike other sixteen-year-olds, I have basketball teams and athletes stuck on my walls, rather than Blondie or The Jam. It's hot and I feel peculiar. I go over to the window and stick my head out, hoping to catch a cool breeze, but there isn't one. I feel tingly and wet between my legs. I lie down on the bed and pick up a book, but all I can think about is this funny feeling down there.

Da comes into the room.

Click, click.

'You, in here.'

I feel so disgusting. I don't want to go with him. He'll know I'm all wet and think it's for him. I want to get sick.

'No,' I say sheepishly.

I can't go. There's something wrong with me. I'm as horrible as him. He'll think I want it. He looks shocked.

'Get in here. Now.'

'No.'

He stands there and I turn towards the window, afraid that he'll know what I'm thinking. It seems like a lifetime before I hear him walk out of my room and go downstairs. Oh, Jesus, he'll kill me. But why did he take no for an answer? I'm so confused. I don't know what to do next. I panic and, as quickly as I can, I sneak down and run out the door before he can catch me.

I'm standing outside the house waiting for my friend Brigid to come; we're going to the cinema, to see *Kramer vs. Kramer*. Now I'm sixteen, I get to do stuff on my own. I watch Da and the boys while I'm waiting. They are digging a big hole in the ground and have pipes and tools all over the place. Da is shouting as usual and I'm mortified in case anyone hears.

'Hook that pipe into the grey one,' he shouts at Kevin.

'It's a different size. It won't fit,' Kevin says.

'Just fuckin do it. Make it fit,' Da replies.

A man interrupts Da, saying he's from the Corporation.

'What are you doing there, Mr Kavanagh?'

'Knitting a jumper, what does it look like?'

'Sorry, Mr Kavanagh, but you don't have permission to dig here.'

'I have no sewerage in the house and you useless fuckers won't do anything about it, so I'm doing it myself.'

'But you can't just pipe into the main sewerage system without permission.'

'Let me tell you, I have ten children and they all crap a lot. If you don't fuck off, I'll get each of them to shite in brown paper bags and deliver them in a wheelbarrow to your door, every day. Now fuck off. Let me finish the job.'

Da continues to shout instructions to Kevin. The boys are laughing so much as they imagine having to shit in bags, it's hard for them to work. Da tries to be serious, but ends up laughing with them as the man stands watching them, unsure what to do.

The Corpo man looks scared; he's clearly shaken and mortified as he looks around to see if anyone else has heard the conversation. He silently turns and walks away. I feel so sorry for him. He's obviously new, because everyone else in the Corpo knows what Da's like. I'm sure they all hate the thought of dealing with him. They know they can't win because he makes up his own rules and is afraid of no one. They must all be scared of him because they never pursue him or charge him. He's a big bully. Where the hell is Brigid? I need to get out of here.

Paula: 1980

Our basketball team won the tournament in Killarney, and I'm delighted. I'm team captain, even though I'm only seventeen, so I get to take the trophy home first. It's huge and I can't wait to show it off. Ma is standing at the sink peeling potatoes when I show her the trophy, all excited.

'Look, Ma, we won!'

Ma looks at the trophy.

'Wow, that's great! Jesus, that's a big trophy.' She looks so happy for me.

'It was great, Ma. We won all our matches, and we played a really good team in the final and beat them. We got our picture taken for the papers.' I'm so thrilled with myself and talking so fast, I'm sure Ma doesn't hear half of what I'm saying.

'Well done! You must be delighted after winning all those matches. Go show your da. He's in the sitting room.'

I run into the sitting room, holding the trophy with both hands because it's heavy. Da is sitting in front of the telly.

'Da, look, we won.'

He barely glances in my direction.

'We won the final.'

'Shush, I'm listening to this,' he says, glancing in my direction. He gestures with his hand for me to go away.

I feel a sick sensation in the pit of my stomach. The disappointment is overwhelming. My head is spinning. He didn't even acknowledge me, never mind the trophy. *Dad's Army* is more important to him than my team winning the tournament.

I walk out of the room and go up to lay on my bed.

Fuck him. I hope the telly blows up. He doesn't know how good I am, he's never made any effort to see me play. I bet if it was Joyce or June, he'd make a big deal out of it. I clear a space on my dressing table to place the trophy on it. What's the big deal? It's just a silly basketball game. Why did I expect anything else from him? What's wrong with me? Will I never learn? He doesn't care, never has and never will.

I try to recapture the feeling of winning, but I can't. I turn on my telly and lie back looking at the trophy that a few minutes earlier had made me feel so proud. Now it's meaningless – the trophy, the game, even being captain, it's all pointless. I can't understand why I even bothered to show it to him. I slowly get up off the bed, and put the trophy in the wardrobe. I lie back on the pillow and stare at the empty space on the locker. I didn't deserve to win it anyway; it wasn't me that won the game. That'll teach me for getting ideas about myself.

Paula: 1981

My pals are going to America. They reckon there's loads of work in the States, and some of them have friends and cousins there who'll help them get jobs. They keep asking me to go with them. It'd be great, and I'm eighteen, I should go. They keep asking me why I'm hesitating.

'You hate it here,' they remind me. 'Why would you stay?'

Good question. Because I'm a coward. I haven't got the guts to go. I've never had to look after myself. I've never had to make a decision. The idea of all that freedom, that responsibility, terrifies me. Shit, I wish I could be brave, like Joyce, and just head off, but I can't. Bad and all as this is, at least I know I can deal with it. I can't handle the unknown. I have never worked for anyone other than Da, and, anyway, who would give me a job? No, I am better off staying where I am.

Paula: 1985

It's been over three years since I fell in love. It's been wonderful and terrible; all-consuming and desperately painful. I'm still confused. I'm not attracted to other women in the same way, so I don't think I'm gay.

It has taken so much energy to hide the relationship, pretend we're just friends, find time to be together, and we've been arguing a lot lately because we never get time on our own, so I decide it's time to move out and get a place of my own. A friend offers to rent me a small house off Church Street in the north inner city, and I arrange to view it after work. It's tiny, in the middle of a warren of narrow streets near the Liffey that I never knew existed, but I fall in love with the house as soon as I step inside. To the left is a small door that leads into a bedroom that faces out onto the street. Straight ahead is a small sitting room with two doors, one that leads into a main bedroom and the other a small kitchen. The décor badly needs updating, but the sitting room has a fireplace and all I'm thinking of is the romantic evenings sitting in front of a blazing fire with Alice.

I go home and tell Ma I'm moving out. She looks shocked and asks if I think I will be safe. Can I afford it? Do I not think I will be lonely on my own? I assure her that I'll be fine. I ask her to speak to Da, because I don't want to face that drama, and she agrees. I can hear them in the other room. Da is going ballistic. 'What's fuckin wrong with her? Why does she want to move? She has everything she needs right here; she gets paid, never has to hand over a fuckin penny. She'll never be able to cope, just you watch, she'll be back here next week, begging to come home, but she can fuck off. If she leaves this house, that's it, she's never getting back in here, the ungrateful little cunt.'

He stops talking to me, ignoring me, pretending I don't exist. It's not the reaction I expected. I thought he'd go mad and call me all the names under the sun, and I don't know why his silence bothers me. I should be glad – at least he's not shouting at me – but actually it hurts when he won't even look at me. I'm more determined than ever to prove him wrong.

I move my stuff into my new home and relish cleaning it up and arranging my things to make the place look lovely. I light the fire, even though it's not cold, because I want the place to feel cosy. It takes me ages to light it but when I finally get a flame going, I'm so happy I did it all on my own. I spend my first evening happily snuggled up on the couch, imagining the new life of freedom ahead of me.

Over the next couple of weeks, I cycle the seven miles in and out to work. Going in only takes me half an hour but coming home is so hard because of Infirmary Hill. As I reach the bottom of the hill each evening, I feel like crying, knowing the pain ahead of me. Da still isn't speaking to me but I'm seeing the benefits of not having him screaming at me every day. My day is a lot more peaceful.

I realise very quickly that independence is not all it's cracked up to be. I'm totally broke, even though Ma's great, filling a bag full of food every few days, so at least I have something to eat. I have no money for coal to light the fire and it's freezing. My arse is so sore from the saddle on the bike that I cry every night and have nightmares about having to cycle up that fucking hill.

Alice hasn't stayed once since I moved in and I'm fed up not being able to go out for a few drinks with the girls because I'm broke. My dream of having a love nest has disappeared.

It's Christmas and I just got paid, so I go out and buy a four-foot plastic tree, some decorations and a set of lights. It takes me ages to get the place looking just right, to place each little bulb in just the right spot so it has maximum effect, every cheap bauble where it will best catch the light. I beg Alice to come over on Christmas Eve and spend some time with me. She says she'll try, and I spend all night waiting for her to arrive but by eleven o'clock I have to accept that she's not coming and I cry myself to sleep. My Christmas dinner consists of a crisp sandwich.

After six months of cold mornings and a damp bed, being broke and miserable, having a sore arse and feeling lonely, I finally decide to give in and accept that I am a complete failure. Da is right: I can't manage on my own. Most of the time, I have no money to feed myself or buy coal to light the fire. The worst is not having any money to go out with my friends. On the occasions I do go out, I have to face the cycle back home because I don't have the money for drink *and* a taxi.

I finally get up the courage to ask Ma if I can come home. Her face lights up, she smiles and says, 'Of course you can. This will always be your home.' I ask if she will talk to Da and she tells me not to worry, that she will speak to him later. I'm so worried that he won't let me come home. He hasn't spoken to me in months and I know that he can keep that up for a long time yet, stubborn bastard. I can't sleep. I feel a complete failure for not making it on my own, for relying on him to take me back, for being such a coward that I can't even ask him myself, but I have nowhere else to go.

The next morning Ma tells me it's OK to move back, so that evening I'm standing at the front door searching for my key, surrounded by my black sacks of clothes. I look about, hoping no one will see me. I'm so ashamed to be back here. I failed in my one attempt at independence. I'm almost twenty-three and yet I'm useless, like a child. I can't do anything on my own. I feel sick thinking how Da will gloat about the fact that he knew I could never survive without him.

When I get in, I head straight upstairs to unpack, but I haven't even put the bags down when Da shouts at me. 'Hurry up, you, and give your ma a hand with the dinner.'

Oh, God, nothing has changed. It's been six months since I moved out and I can't believe I'm back. My room is the very same as the day I left and Da is already shouting orders. You'd think he'd give me time to unpack before he started. I hate him. I'm such a stupid cunt. I can't do anything right. I'm so useless not being able to make it outside of this hell hole.

Why can't I go out and get a job? I wouldn't have to be here if I wasn't such an idiot and could work somewhere else. I can't spell or add, so that rules out working in an office or even trying to work with June in the restaurant. I'm stuck here for the rest of my life, trapped in this one room with nothing to look forward to. Da was right: he knew I would come begging, that I wouldn't be able to survive without him. There is no point in hoping that I'll make it on my own or that I'll ever get away from him. I'm just a fuckin loser.

I rush about, putting my things in the wardrobe before he

starts screaming up the stairs for me. This is the best it's ever going to be for me. I will never be able to survive outside. This is all I can do and I don't even do that well.

June: 1972

Da always makes us get up real early during the school holidays. He hates to see us in bed late, so he strikes a deal with us to get all our chores done early. If we do them well, he lets us stay out late in the evening. Me and Joyce are really excited about this as we usually have to be in at nine and our friends are allowed out later, so, of course, we work extra hard to get our jobs done. He says we can stay out until half ten, and gives us a watch so we know the time. I'm delighted to be able to stay out as late as Joyce because she is sixteen and I am only eleven.

We go around to the playground to meet the gang of boys that Joyce and her friends hang out with. One of them is Joyce's boyfriend. He says she looks really good in her yellow leather hot pants. Lorraine and Denise are giggling in the corner talking about David Cassidy from *The Partridge Family*.

'He's gorgeous, isn't he?' Lorraine asks.

'Yummy,' says Denise.

One of the lads has a radio; it's small and doesn't sound great but we all sing along to 'Ben' by Michael Jackson. We laugh because we are all out of key and can't reach the high notes. It's getting dark, but when I check the time on the watch, we still have plenty of time before we have to go in.

We decide to go for a walk and end up over the bridge, just up the road from our house. It's so exciting to be out with Joyce's friends, I've never been out this late before. I feel so grown up.

I look at the watch and it says ten o'clock, but it was ten o'clock ages ago! Joyce is busy with her boyfriend.

'Joyce, I don't know what time it is.'

'We've lots of time. Don't worry.'

'I don't think this watch is working. I think it's stopped.'

'What? It's only about half nine, June. Relax.'

'I don't think so, Joyce.'

'Are you sure, June? Has anyone else got a watch on them?'

No one else knows the time.

'Oh, Joyce, what are we going to do?'

'It's all right, for God's sake. Stop worrying!'

She looks down towards our house and her face drops.

'What is it, Joyce?

'Oh fuck, it's Da.'

I turn around to see him marching up the road and I can tell by the way he's walking that we're in trouble.

'Quick, lads, scarper. It's Jughead,' shouts one of the lads. They run up over the bridge. Me and Joyce run towards Da.

'You and you, get down to the fuckin house now,' he says, swinging an iron bar in his hand.

We pass him as fast as we can but he keeps walking towards the lads. We run to the house terrified, wondering what he is going to do to us. We dash into the parlour and dive onto the couch. Joyce sits me on her lap. She is shaking. It takes me a minute to realise that this is not the best place to be, so I jump up.

'No way, Joyce. You're not hiding behind me.'

'OK, then. Let's hide in the bathroom.'

We go into the bathroom and close the door. Now we're both trembling.

'What's keeping him so long?' I ask.

'I don't know.'

We hear him charging into the house screaming for the keys of his van.

'Oh, God, Joyce, what's he doing?'

'He must be going after the boys.'

We hear the screeching of the tyres as he drives off.

'Oh, Joyce, I don't want to stay here. He'll kick in the door and batter us.'

'Shit. We'd better get into bed before he gets back.'

We run upstairs and sit on the bed.

'Will we hide under the bed?' Joyce asks.

'No, Joyce. He'll bash us.'

'Will we get into bed?'

'Yes, come on quick, before he gets back.'

As we start to undress, we hear the van pulling up outside. We freeze for a moment.

'What'll we do? What'll we do, Joyce?'

We hear him thundering up the stairs. He bursts into the room, nearly taking the door off the hinges, the iron bar still in his hand. He drops the bar and raises his foot to kick me because I'm the closest to him, but before his foot reaches me, I throw myself on the bed screaming at the top of my lungs. He storms over to Joyce and lashes out with his fist but before he gets her, she dives on the bed and starts screaming too. We are yelling so loudly, I can hear Ma shouting.

'Kevin, Kevin, leave them alone!'

We pull the covers up over our heads for protection but keep screaming as he continues to hit us. Ma is behind him, trying to pull him away. He finally stops and leaves the room. Ma tries to get past him to see if we are all right, but he won't let her. She's frantic, but he screams at her. 'You fuck off. Leave them alone. Don't fuckin go in there! I'm warning you.'

We wait until there is no sound outside and slowly lower the covers.

'He didn't hurt me. Did he hurt you?' we both say together.

'No, he didn't hurt me.'

We giggle but real quiet. We want to go tell Ma we are all right but we can't.

June: 1974

'You and you.' Da points at me and Leonard. 'Come on, we're going to the cash and carry.'

Da has on his big brown coat that he wears for shopping and I know enough to move when he calls, so me and Leonard run out to the van. Leonard is older than me, so he gets to sit in the front and I'm in the back. I'm really strong and, even though I'm only thirteen and Leonard is fifteen, I can lift as many boxes as him. That's why Da brings me.

When we pull up outside the cash and carry, Da tells us to put two boxes of butter and three boxes of sugar into the van while he gets the rest of the shopping. I rush in the door. I know exactly where everything is and me and Leonard race to see who can carry the most. Leonard tries to pick up two boxes of butter at once but they're too heavy and he puts one back. I grab a box of sugar and head for the van. I'm on my way back for the second one and Leonard is only getting to the van. He's raging because I'm quicker than him. I have three boxes of sugar in the van before he has the butter in and I am chuffed with myself. Da says we have to wait in the van until he calls us to carry out the rest of the shopping and we normally do, but I want to tell him that I have beaten Leonard, so I go back inside to find him. He's at the cash desk paying for the shopping in his trolley.

'Da?'

'Not now.'

'But, Da.'

'I'm busy.'

I stand there looking at the man who counts up the cost of the shopping.

'Is that everything?' he asks Da.

'Yes, that's everything.'

'What about the sugar and the butter we put in the van, Da?' I say.

'What?' The man looks at Da.

'Oh yeah, that's right, I forgot. Add that on to the bill,' Da says.

I know by the look Da gives me that I've done something wrong. 'I'll fetch Leonard to help with the shopping.' I've a feeling I'm best getting out of his way.

When I get to the van, I tell Leonard we have to help with the shopping and repeat what I said to the man.

'Da doesn't pay for them.'

'What? Oh, God, he'll bash me.'

'There's lots of stuff he doesn't pay for. Why do you think he wears his Aspro coat?' Leonard says.

'That brown thing? Why is it called an Aspro coat?' I ask.

'Because he slips sheets of Aspros along with anything else that'll fit in the pockets he cut out of the coat.'

We hurriedly get the shopping loaded and when Da comes back to the van, I get a whack across the back of the head as he spits out the words, 'You stupid cunt.'

I'm so embarrassed. I hope the people in the shop didn't see. Thank God I'm sitting in the back so I can hide. When we get home he walks into the shop, leaving me and Leonard to carry in the shopping. He never says another word about the shopping trip to me.

June: 1976

I'm lying on my bed and I can't stop crying. All I want is to go into town with Joyce and her friend, but she won't let me. The bitch. Why won't she let me go with her? It's not as if she's going in for anything important. I heard her saying she is only going in for a doss. She doesn't care about me; nobody does. I even asked Da if I can go with her and he said no. I hate him, and that little bitch Paula had better not come in the room or I'll kill her.

Joyce doesn't need me now she has Freda. Well, fuck her, I don't need her either. She knows I have no one. The tears roll down the side of my face into my ears. I need a hanky but there's nothing I can use, so I pick up the edge of the bed sheet and blow my nose. I can't stop crying. I thought Joyce would come back for me but it's too long now – she's not going to do that. She doesn't care, and nobody realises just how upset I am. I may as well be invisible. She just left me standing there crying. She'll be sorry. I'm never going to talk to her again.

My head hurts and my eyes are stinging from all the crying. I'm fifteen now. I'll find my own friend and she can go fuck herself. I don't need her or anyone else.

Click, click.

I hold my breath. I look over my shoulder and see Da standing at the bedroom door. Maybe he's going to bring me into town or do something really nice to make up for not letting me go with Joyce. He nods for me to go into the other room. He wants me to do 'that' now. What's wrong with him? Can't he see that I'm crying? Does he not care about me at all?

The look on his face annoys me. He doesn't care how I'm feeling. How can he? All he cares about is himself. Surely he'll leave me alone now that he can see my face. Maybe he doesn't realise how upset I am. I turn my back on him and look at the wall.

Click, click.

'What?' I snap at him without turning around.

'Come on.'

'No.' I feel tired from all the crying and I'm very angry.

'What?' He's angry and I'm shaking, but I'm not going to turn around.

'No,' I say and hold my breath, waiting for a clatter. But the clatter doesn't come. He stands behind me in silence for what seems like forever before he moves. I can hear him going into the other room. All of a sudden I don't care about Joyce going into town without me. I stop crying.

I sit up on the bed. What have I done? Oh, God, what'll he do to me? Please don't let him kill me! Somebody help me. Oh, Mammy, Mammy, what am I going to do? I wait for ages but he doesn't come back. This is confusing and I'm scared now. What's he doing? I can't even get out without passing through his room. I listen for any sound but I can hear nothing. Finally, I stand up, my legs trembling. I go to the door and can't believe he isn't in his room. I was so sure he'd be waiting for me. Where is he? I listen again, but can't hear him. What's going on? I don't understand this.

I fall over my feet getting down the stairs. I'm terrified and confused; this isn't what I expected. There is still no sign of him. Where will I go? I run down the hall and out the door as fast as I can, trying to be quiet, all the time waiting for him to appear. I run up to the little field over the bridge to see if there is anyone there to play with. My heart is pounding and I keep looking down the road to see if he is following me, but no one is coming. Maybe it's because I'm upset that he didn't go mad. Maybe he'll get me when I go back in. Maybe he's too busy to batter me now. I'll just stay out of his way for as long as I can. But when I go home later, he ignores me, acts like I'm not there at all.

I keep expecting Da to call me in again, but he doesn't. In

fact, he seems to be avoiding me. Maybe there's nothing he can do about me saying no. I feel guilty and confused. If it's that easy to say no, why didn't I do it sooner? I could have stopped it before now. Maybe it is all my fault.

Later that week, I'm in the factory and he says, 'I know you're smoking.'

My eyes widen, but I say nothing.

'Well, you know, we all have our vices,' he says, with this horrible grin on his face.

'What are vices?' I ask stupidly.

'Smoking is a vice and you know what I do – that's a vice too.'

I'm confused. I don't know what he's trying to say, but I know I don't like it.

He continues, 'If you allow me my vice, I'll allow you yours, but if you don't, you know I can make your life very difficult.'

It's too late. I realise there's nothing he can do. He's almost desperate, trying to bribe me, and I know everything has changed now. I look at him and say 'no', really clear for him, as I turn on my heels and walk away. I'm not scared any more.

Joyce: 1971

It's been days since Da called me to the room and I wonder what's wrong. He hasn't really talked to me much since I got my periods. I was the last one to get them of all my friends. At sixteen, they all had theirs but I am nearly seventeen and I only got them a few weeks ago. I try to remember if I did anything to annoy him, but I can't.

When I finish the housework, I hang around with girls on the road. It's great he doesn't even call me in when I'm playing, but I'm worried. I wonder what he's up to. He's not even grabbing me when he passes, which is very unusual. Something has to be wrong but he isn't saying anything and I don't want him to know I've noticed. I can't really enjoy anything because I'm waiting for something to happen.

I keep dreaming of him coming into my bed and touching me. It's always really nice and we are in love. I like it and I want him and then when I wake up, I'm all wet down there and I can smell him. I don't know what's happening to me. I've waited years for this to stop, so why am I not happy?

I feel a constant pain in my body down there, but it's not a normal pain. How could I want him? I've always hated him near me. I remind myself of the pain and the smell, but the feeling does not go away. There is a constant dirty pong off me, and my knickers are always damp and smelly. I stink when I wake up and feel awful all the time. I really am a horrible person. I should be happy, so why am I not.

Joyce: 1974

Saturday night is ending perfectly. Gerry, the fella I fancy, has finally asked if he can leave me home. I have liked him for ages, and he's noticed me at last. I knew I looked good tonight, in my new green and brown maxi dress, with the cork wedges that hurt my feet but make me look tall and slim. I'm so happy to be walking along with him, waiting for him to stop and hold me, kiss me gently. But then he suggests we go to his friend, Joe, for coffee after the pub. I don't want to let this opportunity go because I like him, but I know going for coffee will make me late and cause serious trouble. I'm nervous, so I explain to Gerry that I have to be home soon.

'For God's sake, Joyce, we are only going for coffee. I haven't seen Joe in so long. We won't stay long. I can explain to your Da if you're worried.'

I agree, but I'm nervous. I'm too embarrassed to say any more. I don't want to admit that at nineteen years of age, I am still under such a strict curfew. I know Da will be waiting for me and there will be trouble. I try to relax as we walk down the street towards Joe's house but I can't stop myself watching the clock as we drink our coffee.

I'm so relieved when Gerry finally stands up to leave, which is obvious by the way I jump up from the chair. Joe and Gerry both laugh, saying I want Gerry to myself. I don't care what they think. I just want to get home. Gerry and I have a laugh on the way back to my house and he stops several times to kiss me. I think I am in heaven. As we get close to home, I'm worried but I'm also very happy – the happiest I have ever been.

I am jolted back to reality as we come to the corner of my street. I spot Da coming around the corner. He has obviously been out looking for me. I whisper to Gerry, 'Please don't say a word to him, no matter what he says. Just go and I'll talk to you tomorrow. Please, please.'

'Do you want me to explain what kept us late?'

'No, please, just go, and don't say a word.'

Da's step is quickening now and I can tell I'm in big trouble by his walk. I again ask Gerry to go, but he continues to stand there. He looks shocked at how afraid I am, but I can't deal with that now.

'You, cunt, get inside now!' Da says, pointing at me. He turns to Gerry and says 'You, fuck off.' Gerry looks shocked. I again whisper to him not to respond and beg him to go. I am hugely relieved when he takes another look at Da and says goodnight to me, before quickly walking away.

I stand and watch him leave and then feel Da grab my arm and drag me in the door. He slams the front door shut and starts shouting at me that I'm a slut, an ungrateful cunt. I compose myself as I hang up my coat, taking a deep breath before I turn around to face him. I'm furious; I can still see the shock and disgust on Gerry's face. Da is roaring but I'm thinking of Gerry and me. Will there be a Gerry and me after tonight? I am disgusted. God, it's only half eleven! Some of my friends are married with children and here I am rushing home because I might upset my father. I zone in on his whinging voice and scream back at him. 'Fuck you! I'm nineteen and you won't tell me what to do!' I point my finger at him, shouting that he isn't going to ruin my life, that I'm an adult now.

He looks shocked and I'd swear he's frightened. I continue to yell at him to leave me alone. My only thought is the expression on Gerry's face as Da told him to fuck off. I will probably never see him again. I can feel the anger inside me. My face is hot and my eyes are burning, but I focus all my rage on the bastard in front of me.

'You won't talk to me like that,' Da says, but he doesn't sound as controlling as usual.

'What will you do about it?' I ask, my face right up against his. I can smell his breath, see the bristles on his unshaven chin. It's a long time since I've been this close to him, and I am amazed to realise that I'm not frightened of him, that I actually feel like I'm in charge. He gestures that he's going to hit me but, instead of running away, I move closer, shouting in his face. 'Go on, hit me! Go on.' I say it over and over.

Ma jumps in between us, but even she hasn't the strength to hold me back. I have no idea what I am going to do but, at that moment, I want him dead. My arms flail about, and I desperately want to slap him across the face, but he scurries away sheepishly, muttering under his breath that he isn't putting up with this. Ma continues to hold me back because

I'm clearly not finished. I continue shouting at him, telling him I'm leaving because I don't want to stay in the same house as a prick like him.

Ma whispers to me to go to bed, but I insist I'm going up to pack; I'm leaving. I storm up to my room.

June and Paula obviously heard the commotion and are wondering what it's all about. They are sitting anxiously on the bed, whispering to each other when I open the bedroom door. Snivelling little fuckers – imagine me having to share a room with these two. I should have done this ages ago. I continue to shout at the top of my voice. 'Fuck him,' I repeat loudly, explaining to them that I'm leaving. Hurriedly moving around the room, pulling out my few bits of clothes, I feel the adrenalin pumping in me, the rush of power, completely new and unexpected, and I relish it. The two girls look at me in awe. I'm their heroine!

They fire questions at me: What happened? Who was the guy? Did Da catch you kissing? Where are you going? Can we come too? I sit on the bed, calmer now, wanting to explain it all to them, relive the magic of getting one over on the bastard, but the moment I touch the bed, I suddenly feel so tired. I'm drained and have no energy; the idea of going anywhere now is exhausting. All I want to do is sleep. I climb into bed and tell them I'll go in the morning.

I recall the fear on his face and drift off to sleep feeling powerful, in control. There is a smile on my lips as I nod off.

The moment I wake the next morning, the memory of the night before comes flooding back to me. I no longer feel so brave. What will I do? What will I say to him? What if he makes me leave? Where will I go? Oh shit, what have I done? It takes me ages to pluck up the courage to go downstairs, my legs shaking on every step. As I reach the end of the stairs, he walks by with his coat on; he has obviously been out already.

'I bought tickets to England, so I will be leaving soon,' he says as he walks by. Fuck him, I think to myself. I know better than to believe him; he threatens to go to England all the time, but never does. I'm shocked he's not shouting at me about last night. I'm just glad I'm not being asked to leave. I decide my best move is to play along and say nothing.

Joyce: 1975

I can't make out what's going on. I'm at work in the local pub, which usually makes me feel good, but I'm really low. I'm just going through the motions here as I laugh out of politeness at the usual jokes and comments from the lads. I try to shake myself out of this mood and sing along with the local band's version of The Eagles' 'Take it to the Limit', but nothing is taking away the pain. I don't know what this dull ache is but it's been there for a long time now and it won't shift. If I can just get out of here, things will be fine, but where can I go?

All these thoughts go round in my head as I move from one table to the next serving drinks without really paying any attention to anyone. Some of the girls ask if I'm OK and I tell them I'm tired. I'd love to explain, but I can't even do that for myself. Where would I start? I don't understand what's wrong with me. I place drinks in front of two ladies and force a smile while I wait to be paid. I overhear them discussing their weekend in Scotland. I light up as I think about my sister Pam in London. That's where I can go! It will be great to get away.

I ask for a smoke break and immediately ring Pam from the pub phone. When she answers the phone, I burst into tears.

'What's wrong? Is someone hurt?'

I want to reassure her but can't get my voice to work through the tears. I take a few deep breaths and ask, 'Can I come and live with you for a while, a couple of weeks maybe?'

'Of course you can. Why? What's wrong?'

'Nothing. I don't really know, Pam, but I want to get away.'

'Does Ma know you're ringing me?'

'No, not yet, but I'll tell her.'

'When do you want to come over?'

'As soon as possible, Pam. Give me a week to organise it and get some money together.' The money is running out on the phone. What with the beeping of the phone and the noise of the Bee Gees' 'Jive Talkin' in the pub, I'm struggling to concentrate. 'I'll ring you tomorrow, Pam.'

The phone goes dead. I already feel better, so I run in to tell Freda, my best friend. She's as confused as I am about this sudden decision, but she's very supportive and agrees it would be good for me to get away. The next day I book a flight. That gives me time to tell Ma. Over the next few days, I perk up. When I tell her, she says nothing but looks disappointed. I don't care; I have to get out. I leave her with her disappointment and walk out of the room.

I spend the rest of the week deciding what to take with me. June and Paula are upset but I tell them it won't be forever. I have to soften the blow because I haven't the energy to deal with anyone's pain but my own. I know I need to leave this house. The sadness, hurt, constant tension are eating away at me. I can feel myself withering.

Freda brings me to the airport and we cry in each other's arms. I'm still crying as I board the plane to Heathrow and only then does it dawn on me that it is my first time to fly. I sit near a window and stare out into the darkness. I don't know what's going to happen when I get there. What will I do. How long will I stay? I reassure myself that I'll work it all out, like I always do, but then I panic as I realise Pam will have loads of questions and I have no answers. What will I tell her?

Pam and her husband Sid are waiting for me. Sid smiles and tries to calm down their two-year-old son, Daren. Daren's eyes light up as he struggles to get out of his buggy, even though he doesn't remember me. I haven't seen him since he was ten months old. His big brown eyes stare up at me as I run to Pam, holding her really tightly for the longest time. I want to stay like this but I know that isn't possible. No sooner has the grip broken than she fires questions at me. I don't listen, just talk over her, saying that I need a change. She seems happy enough with that and immediately plans to get me a job in the pub she works in. We are both excited about the idea of working together. We stay up late, talking and laughing into the early hours.

For a while, everything is fine. Pam and I work together in the pub where she has been a barmaid for a couple of years. The English find my accent very funny and I enjoy the banter as we tease each other back and forth. I get a few offers from guys in the bar, but I'm not interested and Pam shoos them away. The good humour doesn't last long, and within a matter of weeks, I'm feeling just as bad as I did at home. I'm depressed but I ignore it and carry on as best I can. I don't discuss it with Pam, hoping that my low spirits might go away.

Each day I find it harder to function, to plaster a smile on my face and make small talk with the customers and chat with the staff. I'm really struggling to hold it together in front of Pam and Sid; even getting out of bed in the morning is becoming impossible. I try to distract myself with Daren, but that doesn't work. I continue to work but I can't shake this hollow, empty feeling, and the energy it takes to hide it is exhausting.

It's Friday night and Pam has the evening off, so I get dressed up and head to work. Friday is always an important night in the pub, and we all have to wear evening gowns. Luckily Pam has plenty to lend me. I stick to washing glasses for most of the night, so I don't have to deal with customers and, by closing time, I'm fit for bed. I don't speak a word on the way home. Bill, the driver, tries desperately to get a conversation going but I tell him I'm tired and he continues to do all the talking. I'm grateful to him for filling the night's silence, and stare out of the window until I arrive at Pam's.

Everyone is in bed, so I go into the kitchen to make some tea. I'm glad to be alone. I look in the cupboards for something to eat and spot Pam's medication. There is a huge variety of containers with every colour tablet you can imagine. Pam was always a bit of a hypochondriac, and the fact that she hoards everything means she has accumulated quite a store. I immediately think this would be the perfect way to end the pain. I can't bear it any longer and as I gently touch each bottle, checking out the names, and slide out the sleeves of tablets, putting them into neat rows, I know I have finally found the answer. If this is life, I don't want it any more. I turn off the kettle, take out all the containers, and sort the ones with names I don't recognise. I know aspirin won't be strong enough and the ones with names I can't pronounce sound really impressive, so I reckon they must be good. I set the good ones up on the coffee table and look in the drinks cabinet for something to go with them.

I haven't been this excited in ages. Already I feel better, knowing I won't have to feel like shit for much longer. I pour myself a vodka and coke, adding plenty of coke to kill the taste. I empty one container of blue tablets, take a handful and put them in my mouth, washing them down with the vodka and coke. Wow, that was easy! I prepare the next handful, and swallow them in one go. I'm heaving now but still manage to get them down. I work my way through each container until they are all empty and then sit back, sipping the rest of the vodka and coke. The tears roll down my face. I feel ill and not at all relaxed, the way I imagined I would. I cry for a while and it dawns on me that I'm going to die.

I'm not ready to die. What am I doing? What will I do now? Will I sit and just wait to die? Oh fuck, I'm going to be sick. I stagger into the bathroom, gripping the wall to keep me steady as I bend over the toilet, but nothing happens. I stick my fingers down my throat, but I can't get sick. I feel panic. I didn't think this through at all. I'm a stupid cunt. My legs are going from under me now and I feel really weak. Everything is getting very foggy and I want to sleep, but I know that's not the right thing to do. I need to call Pam but I don't want to wake Sid. I make my way upstairs and open their bedroom door. It's pitch black and I can't see a thing. I turn on the landing light and try again. The room is still black, but I get on my knees and crawl over to Pam's side of the bed. I shake her and have to call her a few times before she wakes.

'What?' she shouts, partly in shock at being woken up and partly because she is annoyed at being disturbed. I am sobbing now and finding it hard to speak anything other than her name. She turns on the lamp beside her bed, waking Sid.

'What's wrong?'

'Pam, I took some tablets and I don't want to die.'

'What? What tablets did you take?'

'I don't know. They were in the press.'

Sid sits up in a daze, rubbing his eyes, trying to make sense of what's going on.

'She took my tablets.'

Pam takes my hand and leads me downstairs. I have trouble

balancing myself and trying to keep up with her. I fall on the couch and point at the containers I emptied. Sid follows us, still looking dazed.

'She took all my fuckin sleeping tablets!'

'We'd better take her to the hospital.'

Suddenly I am very relaxed and really want to sleep. I'm no longer afraid and that awful feeling is gone; maybe this wasn't such a bad idea after all. I'm feeling soft and fuzzy, and all that tension is leaving my stomach. I watch the two of them rushing around, clearly worried, all the time shouting at me, 'Don't fall asleep.' I want to tell them to calm down, stop panicking, but my throat is dry and my tongue feels swollen. They'll work it out themselves, I think as I lay my head back on the couch.

Pam tries to keep the panic out of her voice, but she can't. Sid is on the phone to Sylvia next door to come and babysit. I fade in and out of the room, feeling very giddy. Sylvia arrives in her housecoat and Pam and Sid lift me to my feet and throw a jacket over my shoulders. I'm still wearing my evening gown as they struggle to get me out to the car. I feel good, safe and relaxed. Pam sits in the back of the car with me and constantly smacks my face to keep me awake. The tears flow down my face but I feel happy, and if I had the energy I'm sure I would laugh. They practically carry me into the hospital, my feet dragging behind me, as they hoist me from under my arms. They are putting me on a trolley and they are hurting my arms. Why are they being so rough? There's no need for that. Everything else is so quiet and gentle, I'm wrapped in a cloud – maybe I'm already dead. I watch the white lights flickering as they wheel the trolley into another room. I'm sorry for the pain I can see on Pam's face, but mine is gone. Surely they can understand? Now there are lots of people. Doctors maybe? Nurses? Or angels possibly? I don't know. My dress is taken off and I'm placed on my side. I'm sobbing but I can't answer the questions they are asking me.

'How many tablets did you take, Joyce?'

'Did you get sick? This is going to be uncomfortable for a while.'

I can hear Pam outside trying to explain that she doesn't know how many tablets she had in each container. The cloud is beginning to lift, and I can feel my mouth and legs again. Suddenly I realise I don't want to die.

The nurse holds me while someone puts a tube down my throat. I'm heaving.

'That's it. Good girl. Get it up.'

I'm placed in a ward, as the nurse explains to Pam that the procedure was successful. I let out a sigh of relief and fall asleep.

Three weeks later I move back home and return to work in the factory during the day and get my old job back in the pub at the weekends. In some ways, nothing has changed.

2010

A fresh pot of tea is placed in the middle of the table, and Paula gets up to empty the ashtrays. The women have spent another day at Joyce's kitchen table, talking, writing, crying, laughing. Time passes as the work is edited, omissions identified, memories dissected. They enjoy the time together, the connection, and they realise that, in many ways, completing the book is merely the vehicle for their journey, not the destination itself.

'You know what I found so difficult about you, Paula?' asks June.

'No, but I've a feeling you're going to tell me!'

'I hated quiet people because I couldn't read them. I like to know what someone is thinking, and with you I never could. You didn't

share anything; I had no idea what was going on in your head.'

'Yes, I felt that too. We were all trying to survive and you didn't think about how your behaviour affected other people, but it did,' says Joyce.

'I never understood that my not talking to people at home had an impact,' says Paula. 'I get it now, but only because you've explained that to me. I had no idea at the time. I hated all of you, so all I ever thought about was how awful you all were to me.'

'I always thought you hated us; you didn't want us in your life,' says Joyce. 'You deliberately went out of your way to cause trouble; whereas I was so afraid, I did anything to avoid it. He didn't need any triggers; he was bad enough without any agitation, so your behaviour, you setting him off the way you did, was a real problem for the rest of us. We didn't understand then that there was a different dynamic going on with you and him.'

'Whereas I assumed you knew how badly he treated me but just didn't give a fuck. I couldn't get over how none of you cared about me. I couldn't figure out what I was doing wrong. When I stayed out late, or did other things to annoy him, I wasn't thinking about anyone else but him. It never occurred to me that it would upset other people.'

'It was tunnel vision, I think,' says June. 'We stayed in a cocoon, and were oblivious to what was going on around us. For me, that was survival; it was driven by fear. My own world was the only world, so I was totally ignorant about how he treated you.'

'I'm ashamed to say it, Paula, but I really never noticed how he treated you either. I just never saw it. But, like June says, I wasn't able to think about anyone else. My God, how different our lives would be if we had spoken to each other!' Joyce shakes her head, the regret deep.

'Why didn't we speak to each other?' asks June. 'What stopped us?'

'Because he set it up that way from the beginning, that we didn't trust anyone. And I hated you, with a passion.' Paula can still feel the anger, the isolation, that sense of exclusion which has only begun to heal in recent years. The wounds are still raw and she knows to mind them.

'But I didn't hate you,' says Joyce, laughing, amused at the power of the response, 'although I didn't love you too much either! I did love June, though, and we told each other everything, but we never discussed the abuse. So, why was that?'

'I think it was self-hatred,' June says. 'It was too difficult to talk about. And believing it wasn't happening to others, thinking it was only happening to me, at whatever level we felt that, and the shame that came with that, stopped us from being able to name it.' She rubs her temples gently, and asks 'Has anyone got any Solpadeine? My head's killing me.'

'It's not that we didn't talk about it though, not completely,' says Paula, rummaging in her rucksack through her copious supply of painkillers. 'I remember when we had that conversation, June. I was about thirteen or fourteen, and you came into the bathroom when I was in the shower. There was lots going on in the street with the other kids being blood brothers, and keeping secrets and we were talking about it. I said to you that I had a secret that I would never tell anyone and you said you bet you knew what it was. I was sure you couldn't know, until you said, "I do, it's about Da, isn't it?" It's funny, the fact that I was behind the shower curtain made the conversation easier because we couldn't see each other. We probably would never have said that face to face. I couldn't answer you. I remember thinking I was going to physically pass out in the bath, with the fear of someone knowing. I still didn't make the connection that if you knew, that it must be happening for you too. I just couldn't understand how you knew my secret. And I was terrified that you would tell someone.'

'I was glad we'd had the conversation' says June, swirling the tablets in a glass of water. 'I felt closer to you after that. Even though the conversation didn't go any further, it created a bond of some kind. I had just told Emily, and I think I was starting to need to talk about it.'

'When did you tell Emily?' asks Joyce.

'We were sitting at the sewing machines, so we must have been seventeen or eighteen, which means our conversation in the bathroom was later than you remember it, Paula. We told each other everything and when I told her I had a secret she said she could guess. I didn't think she could possibly know, but she said, "It's to do with your father, isn't it?" I was so shocked that she knew. And you told Kevin, didn't you, Joyce?'

'Yeah, when I was about eighteen or nineteen. He was giving me a lecture about the fella I was going out with because he thought he was too old for me, and he warned me not to have sex with him. I said it wouldn't be the first time and he went mad, so I told him about Da. It was stopped a good while with Da at that time. I had been getting my periods for a couple of years then, and he never came near me again after that. But Kevin took me to the GP anyway, and he was really good actually, doing most of the talking for me. The GP told me not to worry and that everything would be sorted, that he would talk to Da the following week. That's when I spoke to you, Paula. The GP told me to explain to the two of you that Da wasn't allowed to do it any more, and for you to say no if he tried.'

'I remember that – you telling me that the doctor was going to sort it, that it would never happen again,' Paula says angrily. 'I absolutely believed you. I was so happy, thinking it was over. And I remember leaving the house immediately after, and I didn't even get down the road when he called me back and raped me. I wanted to string you up. I hated you, Joyce. I blamed you for it. But I hated myself too, because I thought I was so stupid for believing you.'

'And, Paula, when you did say no, did you remember that conversation, and me telling you to say no?' Joyce asks, gently but persistently. The writing process has given her an opportunity to challenge her youngest sister, to confront her about her behaviour, and she is determined that Paula must face her own responsibilities in this too.

'Much later I did, but it took a long time for me to make that connection,' Paula answers. 'The abuse didn't stop until years later for me, and that brought so many other issues with it that it took me a long time to work through. To be honest, when it stopped was probably the worst time I've ever had because I turned all that hatred for him on myself. I couldn't understand why I hadn't said "no" sooner. I never realised I had a choice. I know now I didn't, but I despised myself for years, believing I was a gutless coward.'

'It's funny,' says June, 'I didn't react like that after Joyce gave us the doctor's advice, because I don't think I believed it was possible for it to be stopped. I didn't feel let down because I just felt it was out of anyone's control. I just accepted it and didn't give any real thought to the idea that someone was going to stop it. But, like you, Paula, the later years were harder. I felt such guilt about wanting sex when I got older, and, to be honest, that guilt has never really gone away.'

'Me too,' says Joyce. 'I found it so difficult when I had a desire for sex; how could I live with that? I prayed all my life for it to stop, and now I wanted it – it didn't make sense. So I began asking myself, thinking maybe it's all my fault, maybe I wanted it all along.'

'Well somehow you got over that, seeing as you've got five children and are on your third man!' Paula laughs.

'Ah, well,' Joyce giggles through a coughing fit, 'life's too short not to get over shit like that, isn't it!'

Chapter 5: Healing

July 1989

On the dot of one o'clock, the sisters switch off their machines, gather their fags and empty teacups from the work benches and head to the kitchen for lunch. June and Joyce have come back to work in the factory to help try and make a go of the business while they're waiting for the court case. Joyce's marriage ended a couple of years ago and since then she and June had lived together until recently. They worked hard, getting their own sewing contracts and working in fast food outlets, and earned more money than they would ever have scraped together working for their father.

They put considerable energy into spending it too. When Joyce's children stayed overnight with their dad, the two women became regulars at the local nightclubs and pubs. The relationship between the two sisters has strengthened even more during this time, as they shared their first real experiences of freedom and relished their opportunities to make choices for themselves. Joyce began a new relationship a number of months earlier and recently started living with her new man, Trevor, while June and Eamonn are now living together almost a year. Now that their father has left the family home, and the abuse is out in the open, they have returned to working in the factory, so the three sisters spend each day working together, a rhythm slowly developing between them. They have continued making tentative steps towards discussing their shared experiences, but they are still careful and cautious. This is very uncertain territory for them.

Paula already has the kettle on when Joyce gets into the kitchen. She's always the first up from her seat when it's time to stop work, and the last one in every morning, despite the fact that she's the only one of the three siblings still living in the family home. She got into the habit of doing it over many years, as a way of annoying her father, and has continued with it, despite the fact that he hasn't been around for months.

June has a batch loaf out and is buttering bread, so Joyce puts the TV on in the sitting room and empties the ashtrays.

'Come on, girls,' she calls, 'Oprah is on.'

It's the summer of 1989 and the sisters have been following *The Oprah Winfrey Show* for a couple of weeks now on their lunch break. They often spend the afternoon talking about the programme over the noise of the sewing machines. June comes in with a plate of ham sandwiches and Paula brings in the teapot. There is a relief in the air since their father left the house, a novelty about being able to watch TV in peace, not constantly keeping an eye on the clock, and, whilst it's unspoken, the sisters know they are all relishing every moment of it. So they settle into the chairs with tea and fags, and the hastily made sandwiches.

They can tell from Oprah's voice that it's going to be a sad guest today. Sometimes they are upbeat and funny, but her tone is very serious and quiet. Joyce isn't really listening to her, and has her eyes half-shut. She's tired, her seven-year-old daughter Audrey had her up half the night with a tummy bug, so she hardly slept. She is suddenly alert when she hears the topic of the show.

Oprah's eyes are filled with tears and she seems really emotional. The woman beside her is also looking very upset.

'Child sexual abuse is something we all know happens, but none of us want to believe it is happening in our street, our town, our family. We are so grateful to you for coming here to tell us about your experience,' Oprah says.

The sisters listen intently as the woman describes her childhood pain, and exposes the fear, guilt, feelings of being dirty which characterised her early years. But then she goes on to talk about accepting her innocence, recognising that she was only a child, being able to see that she wasn't to blame. She talks about counselling and healing and how it's slow and gradual. The adverts come on but the room is still quiet and no one moves, even though they should be back at their machines by now. Eventually, Joyce gets up and quietly leaves her cup and plate in the sink and returns to her bench. June and Paula follow her shortly after and the sisters settle back to their work for the afternoon, but the silence remains. None of them speaks a word.

Paula: October 1989–1999

Joyce arrives in the factory and, looking at June and me, throws two cards on the bench saying, 'There's your appointments for the Rape Crisis Centre.'

I don't even look up from the work bench. I'm horrified and immediately angry because I don't want to go to counselling. The appointment is a few weeks away and that only makes things worse because I have more time to think and worry. I know I need this; the court case will start progressing over the coming months, and that's going to be tough. Giving the statements was bad enough, but the thought of telling a courtroom of strangers what happened with Da is too frightening.

My first appointment is early in the day and I arrive outside the big purple door with Rape Crisis Centre written on a plaque on the wall. I want to shrivel up and die. Everyone will know why I'm here. I ring the bell and wait for what seems like an eternity for someone to answer the door. A young woman opens it and I quickly step inside, hoping that no one has seen me go in. I'm shown to a waiting room and I sit on one of the chairs placed around the walls as she goes to tell the counsellor I'm here. I have no idea what I'll be asked or, furthermore, what I'm willing to tell. Fuck. I don't want to be here. I'm such a coward. I'm only here because I don't want Joyce and June to get well, and me to stay the way I am.

I want to walk out but I'm afraid to move. A woman comes in, introduces herself and leads me to a small room with two big chairs facing each other. She sits on one and gestures for me to take the other. I sit on the edge of the chair, ready to run if I have to. I can't stop my legs shaking and she asks me to say a little about why I'm there.

I tell her as little as I can about Da and that we are in the process of taking him to court. For the most part, she just listens and nods like she understands. The hour passes slowly, with a lot of silences that go unfilled, until she finally says, 'Our time is up.' She hands me a card with an appointment for the following week.

I attend my second appointment because, again, I listen to Joyce telling me that it will do me good. I don't believe her, but I know I need help, so I'm willing to try again.

This time, I'm led into a room full of women sitting around on beanbags. In the centre of the room is a small single mattress. I'm such a fucking coward. I want to run, but instead I sit on one of the beanbags. They have obviously put me in the wrong room. I want to cry. Just then, the counsellor I'd met the previous week and another woman enter the room and sit down. I want to get out, but I don't want to walk across the floor and draw attention to myself, so I wait for the counsellors to speak.

My counsellor asks everyone to introduce themselves and say something about why they are here. Slowly, each of the women tells a little about herself until it's my turn. I have no idea what anyone else has said. I can't hear them as I'm too focused on working out what I'll say when it comes to me. I stutter through my name, finding it difficult to breathe. I can feel my face getting redder and redder.

'I'm here because my sisters and I are taking my father to court for sexual abuse.' I put my head down and wait until they move to the next woman.

When the introductions are over, the counsellor explains that we will be doing some mattress work. I have no idea what that means, so I try to sink into the beanbag and make no eye contact. She explains that the point of the mattress work is to go into a memory, using your breath. By doing this you will let the memory go. I have no idea what she's talking about and I just want to go home. She asks for a volunteer. The girl in front of me says, 'I'll do it. I want to get it over with.' She moves over to lie down on the mattress.

The counsellor speaks to the woman, telling her to take long, slow breaths and to concentrate on her breathing. The room is dead silent and everyone sits still, staring at the girl in the middle of the room. After a short while, the girl begins to cry and her body is shaking. She then starts to wail, throwing her body all over the place, while the counsellors speak to her, telling her not to be afraid, that she's safe, nothing can happen to her.

I think these people are fuckin mad. There is no way I'm doing that in front of them. I don't even know them. I manage to sit and listen to some of the other girls telling their stories, each one more horrific than the last. All the time, I'm shrinking into the beanbag and moving my position so that I'm out of eyeshot of the counsellors, ensuring that they won't call on me.

Over the next six months, I sit in the group without ever doing any work, never contributing, just listening to the women telling their stories. When the counsellor asks me to participate, I just say I don't want to talk. When they try to push me, I just sit looking at the floor until they give up and move on to someone else.

Over the coming months, I find it harder to function. I don't know what's wrong with me, but I'm constantly tired and dread the thought of getting up in the morning. It's like being back at school, trying to find excuses to avoid the day. I don't want to talk to anyone, engage with anyone. I just wish they would all leave me alone.

The only thing that keeps me going is my individual session with my counsellor which happens every three weeks.

One day, Joyce arrives at work and tells us that she has finally got Ma into the Rape Crisis Centre. She tells us that Ma will be working with my counsellor. I'm so hurt. I know Ma needs help, but why does it have to be from my counsellor? This is the only person I have even come close to telling my story to, and now I feel that I can't trust her. It feels so unfair. The fact that I was never consulted or asked if I minded just confirms to me that no one can be trusted and no one cares about me. I can't tell anyone how I feel. I know I am being totally selfish and Ma needs help too. Maybe I'm just being unreasonable. I can be so horrible. I don't think about other people the way June and Joyce do.

Some of the women in the group are always saying how lucky I am to have my sisters and how it must be great to have someone else who understands what I'm going through. It's true: June and Joyce talk about the sessions. They're always on about what happened in their last session, what they had to do, what they said, what their counsellors said. Why don't they understand? I don't give a fuck! I don't want to hear about how great they're doing, how amazing their progress is, how brave they are. They do stuff I could never do or say. They are talking, participating, engaging. I'm sitting in silence looking at the wall. Jaysus, I feel inadequate enough without having to hear about the fantastic work they're doing. It only reminds me of what a failure I am. Why can't they just let me do it my own way?

It's strange, though, because over the months I have become dependent on the sessions. I've been seeing my counsellor for almost two years now, and even though I still don't say much, I do share sometimes and I recognise that I need the space. It's costing me a fortune, but I don't care because my counsellor is right: if I don't show that I value myself, then who will?

I decide it is time to look for another counsellor because it doesn't feel right with her seeing Ma as well. One of the girls tells me about a counsellor who has left the Rape Crisis Centre and gone out on her own and who is very good. I know I'm not cured yet, but maybe with the right person I will make more progress. I can't continue with this existence; it's too miserable. I have no option but to try again, so I call and make an appointment. This begins another long and slow process of building up a relationship with Rose, my new counsellor.

I've been going to Rose for over two years now. It was difficult to work with someone new, and it has taken a long time, but I am finally beginning to build up a trust with her. The business at home is going down the tubes, and we decide to close down the factory, which means that I no longer have the money to attend counselling. I have been spending about £500 a month but I need to make that investment in myself. I don't know what to do now that I have no job. Rose tells me not to worry, that I will be OK. I am chuffed, and feel supported, understood and cared for. The following week, Rose calls me into her office and informs me that I am already behind in my payments and need to settle up before it becomes unmanageable.

I leave the counselling centre for the last time, furious with myself for trusting her, angry for allowing myself to think anyone would care about me. What kind of fool am I? I swear to myself that I'll never make that mistake again. I'm thirty-one years of age, the work in the factory has all but dried up, I have no qualifications, still live in the family home, despite various attempts to move out, and see no future for myself. I'm spending more and more time alone in my room, just staring at the walls, thinking about how my life could have been better, but doing nothing about it. What's the point? It's always going to be shit.

June phones one evening and somehow talks me into joining a meditation group and enrolling in a reflexology course with her and Joyce. I don't know the first thing about reflexology and agree only because I'm afraid of being left behind. We're all still going to various forms of counselling, and I know they're doing better than me, so I can't let this widen the gap even further.

The first night we go to the college, we're nervous and giggly, like schoolgirls. We sit near the back of the big hall, which is freezing, but I quickly feel the heat rise and my hands sweat as I listen to the teacher explaining the modules we'll have to complete and the coursework that lies ahead. This is way beyond my reach; I was mad to sign up for this. What was I thinking? I can't even pronounce the words, never mind spell them! The only reason I don't run away is because of the other two, and I think that maybe we can help each other through this.

I quickly realise that I love studying and preparing lesson plans but hate going into the class itself. I feel uncomfortable around the others in the class and avoid having to work with anyone other than June or Joyce. I panic when the teacher splits us up. My hands sweat, my stomach churns, my head goes fuzzy and I want to cry. I have to really concentrate to remain focused on what's being said. Outside of the classroom, I throw myself into the work, study for hours on end, plan weekly study sessions for the three of us and fall in love with the whole idea of learning something new. I particularly enjoy the anatomy and physiology classes and learn each system by heart. I'm so competitive, I have to know the information before our study group begins and June or Joyce are not allowed to differ from the answers I prepare. We have a great time with lots of laughs as Joyce always manages to grab strangers off her road to be our guinea pigs for the practical work.

A few weeks before I take the final exams, I meet Siobhan. I'm instantly caught up in her life and we fall madly in love. Things move fast between us and, within a week, we move in together. It's exciting being with her; I love sitting up for hours talking. We talk so openly about our lives, past relationships, our friends and our families. I tell her all about the abuse. Nothing is held back. I want this relationship to be different. I want it to last.

For a while, my enthusiasm to study is dented, as all my energy, thoughts and motivation centres around being with Siobhan, but eventually I knuckle down and we all sit our exams in July 1999 and manage not only to pass, but to get high marks.

With the exams finished, I have no idea what I want to do with my life. Studying has filled my days for the past year and now I'm lost again. I don't feel qualified enough to work as a reflexologist and, strangely, my hopes for any future career haven't improved. I still struggle to see myself in a role I'm capable of fulfilling, or doing something I'm good at. I talk Siobhan into taking a year out of work to explore other options and we spend every minute of every day together. We are never out of one another's sight. We drink a lot, cry a lot and really get to know each other.

Months later, out of boredom, Siobhan signs us up for a six-week creative writing course. We arrive to the first session a little late and take the last two seats by the window. The facilitator asks us to introduce ourselves to the rest of the group. By the time it's my turn, I'm in an awful state; I'm panicked about what to say, how to introduce myself. I can barely breathe and I'm sure no one can understand a word I say. I feel so stupid. He goes on to speak about how best to write a story, explaining how, firstly, it is important to connect with an event or emotion you have personally experienced. He suggests we go home, write something and return the following week for feedback.

I begin to write what I subsequently realise will be the first chapter of the book my sisters and I will write together. The following week, I go back to the class, more confident this time, and I read out what I have written. Their response is great: I get a round of applause and blush with pride. The facilitator is very encouraging and tells me to continue writing and see where it leads. I love the course and I'm disappointed when it comes to an end. I show June and Joyce what I have written and suggest it would be a good idea if we all write together.

Over the coming year, I do a few short courses, mainly to fill in my time, but, as much as I enjoy learning something new, I still have no idea where they might lead me or how I will get a job, let alone a career.

Siobhan returns to do her Leaving Cert. and I take a two-year holistic healing course. It's unlike any other course I have done, because this time I'm on my own, with no one to shield me. I love the coursework and I have some excellent tutors, but I still struggle with the social side of college. I hate being around others and feel stupid if I have to make small talk. I have nothing in common with anyone, even though there are other mature students; I feel awkward and extremely uncomfortable at break times. I spend a lot of time texting Siobhan for help. She's great at calming me down and encouraging me to go on; there are plenty of days when I would easily walk away if it wasn't for something positive and upbeat in her text, telling me I can do it, to be brave. I focus on studying and the academic course work which I'm good at. I begin to understand what they mean by your comfort zone!

I pass all the exams with distinction but still feel like I know nothing. After two years of full-time study, I realise that I would have difficulty naming any of my fellow students.

I think about setting up on my own, but I'm afraid I will fail. Siobhan talks me into booking myself an appointment with a qualified counsellor to see how a real reflexologist works. I'm so disappointed with the session and feel I can do better, so I decide to convert the front room of our house into a healing room. I spend a fortune getting every detail just right; it takes me three weeks just to select the right music to enhance the experience!

I even manage to get some paying clients, but I still feel I know nothing. I take it personally if clients do not book repeat appointments. I'm very aware that I'm not the picture of health and happiness and don't practise what I preach, so I feel like a fraud. I convince myself I'll never be any good. The biggest struggle for me is the fact I will almost always be dealing with strangers even though I tell the clients not to speak through the treatment so they can be totally focused on themselves, really it's just a way for me to avoid having to talk to them or be put in a situation where they ask a question I don't know the answer to.

I tell Siobhan how I'm feeling and she's great; she tells me that I don't have to continue if it isn't for me and maybe I should consider going to college to try other things. I find a degree course in Leisure Management running in the Dublin Institute of Technology that doesn't look too difficult and it includes some of the subjects I've just studied, so I apply and I'm offered a place.

During the first week of the course, I am informed that one of the modules is around team-building. All the class will be going away for a week to an outdoor adventure centre in Killary, County Mayo. All the activities are designed to stimulate bonding among the group.

I don't want to go, so I try to come up with an excuse, but I'm informed it is compulsory to attend. We are to stay in dorms and that alone makes me want to leave the course. Siobhan spends hours telling me it will be OK; that it's only a week. How hard can it be?

The day we arrive we drop our bags into the room and are immediately brought outside towards a lake where we are instructed to change into wetsuits. I hold up the smelly, clinging item in disbelief, looking around me to check if it's a joke. I've never seen a wetsuit before and don't understand how I'm supposed to squeeze my considerable body into this tiny, skinny piece of elastic. I'm so conscious of my weight, and my sensitivity isn't helped by the fact that all but two of the other students are aged eighteen or younger and are skinny. I want to run home. I'm trapped. If I make a fuss, I'll look even more stupid than I feel.

I spend ages trying to pull this impossible tight wetsuit on. It highlights every lump and bump. When I eventually get it on, we are handed a tiny luminous orange life jacket that I manage to pull over my head. It reaches just below my chest. I'm sick. I look ridiculous; all I'm missing is a tutu and I could easily pass as one of the Michelin Men! I pray for the ground to open up and swallow me. But it's not the end of my humiliation. The instructor hands me wet runners, a yellow helmet and insists we pose for a picture.

I'm physically sick and have to fight back the vomit in my throat. My legs are shaking as we set off to walk the wrong way up a gorge, and it's terrifying. I'm so unfit, fat and feel stupid. The others have no difficulty with the slippery rocks and the sudden drop into ice-cold water. When we finally get to the top, the instructor leads everyone to a mud slide just above a cliff face with an option of jumping into the water below. I have a long lonely walk back to the house while the others jump happily off the cliff.

I decide I'm going home. I cry all the way back down the mountain, and I'm clear I've had enough. I want to get the hell out of here and fast. I don't care if they throw me off the course, I'm going home.

When I eventually get back down the mountain, I go to my room to call Siobhan but there is no signal. I walk outside the building but still there's no signal and there's no phone in the dorms. I fall apart, I'm so upset. The only phone is in the instructor's office but I'm too embarrassed to ask if I can use it and I don't want everyone to see I've been crying, so I go back inside to take a shower and get dressed. I try to convince myself that the worst is over and I don't have to ever get into a wetsuit again.

That evening, we play puzzles which I really enjoy and when the girls ask if I'm OK, I tell them I suffer with allergies anytime I go away. I'm sure they don't believe my excuse for red, puffy eyes but at least it stops them asking.

The next morning, we're taken by boat to a small cliff face and told we will be climbing to the top and abseiling down. I want to die. I'm terrified of heights and don't want to do this, but I feel such a gobshite for falling apart yesterday. I say nothing as I move to the end of the line. The rest of the class practically run up the cliff until it's my turn. I'm in such a state my legs are wobbling just putting on the harness. When I get to the foot of the cliff the instructor explains how important it is to stay back from the wall so that we can see our hand and footholds. I take the first step off the ground and stick firmly to the wall. I can't move a muscle, the fear is overwhelming, my legs are shaking and I start to cry. I can barely hear the instructor talking in the background, and I'm so afraid of moving either up or down that I lock myself in position with my fingers turning white. Finally, the instructor steps up beside me and tells me to let go. I'll be fine if I just let go. Out of embarrassment, I eventually let go and feel such an idiot when I realise I am only four feet off the ground!

The next morning as we board the train, the tutor asks us all to write a report on the week, outlining the highlights and learning from the experience. I describe how the highlight for me is getting on the train to come home. I'm thirty-eight years old and so humiliated. Despite being the oldest student, I acted like a complete idiot. How will I ever learn to socialise with these people?

June: October 1990-1992

What am I doing in the Rape Crisis Centre? Why did I agree to do this? How have I put myself in this position again? I'll never learn. I'm doing a weekend of intensive counselling and it's supposed to speed up the healing process. I've been coming to the Rape Crisis Centre for a long time now and I'm still a mess. When will it end? I thought I would be here for a month tops, and my life would be sorted. That was some mistake. Maybe this weekend will fix me. I heard it's really powerful, and I have to get better soon. I just have to. I don't even know anyone here because this is not my usual group. It's bad enough having to do this counselling, but spending the whole weekend with a bunch of strangers is going to be really tough.

Then I see Margaret and Angela. Thank God they're here. It's good to see familiar faces. I'll sit beside Margaret. Oh no, I didn't know there was going to be a male counsellor here.

'Who's he, Margaret?'

'That's Martin; he's supposed to be very good.'

I'm not comfortable with this, but at least Celine is with him and I really like her. I don't want to tell my story in front of a man.

As the day kicks off, a few people share some memories but I still feel nervous, because I know I'm going to have to talk soon. Usually I would jump in, but I don't feel safe.

After lunch, we are all sitting on the floor in a circle and then Martin looks at me and says, 'June, we haven't heard from you today. Would you like to share a memory with us?'

I knew I was going to have to speak before the day was out

and I've been trying to rehearse something. I relay a childhood memory of playing with a few friends in a nearby graveyard when a strange-looking guy jumped out on us with a small hatchet in his hand. My friends ran off and left me, because I was too small to climb back down the wall without help. I threw myself off the wall, badly grazing my knees. I ran home crying and told my mother what had happened. I thought she could see how frightened and upset I was, but she just sent me to the shops with Joyce.

I take a deep breath as I finish sharing this memory with the group, relieved it's over.

'Well, June,' says Martin, 'I heard you say that your mother never saw you were upset. How did that make you feel?'

'Invisible.'

'I see. Well now, June, I want you to stand up here in front of everyone and say the words "look at me".'

'What?'

'Just stand up here in the middle of this group and say, "look at me".'

Oh, my God, I'm so embarrassed. I don't want to appear like a stupid child, so I get up and say, very sheepishly, 'Look at me.'

'Louder,' he says.

'Look at me.'

'Again.'

'Look at me.' I'm getting hot and sweaty, and I know my face is really red. I feel stupid. He looks a bit disappointed in me and says, 'Just pace up and down here, and say it with more feeling.'

I want to die. How can I get out of this? Please, leave me alone. Can you not see how hard this is for me? Somebody stop this. I can't see a way out, so I walk up and down the room saying, 'Look at me, look at me,' over and over. Every few seconds, I look at him to see if he's finished with me and will let me sit back down because my legs are shaking and my heart is pounding. I know I'm not doing it right because he still looks disappointed. Then he says, 'I want you to get on your hands and knees and shout, "Look at me".'

I'm shaking. Everyone is looking at me, and I feel like such a failure. I know he wants me to cry, and I think everyone else does as well, but I can't. I'm too embarrassed with all eyes on me. I can't take this.

'Come on, June,' he says. 'Get on your hands and knees and shout, "look at me".'

He's more forceful now, but I can't do it.

'I'm sorry. You can throw me out if you want to, but I'm not doing that.'

He looks surprised, and I think he realises it's not going to happen. Then he says, in a different tone, 'It's OK, you can sit back down. You don't have to if you don't want to.'

As I go back to my seat, I want to die. I feel everyone's disappointed with me. I can't do anything. Why am I so afraid? I've just wasted an opportunity to get better.

Even though I'm coming to the Rape Crisis Centre for over two years, I'm still conscious of being observed entering the building, so terrified of being labelled. I ring the bell, and when they buzz the door, I nearly fall over myself to get in as quickly as possible. Today, I'm going to attend a groff for the first time. A groff is a very intense counselling session, from what I've heard, and it's supposed to move you forward much faster than one to one or group counselling, and I'm in a hurry to finish counselling as quickly as possible. Eamonn and I have been living together for a couple of years now, and I love him to bits, but I have such guilt about sex, about wanting it, so I can't initiate it, and he gets hurt by that and thinks I don't love him. And yet being attractive, him wanting me, is so important too. I need that reassurance. Christ, I'm still so fucked up, this thing had better work.

I'm very nervous because I've heard the groff is good but I don't really know exactly how it works or what is involved. I know a couple of people who will be here but the majority of them are strangers. As I walk into the room, there are twenty or thirty small mattresses on the floor and beanbags scattered everywhere.

'Just grab a mattress,' someone says, so I pick up the first one in front of me because I'm too embarrassed to look around the room. The curtains are pulled shut and the lights are out, so we're lying in the darkness with music playing. I think it's the most beautiful piece of music I've ever heard. 'It's the soundtrack to *The Mission*', I hear someone whisper.

Almost immediately, someone down the back of the room is screaming and shouting. It sounds like she's punching a beanbag. I panic, wondering is that what we're supposed to be doing because if it is, I can't do it. I hear people sobbing and wailing and I freeze, thinking, how can I get out of here? I decide to just tune in to the music and ignore all other sounds.

I can feel someone beside me. I open my eyes, struggling to see in the darkness, only to find no one is there. I feel really sad and, before I know it, I'm crying. I'm afraid to even raise my hand to wipe away the tears. Suddenly, I feel someone's hand on my stomach. It startles me and I open my eyes to find one of the counsellors kneeling beside me. She whispers to me, 'Breathe, June.'

I realise that I have stopped breathing.

I've had something on my mind for some time and feel I need to talk about it. Although I've always remembered the abuse, there's one memory that I've never spoken about because I feel it's so shameful. But here, in this space, I feel it's the right time, so I ask the counsellor, 'Can I ask you something? Is it normal to feel something "down there" when you're being abused?'

'What do you mean?'

'Once, when my father was abusing me, I felt like I had an itch, and I moved slightly in order to scratch the itch.'

'Yes,' she says. 'It's perfectly normal. You have to understand that your body has been sexualised from a very young age.'

She thinks I am satisfied with this answer and, after a few moments, leaves my side and moves on to someone else. But I'm not happy because I haven't been entirely honest with her. After I had moved slightly, Da noticed immediately. He looked down at me with a pleased look on his face and said, 'Are you enjoying this?'

'No,' I replied, as quickly as possible, and looked away from his smug face, feeling repulsed.

He then responded with the words that have stayed in my mind, words that even now I can't shake from my head.

'You're the best.'

I lie here and feel awful for the longest time and can't wait for the groff to be over. It lasts for three hours, and I leave feeling wretched, ashamed, abnormal. I'm never going to be fixed.

Joyce: 1991

The sexuality course is the ultimate, the epitome, the critical last leg of the journey. This is a sign of being cured. Even being put forward for this course is a testament that I'm ready for the final hurdle, so I'm thrilled when they invite me to go on it. It's like receiving a medal, recognition that I've worked through my stuff and I'm ready to take the final step. Trevor and I have been together almost four years now, and I know he wants us to have a child together, and even though I know I'm getting better, I haven't felt ready for that. The depression that hit me after each of my first three children still scares me and I really need this course to make me better so that I can leave that behind.

I'm both excited and worried about the course. There aren't many clients in the centre who know much about it, and the counsellor isn't too forthcoming with information about what it entails. I did hear some rumours about the course requiring nudity but I can't even imagine that, so I dismiss it.

The course takes place on a winter's night. It's dark and cold as I arrive at the Centre. I meet with the other girls in the kitchen and we drink tea while we wait to be summoned to the room. We laugh and joke about what to expect and nudity is mentioned again. Christine, my friend, is clear that baring all is required, but the rest of us can't imagine sitting on a beanbag in the nude, so we joke it off.

Angela comes down the stairs and says we are ready to begin. My stomach churns and my legs go wobbly as I try to get up from the chair. I don't want anyone to notice how nervous I am, so I bend down to pick up my bag while I compose myself. The course is taking place on the top floor and the stairs look like a mountain. I try desperately to calm myself as I listen to the others chatting and laughing.

Fuck it, I have to do it now, I realise, following them up the stairs. Maybe it won't be as bad as I think, and after tonight I'll be cured. Angela says we have nothing to worry about and that she'll be participating fully in the class. I try to think about whether this makes me feel any better, but I'm quickly distracted by the loud beating in my chest.

The ten of us enter the room and take up our positions on the beanbags which are placed in a circle. I adjust myself on the beanbag and place my bag on the floor beside me. Angela welcomes everyone. We laugh and giggle. I guess I'm not the only one who's nervous at the prospect of being cured at last. Angela speaks quietly as she explains the purpose of the course, telling us that many of us have disowned our bodies as a result of our experiences and this course provides the means to reclaim it. On one level it makes sense but on another, the thought of getting naked in a group is very frightening. I have trouble getting naked in front of my partner, never mind a roomful of strangers.

The lights are dimmed and there are candles lit on the corner tables. The atmosphere is calm and there is an air of anticipation as we wait patiently to cross the final hurdle.

Angela asks if anyone would like to be first and there is an inevitably long, awkward silence. I want desperately to get it over with but there's no way I'm starting off. Angela decides to be first in order to relax the group. She slowly takes each item of clothing off and stands beside her beanbag. She observes her body slowly from her toes up. I'm embarrassed to look but feel compelled to at least glance in her direction. I focus on her face, wondering all the time if my discomfort is noticeable. The silence is once again broken as Angela speaks. She explains the objective, which is to choose one part of the body and discuss all its positive aspects. What you like about it, how it feels and, if you wish, how you felt about this body part before counselling.

I need to go to the toilet. I'm convinced my bowels are about to open but I focus on trying to look relaxed about what's happening. I'm not succeeding.

One at a time, the women follow Angela and I'm getting more and more agitated because I know it is only a matter of time before it's my turn. I'm struggling to rehearse which part of my body I'll choose, as well as why I chose it. I can't decide on any body part that I am particularly proud of and we are not allowed to criticise, so I'm panicking. The anxiety is creeping up my neck; I can feel my throat going dry and I'm sure I won't be able to speak.

Being invited to join this group is an indication that progress has been made, that you're coming to terms with your past and are ready. How the hell did I get here? I'm not ready for this. There's a sense of danger and I'm scared that if I don't proceed they will all get on my back or be disappointed in me. I can't run or I won't be able to face them again. Angela assures us we will not be forced to do anything against our will but, fuck that, we have no choice.

I jump up and ask to go next. It's do or die. I can't breathe but I have to get it over with. I remove my clothes as quickly as I can. As I bend to tuck my pants into my jeans so they are not on view I realise that my naked bum is in the air, so I stand up too fast and feel dizzy.

I stand beside my beanbag, fumbling with my hands, trying to look like I'm studying my body, while all the time rehearsing in my head what I'll say. Nothing has prepared me for this. My body looks as disgusting as ever to me and I'm cold. I really want to get dressed but know I have to say something before I can do that.

I scan my body, desperately looking for some part I can speak positively about. I go through the various parts one at a time in my head. My legs, but then I remember my varicose veins; my feet I wonder, then remember my bunions and corns, and, as for my tits, well they hang over my sagging belly. I pick a spot on the wall behind Angela and move my eyes from there to the ground as I speak. I take a deep breath and tell myself it'll all be over shortly.

I quickly dismiss one body part at a time as I know I can't

speak negatively. I can hear the shaking in my voice and I want to cry. I raise my hands and suddenly realise I like them. I stand for a minute talking about my hands, thinking all the time I didn't need to undress to speak about my hands. I sit back down and quickly reach for my clothes. The group echo their congratulations as I stumble to get dressed. I feel relief: it's over, the pressure is off and I can feel my heartbeat beginning to calm. I don't recall much of the rest of the evening, but I do feel proud that I've crossed another hurdle. So why don't I feel cured?

2010

'It seems so long ago, doesn't it?' June murmurs, as she picks through the pages she has just read. 'We were so innocent, or naïve. We really thought there was a quick fix.'

'We were fuckin eejits!' laughs Paula. 'No need to dress it up!'

The women light new fags simultaneously and Paula opens a bottle of lager. She nods at the other two women from the fridge, indicating she will get them drinks, but they both shake their head. There is silence in the room as they each reflect on the journey they have taken since those hard, painful days. Joyce's relationship with Trevor eventually ended, but not before she had two very happy pregnancies, bringing Sarah and Nicole into her life. Her three older children, Paul, Derek and Audrey, have all left home now but come back regularly and she is tremendously proud of each of them. She smiles as her partner Mark pops his head around the door to let her know he's going to the bookies. He kisses her quickly on the top of her head and leaves the women alone.

June has three sons now, and herself and Eamonn continue to fight over the housework but love each other deeply. She had two very difficult labours, but the third was a home birth, with Joyce and Eamonn holding her hand, and rejoicing in her screams, as she brought Adam into the world. Their middle son, Christopher, has special needs, and they have had difficult times battling with bureaucracy and near-absent services, trying to ensure he receives the interventions he needs. June has learned a great deal about how to negotiate through this process, but she is tired. She runs her finger across the pages and wipes away a slow tear as she considers how hard she has worked to give her sons the best, and how much joy they bring her.

Paula sips her lager, and in her mind ticks off the multiple courses she has completed in the past two decades. Her love of learning has taken her down many paths, but the Diploma in Life Coaching was particularly significant for her, giving her a deeper understanding of how and where to take responsibility in her life. She leans back against the sink and watches her two sisters, with whom she now has such a bond, and she takes a moment to give thanks for the opportunity to hold them, and be held by them. In recent years, this relationship has extended to include Siobhan, and she has a sense that the path ahead is going to be an easier one. She takes another drink, and then returns to the table, smiling gently to herself.

'It is a long time ago, over twenty years,' confirms Joyce, 'and so much has happened since then. When you think about it, we started counselling before the court case got under way. I know we don't think it did us much good, but let's face it, we might have been complete basket cases without it!'

'What was the motivation for you, Joyce, in making us go to counselling?' June asks. 'Neither Paula nor I would ever have got round to organising it, and we only went because of you, so what was that about?'

'I suppose it was Oprah really, and the people she had on talking about their own experiences and how they have managed to come

to terms with abuse, and I figured we needed some help with that. And then do you remember that TV programme we saw, years ago, where they showed this woman who had been abused by her father, and the programme followed her going back to the family home, and then spitting on her father's grave? That was the first time we ever really began to think about the possibility of getting help with our abuse issues. Up until then, I didn't know where to start, where to look for help, but the number for the Rape Crisis Centre came up at the end of the programme, so I rang and put our names on their list. When I explained to them that we had the court case coming up, they did what they could to help get us in, because they knew we would need support to get us through that.'

'Well, they were right about that! We needed help, that's for sure, because we all had such different things going on,' says Paula. 'I was so angry; it was eating me up, whereas you two were feeling guilty about it, which I just didn't get. So we certainly needed support, but I don't know that counselling was necessarily what we needed at the time. In a strange way, I never really felt that the people at the Centre understood me.' She starts clearing away the papers on the table, making room for the tea, stacking their work into an ordered pile.

'I know what you mean,' says June. 'Anyone who has experienced abuse needs support, and it was great to have a place to talk, especially when we were preparing for the court case. But what kind of support you need depends on the individual. We all heal in different ways and need different things, which is inevitable because we're different people. I mean, look at us: three sisters, all abused in the same family by the same man, but how we've dealt with it and how it affected each of us is so different. But I'm not sure the counsellors recognised that. They didn't seem to consider what might suit each of us best, but simply slotted us into what was available.

Group work was great for me, but, Paula, you hated it, didn't you?'

'Oh, yeah,' Paula says emphatically. 'I used to break into a sweat just going up the stairs for those sessions. I didn't speak for months, but no one ever asked me if the form of counselling was the problem, or suggested trying something different.'

'People we were in counselling with were so raw,' says Joyce, sighing deeply. 'They held nothing back, and that made me feel completely inadequate. I didn't like the group work either because of that. I couldn't stop myself comparing my pain with theirs, my progress with how they were doing, so it just didn't work for me. It didn't feel safe. But the one to one work was great; I really did get a lot out of that.'

'I felt like that about the groups too,' says Paula. 'I thought, here is yet another place where I have underachieved and I minimised my own experience, because everyone else's story seemed so much worse.'

'That wasn't how I experienced it at all,' says June. 'I actually felt relieved to discover that I wasn't the only person with all this terrible stuff to carry around with me, and the bond I felt with people after sharing at such a deep level, that was great healing for me.'

'That's the difference for you, June. You did share,' Paula nods to her sister. 'I just didn't do that in the group sessions.'

'It's not just the method, but different personalities will suit different people too,' June adds. 'We all look for different qualities in people and that must have an impact on your relationship with your counsellor. It's really important that people recognise they're entitled to be fussy, that they should keep looking till they find the right person. You're going to disclose your most intimate secrets to your counsellor, so why would you do that with the first one you meet? The relationship needs to be respectful. We never knew we had a choice about what we participated in, that we had the option *of refusing to take part. Feeling you aren't in control is so typical of a victim of abuse that they need to really emphasise the importance of taking control. You really must surround yourself with people who care about you, and will be honest with you, don't you?'*

'I didn't always want honesty, I have to say,' says Paula. 'I found that hard; it was challenging, even though I actually did have trust in my counsellor eventually. It just took a long time.'

'I built up a good relationship with my counsellor,' says Joyce, 'and she considered me one of her top students! I was prepared to do whatever I was instructed to do without question. I believed she knew best. I did whatever I was told and didn't understand why I wasn't getting better. I thought if I conformed, did everything I was told, I would be OK. I didn't understand that ticking the boxes won't do it, that you have to get beyond the hurt and learn to live with it. I gave myself over to counselling completely. I wouldn't do that now. I would take more responsibility; I think that's probably what was missing for me, why I took so long to feel any change. I thought counselling was something they did to me, not something I did for myself.

'I don't think they really understood how much growing up we still had to do,' continues Joyce, pouring the tea and putting out biscuits on the table. 'Counsellors don't always recognise how much of the child is still with you, and they expect you to make rational decisions, to think logically, to act like an adult, but I wasn't able to do that for years.'

'Some of us are still trying to get there!' Paula says with a laugh.

'Jaysus, tell me about it!' June lights her cigarette, 'You're not capable of making decisions or questioning things you don't agree with. That's what I meant about needing to be told you can make choices. We just didn't know that.'

'They treat you like an adult, but when you don't have the

vocabulary, or understand your own feelings, the counselling just doesn't make sense,' continues Paula. 'I went out and bought all the books, and read everything I could get my hands on, thinking I would find myself in a book somewhere. But I couldn't because I didn't recognise myself. I needed a different way to connect my behaviour and the past. The life coaching worked for me because you didn't have to relive an emotion to understand it, whereas the counsellor insisted you had to go back there. When you think about it, and what we observed, girls screaming and wailing, thrashing around, and listening to all these horror stories, why would you want to do that? How could that be a good thing for you? Coaching is about identifying your own responsibilities, and finding solutions. That just makes more sense to me.'

'Whereas counselling is about dredging up all your crap and feeling the pain,' June says. 'Take it out, look at it, and then it's sorted. Bollox!'

The sisters laugh for a moment, as they reflect on the journeys they have taken. The years of counselling seem such a long time ago for them now.

'Remember how we used to shut down?' June asks. 'We all did that, didn't we? I remember being able to describe myself standing behind him when he was doing it. It was like an out-of-body experience: the real me used to just leave and watch, dispassionately. It was like making yourself dead on the inside, so I wouldn't have to deal with it. Now I know it's like the spirit leaving the body.'

Paula says, 'I felt it was like a shutter coming down, that's how I protected myself. I went inside, not out. I think that's part of my problem. Maybe I would have been better if I had gone outside.'

'That was the really hard bit of counselling,' says Joyce, 'because we had to bring those two people together. That dirty bitch back there was someone else, but in counselling I had to recognise that it

was me, the same person. I used to come out of counselling feeling like I had no skin, I was so raw. They strip you back, expose you, but somehow don't put you back together again to get on with your life.'

'I felt like a foreigner leaving a session,' says June, struck by her sister's analogy. 'I didn't know how to function, I would forget where I was, how to get home, mad stuff. It's so hard to manage everyday life when you start unravelling all these emotions, and then you can't stop it either, it just runs through your fingers, you can't hold it. Some of those sessions should have been residential; you shouldn't be expected to walk back to your life and just pick it up where you left off. They didn't give you the tools to cope, did they? Now I think about it, there were some real gaps in what we went through. I think they were making it up as they went along, to be honest. It was new to all of them, and I think they were all struggling to find a way that might work, or at least wouldn't do any harm.'

'Well, I never got how embarrassing myself in front of a room of strangers was going to help me, so I just wouldn't do it,' says Paula angrily. 'That was verging on harmful, wasn't it? What they made you do, June, "Look at me". For fuck's sake! And I'm not even going to go there with you and your "get your kit off" session, Joyce!'

There are more giggles, and Joyce shakes her head, laughing at the memory of stripping off. 'I know. What feckin eejits we were!'

'I did it because I wanted to belong,' says June earnestly. 'But it was wrong; some of the things we did were never going to help.'

'Looking back now, you'd wonder how could you integrate anything, or have time to reflect, when we were having two and three sessions every week?' says Joyce. 'We became dependent on the sessions too; I know I got to the point where I thought I couldn't manage without them. And some of that was to do with our expectations. We didn't realise that healing and counselling are slow. We all went into it thinking we would be fixed quickly, that *there was some miracle cure.'*

'I suppose it was a long time ago,' says Paula. 'They didn't really know what they were doing themselves, did they? Sexual abuse was only beginning to be discussed and dealt with openly, and I think the counsellors were as unsure as we were. But things have moved on, thank God. It would be different now.'

'Do you know how I first realised that I wasn't going to be "cured" in a session?' asks June. 'Oprah! She was able to explain what those counsellors never got me to understand; that all the counselling in the world will never make the abuse go away, that it can never be undone, but I can learn to live with it, that I don't have to allow it to define me.'

'Oh, you're so right. She inspired us all,' says Joyce. 'Her honesty, sharing her struggles, being so open about not being perfect. Louise Hay's books made it all so simple, too easy. Oprah made it real.'

'When she talks about her weight issues, I'm sure every woman in the country recognises her insecurities; she's amazing,' says June. 'And she doesn't try to sell a new diet or exercise DVD; she always says it's about resolving the internal issues.'

'Mind you,' says Joyce, 'she's also the reason why I think the three of us are well and truly fucked! I mean, if she can't sort herself, with all her money and support, what chance have we got?'

'Education has been as much a part of our healing as counselling though, hasn't it?' says June, lighting a fag.

'God, yeah,' agrees Joyce. 'I started because of the kids. The first course I ever did was that Beginners Irish, remember, June? We both had our kids in the Irish school, but hadn't a word of it ourselves, so I figured the only way I'm going to be able to help them is by learning the language too. And then we took the car mechanics course, thinking we'd save a load of money if those fellas couldn't rip us off!'

'So how did that plan go, then?' laughs Paula.

'My interest was always in personal development and healing,' says June. 'I was constantly looking for an answer, reading every self-help book I could find, and spending years doing all kinds of courses, thinking I would find myself in them. I think I was hoping someone would give me the answers, tell me how to live my life. It was a search for happiness; it's that basic really.'

'And yet, when we took on serious courses, like the reflexology and holistic healing, Paula, your degree, despite all our hard work, and the fact that we always did so well in the exams, it never meant anything to us,' reflects Joyce. 'We never believed it was our achievement. I didn't realise how that was a common experience for all of us until we wrote about it, but we have all struggled to accept success.'

'In fairness, we learned by rote, the way we did at school,' says Paula. 'I loved preparing our study groups, listing the topics likely to come up, doing all that preparation.'

'And you were great at it,' interrupts June. 'We'd never have got through it without your organisation, and the hours you put into that.'

'But it wasn't real learning,' explains Paula. 'We didn't learn to develop an understanding; we learned to pass the exams. It took me a long time to understand the difference between those two things.'

'Yet having a career, a profession, is important to us, so you'd think we would have approached studying differently, wouldn't you?' asks Joyce.

'I know that the time I went to the States on holiday,' says Paula, 'and was able to fill in 'reflexologist' on the card, beside the question about profession, I was so excited. I really thought I'd made it. But that feeling didn't last because I didn't believe in myself. I didn't feel I'd earned it.'

'That's the fundamental problem, isn't it?' says June. 'We still doubt ourselves so much. We have never really shaken that childhood belief that we're stupid, that we don't belong, that we're not good enough. We all strive for perfection, especially you, Paula. Even though we have big ideas and, Joyce, you think you can change the world.'

'I can! Just give me time!' laughs Joyce.

'But alongside that optimism are our self-doubts and our default position: that we're stupid, it's our fault – we are all getting better, there's no question about it, but we still go back there more readily than we should.'

'Do you think you ever get over abuse? Is it possible to ever completely recover?' asks Paula, very sombre now. She avoids looking at her sisters as she reaches for the cigarettes. This is a question she has managed not to ask for a very long time.

'I think there is something in your core which will always be damaged,' says Joyce. 'It's like the building blocks were never put in place. We were so young, I think we didn't reach all our developmental milestones, emotionally, you know? But I don't feel as messed up by the abuse now as I have done in the past. I don't consider myself a victim all the time now. That's just one part of me, but, it's like June said, it doesn't have to define me.'

'I suppose I went into counselling thinking there was a cure,' says Paula, 'that some day I would wake up and it would all be gone – the pain, the hurt, the mistrust. But now I don't know that you ever truly recover; I think you can make the best of what you've got, but the most you can hope for is that you live a better life than before.'

'Jaysus, Paula, that's a very depressing view,' says June, uncharacteristically sharp. 'I'm not being naïve, but I think that's really sad if you believe that's all you can hope for. And it's not true; you've made amazing progress in the past couple of years. Look at how you've managed all the changes at work, and taken on a front *of house role that you would have hated before. You'd never have done that a few years ago. And you manage conflict so much better now. You don't run away and disappear from us every time there's a tiff, like you used to.'*

'That's only because I have to see you both at work; it's not out of choice!'

'But the fact is, you do it.' June is determined to challenge what she sees as her sister's negativity. *'And you've said yourself many times how the coaching course has helped you to take responsibility, and by God you needed that love!'*

'And we've got to know you,' says Joyce. *'For the first time, I feel like I actually know you, that you're part of my life. We never had that until we started writing this book, and we shouldn't take that for granted. It's a blessing.'*

'You're right,' acknowledges Paula. *'That's all true. And of course I know I have made progress, and I do believe now that I can make my own choices, that I don't have to be a victim. But fear still stops me. I am terrified of revisiting those feelings of being stupid, being left out or laughed at. That is such a barrier for me.'*

'I think a lot of what we do is done out of fear,' says Joyce. *'Fear and self-doubt. I can't even take a compliment. My tutor on this degree course told me the other day that I am almost top of the class, but I dismissed it and just wanted to talk about what I need to do to improve. See, conformity again! Just give me the boxes and I'll tick them!'*

'I read back through the book last weekend,' says Paula, leafing through the ever-growing manuscript on the table. *'I thought that, by now, with all the work we've put into it, I would be proud of it, that I would like myself. But I was gutted when I read it because I don't like myself. I'm so angry in it. I was really shocked by that. That's why I had a meltdown when we finished the first draft. I thought the*

writing would help the healing, but I still don't like myself.'

Paula looks down at her lap and heaves a deep sob. Her face is flushed and the tears are suddenly streaming down her face. Joyce and June look at each other, their eyebrows raised. They hadn't seen this coming.

'We all had high expectations of what the book would do for us,' says Joyce gently. 'We all thought we would be healed through the writing, and there has been some of that. Revisiting the abuse isn't nearly so painful now as it was a few years ago. But none of us is where we want to be, that's for sure.'

'I can't believe we're so close to finishing the book.' says June. 'Every time we've worked on it, I've been left feeling heavy, tired, grieving almost. And that hasn't really gone away; I thought it would, that it would somehow be purged through the writing. So I am disappointed by that, but I realise I was probably unrealistic in my expectations. And also, I know that finishing writing the book isn't the end, it's the start of a new phase. And that's exciting.'

'We all resist accepting that we've done something amazing,' says Joyce. 'We're great at affirming others, encouraging people, giving advice, but we all struggle to believe we've done something good here, to take ownership of it. That's part of why our expectations aren't being met, because there is a part of us that won't accept that we've done what we set out to do. And that's because we still have such confusion about taking responsibility.'

'But there's a contradiction, isn't there?' suggests June. 'I know exactly what you mean about us having difficulty taking ownership, but, on the other hand, we all believe we can change the world; we can do anything. Some of the things you do at work, Joyce, are incredible; you always think on such a grand scale, nothing is too much for you. And I love that about us, that we're dreamers, that we believe anything is possible.'

'No wonder we were in counselling for so many years,' says Paula, trying to smile through her swollen eyes. 'We're a right mess, aren't we? I'll really miss the process, the time together.' Paula catches her breath several times as she struggles to hold down her tears before she can continue. Her sisters wait patiently, and eventually she smiles at them, a mischievous look on her face. 'But I tell you what I won't miss. I won't miss being asked to explain every fuckin emotion, every behaviour. Jaysus, if I get asked one more time, "What are you feeling now?"!'

'Well, you know what,' says Joyce, reaching across the table, taking a hand of each of her sisters, 'this book may not have cured us, and it will probably never make us rich, but it has given us so much special time together. This is what I'll grieve for when we finish writing. These times when we talk about real things, when we are honest, challenging, raw, yet safe. It's such hard work, but it's been necessary, not just for the book, but to strengthen the bond between us, the connection we have with each other. And I will always be grateful for that.'

Chapter 6: Justice

24 May 1990

The family arrives at the Circuit Court together. Not a word is spoken as they jostle for a spot in the packed lobby. It's a big group, with the four sisters, their mother, brother Kevin and June's partner, Eamonn. They are pinned up against the wall, all anxiously trying to avoid being split up, trying to hang on to one another without looking desperate. The building and level of activity is much more intimidating than Kilmainham Court and they are unprepared for the fear they each feel. Close by, a garda is handcuffed to a man who is staring at the ground, while the lobby is full of groups of people huddled together whispering.

The siblings see their father walk in and there is a collective gasp as they notice his dirty T-shirt and his unkempt white hair. He is wearing a newly grown beard.

'He looks a bit like David Attenborough,' June whispers nervously.

Their father is holding a plastic bag with butter, bread and tea bags clearly visible.

'Look at his groceries,' Paula says. 'He obviously knows he'll be going home today. This is a sham.'

He spots the family and nonchalantly nods in their direction. June decides to stare him down, but can't hold his returned gaze and is gutted when she has to turn away. A man from the barrister's office approaches the group and asks those who have made a statement to follow him. Walking down a long corridor, the four sisters are brought into a room at the back of the courthouse with nothing in it but a large table and some chairs. Their barrister is seated at the top of the table and the man who escorted the women joins him there as the barrister begins to talk through the papers in front of him. The women are invited to sit, feeling like school children who've been called in for a telling-off from the headmaster. He avoids any eye contact and remains focused on the documents as he informs them that the case is likely to be heard today. He constantly clears his throat as he flicks through the pages, and mutters to his colleague, who listens intently and makes notes in his book.

'Your statements will be read out, as well as your father's, but since he has pleaded guilty on the basis of your statements, there will be no need for any of you to be called as witnesses.'

Joyce lets out a gasp, and he glances up.

'How has he had access to our statements and yet we have never seen his?' Joyce asks, incredulous that their father has the upper hand, even at this eleventh hour.

The barrister looks shocked and a bit rattled, but he gathers himself quickly. 'Would you like to see your father's statement now? And maybe review your own, given that it's over a year since you made them?'

The sisters exchange glances, surprised at being given the choice and, without a word, nod. Copies of the statements are passed around the table and the sisters read them. The room is quiet, the pages crackling with each turn. Soon, the sound of sobbing fills the room as June and Joyce and Pamela sniff and wipe away tears, shaking their heads as they read the documents.

'Not only did he know us, understand us, but he used our different personalities to describe how we coped with the abuse.' says Joyce.

'I know,' June says. 'I can't believe he knew us so well. It's worse than that, it's the fact that he used that insight to shape how he abused each of us.'

'But look at how he's admitted only to the things we said. He hasn't said anything more than what we described. He just agreed with our statements which indicate that his statement was made after he'd read ours,' says Paula with a mixture of sadness, confusion and anger.

The barrister waits a few moments before explaining the likely outcome of the day.

'Because your father is now sixty-nine, it is highly unlikely that he will receive a custodial sentence.'

'Where will he go? What will he do if he doesn't get a custododial sentence?' Paula asks, panic-stricken at the possibility of him returning home.

'You should not think he's getting away with anything. Just because he isn't getting a custodial sentence doesn't mean he will be free.'

'But how is that justice?' says Paula. 'Of course he'll be free if he doesn't go to prison. What if he does it again?'

The sisters talk over each other, demanding answers, questioning what the whole point has been, wondering why they have bothered putting themselves through this past year. The barrister ignores them and simply explains that their father will more than likely be placed on probation. He excuses himself, offering the women the room for five minutes to compose themselves.

Back in the lobby, the sisters explain to the rest of the family what they believe to be a fundamentally unfair system. The shared sense of disgust is heightened as they divulge the barrister's expectations of the outcome. Their mother mutters, 'Bastard! The dirty bastard!' The family are still startled by her uncharacteristic outbursts in relation to her husband, and the sisters giggle as they catch each other's eye, noting their mother's increasing use of bad language.

'He's got the upper hand again,' Paula mutters through gritted teeth.

The mood is dark, crushed, as the family members consider their place in the slowly unfolding legal process. There is an air of defeat as they talk in hushed tones, muttering about the inequity of their treatment. Paula shifts from foot to foot, desperate for a cigarette but afraid to move in case they are called. Inspector Mick Carolan approaches the group, the frown on his face indicating further problems. He takes Joyce to one side and they have a short, whispered conversation before he nods to them all and leaves.

'What did he say?'

'We can't all go into the courtroom. There are too many of us.' Joyce can't look her siblings in the eye as she imparts this devastating news.

'What? I don't understand. We can't all go in?' June's eyes are full of painful tears, and she clutches her cramping stomach as she looks about the group, trying to make sense of the news.

'What are we supposed to do? Draw straws?' Paula holds her head in her hands and closes her eyes, trying to shut it all out. They can't exclude them now, not here, not today, not after all they have been through.

'Mick's gone to see what he can do,' says Joyce quietly. 'We just have to wait and see what he says.'

June hugs her mother and holds her tight, each crying gently, and the men shift uncomfortably, looking at the floor, as the family stands, broken, an oasis of silence in the thronged lobby.

The minutes slip by painfully slowly. They take turns going for a smoke, and someone finds Ma a chair. There is no conversation, no chatter, just a collective sadness.

Eventually, the big doors open to the courtroom and a man in a gown calls out 'DPP versus Kavanagh.' The siblings, partners and their mother all move towards the door to enter, several of them holding hands, anxiously trying to avoid drawing any attention to themselves in case they are refused entry. They find an empty row of seats near the back of the courtroom and sit silently, taking in the walls lined with gardaí who have been involved in the case. Joyce, June and their mother cry quietly and clutch each other's hands. Emotions are high as they now contemplate their statements being read out in this packed room.

June is distraught as the reality of the hearing becomes tangible for her. 'Joyce, I don't think I can bear it. They'll all hear what he did. They'll know it was us.'

'Shush,' says Joyce gently, rubbing her sister's arm. 'It's OK. It's what we've been waiting for.'

Eamonn puts his arm around June, and gradually her breathing steadies, until they see their father enter the court, the bag of groceries dangling from his arm. He looks around the room apparently deciding where to sit, then walks over and sits himself in the row opposite the family. There is an audible gasp as he sits within touching distance, and the sisters squeeze themselves as far back into their seats as they can, trying to put some distance between them and their abuser.

The judge enters and everyone stands. Paula uses the noise of the movement as an opportunity to ask June why there are reporters in the court. 'I thought it was supposed to be private. You know, in camera?'

June shrugs. She doesn't understand either, but the presence of the journalists is nothing compared to the impact of her father being able to sit wherever he likes.

Paula looks up and down the row, hoping to catch someone's eye who might explain what is going on, but all eyes are cast down, shoulders are hunched, and some of her family have their eyes closed. The press of bodies in the tightly packed room means that they are all warm and uncomfortable, yet each is alone in their confusion.

The barrister stands to speak, and there is an immediate shuffling in the seats as everyone sits upright to get a good look at him. The family lean forward, straining to catch every word. It's hard to hear, and even when they are able to do so, the legal jargon is incomprehensible, and they look at each other, perplexed, disappointed, frustrated. Paula sits back heavily in the seat, despondent at not being able to follow the proceedings, but Joyce and June remain on the edge of their seats, determined to hear everything that's said, even if they don't understand it all.

After a number of minutes, the barrister starts to read out Joyce's statement, but he gets through only the first few lines when their father jumps up in his seat, waving his arms in the air and shouting, 'Stop, stop, stop! I pleaded guilty, what more do you want?'

'It's a pity you didn't stop all those years ago,' Ma shouts.

Everything goes quiet for a moment as the barristers at the top of the room look at each other, deciding what to do. The barrister begins reading the statement again, but the judge interrupts, waving his hand, saying that he will consider the statements in chambers.

The family look up and down the row at each other, at the

barrister, over at the gardaí, seeking out Inspector Carolan, desperately looking for someone who will explain what's happening.

Their father's barrister steps up in front of the judge. There is more technical language and then a priest is called up to the witness stand.

'This is a joke,' Paula spits quietly. 'He's the fella Da is supposed to have gone to for that spirtual guidance programme.'

June whispers back, 'I know. Do you think he asked forgiveness from him? That would show he was sorry, wouldn't it?'

Paula's withering look leaves June clutching her stomach again and wondering why she keeps trying to forgive her abuser. Eamonn softly rubs her hand as she wipes away more tears.

'Father, can you please tell the court of Mr Kavanagh's participation in your programme?' their father's barrister asks.

'Well, he turns up regularly,' the priest responds in a flat, dull tone. 'He is an old man and is very worried that he is going to hell as a result of his deeds. He shows shame, and keeps referring to a quote from the Bible which states that if you harm a child, you may as well go into the middle of a lake and tie a stone around your neck.' The priest's tone is cynical and suspicious. He clearly doesn't believe that forgiveness has genuinely been sought.

'That's great!' Joyce whispers to her mother. 'The priest's no fool, and didn't fall for the old fella's games.' Her mother rubs her hand back.

The barrister calls Inspector Mick Carolan up next, and there is consternation in the row as they look about, trying to understand why he is being called by their father's defence counsel.

'I can't believe this.' Joyce is wiping her sweating hands with a damp tissue. 'He's a policeman, for God's sake. He's supposed to be helping us.'

'Sshh,' their mother hisses. She is terrified that all the talking will get them thrown out of the courtroom, and doesn't seem to have noticed that everyone is talking throughout the hearing.

The inspector starts to give his statement, so everyone leans forward, listening intently.

'Mr Kavanagh came into the station of his own free will and simply rattled off his statement, constantly talking about how he is haunted by the terrible deeds he has committed.' The inspector's responses are brusque, and he is clearly unhappy about being called to the stand. The barrister eventually gives up in frustration.

'Good man, Mick!' Joyce is whispering as the inspector steps down from the stand. Even Paula has to restrain herself from giving him a round of applause as he looks to the back of the room and catches the eyes of the entire family.

There is an excitement in the room now. Spirits have lifted with a feeling that this process might prove to be an honest one after all. The siblings exchange glances, when suddenly they are all thrown by a question from the judge.

'Would anyone from the family like to speak?'

The courtroom is silent. Everyone looks at the family, who stare back at the judge, shocked, unable to answer.

'Do you want to get up and speak?'

'No, do you?'

'I can't.'

'Neither can I.'

They are all terrified and shocked because, up to now they felt lucky to be allowed into the room. The judge's request has confirmed that he is aware of their presence.

'Why didn't we prepare for this? Typical. We're so stupid.'

'We can't let this opportunity pass.'

'I'll do it,' Joyce says.

The relief in everyone is evident as Joyce gets up to take the stand. She is shaking and has to pass her father on the way, but she keeps looking straight ahead at the judge.

'Tell me a bit about your father. What kind of man was he?'

'He was never a good father. He was never nice to us and in the statements it says that the abuse started at age seven or eight but in fact it began much earlier than that.' Her voice is trembling but she continues. 'He took away our childhood. Even at Christmas, he would buy lots of toys but then he didn't allow us to make any noise or play with them. We were always afraid of him.' Joyce's voice falters and stops. She looks at the judge, uncertain whether she should continue or not.

'Have you any questions?' the judge asks, but the barrister shakes his head and remains focused on the bench in front of him.

The judge thanks Joyce and tells her she can stand down. Joyce is disappointed that it has ended so suddenly. There was so much more to say, but she steps down and joins the others. The room is informed that there will be a break for lunch, and the family walks out together, feeling dazed and numb.

In the pub across the road, everyone tells Joyce how brave she is, how proud of her they are.

'I'm raging now I didn't get up too,' says June.

'Me too. Fucking coward!' Paula gulps back a glass of lager, furious with herself.

'You might get another chance,' Joyce consoles. 'It's not over yet.'

Lunch is a tense, nervous hour interspersed with long silences as the family comtemplate the possible outcomes, the impact of the judge's decision and the power he has over their lives. They hurry the food leaving most of it behind and return to court determined to get central seats to reflect their place in the drama.

As they settle themselves on the hard bench, the family are informed that the hearing is over and that the judge is about to pass sentence. June and Paula feel a mixture of disappointment and relief that they will not, in fact, have the opportunity to speak.

The judge and barristers talk in legal terms and none of the family understands any of what they say. Then suddenly there are cheers from the gardaí around the room. The atmosphere is charged; it's electric. The sisters jump up, still not understanding the proceedings, but knowing that something significant has taken place.

'What's happening?' June asks over the noise that has now engulfed the room.

'I don't know,' says Paula, stretching to see over the people in front. Everyone is standing now.

'It's over; it's over!' Joyce says.

'What do you mean?'

'He's going to prison, and it's over.'

Everyone is hugging, crying, laughing, still confused but knowing that a sentence has been given. The family is elated, vindicated.

'See, they were on our side all along!' shouts Joyce over the noise as she grabs Paula and hugs her.

'I can't believe it. We fuckin did it. They're locking him up!' Paula jumps up and down, still holding Joyce, and pulling June into the embrace.

Eamonn joins the hug and strokes June's hair, whispering into her ear, 'I'm so proud of you, love. You did it.' Even their mother is laughing, caught up in the excitement.

The room is beginning to quieten as the journalists rush out to submit their articles in time for the evening editions. It's quiet enough now to hear their father as he shouts over at his barrister, 'Do you call that justice? You're fuckin sacked!' He looks at his wife, his son, and his four daughters as the gardaí put him in handcuffs. He shouts over to them as he is walked out by a garda.

'Well, are you fuckin happy now?'

'Yes we are,' Eamonn retorts.

They all laugh with glee, the adrenalin pumping through the room.

Joyce goes over to talk to the barrister as he is packing up his papers.

'Seven counts of seven years to run concurrently because of his age,' Joyce explains.

'What does that mean?' asks June.

'That he'll be locked up for a good few years!'

The group leaves the court together, feeling that finally their hurt has been heard. Linking arms, they cross the road to the pub, a very different group from the one that had sat there so despondently just a few hours earlier.

'Right, ladies, pints all round?' Eamonn and Kevin say as they head to the bar. The family settle into the snug and light up fags.

'Jaysus, can you believe it's over? It's incredible, isn't it? Seven years!' Joyce hugs her mother, who is smiling but drawn.

They all clink glasses, make toasts, shed tears, laugh and congratulate each other. 'It's like we've won the Lotto, and are holding a wake, all at the same time,' June laughs as she takes the pint of lager being handed to her.

'We have to remember this feeling,' Joyce says. 'We'll never get this feeling again. Finally, someone believed us. They saw through him for the lying bastard he is.'

'You were so brave, Joyce, getting up to speak,' June says. 'I'm raging now I didn't get up too. I wish we could have said more about how bad it was. They didn't get the full picture.'

'Yeah, I should have got up too,' says Paula. 'I wanted to say what a bastard he is. He didn't just abuse *us*; he was a horrible fucker to everyone.'

'Ma, you were great, shouting out in the court like that,' says June. 'I was terrified. I couldn't move.'

'And what about him sitting beside us?' says Kevin indignantly. 'I never thought it would be like that. I couldn't believe they'd let him sit so close to us.'

'I know. It's not like that in the movies, is it? It was really intimidating,' says June. 'I was so determined to stare him out, but I couldn't. I'm so weak.' She is crying, her mood suddenly changed from jubilation to sorrow. 'Even though he deserves it, I hate the idea of him suffering. I feel terrible thinking about him being battered in prison; you know what they say happens to people who get locked up for doing things to children. I really believed he's sorry. He must be frightened, don't you think? He has to be worried and scared that he won't be able to cope. I know I shouldn't be concerned about him, but I couldn't help feeling that I didn't want him to be hurt.'

'What?' Paula says scornfully. 'Are you for real?'

'That's how I was feeling,' says June, 'right up to the time he caused a scene in the courtroom, sacking his barrister, and then asking if we are all happy – that settled it for me. It's obvious he was still only thinking of himself, so at that point I just thought, fuck him.'

'We're amazing. Stop thinking about him, and enjoy the moment.' Glasses are clinked, cigarettes smoked and hugs shared as the group revists every moment of the day. 'Mind you, it was horrible in there, wasn't it?' Paula is quiet, reflective. 'When we read his statements and saw how he had described us and our personalities, that he actually knew us, that was really shocking. It never crossed my mind that he knew who I was or had worked out anything about how I had behaved. Remember he mentioned the fact that I couldn't get out of the house quick enough? I can't believe he knew that about me.' Paula shakes her head, clearly disturbed by the revelation. 'I feel like I have to re-evaluate everything I knew about the man. He's not who I thought he was, this distant, remote power, who doesn't actually think about me and who I am. I don't know if it's better or worse to find that out about him.'

'Yeah, I was shocked too,' says Joyce. 'He got how we're different from each other. He understood us and what makes us tick. I didn't expect that.'

'It's kind of sickening; it brings it all to a different level,' June adds. 'The fact that he knew us so well, it makes the abuse go deeper somehow, doesn't it? Maybe that's how he was able to do what he did. He could manipulate us because he knew us so well. We never gave him credit for that.'

'I wanted him to pay,' Paula says. 'Pay for all the hurt and pain he caused for so many years, but I didn't want them to read out my statement. I still feel ashamed. I didn't want to hear what he did to me read out loud in a room full of strangers.'

'Me neither,' says Joyce. 'At least the bastard got that right, stopping them being read out. The shame of it.'

'Come on, girls,' says Kevin. 'Drink up. We're celebrating, not in mourning!' More drinks land on the table and the mood lifts but inevitably stories begin to emerge about their father.

'Do you remember the cartoons he used to make?' Kevin says. 'In fairness, he was very creative. What about that time he made a whole village out of cardboard? He had these drawings of a whole town, with all the streets, and he made little model houses and people, and he was going to film a cartoon with it.

He spent hours taking a photo, then moving something for the next photo.'

'And then I came in and moved it all!' laughs Paula. 'I didn't know this was part of some master plan. As far as I was concerned, it was just his usual shite. He went fuckin bananas.'

'And he was convinced he'd invented wooden clogs, the ones they wear in Holland, wasn't he, Ma?' June says. 'He said you'd stopped him from making a fortune cause you reckoned they would never catch on, and how he then heard that some other fella had made a shitload of money from his idea.'

Their mother laughs with them, and sips her gin and tonic, happy to watch her children having fun for the first time in so long.

'What about the time we all got shocks from the sewing machines because he forgot to earth them?'

'Or when he had a cold and he'd cut an onion in half, strap it under his nose, and lie on the couch for the day.'

'Jaysus, as if he didn't smell bad enough!'

'Kevin, tell us about the time he went with you to the bank,' June asks, wiping away the laughter from her eyes.

'Ah, that was some day,' says Kevin, recalling the meeting they had with the bank manager. 'I did my best to get out of the house without him. I really didn't want him with me. I was trying to make a good impression, start well with the banker, you know? I didn't want him coming along with all his hare-brained ideas, messing up the meeting. Well, there was no way he was letting me go without him. When I saw him coming out to the car in his piss-stained trousers and with no teeth in, ah, Jaysus, I was mortified. We were late leaving, so he insisted on bringing a cup of coffee with him, and, as we pulled away, he spilled the coffee all down his front. You should have heard him. He was ranting all the way to the bank, calling me names, as if it was my fault!

'He was amazing in some ways though, wasn't he?' muses Joyce. 'I mean, he took crap from no one, and he was convinced he was always right. I know that's what made him such a pain, and so arrogant, but he was ballsy with it. He really believed he could do anything.'

There is laughter around the table as the memories flow as readily as the rounds of drinks. One after another the siblings tell stories of their father's disregard for authority, his overstated sense of self-importance, his wacky attempts at fame and fortune.

'The stories he wrote, thinking he was going to be the next big thing in children's literature.'

'When he bought the drum set and guitars after seeing some programme about the Jackson Five and he thought we could be the Ballyfermot version!'

There are howls of amusement, giggles and snorts as they outdo one another with their tales, all recognising the distinctiveness of the man they have just seen sentenced, all waiting for the moment when they begin to reflect on the ultimate impact of their father's self-obsession. Amongst the hilarity around the table, there is an unspoken fear of where the conversation will lead them, permeating the air as thickly as the ever-increasing cigarette smoke. Eventually the stories begin to dwindle and there is a moment of silence. Glasses are swilled, cigarettes flicked and eyes averted.

'When he did things like that, you know, when he had such a hard neck and didn't give a fuck about anyone else, it did make you feel he was untouchable.' June takes a deep breath before she continues, knowing she has everyone's attention. 'You could imagine people down in the Dublin Corporation offices arguing about who would have to come down to the house, because everyone who came to that door got run out of it. Remember that time I was supposed to go to the States with my friend Julie and he didn't want me to go? He reported the two of us to the American Embassy, saying we had no intention of coming back, so when Julie went in to pick up her visa, she was called into a room and interrogated. It was really frightening. I never bothered going for mine. But the point is that there were times when you thought he was invincible, all-powerful, you know? It was like there was nothing he couldn't do, no part of your life that he couldn't touch. And sometimes that felt really reassuring, but mostly it was terrifying; it was like there was no escape from him.'

The atmosphere in the snug in subdued now, contemplative. There is sadness as the family begins to unravel their stories and the threads of their mother's and father's influence.

'That's why we have such mixed feelings about him, why we're confused about our relationship with him,' says Joyce thoughtfully. 'Despite all the awful things he did to us, we were dependent on him for so many things. Paula, you never went to the States because of your fear of the unknown. He created that fear in us, he made sure we needed him, that's part of how he managed to do what he did. I remember one time, when he was abusing me, he said to me that if anyone else ever did this, he'd kill them. And you know what I thought? I reckoned I was as safe as houses, because he was looking after me. That's pretty fucked up, eh?'

June elbows Joyce discreetly, nodding to their mother, who is looking at her hands held tightly in her lap, sad tears gently trickling down her wrinkled cheeks.

'But he wasn't all bad, was he?' says June, eager to shift the focus of their thoughts, uncomfortable with her mother's obvious distress. Paula looks at June sharply, confused at this new tone, but immediately understands the strategy when June nods in their mother's direction.

'He was funny, you have to give him that,' Paula manages to offer. 'He gave us all a great sense of humour. It's never a bad thing to be able to laugh, eh?'

'And he was good to his brothers and sisters,' Joyce adds. 'They all came to him whenever they were in trouble, and for money too, isn't that right, Ma? I know he helped them out at Christmas many times. They'd have really struggled if it wasn't for him.'

'And I know this might sound strange,' says June slowly, drawing deeply on her cigarette, 'but he gave us each other, and the belief in family. He did really value family life, all of us looking out for each other, minding each other. And I think we have a depth in our relationships that is powerful. I couldn't have got through the past few months without each of you; I can't even begin to imagine how it would be if I had to do this on my own. And in whatever way it happened, Da was part of what created that connection.' June's eyes are welling with emotion as she looks around the table, acknowledging her gratitude to her siblings with each nod and watery smile. Joyce squeezes her hand, and smiles back as she reaches over and rubs her mother's arm.

'We're lucky to have each other, that's for sure. Here's a toast to each and every one of us. We are brave, courageous and strong, and we've done an amazing thing today. I love you all,' Joyce says. 'To us!'

Glasses clink and tears are wiped away, as the family collectively echoes the toast.

'To us!'

Kevin goes to the bar for another round of drinks and rushes back waving the evening newspaper over his head. 'Look at this,' he says, holding up the front page. "Father of Evil is caged – daughters lives scarred for ever." says the headline.

'Jaysus,' says June. 'Give us a look at that.' June glances over the front page and then tries to quieten the noise that has erupted around the table. 'Listen to this. This is incredible. This is what the judge said. "This has been the most distressing, disturbing and upsetting case I have ever had to deal with. I have watched tear-filled, anguished faces of your family, and their anguish and distress must be minimal to what they have suffered in the past."'

There is silence now, the euphoria gone, spirits deadened.

Chapter 7: Ma's Story

2010

'Do you think she knew?'

The words hang thickly in the air, caught in the fog of cigarette smoke.

Paula hunches over the table, pulling deeply on her cigarette, avoiding eye contact and wishing she hadn't voiced the question that has silently pervaded the sisters' thoughts for so long.

The ashtray brims over between the half-drunk cups of tea, as they each flick their cigarettes in its general direction. Another pull on the fag, another smoke ring in the air, another long and wistful sigh.

'She knew in the same way we all knew,' says Joyce, straightening herself in the chair, and looking each of her sisters in the eye. 'We all claim we didn't know he was abusing the others, but when he came into that room, and clicked his fingers, all we thought was, Please don't let it be me, so, of course, we all fuckin knew. But there's knowing and there's knowing, isn't there? I could never believe she knew, not for a minute, not while it was going on. If I thought that, I'd have no parents. I already have no Da.'

'We confronted her that time, do you remember, June?' Paula asks.

'Yes, of course I do. I'd come home after a counselling session, so it must have been after the court case had begun. We were sitting in the factory. Ma thought everyone was talking about her because it was the talk of Ballyfermot by then, and she didn't want to be seen out in public, do you remember? I confronted her first,' says June.

'Where was I?' asks Joyce.

'I don't know; there was only me and Paula in the factory. I just spat the words out while I had the courage. "I always thought you knew, Ma," I said.'

'How did she respond?' asks Joyce.

'I'll always remember her answer,' June says. '"No, I didn't know, but I did think he was peculiar, and he liked looking at girls' pants."'

'That's when you joined in, Paula.'

'Yeah, that's right,' continues Paula. 'I said to her, "Wasn't that bad enough? Did that not make you suspect something wasn't right?" Ma said she thought he was harmless because he was always grabbing at women. She then said that she remembered walking into the bedroom to find him kneeling on the floor beside me. She said she was suspicious then, but when she asked what he was doing, I said nothing.'

'"That wasn't Paula, Ma, it was me," I told her,' says June.

'What did Ma say to that?' Joyce asks.

'Well, to be honest, Paula didn't give her time to respond because she asked her about the time when her insides fell out.'

'She said she was worried about me going on holiday,' says Paula.

'Well, I believe she knew as we knew,' says Joyce. 'I mean look at the state of her, she is so removed and distant, that's learned behaviour. Who's to say she wasn't abused herself as a child, long before Da got his hands on her. That's something we will never know. I do know one thing: I couldn't bear to be without her when I was younger.'

'*I know exactly what you mean,*' June says. '*I realise now that, actually, the feeling of not having a mother was harder than anything he ever did to me. It took me a long time to recognise the impact of not being loved by her. What he did was visible, but what she did wasn't, and, in some ways, that's harder. My focus was always on the abuse. I didn't look at my relationship with her, or the fact that she just wasn't there physically or emotionally throughout my life.*'

'*I know she knew,*' Paula says angrily. '*That day in the bathroom, when she called him, I know she knew then. Why else would she call him? And if you saw the look on his face, the way the blood drained from it. And the next day, when she insisted that I go to the hospital, that was the only time I ever saw her angry. I thought she was going to tell the doctor. There was another time too, when my friend came home from school with me and we were out in the factory looking at the stuffed toys. Da sent me into the shop to get something, and Ma says to me "Has your friend gone home?" I said "No, she's out in the factory." The look on her face, she fuckin knew. "Get out there now," she says, real sharp. She knew young girls shouldn't be left alone with him.*'

'*I believe she was as much a victim as we were, and it would have killed me to tell her and then have nothing happen. It was easier to live with the secret than to admit that no one could help,*' June says thoughtfully, stubbing out her cigarette.

'*I never saw any point telling her either, because I knew she wouldn't do anything,*' Paula says. '*But then what were we all so worried about, the day it all came out? Isn't that weird, how we all panicked because finally she knew, when we're all saying now that she knew all along?*' Paula is confused, and lights her cigarette as she watches her sisters, waiting for an explanation.

'*It's like I said: we all knew at some level,*' Joyce says. '*But acknowledging it, voicing it, that's a very different thing. None of us could say that she knew because then we would have to understand or accept why she did nothing. In the same way, we couldn't admit we knew about each other being abused, because we would then need to take some responsibility for not intervening.'*

'There are so many contradictions, aren't there?' Paula says. 'All these mixed messages. So we all knew somewhere inside us that she knew, but we did everything we could to stop her finding out, to protect her; we all worried so much about her when the abuse was exposed, yet we all believe she knew anyway.'

'And when it all came out,' June says, 'remember how she was? So hurt.'

'So fuckin angry,' finishes Paula. 'Do you remember we all thought she was going to hire a hitman to kill him?'

'She would have as well, if she'd known one. Unfortunately, the only mad bastard any of us knew was Da!' Joyce says.

The sisters laugh, and the tension breaks. Paula's shoulders relax and she finally looks up from the table, watching Joyce and June wiping away tears of laughter.

A fresh pot of tea is placed on the table, and cups are refilled. The room goes quiet again as cigarettes are lit. June opens a window to clear the room of the smoke, which is thick and yellow.

'It's funny,' Joyce says thoughtfully, 'we all operated out of fear of his threat that she would leave if we told. We were all afraid of her leaving, and how we would manage if she left, yet none of us felt we had her in the first place. We all felt abandoned, so what were we afraid of missing? I think that not only did she know, but she blamed us. She believed we were having fun. We washed his feet, we sat with him watching TV. We were always around him, not her.'

'Do you think she was jealous?' June asks, looking startled at this possibility.

'I do remember her saying to me one time,' Joyce says. '"If there wasn't a bad woman, there'd never be a bad man." She was telling me that it was all our faults, so, yes, I think she probably did blame us. But jealousy is something else.'

'How would any of us know what she was thinking or feeling?' Paula asks. 'She never showed any emotion, or spoke to any of us, or told any of us anything. Well, except you, Joyce; you had a better relationship with her than us.'

'Yeah. I want to know what happened to her that made her shut down,' June says. 'Why was she never able to show affection? Why was she emotionally so unavailable? Why would she never let any of us know her? The only birthday I ever remember being marked by her was my eleventh birthday. I came home from school, and she met me at the shop door, which was unusual. She took my coat off, and then bundled it up and gave it back to me. I didn't know what she was doing. I went into the hall to hang up my coat and out dropped this box of Dairy Milk. She came up behind me and says, "They're just for you, love, happy birthday." It was so special. Jesus, we didn't ask for much, did we? Imagine your own mother not celebrating your birthday. There was something very wrong in that. I never had any kind of relationship with Mammy. I had no physical contact with her; I don't remember ever sitting on her knee, or being hugged by her.'

June looks down at the floor, shaking her head, thinking about her own three children and what she wouldn't do to ensure they never felt that loss or abandonment which is still palpable for her. Each of the sisters struggles to understand her mother's role in her life.

'She told me she didn't want to bring me home from the hospital,' Paula says. 'She said she jumped off chairs to try and get rid of me when she was pregnant. I didn't realise until much later that I was a sickly child, and she was afraid she wouldn't be able to look after *me, but she shouldn't have said that to me. You just don't say that to a child. The only time she showed any warmth was when I was ill. I used to love having to stay home from school, and she'd let me get in her bed, and bring me up comics from the shop. It's the only time I remember feeling really safe.'*

Joyce is torn. She can feel her sister's hurt and sadness, but she has sympathy for their mother. She sits quietly for a few moments, wondering how to balance these relationships, then sits upright, lights another cigarette, and says, 'Let me tell you about Mammy, because, God love her, she had nowhere to go. Bad and all as he was, he was all she had, the poor fucker. When I was about fifteen, Da made me work in the shop. I didn't mind, because I liked helping Ma, and it meant I got time with her, which, as you know, we didn't get much of. She was more relaxed there too. So over those few years, she told me about herself and her life. As you know, she grew up in England, in Edgware, Middlesex. She was the third of six children, and, by all accounts, her parents were always fighting. She was unhappy as a child, had no self-confidence, and thought of herself as ugly.'

'Well, we've something in common there then,' Paula says laughing.

'As a teenager, she only had one friend, Imelda.'

June is stuck to the edge of her seat. Finally, she is going to learn something about this woman whose attention she has craved all these years.

'Imelda and Ma used to go to the dance every Saturday night. That's where she met Da. All the girls were mad about him.'

'Mad about that fat fucker?' Paula asks incredulously.

'Yeah, but he had the gift of the gab, didn't he?' Joyce says. 'And he could be charming when he wanted. Plus he was Irish, and that must have been a novelty factor too.

'So, *this particular night,*' Joyce continues, '*he asks her to dance, and she's thrilled, not just because he asked her, but because she's the envy of all the girls, and they started dating regularly after that. She was happy and he was good to her. Two months after her seventeenth birthday, she realised she was pregnant. She didn't tell her parents until she was three months gone, in case they made her get rid of the baby. They had taken a real dislike to Da. He was great about the pregnancy, by all accounts, and said they'd get married. When she finally told her parents, they were furious and disappointed. Her mother never really forgave her, and the only time her da ever discussed it with her properly was not long before the wedding. He offered to look after the baby for her if she didn't marry Da. Imagine how desperate he must have been, offering to do that? This was 1946, for God's sake. People just didn't do that.*

'*Not long after they announced they were getting married, Da turned up at the door one evening with his suitcase and informed them he was moving in. There was a big row because her parents were having none of it, but he just stormed past them and up the stairs. Ma was amazed at how her parents gave in to him, but kind of proud of him for being so strong and determined. She thought he must really love her to want to be with her so much.*

'*One evening not long after he moved in, two women came to the door looking for Da. He pushed Ma into the kitchen, so she wouldn't be able to hear, but of course she did. The women were shouting at Da, saying he had got the younger one pregnant and what was he going to do about it? "Didn't I offer to pay for the abortion?" he says, and he slammed the door and sent them packing. Later, he told Ma she was lucky that he had picked her.*

'*She had to buy her own ring and, on the day of the wedding, only Imelda and her husband turned up. When it was over, they stood on the steps of the registry office and Da shook hands with them,* saying, "Well, I don't know what you're doing, but we're going to the pictures." Ma was mortified, he didn't even buy the couple a drink or take them for dinner. They went to the pictures and Ma put her hand on his but he brushed her away, saying "I didn't come here for any of that nonsense." The new Mrs Joyce Kavanagh spent her first evening as a married woman sobbing throughout the film.

'Eventually Pamela arrived, and Ma was delighted with her. Apparently, Da was very good, coming to the hospital every day, although he never brought a gift for the baby, or Ma, but Ma didn't care. She had her baby now.

'During this whole time, Da had various jobs, sometimes working for himself, other times in a factory. As you know, he never stuck at anything for very long. After a back injury at work, he decided the only solution was to come home to Dublin, and he went on ahead of Ma to sort things out. But he was afraid she wouldn't follow him, so he took Pamela with him and said he would send for Ma when things were ready. She heard nothing for two months.'

'How old was Pamela then?' Paula asks.

'About nine months.'

'Oh, God, that must have been terrible for Ma,' says June, her eyes watering. 'Imagine not seeing your baby for all that time, or knowing who was looking after her? God love her, she must have been distraught.'

'Yeah, apparently she was really depressed, lost loads of weight and couldn't sleep. It was an awful time for her. So when the letter finally came telling her to get the boat to Dún Laoghaire, that's exactly what she did. She was terrified, knowing nothing about where she was going, but she was excited too, at seeing her child again and about the promise of a new home.

'Da collected her off the boat and brought her by horse and cart to his family home in Church Street, near Smithfield. It was a very small terrace house, two up, two down. The evening she arrived, it was brimming with people. Ma assumed it was family and neighbours come to greet her, but she soon realised that most of them actually lived in the house! Almost as soon as they arrived, Da said that he had to go out, and he left her with all these people she had never met, who laughed at her accent every time she spoke. And when she saw Pamela, the poor child made strange with her, so her heart was broken. She lived in that house for three years.

'After Tony was born, Da went to the Corpo and they got allocated a house in Ballyfermot. Ma was delighted, especially when she realised it had a front and back garden for the children to play in. They had very little, but Da was great at getting the house ready, painting floorboards and making the place nice, and Ma felt that finally they could be happy together.

'Da lost his job again shortly after they moved in, and for the next three years he worked in England, sending home twelve pounds a week to Ma, which was a king's ransom then. For the first time in her life, she had enough money to pay the bills and have something left over to buy nice things for the house. There was no tension, the children were happy, and she was very content. But each time he came home, he was annoyed that she was coping so well. He expected her to fall apart without him, but she was doing fine and, even worse, she was happy! He did take time to play with the kids, but he had very little patience, and it wouldn't be long before he'd get angry or let fly at one of them.'

'He did some horrible things, didn't he?' June says.

'He was so unpredictable, that was the worst of it,' Joyce admits. 'You just never knew what would set him off. Ma told me about this one time she gave Kevin money from the drawer so he could play cards with the other boys. When Da came in and realised the money had been messed with, he went bananas. Poor Kevin admitted *taking it, and before he could explain that he had permission, Da battered him up and down the hall, whacking him over the head, kicking him, until Ma came running out and pulled Kevin away. She was furious. "What's going on?" she asked, and Da said, "That fucker was at my money." "I gave him the money," she says. And do you know what he did then? He says, "Oh, that's OK then," and walks off. That was it. No apology, nothing. Kevin was black and blue for weeks after. He was only six.'*

'She had a hard life, there's no doubt about it, trying to contain him,' says June

'Anyway, his visits became more frequent, and the amount of money he sent home got smaller, until eventually he gave up the job in England. By 1955, she had five children and another on the way. She began to realise that one of the things that really set him off was her showing any of us affection, so she started consciously withdrawing. He would get mad if she hugged any of us, or sat us on her lap, so she stopped doing it. The odd occasion where she would threaten to leave, he would simply respond, "Go ahead, but you're not taking my children." It was an empty threat anyway. She had nowhere to go, and had no money. Her mother wrote regularly, but she didn't reply. She didn't want them to know the misery she was living in. She had come to hate him, wish him dead, but she was trapped and alone with no one to talk to. She was very lonely.'

'I think she felt unsafe all the time. He was so volatile. It's like she made some kind of commitment to herself that she would focus on keeping the peace, not rocking the boat.

'When he came back from England, he decided to buy a van to start up the mobile grocery business. He sold to all the local estates because there were no shops nearby. Neighbours often knocked on the door to buy something after the shop had closed up for the night and he would fly into a rage, shouting abuse at them, calling them stupid cunts. It wasn't long before he parked the van outside the

house and left all the work to Ma. The van was very popular and convenient for everyone and people liked dealing with her.

'Da's only involvement in it was to use it as an opportunity to feel up the women in the shop. He'd grab them by the breast or put his hand up their skirts, letting out a roar at them, laughing and joking all the time. "Give us a feel," he'd say. Some women thought it was funny and those who didn't were told in no uncertain terms that they were the ones with a problem. Everyone came to accept this was the way he was. Most women liked him because he'd talk to them for hours about their problems, always having a sympathetic ear. I'm sure they were all envious of Ma, thinking he was a great husband.

'Ma consoled herself with the fact that he was a good provider, he rarely drank and never smoked. She didn't get battered, like so many of the women in the area. He still demanded sex every night, and would sometimes go to the priest to complain that she wasn't fulfilling her wifely duties. The priest would tell him she wasn't allowed to do that, so that gave him permission to do as he pleased with God's blessing.

'Over time, Ma tried different tactics to manage Da's outbursts, like trying to reason with him, or giving him the silent treatment, but he'd just beat us until she gave in. He knew it was the only way to get at her. When she discovered she was pregnant again with me, she took hot baths, drank gin and jumped off chairs in an effort to get rid of me. So it wasn't just you, Paula. I guess each child she had made her feel trapped. Seven years later, Da decided he wanted to extend the business, which meant we had to move. That's when they bought the house on Le Fanu Road. Ma was happy we were at least staying in Ballyfermot, but I don't know if you remember how derelict it was? Jaysus, it was falling apart. There were no floorboards, nothing, but it had the potential to develop into a bigger shop, and Da saw it as an opportunity to make money and, in fairness, he was right.

'Ma was pregnant with you, Paula, so that was 1963, right? She wasn't consulted about the decision to move, but simply followed orders. And when the side of the house was converted into a shop, she got the job of standing behind the counter from nine in the morning until eight at night, and was then expected to clean the house and look after us. Da worked for a while in the shop, but he was so rude to all the customers that people stopped coming in while he was there.

'Da was in control of everything in that house. Ma was undermined and contradicted all the time, till she got to the point that she didn't trust her own judgement on anything, and had no faith in her ability to make decisions. She even used to check with him about taking us to the GP if we were sick. She just had no confidence. After having a miscarriage on what would have been her eleventh child, she went on the pill. The doctor suggested that Da should get sterilised because he was concerned about Ma having more children, but you can imagine Da's reaction! "Fuck off," he said to the doctor. "Do you want me to walk around like a eunuch?" After that, Da organised separate beds and never showed any sexual interest in her again.'

Joyce finally pauses and watches her sisters absorbing their mother's story. June wipes away a tear, and sighs deeply. 'I feel so sad for her, for her life. Understanding all that helps make sense of things, doesn't it?'

'Actually, no, not for me.' Paula is angry, resentful. 'I'd love it to make a difference, to feel the way you do, to let her off the hook. But I just can't do that.'

'I know I have huge resistance to blaming her,' says June quietly. 'I can't help but take her background into consideration. I can understand how difficult it was for her; how she felt she had no choices. We're so different in how we deal with this, Paula. You were the same with Da. Me and Joyce struggled to get angry with him, but that's your starting point. Look at all she missed out on.

The lack of closeness, the lack of intimacy, and her life is so full of loss. I just think it's so sad.'

The sisters reflect on their memories, and the abandoned childhoods they share. There's a heaviness in the room, a deep sadness and regret.

'Ah, Jaysus, lads, this is no good,' says Joyce. 'Open a bottle of wine there, will you?'

Chapter 8: Exposure

1992

It's been two years since the court case and Joyce is excited as she boils the kettle, waiting for June and Paula to come round and discuss the RTÉ proposal. She was astonished when she got the call, out of the blue, asking the sisters to be part of a television documentary about sexual abuse. 'With your court case over,' the researcher said, 'you would now be in a position to do a face-to-face interview.'

Joyce didn't hesitate in her response and is sure the girls won't either. She can't wait to talk it through with them, and rushes to open the door when the bell rings.

'Well, everyone I care about knows all there is to know, so that certainly wouldn't be a concern of mine,' says June, after Joyce has repeated, word for word, the conversation she has had with the researcher on the phone.

'And maybe if there is some publicity about what we went through, other victims will hear the most important message of all: that they are not responsible,' adds Paula. 'That would be my interest in doing it, raising some awareness, getting people thinking about their own situations. And reminding people that abuse is still going on, that it's still such a secret.'

The girls jump at the chance to go on the programme, and, the following week, Moya Doherty, the producer, calls to meet them. She talks about how their story might be perceived by some members of the public and wants to be sure they are prepared for the possible kickback. 'Not everyone will be sympathetic to you,' she says. 'Everyone will know about your abuse – people in the shops, in your local pub. Are you sure you're ready for that?'

'Yes,' they reply eagerly, impatient that she seems to be trying to talk them out of it. For God's sake, what could go wrong, they wonder? Haven't they got good intentions?

The women spend days discussing and planning for the filming, thinking about what to wear and considering whether or not to get their hair cut. But when the day of 'shooting' arrives, they realise that actually these things aren't important and they manage their intense jitters by nervously laughing their way through the day.

Each of the sisters is interviewed separately, and the process proves far more harrowing than any of them had anticipated. Filming is stopped many times to allow them to compose themselves, and the day ends with each of them feeling a wrenching despair and hurt at the realisation of how much trauma they have lived through. It takes a few days for them to feel any sense of achievement but this does come in time, and they share their pride in what they have done, and a belief that they have done something worthwhile for other victims of sexual and emotional abuse.

Some months later, the sisters gather in their mother's living room, settling into their seats with bowls of popcorn, glasses of wine and nibbles ready at hand for the big premiere. They have decided to watch the programme together, since they have no idea what to expect.

'I wonder how they managed to cut out all those places where we started laughing?' Paula wonders. 'Jaysus, they were so patient with us, weren't they?'

Joyce is quiet, anticipating the emotional evening ahead, and knowing she will have to be strong for her sisters. This is going to be incredibly difficult for them all, and she knows June and Paula don't understand that yet.

The excitement fills the air and there is still half an hour to wait. They fill the space with chat about who might be watching the programme, which of their colleagues they have told, which family members will be unhappy about it, anticipating the reaction of others to their lives being set out for them to scrutinise and mull over. Their mother joins them. She was interviewed too, and is somewhat bewildered by all the attention and activity. She, too, is nervous about how she will be portrayed in the documentary.

The phone rings and Joyce jumps up to answer it.

'When you answer that, take it off the hook so it doesn't ring during the programme,' June says. There is a moment of silence as Joyce listens on the phone, then June and Paula stare as they hear Joyce reacting.

'What! How can he do that? How is that possible if he's in jail? The bastard,' Joyce says as she holds the phone close to her. 'But he was convicted in court, how can he contest that?'

'Who is it? What's going on?' June demands, but there is no response as Joyce nods in response to whatever she is hearing on the phone.

'I don't understand what that means, what's going to happen now, Moya?' she asks.

'Oh, shit, something's wrong. It's Moya,' June whispers to

Paula and her mother as she huddles nearer the phone, trying to catch the conversation.

Eventually, Joyce comes off the phone and sits down in the armchair, the popcorn miserably unfestive at her feet. 'Da has taken out an injunction against the programme. It won't be on tonight.'

'What!' everyone shouts together.

'He says that if the programme goes out before your separation case is heard, Ma . . .' Joyce nods at her mother's anxious face, 'he won't get a fair hearing. So he's taken out an injunction against the programme. It won't go out tonight.'

'But he's in prison, how can he do that?' Paula asks angrily.

'Look, I don't understand either. Moya says we're to watch the news.'

'Fuckin bastard. Will he ever let go?' June paces the room, unable to sit, trying to make sense of how her father can still exercise such control over their lives.

'It's almost nine, so turn on the news and let's get more information.'

They listen intently as the newsreader announces that a convicted father has taken out an injunction against RTÉ for the programme in which his daughters will discuss the sexual abuse they suffered for many years. The broadcasting of the programme *Tuesday File* will now depend on the outcome of the hearing.

Everyone is furious. They each feel the deep injustice of what is happening and the fact that, even in prison, their abuser seems to have more power than them.

'Moya says she'll phone us with an update as soon as she hears anything.'

'Surely he can't get away with this?' Ma says. 'He's a convicted criminal, for God's sake. What is wrong with this country?'

They sit drinking wine and light one fag after the other, watching the phone in anticipation, though they know it is highly unlikely they will hear anything tonight. Moya is furious too but assured the women that they have their best lawyers on the case.

'Let's trust that she knows what she's talking about,' Joyce says. 'Nothing is going to happen until Monday, so let's not brood on this all weekend.'

The doorbell rings and June goes to answer it. She returns with Joyce's friend Annette.

'Hi. I just heard on the news about the programme being stopped. What happened?' she asks before she even sits down.

Joyce explains about the phone call and pours her a glass of wine. The sisters are fed up and don't want to talk about RTÉ any more. They begin to reminisce over childhood games and pranks, people they haven't seen in years, old boyfriends and romances that went wrong, and in no time the room is filled with laughter.

The following Monday, Moya phones Joyce to say the injunction has been lifted and the programme will go out the following night. The judge has watched the programme and could find no reason to stop it. He felt the sisters had spoken about the effect of abuse on their lives and that their father wasn't the focus of the programme. It is all over the papers and on every news bulletin all day long.

'So, you see,' says Joyce on the phone to June later that day, 'he's helped us, in a strange way. Look at how much more publicity the programme is getting now, because of him. Isn't that great?'

Chapter 9: Da's Dead

July 1996

It's been five years since their father was sentenced, and over a year since he got out of prison. He was released early for good behaviour. None of the sisters had any contact with him since his release, although, for a period, there were regular letters from him, often quoting the Bible, or requesting things to be sent on to him. They ignored each letter, although often had a laugh at his attempts at formal correspondence before throwing the letter in the fire.

Joyce now has three more daughters, the youngest being just a year old, but her relationship is beginning to crumble. June has Stephen and Christopher, and is currently feeling some concern about her youngest son, who doesn't seem to be developing the way she thinks he should. She keeps being told not to worry, but something is eating away at her when she holds his rigid little body to her. She keeps telling herself to trust her instincts but constantly doubts herself. Her thoughts are interrupted by the phone ringing.

'Hello, Joyce.'

'Hi, Paula, how are you? I didn't see you all week. Are you ready for our study class this evening? I got three more clients to practise our reflexology on.'

Paula's organisational skills and attention to detail are proving very helpful to June and Joyce as the three women undertake the reflexology course. Paula spends hours preparing study plans and assignments, often involving Siobhan in her thorough research. Her sisters are grateful to hand the respnsibility over to her.

'Joyce, Da's dead.'

'What?'

'Da's dead. He died two days ago of a heart attack or something.'

'Jesus, Paula, two days ago was Independence Day, how ironic is that. How come we are only hearing now?'

'The morgue rang Ma because his sister is looking for permission to bury him. I can't get June on the phone. Do you know where she is?'

'She'll be over here later to study for our exam. You'll be here, won't you? We can't do it without you.'

'Yes, I'll be there and we can talk to June then.'

There is little more to say, and Joyce puts the phone down slowly and stands in the hall for some time, trying to understand what she feels. She is grateful that the house is quiet for once. She needs time to think about this. Going into the kitchen, Joyce automatically puts on the kettle and settles down at the table with a freshly made pot of tea. She allows herself to wonder what life has been like for her father since he got out.

Joyce thinks as she stirs her tea. They heard through a relative that he was living somewhere off the North Circular Road, but no one saw him or knew whether he was working or how he spent his time. He was seventy-five, so he couldn't have been that active. The truth is, none of them was interested in his life; they were all busy trying to keep their own lives on track.

An hour must have passed, and Joyce is still sitting at the kitchen table, nursing a cold cup of tea and allowing her thoughts to meander, when she hears a car pulling up in the drive. She jumps up and quickly goes to the front door. Now that June is here, she realises how much she wants to talk to someone about her father's death.

Joyce is in the driveway before June has even got out of the car. She reaches the car as June steps out, pulling her handbag behind her.

'Da's dead.'

'What?' The sisters hug spontaneously, the shock, the tears flowing. June sobs heavily and Joyce holds her close, both of them overcome by the emotion engulfing them. Eventually their breathing slows and they pull away, still holding each other's shoulders. Their sobs cease, and as they look each other in the eye, they both burst out laughing. They hug again and walk up the drive arm in arm.

Joyce's neighbour steps out as they reach the front door and he nods in their direction, clearly noticing their tear-streaked faces. He isn't sure what to say.

Joyce looks at him, and says with great excitement, 'Harry, me Da's dead,' and Harry walks away, looking back at the house occasionally, shaking his head. The women run into the hall, giggling.

Paula

I stand at the back of the church for a moment, feeling uncomfortable, looking around the church before I follow Kevin and David into the seat. What the fuck am I doing walking into Da's funeral? June and Joyce wouldn't even come, and when I asked Ma, she said, 'Fuck him, I hope he rots in hell.'

I don't know why I felt the need to be here, but some part of me thinks it's important. Maybe it's closure, as they say in counselling. But sitting here looking at the empty church, only Kevin, David and me hiding away at the back, not even included in our own father's funeral, and only a few members of his family in the front row, I feel lost and alone. I can't understand why June and Joyce didn't come. He loved them and they wouldn't even come to his funeral. Da never cared about me and, even now, I'm still trying to get him to notice me, to see that it's me sitting here, not his precious June and Joyce.

What's wrong with me? I spent all my life wanting him dead. Now that he is, all I feel is robbed. I will never get the opportunity to ask him why. Why did he hate me so much? What did I ever do to him to make him despise me and treat me like crap?

I look around as a few of my friends enter the church. I catch their eye as they sit, looking embarrassed. I guess they're as confused as I am. They've only ever heard me say how much I hate my father, and, yet, here I sit, not understanding what I hope to achieve.

Chapter 10: Connecting

2010

'I can't decide whether to have the banana boat or the sticky toffee pudding,' says June, pondering the dessert menu yet again.

'I tell you what, love,' says Eamonn, wearily. 'Let's order both and we can share them.' He is mortified that the waitress has been standing at their table for so long, and just wants to finish the order.

'Lovely!' says June brightly, handing over the menu. 'And another bottle of house white while you're at it!'

'Happy birthday, sis,' says Joyce, raising her glass to Paula.

'Yes, happy birthday, Paula,' they all add, clinking glasses. Eamonn and Mark, Joyce's partner, head out for a cigarette, leaving Joyce, June, Paula and Siobhan to continue their conversation.

'I always found relationships difficult,' says Paula, picking up on the earlier discussion. She gives Siobhan a smile before carrying on. 'I could do the surface stuff, but any friendships I had growing up were difficult. I never allowed myself to get close enough for personal questions to be asked. Whenever I found myself in difficult situations, or someone getting close asking too much, I'd just say that I hated living at home with Da. I never gave a reason. I *tended to pick friends who didn't ask too much. I stuck to groups of friends, rather than to individuals, to avoid any closeness.'*

'*What about boys?*' June asks.

'*Normally when I had sex, I was so pissed, I didn't think about anything. I never used protection but didn't get caught out so I was convinced I couldn't get pregnant. I was a total whore, sleeping with anybody. The ugliest fucker on the planet, and there I was, a prick magnet! I wanted somebody to want me, though, I know that. I wanted to be attractive, but I'd settle for a screw in an alleyway. It wouldn't last long because they were usually as pissed as I was. I didn't care about the way I got attention. I even picked up your rejects, June. I'd hang on the sidelines, waiting for the virgin queen to pass them over. I knew how bad that was, picking up guys who had spent the night chatting up my sister. I'd stand at the end of the night, wondering why the idiots didn't ask me. I was there for the taking, and they didn't even have to buy me a drink!*'

'*Remember when we were on holiday in America?*' June asks Paula. '*That night we met the three Irish fellas? One of them was the ugliest I've ever seen. He had a big whiskey nose, and mad bushy hair. Holy fuck, he was an ugly bastard!*' June turns to Joyce, laughing. '*Paula told me she was going to bed. "Why?" I asked. "It's only eleven o'clock." "Because he's starting to look good to me!" she says!*'

The four women howl with laughter, Paula shaking her head as she wipes away the tears. '*I swear to God, I got a fright that night.*'

'*What about when we went to California when you were eighteen? Remember the pool guy? Ah, Jaysus, you were a sad case then,*' says June, as the two of them start giggling again, remembering their holiday.

'*Oh, him? He claimed to be the manager! I was there on the balcony, and he was down at the pool. He looks up and smiles at me.*

"Come down," he says. I was chuffed. The romance, I'm thinking, going for a swim in the evening light with him. So down I go and get into the pool, and then I realise he has a bucket and a brush. He wanted me to help him clean the pool! Manager my arse! The final straw was the night on the canal boat. I was locked and I picked up a sailor. If he was standing beside me to this day, I wouldn't recognise him. He asked me back to a hotel. Of course I said yeah. I remember walking off the boat with a pint in my hand, classy bird or what! When I woke up the next morning, he was gone and had left money on the locker. I couldn't find my knickers. I had no idea where I was, and had to go out on the street, wearing my evening dress. That was my big wake-up call. I thought, how low can you go? I didn't tell anyone about it. I carried all that stuff for years, but at some level I knew what I was doing was so wrong, so terrible. The lack of delusion makes it even worse. I think it might have been my way of avoiding admitting that I was gay.'

Paula looks at Siobhan, who is sitting back, watching her tell the stories she has heard several times over. She is amused at her partner's sense of humour, but also desperately sad for the years of loneliness she experienced.

'I don't know when I realised I was gay,' Paula continues. 'I never fantasised about sex, but I do know I had a couple of crushes on teachers. I fought being gay because it meant having to admit that I would never have a man to mind me, to pay the bills. We all had this illusion that we were being minded, that we were safe.'

'I remember when you told me you were gay', says June. 'I was gobsmacked. But when I thought about it, it was so obvious, it was staring us in the face. People even used to tell us, "Your sister's gay", didn't they, Joyce?'

'Yeah, and we'd tell them to fuck off.'

'The first time I realised I was gay was when Alice made a move on me. She was the one I moved out of home to be with, so I was mad about her. That night I realised, this is what I want. I still didn't really understand it, because I thought if I was gay, I'd fancy every woman. When I had sex with a man, I never had any sense of satisfaction. When I had sex with a woman, I liked it. I blamed everything on the abuse. The fear of people hating me and thinking I was as sick or perverted as the person who abused me was very frightening.'

'I never knew any of that was going on. I didn't think you even had sex. You were obviously looking for love,' June says. The laughter is gone now, the tone quieter, gentle. 'Let's face it, we all believed sex was love.'

'I ended up having a relationship with Alice for seven years,' Paula continues, 'but she wasn't out, and was in another relationship, so it was all hidden. I didn't feel like a slut though, so I let it continue. It was the lesser of two evils, because at least I wasn't lonely and desperate and out sleeping with a different man every night. It took three months into counselling before it dawned on me that it was a bad relationship, so I ended it. I never opened my mouth in counselling, but obviously something was sinking in.

'After Alice, I had a few relationships and, to begin with, the sex was good, but it didn't take long before I had trouble with not only having sex, but even wanting it. I learned very quickly how to fake an orgasm. I believed at the time that I was doing it so as not to hurt my sexual partner, but in hindsight it was to protect myself from exploring the issues I still had with being intimate with someone. The slightest thing could turn me off, them wanting sex, facial expressions, smells, anything really. I was very content just being close friends, but it wasn't fair on whoever I was with, because women feel rejected easily. I usually ended the relationship and moved quickly into another because I hated being alone and *not having anyone to mind.*

'I had two years, after I turned thirty, during which I didn't see anyone and I was really content. I was living on my own and studying reflexology, so I was busy. I was doing a lot of meditation and, to be honest, I think I was at peace. It was the first time I wasn't out looking for someone, and was happy to be on my own. My energy went into basketball all the time, which is where I met Siobhan. At this stage, the case was over; it had been in the papers, so there were no secrets. I met her on a Bank Holiday Monday, and we had moved in together by the following Friday. We're together fourteen years now, and she's been my rock. Sex is about love, trust. I don't even like using the word sex. I don't have sex; I make love. Sex is about my past and what's happened before. I've left that behind.'

Paula takes a slug of wine, and sits back in the chair with a sigh. Joyce and June look at each other surreptitiously, both afraid to say or do anything that might break this openness of Paula's. They don't want her to stop talking, sharing, so they sit quietly, waiting. Siobhan swills her wine glass, watching the sisters, enjoying the warmth of the conversation, and yet slightly separate from it.

'Jaysus, it's like a morgue in here,' laughs Paula, topping up her glass. 'I don't know where all that came from! What's up with you, Joyce? It's not like you to be so quiet.'

'Oh, I'm just thinking, Paula. I suppose I hadn't realised how much of your life I never knew, or wasn't a part of. And yet it's all so familiar, it's weird. I was thinking about my first sexual relationship, when I was twenty. We had a lot of sex and I enjoyed it. I didn't really allow myself to think too deeply about what I was doing. All I knew was I wanted sex and I believed he loved me. It also meant I didn't sleep around. I had a strong sexual appetite and, although we didn't have much of a relationship outside of *sex, it suited us both. I found comfort in sex and it felt like I was hungry and he was the only one with food. It took some time before I realised I wanted more out of a relationship. So I left him and soon after I met George. I got pregnant and married him within a year.*

'*I cried on my wedding day, all through the ceremony, through the meal, the dancing that night. I was still crying getting on the plane to London for our honeymoon!*'

'*You were the most miserable bride I ever saw,*' *Paula confirms.*

'*You looked like Frankenstein's bride!*' *June adds. There is much giggling as they reminisce about Joyce's smudged mascara and running nose on her wedding day.*

'*In hindsight, I wouldn't say I put any thought into getting married. It just seemed like the next move. I was pregnant but didn't realise how big an issue that was. Ma and Da told me I didn't need to get married. They said I should have the baby first.*

'*When we got back from the honeymoon, back to reality, I remember standing over the sink crying because there were only two cups in the sink. Who's going to look after me? I'd wonder. I can't do all this on my own. It was such a frightening experience. I felt stupid to be feeling that way. I couldn't tell anyone.*'

Mark and Eamonn rejoin the women, but the conversation carries on, as the men order themselves beers.

'*I was only twenty-two when I had my first child. Childbirth was a big shock for me. I couldn't get over Ma not warning me about how hard it was. I thought I was going to die. I'd been to all the pregnancy programmes, and watched the videos of people sitting reading a magazine in between contractions. I was twenty-seven hours in labour. When Derek was born, I was terrified of him. When he was just a few weeks old, I thought he was going to sit up and start talking to me. I was so scared of him; it was an awful time. Maybe that was post-natal depression, I don't know. He had colic too, so for six weeks he never stopped crying.*

'I was still only growing up myself. I don't think giving birth changed my life, the way it did for you, June, but it definitely gave me a new focus. Everyone thought I was really mature, but actually it wasn't true.

'George was older than me. In fairness, I wasn't good at explaining what I needed and he didn't understand what was going on. Regardless of our age, I don't think either of us was ready for the responsibility of being adults never mind parents. It was the first experience either of us had of looking after ourselves, and the added responsibility of looking after a child didn't help.

'Derek was one year old when I got sick. I had panic attacks at ridiculous hours of the night. I regularly woke up at four in the morning and called an ambulance, thinking I couldn't breathe. Believe it or not, Da was very good to me; he seemed to understand what I was going through. I couldn't go out because I panicked when I got any distance from the house. I was convinced something would happen and no one would know me.

'This went on for some time before the doctor suggested I see a psychiatrist in Ballyfermot. I really thought I was losing my marbles. She said my condition was due to my bad experience of childbirth, and told me to have another child to get rid of this terrible fear. So that's what I did. I would never have discussed the abuse with her, and, to be honest, I didn't see the connection. I had two more children after Derek, one after the other, and it was really hard. I felt like I was responsible for everyone and everything. I was on my own.'

'I remember you were in such a dark place,' says June. 'You looked terrible. It was awful. There was obviously something not right.'

'I think it was shock and growing up,' Joyce suggests. 'Funny, though,

that sex was OK for me even during that hard time, provided he instigated it; otherwise I suffered with guilt. I didn't think too deeply about that at the time as I was too busy trying to be the perfect wife and mother. My marriage lasted seven years and I think it finally fell apart because we were too immature.

'*I had custody of the kids and didn't meet Trevor until three years later. He was a nice guy, so for a while things were really good, but shortly after he moved in with me, the whole story of Da abusing us came out and, although he was supportive, we didn't stand a chance. We convinced ourselves that things would get better because counselling couldn't last forever. After sixteen years, we threw in the towel. He was waiting for me to get better, but it never happened.*

'*Sex was always unpredictable for me: the smell, the sound, the breathing, certain moves. I never knew what would trigger me off. When I was successful in having sex, and enjoyed it, I wondered why I didn't do it more often because it wasn't as bad as I imagined, but then I would wake the next day, all those feelings were gone and I'd be riddled with guilt.*'

'*But, Joyce, you said earlier that you were always hungry for sex. I don't get it,*' *Paula says.*

'*Yeah, it's a contradiction, isn't it? But both those things are true. Me wanting sex was the big issue. I couldn't admit it, but once I got over that, it was like I was starved of sex, and I always wanted it. That all changed when I had children. Sex started reminding me of Da, of the abuse, and, of course, once the case became public, and then the counselling started, well, it became impossible to separate those things. The only time I could have sex then was after I'd had a few drinks, but the next morning I would die with guilt.*

'*One of the good things that came from counselling was orgasms! I was thirty-two the first time I had an orgasm. I thought orgasms were only for men, but I learned about it at the Rape Crisis Centre.*

And then I was on a mission to have one! I wanted to know every detail. I'd ask women how to masturbate. I wanted A to Z instructions. And then it took me hours! Jaysus, the batteries would be gone in the fuckin thing and I'd still be waiting!'

They all laugh at Joyce's frankness, her animation. Eamonn gestures to the waitress to bring another round of drinks.

'And now I have my honey,' Joyce says, snuggling up to Mark. 'Nothing distracts him from how he feels about me and he makes it obvious that I'm the most important person in his life. Our relationship began after the abuse came out, so there are no secrets, and that's a great thing. We have a very honest relationship and I think through all the writing I have learned to express myself in bed. I can let him know when sounds, smells and particular noises affect me and we simply change things around and try something else. It's no problem and he has helped me to really enjoy sex.'

'I was always very clear that she needed to let me know if I did anything that reminded her of her Da,' says Mark shyly. 'I would have said that from the start. I love her to bits, and it was so important to me that we were honest, and that she told me if I did anything she didn't like.'

'Initially he was afraid of doing anything that might remind me of my abuse but, honestly, if that kept up, we would be able to do fuck all,' Joyce says, 'but we laugh and talk about it, which allows us to try things without worrying. We do both have to wash straight after sex because the smell takes me back, but we have a laugh about that too.'

'He's good for you,' June nods.

'Yes, you're happy, Joyce, which is lovely to see,' agrees Paula. 'And what about you, June? How have you managed to deal with sex?'

'Well, you remember how I piled on the weight when I was in my teens, so I didn't get much attention from boys. It wasn't until my *late teens that I lost it. I used to listen to Joyce's stories about boys and how they were all after sex, and Joyce told me to learn from her mistakes, so I thought I was ahead of the game. Smart, you know? I never let anyone near me and my arm came down like a vice grip when anyone tried to touch my chest. Mind you, when I say chest, I'm using the term very loosely!'*

'Yeah, you were a late developer all right!' Paula says, grinning.

'Although that's hard to believe now, love!' Eamonn laughs.

'Cheeky fucker!' June elbows her husband in the ribs. *'That definitely added to how I felt about myself. I thought I was ugly, and had no redeeming qualities. I behaved like a frigid nun.*

'When my best friend got married, I felt completely lost. After hibernating for a while, I attempted to have a social life but I never felt as close to anyone as I had with Christine and always felt I didn't fit in. I drank a lot until I was having blackouts. There were nights I couldn't remember how I got home or what I'd said.

'I was desperate for love, but at the same time terrified of sex, and I never met anyone I could really feel for. I was too fussy and decided to lower my standards. Being with someone was better than being alone.

'I was sexually frustrated but very concerned about becoming pregnant, so I decided to go on the pill. I went away with a friend with the absolute intention of meeting someone and having sex, and true to my word I did just that, but because there was no emotion between us, it just left me feeling worse about myself.

'One of the lowest points for me was being in a nightclub wankin a fella. We were sitting on a couch and he was covered with his jacket. He had to tell me to stop. I didn't understand him. I had given up on myself and was very confused. I thought if I gave someone a hand job, they wouldn't put pressure on me for sex and it was usually a one-night stand, so I would never see them again.

But I did realise that I didn't want to continue like that.

'I was suicidal for periods and spent a lot of time on my own until you asked me to move in with you,' she says to Joyce. 'Your marriage with George had broken down and we got on great together. I was happy to slot into your family. You had three young children and we never had a lot of money, but we tried so many different ventures like waitressing, selling clothes and making toys in order to pay the bills. Although we worked a lot, we still managed to go out clubbing. We had some great times living together and laughed a lot but it still didn't fill the emptiness. And then I met Eamonn.'

'I was working as a security man in The Oval,' Eamonn says. 'I remember the first night I saw you working down the road, and you came up to the club to get change. I just thought woah! It was love at first sight, definitely for me.'

'Really?' asks June, her face alive.

'Well, yeah, but you know that! I just thought you were gorgeous; you had such a great smile, really chatty and bubbly. And I asked her there and then to come up to the nightclub later, which thankfully she jumped at. Herself and Joyce came up later, and very quickly we were attached at the hip, going to the nightclub after work every night, and then we moved in together. They were wild times, weren't they, love? We drank a lot in those days, pretty much every night.'

'He was like the Milk Tray Man to me,' says June. 'He did everything for me, which was the commitment I needed. Initially, we had a lot of sex and couldn't get enough of each other. I told him early on about the abuse, didn't I? And it wasn't an issue at the beginning. It was only when I started counselling that sex became difficult.'

'To be honest, I think it went over my head when you first told me what had happened to you. We were drinking so much, and I don't think I took it in; it didn't have a big impact on me, although I do remember you saying that you had expected me to run for the hills after you'd told me. But it wasn't until that night when your Ma arrived over, that's when it all changed.'

'What happened then?' asks Mark. 'I mean, I know about the court case obviously, but why did that change everything?'

'It just took over everything,' says Eamonn. 'They were consumed by it.'

'I know, it's all we could talk about,' says Joyce. 'We really had to start dealing with it then, because it was out in the open, so there was no pretence any more.'

'When I first met Paula, she was consumed by the abuse,' Siobhan adds. 'She brought every conversation round to it, especially if we'd been out drinking. It's what she saw in herself. She had no confidence, and I think she really saw herself as a victim.'

'Jaysus, you make me sound lovely!' says Paula, clearly hurt by how her partner is describing her, but trying to make light of it. 'So what was the attraction, if I was such a basket case?'

'I didn't say you were a basket case,' says Siobhan patiently. 'But the abuse was a constant theme during those years. And bear in mind, we met six years after the court case, so there had been plenty of water under the bridge by then. But the attraction for me was that you were so open, so able to talk about your experiences. I wasn't "out" then, and I really admired your honesty, your ability to talk so candidly. It wasn't until sometime later that I realised it was all you could talk about! But that's changed now,' she adds, seeing Paula's face darken. 'I think going to college was a huge turning point for you, and you did grow through counselling, even though you resisted it so much.'

'Going into counselling made me question everything about my life; the way we were living, how we spent our time, all our *drinking,' says June. 'That's been a good thing for me, for us, but it was hard at the time, wasn't it?' She turns to Eamonn for confirmation.*

'June being in counselling forced me to question things too,' says Eamonn. 'And that wasn't something I would have chosen to do, but it was what I had to do if I wanted to be with her. I ended up going into counselling myself, to deal with my own stuff. Working as a security man, you just didn't think too much about anything, and here I was, having to really look at myself, and that was very hard. It was a horrible time. I absolutely believe we were meant to be together but, during counselling, June started questioning everything, including our relationship, so that completely rocked me. I realised that if I wanted to keep her, I had to change.'

'We had a few hard years too, didn't we, Paula?' says Siobhan. 'We had a number of years where we drank too much, and it was very depressing. Everything was about the abuse. It was a dark time for both of us. But it's funny, we kind of took it in turns to be the supportive one. When I was feeling low, she was strong, and minded me, and then things would turn, and she would need me to be strong for her.'

'And that's kind of how we got each other through college, isn't it?' Paula adds. 'When Siobhan had the opportunity to go back to education, she was terrified, but she wanted to do it, so I gave her the push she needed. And then a year later, she did the same for me, and we kept that going through the degree course. It worked; we both got there and did well, but we both needed someone motivating us, and telling us we could do it.'

'We had a very tumultuous relationship,' says Eamonn, passing his half-eaten dessert to June. 'There were always loads of rows and we said dreadful things to each other. It was really only when you got pregnant with Stephen that things started to settle for us.'

June nods in agreement.

'So what kept you going through all that?' Siobhan asks.

Eamonn doesn't hesitate in his answer. 'The fact that I love her. That's what kept me there. It was either sort myself out or lose her, and that just wasn't an option as far as I was concerned.'

June rubs Eamonn's hand and simultaneously dabs her eyes.

'What about sex?' asks Joyce. There is nervous laughter at the bluntness of the question.

'Trust you to put that out there!' says Mark, placing his arm fondly around the back of Joyce's chair.

'I'm curious. I mean, I know how it's been for the three of us, because we talk about it, but it must have been hard for you as well, Eamonn. And you too, Siobhan. Knowing we've been sexually abused has to affect the partners too.'

'Everything was fine at the beginning; it was great in fact,' says Eamonn. 'It's like June said; we couldn't get enough of each other. But once you started counselling at the Rape Crisis Centre, that fucked everything up. Our sex life just went downhill from then on. It took a long time for me to understand that. I realise now that June needed to be in control of her body, but that was hard for me to grasp.'

'You're right about the counselling changing everything,' says June. 'I suppose part of the counselling was about revisiting the past, and remembering that made sex very difficult for me. I couldn't separate Eamonn from the past. Having sex was his way of knowing we were all right and when that was removed, it filled him with doubt. He acted out of hurt a lot of the time and looked for constant reassurance from me, and nothing but sex would do it for him. My stubbornness and pain could have split us up, but thankfully his persistence kept us together.

'He had to initiate sex because I couldn't live with the fact that I *wanted it. When I had my first child, I realised I had to cop on because I had responsibilities. I needed to manage my life, and I transferred all my affection to the baby, which excluded Eamonn. We were in counselling less than a year after we married. In one session, I heard how he felt, and what he needed, and my heart melted as I realised he wanted the same things as me. I changed my attitude, my focus, and began looking at the positives in the relationship. I accepted he loved me and would die for me, and that was all I needed.'*

'What made the change in your sex life?' Joyce asks quietly.

'My reluctance to initiate sex, to touch him, and my confusion between our relationship and my past took time to resolve. It happened over a long period, and I think it came from my realising I loved him. I figured I'm in this for the long haul, so I'd better make the best of it. I wanted a good sex life. I didn't want to deny that aspect of my life. I wanted to be normal, whatever that is. We both truly love each other and that made me give attention to sex. It was more of a head thing than a physical one in the beginning. The closeness I feel after sex is so lovely and through that I came to think about sex in a nicer way. We're together about twenty years now. It's still hard work, but we've been through so much together. It's still there – I still need to be in control of sex but it gets easier with time, and I love getting older and not worrying about stuff so much. I want to be like Samantha from Sex and the City; *she doesn't give a fuck! The freedom she has around her sexuality and no guilt about sex; I'm so envious of her. We've wasted so many years feeling shame and guilt about sex, and especially initiating it and wanting it. And that wasn't just about the abuse, it was also the culture, the Catholic Church and the whole way that sex was seen as something so bad. The torment we've gone through in having feelings of wanting to be wanted.*

That is getting easier now, finally.'

'What about you two?' June asks, nodding at Paula and Siobhan. 'How have you managed?'

'I've seen a big change in Paula since she went to work in the Childhood Development Initiative. She's got more confidence now. And the writing has been good; it's healing, whereas before it took over everything.'

'Writing the book has been a good thing for you all,' Eamonn suggests. 'When you started writing it years ago, it was different. You seem to have managed it better this time; it hasn't taken over your lives like it did before. And I'm probably better able to cope now too.'

'In what way?' Paula is curious.

'Well, I would have taken everything personally a few years back. I thought if there was anything wrong, or June was struggling with something, I assumed it was to do with me. Now I realise that's not the case. That just comes with a bit of maturity; we're more open with each other. And time has given some perspective too.'

'When you come in after a session on the book,' Mark turns to Joyce, eager to contribute, 'I can tell whether you've had a good session or a hard session. There's no doubt that there are times it has taken its toll on you, you go quiet; and then there are other times when you're really positive and upbeat about it. But it's been hard, you can see that.'

'It's fantastic you've got so far with the book. I think it's really important to you all to get it finished,' Eamonn says.

'I agree,' adds Siobhan, 'It'll be a conclusion for you, and a huge achievement.'

'To the book!' toasts Mark.

They all clink glasses. 'To the book!'

Chapter 11: Moving On

2010

'That was a lovely speech, wasn't it?' says June, pouring Coke over her Bacardi and ice.

'Eulogy,' corrects Paula.

'What?' June throws in a few more chunks of ice for good measure before taking a long gulp of her drink.

'A eulogy. That's what you call it at a funeral. It's not a speech when it's at a burial.' Paula is tetchy, impatient, possibly looking for a row, so June decides to ignore her. That works sometimes when she's in one of these moods.

'Anyway, I thought it was a lovely speech. Fair play to Connor, getting up and talking about his own mam, and saying such lovely things about her. That takes courage, doesn't it? I'd never have the guts to do that, and then I'd have a million things to say after the event! Just like Da's court case, big loser that I am. Always too late!' June takes another sip of her drink and realises that no one is going to join in her conversation, so she carries on regardless. She doesn't want the silence. They are all on edge after their aunt's funeral. Their father's sister was nice, and it was a moving service, but it was also a reminder of the strangeness of their father's death, and June wants to have noise around her, a sense of normality.

'I wonder will any of us speak when it's Ma's turn? I suppose you will, won't you, Joyce? Of course you will. You'll be great; you'll know exactly what to say. I'd love to have that skill; it's a wonderful thing to have, isn't it? Do any of you ever think about your own funeral? You know, wonder what people will say about you? That's a funny thought, isn't it? I wonder who'll speak at my funeral, or what'll be said?'

June's voice trails off into the silence she dreads so much. They are all melancholy, thinking about their father's largely unacknowledged death a few years earlier, and contemplating their own lives in the face of its inevitable end.

'I'll speak at it, Mam.'

June's eighteen-year-old son Stephen blushes as he says this, and looks at the ground, suddenly embarrassed. People shift in their seats. There is a feeling of relief as the atmosphere lifts.

'Will ya, son? What'll you say?' Already June's eyes are welling up as she contemplates her tall, handsome son. His cousins eye him warily, knowing they will be expected to follow suit, praying that he doesn't set the bar too high.

'Well,' Stephen hesitates, and then appears to take a deep breath, knowing he must finish what he's started. 'I would tell people how I go straight to you if anything happens, you know, if I'm worried or upset. I can talk to you about anything, and you always manage to convince me that it will be OK. I trust you I suppose.' He looks up, with a grin on his face and adds, 'And I trust you not to tell Da! You know the way we agree what we'll tell him, or what's between us. I know you'll never break that, so that's great!'

'Is that right?' laughs Eamonn. 'I never knew I was in the middle of all this conniving. We'll have to talk about that!'

'There's never a dull moment around Ma,' Stephen continues. 'She's always laughing, seeing the funny side of things, even when she's crying – like now!' He looks at his mother, who is wiping the tears with the edge of a serviette. 'I wouldn't be able to not talk at your funeral, Ma. You're too important.'

Heads nod and eyes are dabbed as June reaches over and squeezes her son's hand. 'Thanks, love,' she says, deeply moved. She knows there is nothing else to say.

'Next!' calls Paula, breaking the quiet, and causing a nervous laugh to reverberate around the table. 'Come on, let's hear from the rest of you. And don't think that just because I don't have children, you can leave me out! I want to hear what you'll say about your favourite auntie!' Paula is hugely relieved at the turn in the discussion, and sees the opportunity for something affirming for them all. She is determined to keep the energy in the conversation.

'He's right what he says about June always laughing,' says Paul, Joyce's second oldest. 'You'd never know she had any pain in her life; she's always smiling, happy.'

'Yeah, you'd never think she'd been through anything like she has,' adds Audrey, just a few years younger than Paul. She is relieved to have spoken, to be contributing. She can see how upset her mother and aunts are, and, as always, wants to dissipate the pain, offer some solace.

'As for Paula,' Stephen adds, 'well, I never liked Paula!'

'Cheeky fucker!' laughs Paula, delighted with the obvious endorsement from her nephew.

'Seriously, though, I feel like I have one over on me mates, because I have two such amazing aunts,' says Stephen. 'Paula used to take me to basketball, and got me really involved in all that. I loved staying over with her.'

'So come on, what about me?' asks Joyce. 'What'll you say about me?'

'I'd want to say how you're my best friend …' Audrey starts, but she breaks down, crying, sobbing. Everyone gives her time, they are accustomed to tears at this table. Paula pats Audrey's arm.

'Take your time,' she says and Audrey nods, indicating to Paul to go ahead, that she'll rejoin the conversation when she's able.

'What I really admire about the three of you,' says Paul, taking his cue, 'is your openness. There were never any closed doors in our house, no whispering. It was always open; there was a real allowance of us all being part of what was going on. I don't remember actually being told about the abuse, but it was always there, almost like the wallpaper, you know, always in the background.'

'I loved Granda and I remember when I heard he had gone to prison, I felt guilty for loving him. I know you took me and Derek upstairs in Nanny's house and told us that the reason he hadn't been around was because he was in prison. I was about ten then, and I remember I had noticed he wasn't around, and didn't understand why, so that explained it for me.'

'Yes, I remember all that too, although I don't think that's the day we were told about the abuse,' continues Derek, the oldest of Joyce's children. 'It's funny, but I don't really recall the exact time we were told about it; it's more like we just absorbed what was going on. It was done very naturally, no big drama. That's probably what helped us all to deal with it. I never felt a need to worry about you, Ma, to be concerned about what you'd been through, even though there were times when you were obviously struggling.'

'I don't know exactly when I was told either,' affirms Paul. 'In a way, it kind of went over my head. I just thought, Oh right, and then it was over. Granda was great for me, and I thought, that sucks, because I loved him and now he's black-listed. I never had any feelings of malice or hatred towards him, but after being told he was in jail, I felt that I should feel some of that, that it wasn't OK to love him any more. That was confusing.'

'Me too,' says Derek. 'I thought I should hate him after he went to prison, and I felt bad because I didn't, but Ma always told us how important it was to hold on to the good memories, so that made it OK.'

'He was good to us,' says Paul. 'He could draw and make things; he was really creative. I remember one time I asked him for a bathrobe and he came in two minutes later, measuring my arm, and by the end of the day, he had this amazing bathrobe for me. It was tiger skin, I remember that. Jaysus, of all the materials he could have used! And it even had matching slippers! I liked to draw at the time, and I got his attention because of that; he acknowledged me because of that.'

'Yes, he mentored you because you were creative like him,' Paula says. 'He would have seen himself in you, so he would have tried to bring that on. He liked that in you.'

'He spoiled you all rotten,' continues Joyce. 'Every Saturday we used to go to Kilnamanagh shopping, and he always bought you something huge, some really big toy, not some fecky little thing.'

'I feel bad for my boys, because they didn't have any of that experience with Da,' says June. 'I'm glad Paul and Derek got some of that, but I wish it had been real. Listening to you talking about him makes him sound normal and the relationship sounds so lovely. But that wasn't how he was; it's not who he was.'

'I never worried about him with the boys,' adds Paula. 'It never occurred to me to watch him around them. But once Audrey came along, and he started paying attention to her when she was around four years old, I knew what he was doing; I knew he was grooming her. Anything he did for her, I saw the real intention behind it, because it was exactly what he had done to us, and it was frightening to watch it in action.'

'And yet I didn't see that,' says Joyce, shaking her head in wonder as she fills her wine glass.

'I know you didn't, which frightened me more, because I was scared of what might happen if I wasn't keeping an eye out. If Audrey was in the house and you weren't around, I stayed in the room with her. I didn't let her out of my sight, and he knew it and he'd be fuming. He'd try and get me out, giving me things to do but I wasn't having any of it. I wasn't leaving her with him. I remember wondering at the time where you were. I used to be really angry with you for not watching her better. But it also confirmed for me that I was the only one he had abused, because I couldn't believe that if he had done the same to you that you wouldn't recognise what he was doing with Audrey or that you would trust him with her. So I wasn't able to say to you, "Don't leave her with him."'

'I do remember one time when Audrey was about four,' says Joyce, 'and I left her playing in the front room. When I came back in, she was sitting on his lap. Well, I reefed her out of it. God love her, she got such a fright. He knew what I was thinking, and he was furious, but we never said a word about it. I don't know why I thought it was OK to leave her with him. I think on one level, I thought she was too young, and she was so tiny, that he couldn't think of doing anything to her, but that doesn't make sense because we were so young when it started with us, so there is no sensible explanation.'

'What was it like going into school after the TV programme went out?' Paula asks the young people sitting around the table. 'I often wondered if you got a hard time over it.'

'I remember watching it,' says Paul. 'It was called *Tuesday File*, wasn't it? By then, it all felt very familiar, to be honest. I think there had been so much conversation about the court case that the programme wasn't really anything new. I do remember later meeting with this woman who talked to us about abuse.'

'I remember that woman too,' says Audrey. 'She came in and showed us videos, but I was too young to be told then. I don't know that I was ever specifically told about the abuse. It's like you say,' she nods at her brothers, 'I just always knew about it.'

'She was from the Stay Safe Programme,' says Joyce. 'The school arranged for her to come over, and she talked to you all about "yes" and "no" feelings.'

'I remember someone brushing my hair during that.'

'Yeah, we were trying to explain the "yes" and "no" feelings, so I'd brush your hair real nice, and ask, "Is that good" and then I'd drag the brush through, and say, "What about that?"'

'That sounds familiar all right!' laughs Audrey. 'I do remember getting a bang of the brush a good few times! I don't think there was any big deal about the TV programme when it came out. I didn't get any grief at school, and I don't think there was really any conversation about it from my mates.'

'I remember one of the teachers giving me a letter to bring home to Ma,' says Paul. 'He stapled it all around the edges so I couldn't read it, and it said congratulations to her, and well done for doing the programme.'

'I bragged about it to my mates at school,' says Derek. 'I was really proud of you all, and I know I told everyone in the class to watch the programme. I don't remember getting any hassle over it or snide comments. I think everyone was amazed that you did it. It was such a brave thing to do.'

'What about you, Stephen?' asks Paula. 'When did you find out about what had gone on?'

'I know you told me, didn't you, Ma? I was about twelve, though I don't remember the conversation at all. But we watched the *Tuesday File* again recently, didn't we, Ma?' Stephen looks at his mother, partly for confirmation, but mostly to check how she's doing. He knows how emotional she gets and doesn't want to upset her too much. She nods gently at him, and he continues.

'I didn't feel any different watching it. I can't imagine that actually happening. She's my mam, I can't see her in any other way. I can't even picture her as a child, never mind something like that happening to her. You just don't understand it. You don't associate it with the people you know. It feels completely separate. Even after watching it and all the conversations about what happened, and I've even read some of what you've all been writing, it's like it happened to someone else.'

'It's not real,' Eamonn confirms.

'There's no way to react,' says Stephen. 'I don't know how to think or feel about something that I can't imagine. It's confusing.'

'You're right,' Joyce says. 'I can't begin to imagine my mother as a child. How can any of us think of our mothers as anything other than our mother?'

'But also,' adds Paula, 'it's like watching a movie. None of us can really understand someone else's experience. We all distance ourselves from terrible stories we see or hear about. I don't think there's anything wrong with that. I think that's normal.'

'It's strange to be told something so terrible so openly,' says Paul. 'The details came slowly, over a long time, and Ma was very good at keeping things calm, low key, so there was no big drama about it. And then you all laugh and joke about Granda and growing up, so the mood played a role too. It could have been very different if we'd been told in a different way.'

'Did you make a conscious decision to be so open?' asks Eamonn. 'I remember you all sitting around your mother's house talking about it all the time; it was non-stop, particularly around the time of the programme. But I don't know that you chose not to hide the abuse; it's more like it's what you needed.'

'I think you're right,' says Joyce. 'At the beginning, we were so ashamed that we didn't want to talk to anyone. We found it difficult to share our experiences with each other, never mind anyone else. But the counselling definitely helped that, and we probably did all get to the point where we needed to talk, to hear each other's stories, to understand ourselves better. But then when the *Tuesday File* programme was coming out, I knew I needed the kids to understand, and I wanted to protect them. Some of the family weren't happy about us doing the programme, and I knew the boys would get grief from their cousins, so I thought by telling them, I was protecting them. It was especially an issue for Derek, with him being the oldest. He was in secondary school, and I was afraid of what would be said to him, so I needed him to understand, and yet I didn't want any of them losing their innocence; I so wanted to hold on to that. The shame was still there, yet we went on RTÉ! There are so many contradictions in what we did.'

'Paul, would you have been conscious of your mum being upset, say when she came in from counselling or something?' Siobhan asks. She has been sitting quietly, listening intensely, observing the rapport between the children and their mothers.

'I would have been aware sometimes that she was upset. She did cry in front of us, but it was never any big deal. I don't remember worrying about it or anything,' he says, looking to his mother.

'No, that's because you never gave a bollox!' laughs Joyce. 'Seriously, I know I cried a lot. I'd be mashing the spuds and I'd be sobbing my heart out. Remember my computer used to be over in that corner? I used to spend hours sitting there, writing and crying, and I'd say to them all, "Don't worry, I'll be doing this a lot but it's OK," and they got used to it. They might rub my shoulder going by, or bring me a cup of tea, but mostly they left me alone. They knew I needed to do it, and I didn't mind once they understood it wasn't anything to worry about.'

'But you didn't try to hide it from us, Ma,' says Audrey. 'That's what made it OK.'

'I feel like an outsider sometimes,' says Paul. 'I'm listening to you talk about what happened, but I can't conceive of it, I don't understand it. So I feel very separate from it.'

'Well that means we've done something right,' June nods. 'That's how it should be. I am blessed that Stephen has no insight into what I went through. And I feel such pride sitting here listening to you all being so articulate, so able to speak your own mind. It's amazing to see and I am so grateful we've had this opportunity. We've done something right. We must have, haven't we, girls?'

June's eyes are filling with emotion as she turns and nods at her sisters, the pride glowing in each of them.

'You've done plenty right,' says Audrey. 'Look at us, we're great! You gave us so much. I think it's fantastic you've written this book, but I know I'll find it hard to read. I did read some of it, didn't I, Ma? And after I read that chapter, I just thought, How are you even surviving? I don't know how you have managed to hold it together, and you've all been so successful, you've done so much, and you haven't gone totally off your trollies.'

'Well, not totally! Just a bit off the trolley,' laughs June.

'Just the fact of having written this book,' continues Audrey, 'putting all that time into it, being able to share your experiences, that's an amazing thing to have done.'

'But, you know, I don't think you really believe it,' says Eamonn. 'I don't think you really feel like you've achieved anything. That's why this book has been so hard for you to finish, because you still think you're not there yet. If you could only see yourselves the way we see you; how intelligent you are, how amazing you are, the way you juggle so many things, how great you all are with people, but I just don't think any of you see that in yourselves. All of you are always looking for the next hurdle, something new to work towards, and never acknowledging what you've achieved. I really worry that when this is all over, and the book is finished, that you won't value it, you'll still be looking for something.'

'You're right, Eamonn,' says Paul. 'They never give themselves credit for anything, for all they've achieved. That's probably what the constant learning is about: always a new course, a new mission. But whatever you do, whatever the next target is, it will still be you there at the end of it. You'll still be yourselves. And you know what, ladies,' he adds, raising his glass to the women, 'that's not a bad thing.'

July 2011

There is something unfamiliar about Joyce's kitchen table today, as the sisters gather to plan the book launch. The pot of tea is on the table, the ashtrays are already brimming over and smoke has begun to filter through the room, but this time there are no scattered papers, no well-thumbed manuscripts, no laptops. The table seems bereft, empty and the women are uncertain about how to fill the void.

'It's strange, isn't it?' June breaks the silence, pouring the tea as she speaks. 'This is the first time I've been here in so long when we haven't had writing to do, something to edit or review. Don't get me wrong, I'm delighted it's over. It was exhausting, and I'm so proud of what we've done, but I'll miss it too.'

'So will I,' says Joyce emphatically. 'I'm already grieving for this space we've had. The connection it's given us.'

'Did it give you what you wanted?' asks Paula. 'You know, if you look back at that mission statement we did, has it been what you expected?'

'Well, we don't know if it will change how others understand abuse, or make it safer for people to talk about it, and we will probably never know whether or not our story helps people with their own struggles,' says Joyce. 'But there's no question it's been an incredible experience for me, in all kinds of ways. Finding Marian and having her work with us, support us through this, has been so important. You know the way I didn't allow myself to fall apart? I couldn't allow myself to do that; I always felt that I had to stay strong. I especially couldn't fall apart in front of the two of you, you expected me to hold it together, but I could fall apart with Marian. There's been great freedom in that for me. I didn't shut her out. I feel a safeness with Marian that I didn't feel with you two, because I could admit that I wasn't coping and I knew she was OK with that.'

'I know what you mean,' says Paula, dragging hard on her cigarette. 'Remember that first time we went away with her, when I had my meltdown? I had never cried in front of her, not even in front of you two for a long time, and I just couldn't stop.'

'You were in a right state,' nods June. 'I don't think I ever saw you like that before.'

'Marian stayed completely solid. She just kept asking me how I felt, staying with me, keeping me with my emotions. And she kept listening, but it felt completely safe. If I had done that anywhere else, there is no way I would have showed my face again the next day, but it was fine, because I knew she was fine about it.'

'It's been such a respectful process, hasn't it?' adds June. 'We absolutely wouldn't have completed this book without her. She has this amazing ability to see the bigger picture. There were so many times I thought, thank God, she can see the overview, because I would be so caught up in the detail. We knew from the start it had to be someone special to work with us.'

'I think she's very like me, in that people expect her to cope with everything, and can't handle it when she isn't in control,' says Joyce.

'That was really helpful for me, because she could recognise some of what I feel, the pressure I experience. There have been times over the past few years when I have really needed someone to lean on, and Marian gave me that.'

'What I love most,' says Paula, lighting another fag as she stubs out the last one, 'is the fact that Marian keeps pushing me, even when she knows the shit that will go on in my head as a result. But it doesn't stop her encouraging me to challenge myself or asking me to think differently about something, about the choices I make. She has made me go to places I never thought I would.'

'We were lucky,' says June, 'finding her. She's been fundamental to this process, and is so much a part of it. She facilitated the growth in our relationships, and the funny thing is, I reckon she got as much out of it as we did. She's part of the family now, and that's been important to her too.'

Joyce gets up to empty the ashtrays, and momentarily opens the back door to let out some of the smoke.

'Jaysus, Joyce, its fuckin freezing,' exclaims June. 'Close that door, you mad thing!'

Joyce laughs and closes the door, having made a half-hearted attempt to swipe the air clean with the tea towel.

'Involving our partners and the kids was hugely important, wasn't it?' says Paula. 'They felt included, had their views valued, and they got what this process has been like for us. They understood what it's like to be really listened to. I think it's lovely we did that.'

'You know what's been most important in all this for me?' Joyce says. 'I now have a relationship with my youngest sister and I never had that before. Working with you, Paula, gave us an opportunity to talk a lot about the book, and then the two of us doing the coaching course was great for us. It was the first time you saw me as a human being, with all the problems and vulnerabilities that anyone has. You were amazed to discover that I had been through tough times, *that I was fallible. I mean, how could you not have known that?'*

'I know,' Paula laughs. *'I was so closed off from everybody else. In fact, I didn't want to know; I didn't care about anyone else's pain. I was struggling too hard with my own. Also, Joyce, to be fair, you never ask for help. You always put on this front that you're fine. I feel like I've done a lot of growing up as a result of writing this book. At this stage, I think I'm certainly through my teens in terms of my development and maybe my late twenties, hopefully moving into my thirties. I'm finally capable of taking responsibility for myself, what I feel and what I should do about it. I'm not fully there yet, but I have definitely got better at that. And that's as a result of us sharing and me beginning to open up to you.*

'Sometimes I write stuff and you or Marian question me about it,' continues Paula, *'and I have one of those moments where I finally understand something, or the penny drops; I look at you two and realise you already knew it. It's like when I had to think about how awful it was moving back home, you already knew what that was like for me, how painful it was, but it's taken me this long to understand.'*

'There have been times when I have been smiling to myself,' says June, *'because I have thought, thank God, she is finally working out what's going on, what that's about. It's been lovely to watch your journey, Paula.'*

'I'm shocked that I'm still discovering stuff about myself,' Paula responds. *'I thought I had done it all, but it's like the more you know, the more you realise you don't know. And I have to say it's been hard to hear the two of you talking about all those laughs you had, the fun you had that I wasn't part of. I know we had some good times but, when we did, I was usually the butt end of the joke. I have sometimes felt jealous and left out and separate from those stories. And I need to remember that it's not how we are now.'*

'And, Paula, for you to even say that is an indication of the huge

growth there's been for you.' Joyce sits back in her seat, contemplating her youngest sister. 'A couple of years ago, last year even, you'd never have named that, and would have just allowed that jealousy to fester.'

'I know there's been a shift for me, but I still struggle so much more than you two seem to. Living with secrets has been such a part of my life, not just because of the abuse, but then with my first relationship, the first time I was in love, having to be secret because she wasn't "out". And my sexuality has been confusing, too. That's how I ended up in all those poxy relationships, but that never clouded my relationship with Marian. The storyline they had in EastEnders recently, when that young girl is so fucked up and makes a pass at the guy who is nice to her, I so get that, because that's what I would have done. I would confuse admiration, or liking someone, with wanting to sleep with them.'

'That's been hard for you, Paula, and you've had to work that out on your own. Joyce and I had each other. We have had shared experiences that have really helped us,' says June. 'Having children can be such a healing process, and they make you real. And being gay is difficult, even now. We didn't have any of that to contend with.'

'I feel that I have only got to know myself in the past few years,' says Paula. 'Also to accept that it's OK that I made mistakes, and understand why I made them, instead of feeling horrible because of them. Forgiving myself for leaving relationships, the way I walked away from people, was hard to accept but now I can see that it was the right thing to do, not just for me, but also for the people I walked away from. So I am getting better, but my concern is how I will continue to grow without this process.'

'We will so miss this space,' says Joyce. 'I don't want this process to stop, the meaningful conversations, the connections. The bond between us is so amazing, and I feel like I have a deep friendship with you both now, and Marian; that I have always known you in a way you didn't know me, but that's different now; it's real, it's deeper. I think Paula used to see me as a threat. That was never the way with June, but the imbalance has levelled, it's more equitable now. And I'm stronger now because I have Marian. We all need someone who can take our shit, and put us straight. I never had that before, and I thought there was nowhere for me to be minded or fixed. Having that space has given me a real foundation that was always missing for me.'

'The biggest gift for me,' says June, 'has been creating a relationship with you, Paula. I have always regretted that, mourned it, and I am so grateful for this changing that. Writing the book, alongside the fact that you were working with Joyce, meant you were attached on several levels.'

'It was like there was no escape for me!' agrees Paula. 'Working in the Childhood Development Initiative, working on the book, and doing the coaching in work; that combination of things, having to look at every relationship, and my responsibilities in those things, everything came together to make me realise that I needed to get my act together.'

'Writing the book forced us to get real,' says June. 'We had no option but to talk about real stuff. It didn't come naturally though; it was like something that was imposed. We all committed to finishing it, seeing it through, even though there were times each of us would have walked away. And having someone to hold that, keep us focused, that was part of what helped us come back to it. But there has been such growth in it. I can't even imagine not having it any more.'

'I worry that I will lose this – will I hold the ability to name the issues, to take responsibility for my own feelings and decisions now that the writing has stopped? Or will I quickly fall back into my comfort zone of avoiding things?' Paula says. 'That's my fear:

not sustaining the growth, the way I have got so much better at handling things, because I know I can go back to that, it's easier.'

'I guess that's where the personal responsibility comes in, isn't it?' Joyce places fresh tea on the table, and opens a new packet of cigarettes. 'The fact that the two of you understand that I'm not superwoman, that I have as many hang-ups as you, is a huge relief for me, and I need to hold on to that. I'm more accepting of my own vulnerabilities than I was before, I'm not as hard on myself. I was always the leader, the one people depended on, but this process has taught me that I don't have to be that person all the time. I still struggle to ask for help, but my expectations of myself have changed.'

'There have certainly been times when you let your guard down, Joyce. When you let us in there and showed us your pain, but there hasn't been enough of it.' June takes the cup that's been poured for her and continues. 'When I see you down, it's like watching a wounded animal, because it's so hard to watch you push us all away. You don't want us there and I think some of that has shifted. The strength you pick up in Marian and the safe place she gave you broke through that shield of yours.'

'What about you, June? Did you get what you expected from writing the book?'

June takes a deep sigh, and thinks for a moment before answering. 'I'm absolutely a different person now. I have a much stronger belief in myself, although I still have my default position that will always haunt me, where I assume I'm wrong or stupid. But I am more confident that I'm truly a good person, that I only ever mean well. I don't analyse too much, so it takes time for me to notice the change. I have more acceptance of my faults. I still have a problem with the fact that I have a big gob. There are times I love that part of me, but sometimes I think I should keep something for myself, have some boundaries.'

'When you took on to chair the politicians' night, just before the *general election last March I thought you were amazing to put yourself forward. You would never have done that two years ago, and I can see your confidence growing in our degree class, and your enthusiasm for learning new subjects. I think some of that is connected with delving into yourself and being open to learning in a new way,' Joyce says.*

'I agree,' says Paula. 'I think you have got so much better at expressing yourself, analysing your assignments. You get really complex issues, and you can see the love you have of the material. I have read your assignments and wished that I had some element of that when I did my degree. Just to have the insight to see the relevance of what you're learning, to make the connections. And you think I'm the smart one! You write the way you should, because you're actually interested in what you've been learning.'

'You're right, I do love learning.' June's face lights up as she considers her degree course, and the enthusiasm she has found for studying. 'Something major shifted for me. I knew I was out of my depth, chairing that politicians' meeting, but I so wanted to do it. And I knew I would regret it if I didn't. Imagine, me, chairing a session with Pat Rabbitte, Conor Lenihan, Brian Hayes, all the big cheeses!'

'And you were great!' says Paula. 'Seriously, Vincent Browne, eat your heart out!'

'You know, when you think about it, and what we've achieved, we really should acknowledge how amazing we are,' laughs June, looking at the two sisters she loves so dearly. 'We've studied despite believing we're stupid; we have found partners who love us and care about us, in spite of the fact that our childhoods were spent being constantly undermined and abused; we have created homes and families that people love being part of; and we have careers, friends, great friends. I know the abuse and the vulnerability that comes from that will always be with us, but we have done what we

set out to do. We have proved we aren't going to allow it to define us.'

'And you forgot one very important thing we have,' says Joyce, taking each of her sisters' hands. 'We have each other.'

Epilogue

It's October 2011. Joyce sighs deeply as she looks out of the window at the darkening sky. She is tired, and her eyes hurt, but she knows she has another sleepless night ahead of her. She quietly stands and pulls the curtains, stretching for a moment before returning to her seat, this time facing her mother, who is now restful in the hospital bed, the morphine having finally settled her anxiety. June is dozing in the chair on the other side of the bed, her hands holding her mother's protectively, almost fiercely, Joyce thinks. She smiles to herself at the sight of her sister so peaceful, and once again gives thanks that the sisters have this time with their mother.

The door opens, startling June, and Paula squeezes into the overcrowded room, thrusting two enormous Marks & Spencer's bags on the foot of the bed. She eagerly unpacks the various items of nightwear she has bought, oblivious to the calm she has broken. Joyce and June catch each other's eye and stifle a giggle as they silently acknowledge to each other that this is Paula's way of coping – organising the practicalities, and spending money. She feels useful and they know she needs that right now.

More than the others, Paula is struggling with their mother's imminent death. Over the past few days, they have each had many private moments with their mother, and despite the fact that they know she is unlikely to hear or understand them, they have consciously taken the time to tell her they love her, and that it's OK for her to go. June has relished the opportunity to be physically close to her mother, and it is only with great reluctance that she moves from beside the bed and releases the grasp on their mother's hands. She constantly strokes her mother's face, runs her fingers through her hair, massages her hands – anything to be close to her, to comfort her.

Joyce has taken up her usual modus operandi and is focused on managing everyone around her. She has been the liaison with the medical staff, organised the rota for the overnight stays, ensured that all the siblings are kept up to date with any changes in their mother's condition and ensured she has no space left to feel anything. All of this she has done with an awareness that this is what she needs in order to get through these few days, and unlike the past, she doesn't resist it. In quiet moments, watching her mother rest, she has reflected on the fact that, previously, she would have struggled with her instinctive response, but now, having spent so much time writing, talking and thinking about her behaviours, she recognises that this is how she copes. Several times she has openly acknowledged this to the family, stating her need to protect herself, and they have respected this, albeit with some surprise. Joyce articulating her own vulnerabilities is a new experience for them, but the siblings welcomed it.

The fear of losing her mother is paralysing Paula. She has taken every opportunity to tell her mother that she forgives her, that she understands why she wasn't able to protect her, but she knows she doesn't believe it. She is torn between wanting to do the right thing, say the right thing, and being honest. She frequently catches herself wiping away tears as she gazes at her mother's sleeping form, and mourns for what she sees as a wasted life. Her mother's dignity and quietness that she had admired so much as a child came to infuriate her as an adult, because it left no space to know her, or understand what she was thinking or feeling, and Paula now resents this absence in her life.

The three sisters have had many times over the past few days when they have watched their mother, confused and distressed, and wished her time was over. It is a huge relief for them that the medication has now given her peace, and that the panic and discomfort which was so apparent has abated. With her purchases unpacked, Paula settles into the chair at the foot of the bed, and the three sisters take up their earlier conversation about childhood memories, trying without much success to keep their giggles quiet. Within an hour, the room has filled as partners and other siblings arrive, and the noise levels have increased drastically, but the nurses don't seem to mind. In fact, they are clearly enjoying the humour in the room.

Inevitably, the discussion quickly turns to the night of the book launch. The family never seem to tire of retelling their version of the evening, sharing their pride in the event and taking every opportunity to tease each other mercilessly.

'It was a mixture of preparing for the debs we never had and going to the Oscars,' laughs Joyce. 'There were photos of us everywhere, like we were famous or something!'

'And people queuing for us to sign copies of the book,' adds Paula. 'That was weird. It really did feel like we'd achieved something when I saw that massive line of people waiting.'

'I loved the limo,' says June. 'It felt like Hollywood, didn't it? I never felt so glamorous or special.'

'Yeah, well *you* didn't have to crawl on your knees to get into the feckin thing,' laughs Eamonn, recalling the awkwardness of getting his long legs in and out of the car.

Joyce's fingers unconsciously go to her neck, touching the studded star on her necklace that Mark had presented to each of them in the limo. Eamonn had followed with specially engraved silver pens for them to use at book signings. Joyce smiles to herself thinking of the excitement in the limo as they unwrapped these unanticipated gifts, followed by cards from their children.

The room is quiet for a while as they each contemplate the night when over 500 people packed into the Dublin city centre venue to celebrate the sister's journey, acknowledge it and share it. People they had never met before had listened, cried and laughed with them. Despite the overcrowded room, the chatter and buzz as people bought their books and lined up to get them signed, the moment the speeches began, a hush had settled over the audience. June thinks about the recording on her friend's phone and the fact that, despite it having been taken from the very back of the function room, every word had been captured. She smiles to herself recalling her first words on the stage, still delighted that she followed her instincts.

'I've been working on this speech the way I would for an assignment,' she had begun. 'Trying to get every word right, worried about the grammar, not wanting to mess it up.' She had paused, looking out at the rows and rows of friends and family, all watching her, all sharing the emotion in the room. 'And then I thought, fuck it! I'll do it my own way!'

David blushes slightly as he recalls the tears flooding down his cheeks, the sobs of pride welling in his chest, until he looked down the long row of siblings and partners and realised that they were all in the same state.

Kevin thinks about how much laughter there was that night, and how so many had arrived expecting the evening to be sad and intense. Ronnie recalls the standing ovation at the end of the speeches, the thunderous applause, watching his sisters hugging each other, the manager presenting them with glasses of champagne, and every person in the room clapping with such respect and admiration for these incredibly brave women.

Tony eventually breaks the silence.

'I can't stop thinking about you, Paula, standing there shaking like a vibrator!' They all laugh again, as Paula shakes her head, stifling the chuckles, happy to be the brunt of the jokes.

'I am glad Mammy was there,' says Joyce. 'Even if she didn't fully understand what was going on, she must have felt the pride in the room. It was tangible, wasn't it? There really was electricity in the air.'

'And don't forget being on the *Late Late Show*,' says Kevin. 'I mean it was national TV, and you all looked so relaxed. It was like you were meant to be famous!'

'That was almost as exciting as the launch,' says June. 'There was a sense that this was really important, that we had done something significant. And all the radio interviews we did after the television appearance, made us think really carefully about why we wrote this in the first place. We were given a special opportunity to share our story, and what we've learned, and we wanted to get it right.'

'And we did,' responds Paula. 'It was great to see how professionally we handled even the unpredictable questions. I think we were pretty amazing.'

The reminiscing continues for some time, until the nurses come in to turn their mother for the night. As people gather up their belongings and kiss their sleeping mother good night, the emotions in the room change dramatically, as they each realise their time with her is now so very limited. Soon, the room is empty apart from the three sisters, who unfold blankets and shift chairs around, getting ready for another night beside their mother's bed.

June's mobile rings, having been on silent most of the evening. She fumbles through her bag and informs the others that it's Marian, before answering the phone.

'I missed a call from her earlier,' say Joyce and Paula in unison.

They watch June as she fills Marian in on their mother's condition. They are all tired now, and happy to sit quietly so they listen to their sister and absentmindedly fill in the gaps they cannot hear. June listens for a few minutes and then nods, a sad, watery smile on her face as she hangs up. She leans over the bed and whispers to her mother, 'We are number one on the bestseller list, Ma.'

Paula and Joyce look at each other and back at June. None of them are sure how to react. They are delighted, relieved, validated, but the knowledge of their mother's dying inevitably casts a shadow over the good news.

'It all seems so insignificant,' says Joyce finally. 'You know, sitting here, watching Mammy like this; the past few days have been so hard, seeing her in pain and so upset. And now this, such fantastic news, it's what we set out to do, but it really doesn't matter, does it?'

'I was convinced she would go when we told her the book was finished,' says Paula. 'I suppose I've been expecting this, waiting for it. And of course it's terrible, but in some ways, it feels right too.'

'I know what you mean,' says June. 'God, I need time to let this sink in. Our book, a bestseller! It's incredible. And you're right, this is what we wanted, but all our plans, all our ideas for helping people, sharing our story, it's really only the beginning, isn't it?'

The room is still and quiet as the sisters sit around the bed, each of them holding their mother, touching her, wanting to give comfort. They look at each other, their eyes brimming, each one considering their memories of this woman they have loved so much, despite the distance, in spite of her absence. In their own ways, each of them has found a way of understanding her, forgiving her, accepting her. They recognise their pain in her life, they have all seen it mirrored in her eyes. Paula remembers her attempt at compensating for the Easter egg she never received; Joyce lovingly remembers her hours talking with her mother uninterrupted in the shop; June recalls her mother's dignity and poise, her ability to remain calm in the worst of their father's temper. She gently caresses her mother's velvet soft skin, again wondering at the texture of it.

'Ma,' says Joyce tenderly. 'Ma, it's all right, you can go now. We're going to be OK.'

And the tension lifts from each of them, a calmness seeps in, as they each realise, somewhere deep down, that this is in fact true. They really are going to be OK.

Joyce Kavanagh Sr died on 5th October 2011 with her daughters by her side.

About the Authors

Joyce Kavanagh

Joyce was born in 1956 and has six children, ranging in age from fifteen to thirty-one, as well as recently becoming a granny for the first time. She studied holistic healing and is qualified in reflexology and colour therapy. She has a BA degree in Community Development and Leadership, and works for a not-for-profit organisation as a Community Engagement Coordinator in the Childhood Development Initiative, Tallaght, where she also lives. Joyce has been involved in adult education for many years and is deeply committed to community development.

June Kavanagh

June was born in 1961 and is married with three children. She also lives in Tallaght, is qualified in holistic health and works in a women's education centre. She has a BA degree in Community Development and Leadership. June is a community activist, and a Director of the Board of the Childhood Development Initiative, a children's charity, in Tallaght West.

Paula Kavanagh

Born in 1963, Paula lives in Dublin with her partner of fourteen years. She returned to full-time adult education in 2000 and studied holistic therapies for two years, graduating with distinction. She went on to study for a further four years and achieved a BSc degree in Leisure Management. Paula now works as an Administrative and Communications Coordinator for the Childhood Development Initiative, Tallaght.

Marian Quinn

Marian is the chief executive of a children's charity in Tallaght, and has previously been employed in the Department of Justice and the Health Service Executive, as well as a number of not-for-profit organisations working in children's services. She wrote and developed a national youth crime prevention programme, has published articles in academic journals and is currently writing a novel.

Acknowledgements

The success and completion of anything depends largely on the encouragement, love and support you receive from others. It would have been impossible to get through this without the love and support of each other. Sharing the dark times, challenging one another, and the understanding and acceptance that we all travel this road differently was the key to our healing.

The guidance, direction and support we received from our co-writer Marian Quinn has kept us in tow. She ensured we would be safe if we didn't run. She has been our strength. With her constant supply of ashtrays, wine and vigour, she has pushed, shoved and dragged us through so much. We have laughed and cried together and she has become one of us.

Our agent, Jonathan Williams, has had faith in us from the very beginning, and his aspirations for this book began to match our dreams, as our confidence grew with his encouragement and guidance. His vision and empathy are so much deeper than his carrier bag would ever lead you to believe!

We would like to take this opportunity to express our gratitude to our partners – Mark, Eamonn and Siobhan – who have made many sacrifices to enable us to complete this book. Their love, support and deep faith in our abilities, even when we had doubts, made it possible to let go of the past and believe in our future.

Joyce's children – Derek, Paul, Audrey, Lisa, Sarah and Nicole – and June's children – Stephen, Christopher and Adam – have unintentionally supplied us with the inspiration and energy required to finish the book. The very sight of them acts as a reminder of our greatest achievements.

Finally, our thanks to Hachette for believing in us.

1

Mycah's Parents Didn't Get a Vote

MAX BROOKS

No one likes to imagine they're a nobody. That wouldn't be much of a fantasy. When we watch a show like *Game of Thrones*, we imagine we're Jon Snow or Daenerys Targaryen or that cool guy with the eyepatch and the flaming sword. We don't imagine we're the dude who gets squashed by the falling bell when Cersei blows up the Sept of Baelor. Nobody fantasizes about being Random Shmuck #17 who gets stabbed by the Sons of the Harpy when they run riot through the fighting pit of Meereen. And I'd be hard pressed to find anyone who shows up to Comicon dressed like Mycah the butcher's son.

And why would anyone want to be? Mycah was a powerless peasant murdered for being in the wrong place at the wrong time. But imagine if we were that powerless peasant. Or his parents. Who would speak up for us? A lawyer? A reporter? An elected representative? Westeros doesn't have any of the institutions that protect the weak from the strong, the same institutions that too many of us take for granted.

Out here in the real world, we complain about the compromises, inefficiency, and slow-grinding gears of democracy. Recently, some have gone even further, calling for the "deconstruction of the administrative state." And while democracy's enemies continue to strengthen and multiply, too many of its defenders can't even be bothered to vote. Because that's what voting feels like to many of us—a bother, a hassle, a pointless, boring chore.

And why shouldn't it? How many of us have experienced the horrors of totalitarian regimes? Russian assassinations, Venezuelan starvation, Chinese execution-backed censorship. Those real-life events get less attention from us than a TV show like *Game of Thrones*. And that is exactly why *Game of Thrones* is so important for our time; it is a "stark" reminder of why democracy matters.

If we don't like being governed by a deep state, imagine being ruled by a man who literally *is* the state. "King takes what he wants," Ned Stark laments to his wife in season 1, episode 1. And lamenting is all he can do, because any infantile, psychotic impulse is law. From wars to taxes to murdering babies. Like a "wheel," to quote Daenerys, "crushing those on the ground."

And who's going to save us from that wheel? According to the story, the answer doesn't lie in a better system but a better person. The notion of a good king, someone with the supposed right—and by "right," we mean the freak accident of birth—is the only way that more Mycahs don't end up dead on their parents' doorsteps.

At the point of this writing—on the cusp of season 8, the final season—we're supposed to be rooting for Westeros's benevolent power couple, Jon Snow and Daenerys. Both are good people—honest and kind, with a genuine moral compass that, we hope, will point the way to a future of peace and prosperity for all.

But what if it doesn't? What if, as Missandei warns, "it only takes one arrow" to destroy the hopes and dreams of millions? And what if there's a second archer on a grassy knoll that gets Jon as well as Daenerys? Who takes over? And why? Will it be civil war all over again? Isn't that why Westeros fell into chaos in the first place, because King Robert got himself killed in a hunting accident? That's exactly why our codified, legalized, Oswald-Booth-proof line of succession exists today. To ensure that our lives aren't held hostage to chance, that random tragedy doesn't descend into anarchy.

But let's say Daenerys and Jon live to a ripe old age, which in a world of magic and dragon's blood could be centuries long. Who's to say that they'll always remain the benevolent rulers we're getting to know and love. Not every tyrant starts out tyrannical. A lot of them had nothing but the best intentions. If you don't believe that old-timey saying that "power corrupts, and absolute power corrupts absolutely," just ask the ghosts of Fidel Castro and Muammar Kaddafi.

And if that happens, if those Dear Leaders eventually decline into paranoid, vindictive mass murderers? What checks and balances does Westeros have in place to stop them? The army? That's what stopped Daenerys's father, the "Mad King." The only difference now is that Daenerys still has her two dragons, and that is a very powerful metaphor for our world. Despots throughout time have feared coups as surely as popular uprisings. That's why they've kept their own dragons called the Praetorian Guard, the Savak, and the SS.

But let's say there's no need for a king slayer. Let's say John and Daenerys, "Johnerys," rule with the same fair, wise hand as Caesar Augustus. Then what? Would they have another baby-killing prince like Joffrey? That's the inbred danger of passing down power through blood. But if the storyline about Daenerys's barren womb is true and they have to choose an heir, does that make the people of Westeros any safer?

Maybe Tyrion Lannister would rule for a time, marry a nice prostitute, sire a decent heir and maybe even grand heir, but as long as power remains absolute, it leaves the throne open for a future maniac. Our founding fathers understood this from our own history. They knew that any system that allowed Augustus would eventually spawn Caligula.

This is why George Washington, in the footsteps of Cincinnatus, refused an American throne. In 2018 *Game of Thrones* is a fantasy. In 1776 it was everyday life. The framers of our Constitution saw what happens when a handful of drunken, incestuous, and, in the case of King George III, mentally ill mob dons have direct control over millions of subjects. The whole reason our founders established an administrative state was to protect us from a man like Louis XIV, who declared, "I *am* the state."

That is why we are citizens, not subjects. That is why our Constitution is our king. And unlike Aerys, Balon, Brynden, Robert, Randyll, Ramsay, Rickon, Viserys, Drogo, Hoster, Lysa, Joffrey, Mance, Olenna, Doran, Stannis, Robb, Roose, Tommen, and Walder, our ruler is immortal. Cersei had a point in tearing up the last "piece of paper" from her husband. The words spoke for a person whose power died with him. The words "We the people" speak to the power in all of us.

By choosing to live behind a wall of shared ideals, we ensure that no butcher's son can be butchered. Our administrative state protects every child, and while "constitutional democracy" doesn't exactly roll off the tongue quite like "game of thrones," I like the sound of the former much more than the latter. And so should you.

2

A House to Be Feared

JONATHAN P. KLUG

The vibrant nature of *Game of Thrones* starts with the creative genius of author George R. R. Martin and his ability to blend his vivid imagination with the realism of history. His approach includes grounding characters with actual historical figures and combining history with unique personalities, creating an array of rich characters who seem to be alive with motives and personalities—Martin's is not a story of two-dimensional heroes or villains. Apart from the White Walkers and their undead horde, as well as sadistic Ramsay Bolton, the distinction between heroes and villains is blurred or unclear. *Game of Thrones* characters are complex and unique, and Martin makes their decisions carry a price, often causing life in Martin's world to be Hobbesian—nasty, brutish, and short.[1] Individuals must be painfully careful and lucky to survive, and the heads of the noble houses must think strategically if their families are to survive, let alone thrive. House Lannister and its patriarch Tywin Lannister are the best exemplars of the practice of strategic art in *Game of Thrones*, and this is the focus of this chapter. Just as Tywin and the Lannisters unintentionally taught the Starks, they can teach us much about modern conflict, such as the importance of wealth in the exercise of power and the use of military art.

In an interview, Martin points out that *Game of Thrones* is in part homage to England and its War of the Roses (1455–85), as Martin bases the Starks on the historical Yorks and modeled the Lannisters on the Lancasters.[2] In the same way, the historical basis for Lord Tywin Lannister King is Edward I (1239–1307), rumored to have literally scared servants to death and earned the sobriquet the "Hammer of the Scots." From season 1 until his death in season 4, Tywin Lannister leads House Lannister and hammers his foes. Although he will not win any Father of the Year awards, he focuses on his house, its power, and its future. During his initial on-screen appearance, he sets the tone for all his future actions. As he systematically cleans a deer carcass, he lectures his eldest son Jaime: "It's the family name that lives on. It's all that lives on. Not your personal glory, not your honor—family. Do you understand?"[3] These are the words of a stoic, clinical, and experienced strategist attempting to educate his eldest son and spur Jaime to adopt the same long-term, strategic mindset.

While vital, Tywin's strategic mindset would be of little use without resources. The inhabitants of Westeros seem to know the Lannisters' unofficial motto: "A Lannister always pays his debts"; of all the noble houses, the Lannisters are the richest. At first blush, it may appear that the Lannisters are rich because they are powerful; however, they are powerful because they are rich. The Lannisters' major source of wealth is the many gold and silver mines in their territory, the Westerlands, making it one of the richest regions in Westeros. In fact, one of the most productive gold mines lies beneath Casterly Rock, the Lannisters' ancestral stronghold. This fortification sits above the Sunset Sea and the city of Lannisport, which is one of the great ports of the Seven Kingdoms, a bustling commercial center, and the home of the powerful Lannister fleet. Naval theorist Alfred Thayer Mahan would have agreed that the Lannisters were a maritime power, as they politically support maritime efforts, enjoy a large volume of seaborne trade, possess a large trading fleet, and maintain a large navy, although they lack the colonies that Mahan argued were necessary for sea power.[4] Navies, armies, and allies are expensive, but they are necessary to accumulate wealth from mines and maritime commerce and to secure business investments, which overall makes Tywin Lannister the wealthiest man in Westeros.

Lannister wealth underpins their power, not unlike Great Britain during the era of Pax Britannica, or the United States after World War II. From the eighteenth century to the middle of the twentieth century, Great Britain's "sinews of power" started with wealth.[5] In the twentieth century, the United States' wealth was the foundation of the "arsenal of democracy" and the post–World War II superpower.[6] Like these two powers at their zenith, the Lannisters leverage their wealth to build power and, at the same time, used power to make wealth, creating a virtuous circle of building wealth and power.

The Lannisters also understand finances, as they know how to leverage their wealth by securing loans. The Iron Bank of Braavos is the most important source of loans, continually extending the Lannisters credit based on their mineral wealth and Tywin's track record of sound investments. During his short stint as the master of coin, Tyrion Lannister has concerns that the enormous expense of the War of the Five Kings could force the Lannisters to mortgage their future or not be able to win the war due to insufficient funds. Ominously, the Iron Bank previously funded the enemies of rulers who failed to pay what they owed, of which Tyrion is aware. After winning the War of the Five Kings, Tywin reveals to his daughter, Cersei, that the Lannisters' gold mines had run dry three years previously, driving both Tywin and Cersei to trust no one and increase their willingness to accept risk to maintain their strategic position and secure additional strategic advantage. The alliance with the Tyrells was one of these strategic risks, and it would prove to be a costly decision.

To win the War of the Five Kings, the Lannisters often had to accept risk, and accepting risk is part of using military art to achieve your objectives. For those unfamiliar with the term, military art is broken into the following components: strategic art, operational art, and tactics. Strategic art is "defined as the skillful formulation, coordination, and application of ends, ways, and means to promote and defend the national interests."[7] Successful strategic art achieves the desired set of conditions and thereby secures strategic advantage, which the Lannisters did by winning the War of the Five Kings.[8] Operational art is a series of efforts "successively developing one after another, logically connected to one another, united by the commonality of the ultimate aim, each one achieving limited intermediate aims which in their totality represent an operational pursuit."[9] Robb Stark's efforts against the Lannisters, when viewed together as an overarching campaign, are an example of operational art. Tactics are the pursuit of victory on the battlefield through the application of combat power, and Tyrion's use of wildfire during the crushing defeat of Stannis Baratheon at the Battle of the Blackwater is an example of successful tactics.

Strategic art, operational art, and tactics each require a different perspective and mindset to practice effectively, but they are also interconnected and interdependent. As Russian military theorist Aleksandr Svechin wrote more than a century ago, "all branches of military art are closely associated with one another: tactics takes the steps from which an operational leap is formed; strategy points out the path."[10] Because it points out the path, so to speak, strategic art is the most important component of military art, and operational art and tactics are the materials for strategic art. Tactics are the most dynamic component of military art, as they are subject to the evolution of technology and military techniques, which for *Game of Thrones* includes magic and mythical creatures such as giants, wights, White Walkers, and dragons. The changes in tactics may, in turn, impact operational art, as dragons provide a form of operational maneuver, for example. Operational art provides the context for the tactical level of warfare and tactics, and successful operational art, in turn, facilitates strategic art.

Returning to Tywin Lannister's first scene in *Game of Thrones*, he emphasizes the importance of the near term to his son, although still clearly thinking strategically, when he says, "The future of our family will be determined in these next few months. We could establish a dynasty that will last a thousand years, or we could collapse into nothing, as the Targaryens did." His mention of "these next few months" indicates operational thinking about the forthcoming military campaigns and battles that would be necessary to achieve his strategic goals. Concerning military art, his focus on the future of his family underscores that he is practicing strategic art, his campaign design is a demonstration of operational art, and his battlefield leadership later in the series indicates his tactical abilities.

U.S. Air War College professor Everett Dolman describes strategy as "an idea . . . about the future in anticipation of the probable and preparation for the possible."[11] Strategy deals with the highest levels of statecraft and war and is an unending process. However, who wins at the tactical level is straightforward, as it usually is evident when a battle has a victor. This is also true at the operational level, as it is often clear if a campaign has a victor; however, who "wins" at the strategic level is not always so clear, as it is possible to win a war but lose strategic advantage in the aftermath. In other words, victory is not a strategic concept. At first this notion may seem strange, but because strategy never ends, it is a constant competition without an ultimate victory. Put another way, those who practice tactics and operational art maximize choices within the given rules and constraints provided by strategic art. Those who practice strategic art pursue strategic advantage by manipulating the rules and limitations, thereby changing the context and conditions that circumscribe and shape tactical and operational actions.[12]

Earlier in the *Game of Thrones* series, Robb Stark also demonstrates a growing understanding of Dolman's ideas. After the Starks capture Jaime Lannister, Robb brings him before his mother, Catelyn Stark. During this discussion, Jaime Lannister challenges Robb to fight man-to-man as champions for their houses. Robb wisely responds, "If we do it your way, Kingslayer, you'd win. . . . We're not doing it your way."[13] Robb lives to fight another day and marry a woman he loved, but this breaks the arranged marriage that was the basis for the Stark alliance with the Freys. This sowed the seeds of his undoing. Sadly, Robb did not understand that the Freys would turn on him, nor does he foresee the Lannisters changing the nature of the game with a secret agreement with the Freys and the Boltons, which culminates with the Red Wedding assassination of Robb's pregnant wife, Robb, and his mother.

Naturally, and ironically, the Lannisters' practice of strategy writ large teaches the Starks, making those who survive more capable in the long run. For example, when the honorable Ned Stark confronts Cersei Lannister, he naively assumes that Cersei would follow the same norms of honor that he did. Cersei, however, focuses on power, not honor. She explains the simple nature of *Game of Thrones* to Ned Stark and the audience: "You win, or you die."[14] Sadly for House Stark, Cersei's statement is prescient, as her newly crowned son, King Joffrey, has Ned beheaded, ignoring Cersei's protests. Despite Joffrey's short-term sadistic glee, however, this action sets off cascading effects that still reverberate in the story. The only bit of Cersei's advice that Joffrey seems to heed is, "Anyone who isn't us is an enemy."[15] Although Ned, Robb, and Catelyn die, Sansa and Arya live and learn.

Sansa Stark learns strategy the hard way—from her horrible experiences with the Lannisters, Littlefinger, and the Boltons. Cersei Lannister starts Sansa's strategic education, but Cersei's intention certainly is not to help the teenage Stark girl. Nevertheless, Sansa recalls those hard days and comes to understand their bitter lessons. Sansa's second unintentional master, Littlefinger, uses her as a pawn for his advancement, first in his takeover of the Vale of Arryn and then by wedding Sansa to Ramsay Bolton in an attempt to ultimately become Warden of the North. Just before leaving Sansa with the Boltons, Littlefinger points out that she had "learned to maneuver from the very best."[16] Littlefinger, however, does understand Ramsay Bolton's strategic skills and the depth of his sadistic nature. Again, Sansa learns at great personal and familial expense. All of this adds up to a strategic education par excellence. In Littlefinger's short trial, we see this education come to fruition. It is delightful to watch Sansa turn the accused's "little game" and other smug, but extremely instructive, comments against him. "I'm a slow learner, it's true, but I learn."[17] Sansa's final words to Littlefinger before Arya slits his throat are: "Thank you for all your many lessons, Lord Baelish. I'll never forget them."

Arya, too, learns much from the Lannisters. While he fights Arya's older brother, Robb Stark, Tywin Lannister has Arya Stark serve as his cupbearer, although he does not know her identity. With delightful irony, Tywin provides her with valuable strategic lessons and insight. One of the most important examples is when Tywin discusses the history of Harrenhal with Arya, teaching her about unexamined assumptions and manipulating the nature of the contest. The Lannister patriarch's comments resonate perfectly with Dolman's theories when he explains how the great fortress fell to Aegon Targaryen's dragons, as "Harrenhal was built to withstand an attack from the land. . . . But an attack from the air, with dragonfire? Harren and all his sons roasted alive within these walls. . . . Aegon Targaryen changed the rules."[18]

This chapter's discussion on the strategy of House Lannister in *Game of Thrones* underlines the timeless nature of strategy. This is why Sun Tzu's *Art of War*, Thucydides's *History of the Peloponnesian War*, Kauṭilya's *Arthashastra*, Machiavelli's *The Prince*, Clausewitz's *On War*, Jomini's *The Art of War*, Mahan's *The Influence of Sea Power upon History*, Corbett's *Some Principles of Maritime Strategy*, and other works retain so much value today.[19] In fact, Michael Handel attributes the longevity and preeminence of works such as these to "the underlying logic of human nature, and by extension of political action," which, he argues, "has not changed throughout history."[20] To better understand modern conflict, we can use these theorists and other authors' works in conjunction with *Game of Thrones* to help us appreciate the ageless relationship of money and power as well as the enduring mindset necessary to successfully wield military art to maintain or achieve strategic advantage.

NOTES

1. Thomas Hobbes, *Leviathan* (Harmondsworth, UK: Penguin Books, 1968), chap. 13, para. 9.

2. Mikal Gilmore, "George R. R. Martin: The Rolling Stone Interview," *Rolling Stone*, April 23, 2014, https://www.rollingstone.com/culture/culture-news/george-r-r-martin-the-rolling -stone-interview-242487/. See also "Real History behind Game of Thrones (Explained by Historians and George R.R. Martin)," A, YouTube video, 40:14, July 14, 2016, https://www .youtube.com/watch?v=Odw3Nxdqq4o.

3. David Benioff and D. B. Weiss, "You Win or You Die," season 1, episode 7, dir. Daniel Minahan, *Game of Thrones*, aired May 29, 2011, on HBO.

4. Alfred T. Mahan, *The Influence of Sea Power upon History, 1660–1783* (1890; repr., New York: Dover Publications, 1987), 71.

5. John Brewer, *The Sinews of Power: War, Money and the English State, 1688–1783* (Boston: Unwin Hyman, 1989), 32–39.

6. R. Craig Nation, "National Power," in *U.S. Army War College Guide to National Security Policy and Strategy*, ed. J. Boone Bartholomees Jr., 5th ed. (Carlisle PA: Strategic Studies Institute, U.S. Army War College, 2012), 151.

7. Richard A. Chilcoat, *Strategic Art: The New Discipline for 21st Century Leaders* (Carlisle PA: Strategic Studies Institute, U.S. Army War College, 1995), 3.

8. Strategic advantage is defined as a position of strength of a nation, coalition, or nonstate actor relative to another nation, coalition, or nonstate actor. The position of strength could be one of several factors, such as political, military, economic, social, information, infrastructure, physical environment, or time. Chilcoat, *Strategic Art*, 3.

9. Nikolai Varfolomeyev, "Strategy in an Academic Formulation," in *The Evolution of Soviet Operational Art, 1927–1991: The Documentary Basis*, ed. David Glantz (London: Frank Cass, 1995), 42.

10. Aleksandr Svechin, "Strategy and Operational Art," in *The Evolution of Soviet Operational Art, 1927–1991: The Documentary Basis*, ed. David Glantz (London: Frank Cass, 1995), 22.

11. Everett Carl Dolman, *Pure Strategy: Power and Principle in the Space and Information Age* (New York: Frank Cass, 2005), 1.

12. Dolman, *Pure Strategy*, 1–4.

13. David Benioff and D. B. Weiss, "Baelor," season 1, episode 9, dir. Alan Taylor, *Game of Thrones*, aired June 12, 2011, on HBO.

14. Benioff and Weiss, "You Win or You Die."

15. David Benioff and D. B. Weiss, "Lord Snow," season 1, episode 3, dir. Brian Kirk, *Game of Thrones*, aired May 1, 2011, on HBO.

16. Dave Hill, "Sons of the Harpy," season 5, episode 4, dir. Mark Mylod, *Game of Thrones*, aired May 3, 2015, on HBO.

17. David Benioff and D. B. Weiss, "The Dragon and the Wolf," season 7, episode 7, dir. Jeremy Podeswa, *Game of Thrones*, aired August 27, 2017, on HBO.

18. David Benioff and D. B. Weiss, "A Man without Honor," season 2, episode 7, dir. David Nutter, *Game of Thrones*, aired May 13, 2012, on HBO.

19. Sun Tzu, *The Art of War*, trans. Samuel B. Griffith (New York: Oxford University Press, 1963); Thucydides, *The Landmark Thucydides: A Comprehensive Guide to the Peloponnesian War*, ed. Robert B. Strassler (New York: Simon and Schuster, 1998); Kautilya, *The Arthashastra* (New York: Penguin Books India, 1992); Niccolò Machiavelli, *The Art of War*, trans. Ellis Farnsworth (New York: Da Capo Press, 1965); Niccolò Machiavelli, *The Discourses of Niccolò Machiavelli*, trans. Leslie J. Walker (Boston: Routledge and Paul, 1975); Niccolò Machiavelli, *The Prince*, trans. Luigi Ricci, revised by E. R. P. Vincent (New York: New American Library, 1952); Carl von Clausewitz, *On War*, 1st ed. (Princeton NJ: Princeton University Press, 1989); Antoine-Henri de Jomini, *The Art of War*, trans. U.S. Military Academy (London: Greenhill Books, 1992); Mahan, *Influence of Sea Power upon History*; and Julian S. Corbett, *Some Principles of Maritime Strategy* (1911; repr., Annapolis MD: Naval Institute Press, 1988).

20. Michael I. Handel, *Masters of War: Classical Strategic Thought*, 3rd ed. (New York: Routledge, 2000), 2.

3

Fear or Love

Insights from Machiavelli for Those Who Seek the Iron Throne

LIAM COLLINS

In his seminal work, *The Prince*, Italian political theorist Niccolò Machiavelli famously asked "whether it is better to be loved than to be feared, or the reverse."[1] Machiavelli answered that it is better to be feared than loved but warned against fear spurring hatred. In *The Prince*, he offered a number of other useful insights, and his work has been so influential that *Machiavellian* is now a word defined as "being or acting in accordance with the principles of government analyzed in Machiavelli's *The Prince*, in which political expediency is placed above morality and the use of craft and deceit to maintain the authority and carry out the polices of a ruler" or "characterized by subtle or unscrupulous cunning, deception, expediency, or dishonesty."[2] His treatise, or discourse, aims to advise a prince, the sixteenth-century city-state ruler in Italy, how to remain in power. Ultimately, he argues that the ends justify the means.

Who was Machiavelli? Machiavelli was an Italian philosopher, politician, diplomat, historian, author, and has been called the father of modern political science.[3] He was "born in a tumultuous era in which popes waged acquisitive wars against Italian city-states, and people and cities often fell from power as France, Spain, the Holy Roman Empire, and Switzerland battled for regional influence and control. Political-military alliances continually changed, featuring condottieri (mercenary leaders), who changed sides without warning, and the rise and fall of many short-lived governments."[4] In many ways, it was not unlike the world of Westeros.

When addressing "whether it is better to be loved than feared, or the reverse," in chapter 17 of *The Prince*, Machiavelli starts with an idealistic approach, similar to that of a Greek philosopher, stating, "I say that every prince ought to wish to be considered kind rather than cruel."[5] But he quickly transitions to a more pragmatic, or Machiavellian, approach when he writes, "Nevertheless [the prince] must take care to avoid misusing his kindness. Cesare Borgia was considered cruel; yet his cruelty restored Romagna, unified it in peace and loyalty." He continues, "If this result is considered good, then he must be judged much kinder than the Florentines who, to avoid being called cruel, allowed Pistoia to be destroyed."[6] In other words, the prince and the people are better off when ruled by fear, as opposed to love.

Machiavelli quickly dispenses with the notion that you can be both feared and loved, "since the two rarely come together." He argues that "anyone compelled to choose will find greater security in being feared than in being loved."[7] In making his elegant case that fear always trumps love, Machiavelli writes,

> [Men] are ungrateful, fickle, dissembling, anxious to flee danger, and covetous of gain. So long as you promote their advantage they are all yours, as I said before, and will offer you their blood, their goods, their lives, and their children, when the need for these is remote. When the need arises, however, they will turn against you. The prince who bases his security upon their word, lacking other provision, is doomed; for friendships that are gained by money, not by greatness and nobility of spirit, may well be earned, but cannot be kept; and in time of need, they will have fled your purse. Men are less concerned about offending someone they have cause to love than someone they have cause to

fear. Love endures by a bond which men, being scoundrels, may break whenever it serves their advantage to do so; but fear is supported by the dread of pain, which is ever present.[8]

While many kings and lords of Westeros heeded Machiavelli's words and prized fear over love, they failed to mind the advice from the second half of the chapter, in which Machiavelli states, "Still a prince should make himself feared in such a way that, though he does not gain love, he escapes hatred."[9] King Aerys Targaryen, the Mad King, lost the throne when he was slain by Jaime Lannister, a member of his own Kingsguard. While *Game of Thrones* starts long after Aerys Targaryen was deposed, it is clear that while he inspired fear throughout the kingdom, there was little love for him. Even his own daughter, Daenerys, said of him, "I know what my father was. What he did. I know the Mad King earned his name."[10]

King Joffrey was both feared and hated, and thus, he lasted less than three years on the Iron Throne before being poisoned by Petyr Baelish and Lady Olenna Tyrell at his wedding feast. His own acting Hand called him "a vicious idiot for a king."[11] Tywin Lannister, Lord of Casterly Rock, probably the most feared of all the lords, wasn't even loved by his own family. In fact, he inspired so much hatred that it ultimately resulted in his own son killing him with a crossbow.

King Robert Baratheon didn't appear to be personally loved or feared, as he spent most of his time drinking and whoring, but he wasn't particularly hated either. Given that he deferred the duties of running the kingdom to his Hand and his Small Council, it seems likely that the council was able to administer an appropriate level of fear within the population of Westeros, since he was able to maintain his rule for seventeen years.

Both Ned Stark, as Warden of the North, and his son, Robb Stark, as King in the North, chose to rule by love, as opposed to fear, but this did not bear well for either of them. Ned ultimately found his head on a spike, while Robb's decapitated body was unceremoniously paraded around on a horse with his own dire wolf's head above his body. Robb was betrayed by both Theon Greyjoy, whom he viewed as a brother, and Lord Bolton, one of his bannermen. This would come as no surprise to Machiavelli given his belief that men "are ungrateful, fickle," and "cowardly" and will "turn against you" and that "relying entirely on their promises" brings ruin. Given that so few followed Machiavelli's advice, it should come as no surprise that many leaders of Westeros came to a premature end. The Starks failed to grasp that fear works best because you can't trust people to always be loyal through affection.

Likewise, Orys I attempted to rule by love, having been described as a just leader. He was applauded for his reforms by nobles and commoners alike, but in the words of Tywin Lannister, "he wasn't just for long." Shortly after Joffrey's death, Tywin described Orys's fate to Tommen: "He was murdered in his sleep after less than a year by his own brother. Was that truly just of him, to abandon his subjects to an evil that he was too gullible to recognize?"[12]

So why did the rulers in Westeros fail so miserably? One thought might be that it was a tough environment and leaders simply didn't last long. Sure, it was a Hobbesian world in which "the life of man [was] solitary, poor, nasty, brutish, and short,"[13] but even in that era, Robert Baratheon maintained his reign for seventeen years and the Mad King lasted twenty-four. A more plausible explanation is that many of the rulers failed because they simply lacked an adviser like Machiavelli with "subtle or unscrupulous cunning, deception, expediency, or dishonesty." Simply put, success largely depended on having a Machiavellian Hand, and Tyrion Lannister was the rare Machiavellian in Westeros.

Like Machiavelli, Tyrion was a historian, politician, diplomat, and philosopher. While he was disadvantaged, having been born a dwarf in that era and hated by his father for "killing" his mother, he was still a Lannister, so he never had to want for money or work a steady job, at least until his father appointed him acting Hand of the King. When not whoring or drinking, he was a voracious reader. On the ride north to Castle Black, Tyrion told Jon Snow, "My brother has his sword, and I have my mind, and a mind needs books like a sword needs a whetstone. That's why I read so much."[14] While Tywin was away fighting Robb Stark's Army of the North, Tyrion performed superbly as acting Hand to King Joffrey. He found that his study of history made him well suited for the job and that he had a knack for deceit and deception. His genius ultimately saved King's Landing from nearly certain defeat, and he was able to magnificently manage despite a boy king who lacked the maturity to rule.

By comparison, most other Hands failed miserably. Ned Stark was too idealistic and principled to serve as Hand, lacking "unscrupulous cunning" and "deceit." He may have been a great warrior, battlefield leader, and friend to King Robert, but he was a terrible Hand. He refused to condone the killing of Daenerys on the moral ground of her being a child and, thus, left a threat with a legitimate right to the throne alive. And rather than arresting Cersei upon discovering that the father of her children is not the king but her brother, he did the honorable thing and allowed her twenty-four hours to flee the city. A much more cunning Cersei used this time, instead, to consolidate power and plot against Ned. As Cersei tells him, "When you play the game of thrones, you win or you die. There is no middle ground."[15] Ned simply failed to understand how to play the game, and it led to his demise.

Likewise, the Onion Knight, Davos Seaworth, failed as a Hand. Born in Flea Bottom, the poorest slum in King's Landing, Davos lacked the formal education of Tyrion, and in fact, he couldn't even read until the third season. Too often his advice was clouded by his disdain for the Lord of Light religion. Prior to the attack on King's Landing, he convinces Stannis to leave the red priestess behind. While it can't be certain that the outcome would have been different had she accompanied Davos, it is reasonable to conclude that her sorcery likely would have changed the outcome, given that she was able to defeat Renly's numerically superior army without a single sword being drawn. Like Ned, Davos was too principled for the Machiavellian environment of Westeros, where the ends justify the means, and focusing on principled means can often result in death, as Machiavelli writes, "The way men live is so far removed from the way they ought to live that anyone who abandons what is for what should be pursues his downfall rather than his preservation."[16]

Tywin Lannister's performance, having served stints as Hand of the King to the Mad King, King Robert, and King Joffrey, was somewhat mixed. He was a master at placing "political expediency . . . above morality and [using] craft and deceit to maintain the authority and carry out the policies of a ruler." However, the manner in which he executed deceit to accomplish "political expediency" only incited hatred. Tyrion wisely argued that the treacherous feast of the Red Wedding violated acceptable norms of the day. The dialogue between the two shows the nuanced but extremely important difference and why Tyrion is the Machiavelli of Westeros. While discussing the Red Wedding, Tywin asked, "Do you disapprove?" Tyrion responded, "I'm all for cheating; this is war. But to slaughter them at a wedding. . . . The Northerners will never forget." To which Tywin responded, "Good. Let 'em remember what happens when they march on the South."[17] Tyrion understood that even during this anarchic period there are rules as to how the game is played and that you put yourself and your family at great risk with the hatred that is spawned if you violate the rules.

What of the Spider and Littlefinger? While both were on the Small Council and both were exceedingly cunning and operated in a Machiavellian manner, they had different clients from that of Machiavelli's prince. When Varys visited Ned Stark in his cell after being imprisoned, Ned asked, "Who do you truly serve?" Varys's response was clear: "The Realm, my lord. Someone must."[18] While the Spider served the realm, Petyr Baelish, perhaps the most dangerous man in Westeros, served only himself. In the end, both rivaled Tyrion for the ability to operate effectively in the Machiavellian world of Westeros, but only Tyrion's goal was to help "the prince" maintain his rule.

What else can be learned from Machiavelli? Machiavelli is very critical of conscripts, stating, "Mercenaries and auxiliaries are useless and dangerous; and any ruler who keeps his state dependent upon mercenaries will never have real peace or security, for they are disorganized, undisciplined, ambitious, and faithless. Brave before their allies, they are cowards before the enemy."[19] In Westeros there is much debate about the reliability of mercenaries, but their record is fairly strong. When discussing them, Barristan Selmy argues that "men who fight for gold have neither honor nor loyalty; they cannot be trusted." However, Jorah Mormont argues, "They can be trusted to kill . . . if they're well paid."[20]

Yet in *Game of Thrones*, mercenaries and sellswords performed remarkably well and were more reliable than many lords. The Stone Crows, led by Shagga, son of Dolf; the Burned Men, led by Timett, son of Timett; and the Black Ears, led by Chella, son of Cheyk, were reliable and fought valiantly for Tyrion at the Battle of the Green Fork, for the price of a few weapons and a small amount of gold. Likewise, Bronn was extremely loyal to Tyrion, and it was clear that his loyalty was not tied to gold alone. Bronn was anything but "ungrateful, fickle, dissembling, [and] anxious to flee danger."[21] Tyrion put him in constant danger, and never once did Bronn attempt to evade. By contrast, nobles, including Theon Greyjoy, Lord Bolton, and Lord Walder Frey, turned out to be much less reliable.

While the world today is much different from sixteenth-century Italy, or the imaginary world of Westeros, Machiavelli's words still hold true. During the Iraq War, fear held greater persuasive power than love. While al-Qaeda in Iraq subscribed to a twisted version of Sunni Islam, a vast majority of the more moderate Sunni population had no love for al-Qaeda in Iraq, but those same moderates supported the terrorist group out of fear. The brutal tactics carried out by its leader Abu Musab al-Zarqawi held the population in check. But eventually his brutality turned fear into hatred, and the Sunni population turned on him.

There were at least four isolated attempts by Sunni tribes to realign with coalition forces prior to the Sunni Awakening, but each attempt failed, as they were unable to muster the required strength to defeat al-Qaeda. With the coalition unable to provide security, the attempts quickly fell apart, and the Sunni tribes returned to tacit support for al-Qaeda out of fear. The fourth attempt failed when al-Qaeda killed most of the group's leaders. The Sunni Awakening only succeeded because the U.S. surge provided the additional forces necessary to safeguard the Sunni tribes and protect them from al-Qaeda retaliation for supporting the coalition.[22] Had al-Qaeda practiced less brutality, it might have been able to maintain its hold over the Sunni population. Likewise, if the United States understood the power of fear sooner, it might have been quicker to surge troops to support the tribes.

While modern nation-states do not use mercenaries per se, they do use proxies. The United States has used proxy forces in Syria; Iran supported proxies in Iraq; and Russia uses South Ossetian forces to advance its interests in Georgia, as well as street gangs and thugs in the Donbas region of eastern Ukraine and elsewhere. Machiavelli, however, would not be surprised to find that the performance of these modern-day mercenaries can be extremely poor. Criminals often make poor agents, as they are often extremely unreliable and may look for ways to exploit their state sponsor.[23] While the United States might avoid criminal proxies, it is not immune to problems; the United States spent over $500 million to train what ultimately amounted to a mere five fighters in Syria, before shutting down the program in 2015.[24]

In the end, the many kings and lords of Westeros would have fared better if they had had a Machiavelli to advise them. The Stark lords failed because they thought it was better to be loved than feared. Lord Tywin and King Joffrey were right in their belief that it was better to be feared than loved, but they failed because their actions inspired hatred. The most important action that a king or lord of Westeros could have done to ensure regime stability was to select the right Hand and Small Council and heed their advice. As Tywin wisely advised Tommen, "A wise young king listens to his counselors and heeds their advice until he comes of age. And the wisest kings continue to listen to them long afterwards."[25] Unfortunately, few possessed the skills to be a Machiavellian Hand. It required cunning, deception, education, and perhaps most importantly, an understanding that the ends justify the means, and sometimes immoral means must be used to achieve the desired ends. Given that Tyrion was one of the few Machiavellians in Westeros, it should come as no surprise that life in *Game of Thrones* was "solitary, poor, nasty, brutish, and short."

NOTES
1. Niccolò Machiavelli, *The Prince*, trans. Daniel Nonno (1966; repr., New York: Bantam Books, 2003), 65.
2. Dictionary.com, s.v. "Machiavellian," accessed May 22, 2018, https://www.dictionary.com/browse/machiavellian.

3. Mikko Lahtinen, *Politics and Philosophy: Niccolò Machiavelli and Louis Althusser's Aleatory Materialism* (Chicago: Haymarket Books, 2009), 115.

4. "Niccolò Machiavelli—A Brief Introduction," *Niccolò Machiavelli Blog*, October 13, 2017, https://nicolomachiavelliblog.wordpress.com/2017/10/13/first-blog-post/.

5. Machiavelli, *The Prince*, 65.

6. Machiavelli, *The Prince*, 65.

7. Machiavelli, *The Prince*, 66.

8. Machiavelli, *The Prince*, 66.

9. Machiavelli, *The Prince*, 66.

10. David Benioff and D. B. Weiss, "Hardhome," season 5, episode 8, dir. Miguel Sapochnik, *Game of Thrones*, aired May 31, 2015, on HBO.

11. Tyrion tells Joffrey, "We've had vicious kings, and we've had idiot kings, but I don't know if we've ever been cursed with a vicious idiot for a king!" Vanessa Taylor, "The Old Gods and the New," season 2, episode 6, dir. David Nutter, *Game of Thrones*, aired May 6, 2012, on HBO.

12. David Benioff and D. B. Weiss, "Breaker of Chains," season 4, episode 3, dir. Alex Graves, *Game of Thrones*, aired April 20, 2014, on HBO.

13. Thomas Hobbes, *Leviathan; or, The Matter, Forme, and Power of a Common-Wealth Ecclesiastical and Civill* (1651; Project Gutenberg, 2009), https://www.gutenberg.org/files/3207/3207-h/3207-h.htm.

14. David Benioff and D. B. Weiss, "The Kingsroad," season 1, episode 2, dir. Tim Van Patten, *Game of Thrones*, aired April 24, 2011, on HBO.

15. David Benioff and D. B. Weiss, "You Win or You Die," season 1, episode 7, dir. Daniel Minahan, *Game of Thrones*, aired April 24, 2011, on HBO.

16. Machiavelli, *The Prince*, 61–62.

17. David Benioff and D. B. Weiss, "Mhysa," season 3, episode 10, dir. David Nutter, *Game of Thrones*, aired June 9, 2013, on HBO.

18. George R. R. Martin, "The Pointy End," season 1, episode 8, dir. Daniel Minahan, *Game of Thrones*, aired June 5, 2011, on HBO.

19. Machiavelli, *The Prince*, 52.

20. David Benioff and D. B. Weiss, "Second Sons," season 3, episode 8, dir. Michelle MacLaren, *Game of Thrones*, aired May 19, 2013, on HBO.

21. Machiavelli, *The Prince*, 66.

22. Stephen Biddle, Jeffrey Friedman, and Jacob Shapiro, "Testing the Surge: Why Did Violence Decline in Iraq in 2007?" *International Security* 37, no. 1 (2012): 7–40.

23. Mark Galeotti, "The Kremlin's Newest Hybrid Warfare Asset: Gangsters," *Foreign Policy*, June 12, 2017.

24. Paul McLeary, "The Pentagon Wasted $550 Million Training Syrian Rebels. It's About to Try Again," *Foreign Policy*, March 18, 2106.

25. Benioff and Weiss, "Breaker of Chains."

4

The Source of Tyrion Lannister's Unlikely Survival and Success

JOE BYERLY

Of all the players in *Game of Thrones*, Tyrion Lannister would probably not make anyone's short list of likely survivors of season after season of intrigue and violence. He's small in stature, he has a drinking problem, and his chances of catching venereal disease are extremely high. There are many characters who possessed quality traits that made them better candidates for survival, and yet Tyrion outlasts them all: the noble and strong Ned Stark lost his head in season 1; the Achilles-like Oberyn Martell had his skull crushed in season 4; and the ruthless and Machiavellian Tywin Lannister met his demise in a particularly unfortunate setting, also in season 4. Among the heroes and villains of Westeros, how does a man who stands at only four feet five inches and has a penchant for heavy drinking and enthusiastically patronizing bordellos make it so far in the game of thrones?

Tyrion had two habits that became his competitive advantage and enabled him to overcome his many disadvantages. First, he read *a lot*. Through reading, he gained an understanding of history and internalized years of vicarious experiences. These books gave him the mental models with which to maneuver through multiple complex situations within the

22

The Myth of the Accidental Strategist

STEVE LEONARD

Early in the sixth season of *Game of Thrones*, Tyrion Lannister is holding counsel with Missandei, Varys, and Grey Worm in Meereen. With the Dragon Queen, Daenerys Targaryen, missing since escaping the Sons of the Harpy in Daznak's Pit, the four are discussing the progressive decline of her dragons Rhaegal and Viserion, chained in captivity beneath the Great Pyramid. Their conversation is significant, as it underscores the transformation of Tyrion from a comically drunken, lascivious rascal to a trusted confidant and adviser.

> MISSANDEI: They are not eating. They haven't touched any food since Queen Daenerys left.
>
> TYRION LANNISTER: Daenerys is the Dragon Queen. Can't very well let the dragons starve. That's obvious.
>
> GREY WORM: The dragon does not want to eat. How do you force him to eat?
>
> TYRION LANNISTER: Dragons do not do well in captivity.
>
> MISSANDEI: How do you know this?
>
> TYRION LANNISTER: That's what I do. I drink, and I know things.[1]

The youngest son of Lord Tywin Lannister, the powerful patriarch of House Lannister, Tyrion lives a seemingly cursed life. His mother, Joanna Lannister, did not survive his birth, a death for which both his father and sister, Cersei Lannister, blame him. He also suffers from dwarfism, a condition for which he endures persistent prejudice and persecution. Derisively referred to as "the Imp," "Halfman," and "the Demon Monkey," Tyrion is widely known for two unique and somewhat endearing characteristics: his insatiable taste for prostitutes and his uncanny ability to consume alcohol. His family has little respect for him, as do those with whom he associates.

Tyrion's lesser qualities, however, are more than mitigated by a substantial intellect, keen observational skills, and a deeply cynical perspective. While the rest of House Lannister is busy plotting and scheming to retain their tenuous grasp on the Iron Throne, Tyrion is watching, learning, and—without fail—drinking. All the while, those around him continue on, oblivious to the quiet evolution of the accidental strategist.

The Bastard Prince

In the fictional world of *Game of Thrones*, Tyrion Lannister is a Westerosi Niccolò Machiavelli: diplomat, philosopher, political realist. Machiavelli, who served in a variety of influential positions in the Florentine Republic of Renaissance Italy, was an astute observer of the brutal political realities of his time. While in service to the Republic of Florence, Machiavelli bore witness to unrelenting political deceit, deviousness, and unscrupulousness. His treatise on the realpolitik of the era, *The Prince*, remains relevant today as much for its timeless treatment of political immorality as for the subtle brilliance of the author himself.[2]

Much like Tyrion, Machiavelli enjoyed a rich and full life. While credited with being the father of modern political science and a military theorist of some repute, Machiavelli also found time to write poetry, satire, and even carnival songs. In these lesser-known works, he exhibits a wry sense of humor and biting wit honed through years of serving as "the Hand" to Florentine political elites. Even while assembling the ideas that would one day form *The Art of War*, Machiavelli was busying himself with "L'asino d'oro" ("The Golden Ass"), a satirical poem in which the author finds love with a beautiful herdswoman surrounded by the beasts of the enchantress Circe.[3] An irony, perhaps, that was not lost on George R. R. Martin.

In a world steeped in political intrigue, Tyrion is Machiavelli—easily overlooked by the princes around him, deeply intelligent, and quietly observant. In *Game of Thrones* the Italian poet-philosopher is not just a literary prototype for Tyrion; he is channeled through "the Dwarf of Casterly Rock." Even as we are introduced to Tyrion as the drunken castoff of House Lannister in the first episode, we get a glimpse into the character's future during a brief, but significant, exchange with Jon Snow:

> TYRION LANNISTER: Let me give you some advice, bastard. Never forget what you are. The rest of the world will not. Wear it like armor, and it can never be used to hurt you.
>
> JON SNOW: What the hell do you know about being a bastard?
>
> TYRION LANNISTER: All dwarves are bastards in their fathers' eyes.[4]

No two characters in *Game of Thrones* are as deeply connected. Both men are the "bastards" of their respective houses, and both men fight to earn the respect they have been denied for so long. Even as their paths take them in widely different directions for much of the series, they are reunited as the fantasy epic approaches crescendo. In whatever direction fate takes the two, it will take them together.

True to character, Tyrion walks away from the encounter, pulling a last drink from his ubiquitous wineskin.

The Unlikely Sage

Throughout *Game of Thrones* Tyrion dispenses Machiavellian wisdom. In every episode, his words are often noteworthy and inevitably memorable, ranging from the prophetic ("The Northerners will never forget") to the seemingly absurd ("In my experience, eloquent men are right every bit as often as imbeciles").[5] His counsel foreshadows the risks of ill-conceived plans ("It's hard to put a leash on a dog once you've put a crown on its head") and provides important perspective on life ("And a mind needs books like a sword needs a whetstone").[6] His advice can be simultaneously colloquial, comical, and controversial.

In Tyrion Lannister, Martin's choice of sage is at the same time unprecedented and profound. In *The Lord of the Rings* J. R. R. Tolkien channels wisdom through either Gandalf, the aged wizard, or the elves, who convey insight from a time before man. In the *Foundation* series, Isaac Asimov draws on mathematics professor Hari Seldon, who uses "psychohistory" to guide mankind through millennia of chaos. In each volume of *Tarzan of the Apes*, Edgar Rice Burroughs uses his archetype hero as a conduit for the hard-fought lessons of the jungle. Martin, however, chooses the least likely character to deliver the most important knowledge.

As with any sage, Martin bestows on Tyrion a powerful medium through which to channel his rare insight into the world around him. Gandalf had his staff, Hari Seldon his mind, and Tarzan his strength. Tyrion has alcohol, and an abundance of it. From the outset of the series, Tyrion the philosopher casts wisdom from the depths of a wineskin. Whether extolling the virtues of alcohol to Jon Snow ("Everything's better with some wine in the belly") or bemoaning his vice to Podrick Payne ("It's not easy being drunk all the time. If it were easy, everyone would do it"), Tyrion wields his drink with the power and conviction of a great wizard's staff.[7]

While such a choice might seem ironic on the surface, Martin's thinking is ever-so-subtly revealed as the initial season unfolds. In the fourth episode, "Cripples, Bastards, and Broken Things," the series offers what is probably the most significant clue about Martin's vision for the diminutive sage, when Tyrion gives the crippled Bran Stark his design for a saddle that will allow the boy to ride a horse upright:

BRAN STARK: Will I really be able to ride?

TYRION LANNISTER: You will. On horseback, you will be as tall as any of them.

ROBB STARK: Is this some kind of trick? Why do you want to help him?

TYRION LANNISTER: I have a tender spot in my heart for cripples, bastards, and broken things.[8]

In Tyrion, Martin finds a "tender spot" that strikes at the heart. While most fantasy epics leverage characters of lesser stature (dwarves or hobbits, for example) as comedic relief, Tyrion represents a sympathetic figure, a familial black sheep not by choice but by birth. Like Jon Snow, Tyrion has lived his life as an outcast in his own family; unlike Jon Snow, Tyrion provides a unique vessel to serve as Martin's sage, one as unusual as it is improbable.

Martin's sage drinks, and he knows things.

The Influential Hand

In the season 2 episode "What Is Dead May Never Die," Varys plays the role of prophet in a discussion with Tyrion, sharing with him a riddle that shrewdly defines the influence—and power—of a strategic adviser, the right hand to the throne:

LORD VARYS: Power is a curious thing, my lord. Are you fond of riddles?

TYRION LANNISTER: Why? Am I about to hear one?

LORD VARYS: Three great men sit in a room: a king, a priest, and a rich man. Between them stands a common sellsword. Each great man bids the sellsword kill the other two. Who lives? Who dies?

TYRION LANNISTER: Depends on the sellsword.

LORD VARYS: Does it? He has neither crown, nor gold, nor favor with the gods.

TYRION LANNISTER: He has a sword, the power of life and death.

LORD VARYS: But if it's swordsmen who rule, why do we pretend kings hold all the power? When Ned Stark lost his head, who was truly responsible? Joffrey? The executioner? Or something else?

TYRION LANNISTER: I've decided I don't like riddles.

LORD VARYS: Power resides where men believe it resides. It's a trick. A shadow on the wall. And a very small man can cast a very large shadow.[9]

Power *is* a very curious thing, and so is influence. Machiavelli's *The Prince* was not published until 1532, five years after his death, yet it stands today as one of the most influential treatises on realpolitik. Prussian military theorist Carl von Clausewitz died before finishing his masterpiece analysis of political-military strategy, *On War*. After his death in 1831, his wife, Marie von Brühl, edited and published the unfinished, and now classic, work. Major General Fox Conner of the U.S. Army, who personally and deftly mentored George C. Marshall, Dwight D. Eisenhower, and George S. Patton—three of the most impactful military officers of the twentieth century—throughout the course of their careers, ordered his papers and journals burned upon his death in 1951.[10] Were it not for the personal recollections of those he mentored, his profound impact on World War II might never have been revealed.

Each of these men exerted a tremendous amount of influence during their lives, but that influence went largely unnoticed until long after their deaths. They were quietly observant and deeply reflective, possessing a singular, transcendent wisdom. Tyrion is cast in this mold, emerging from the brothels of Westeros to assume a crucial role as Hand to Daenerys Targaryen. As the Dragon Queen's most trusted adviser, Tyrion's wisdom has never been more prophetic ("The world you want to build doesn't get built all at once, probably not in a single lifetime") or timely ("Sometimes, nothing is the hardest thing to do").[11] His counsel offers both restraint ("If that's the type of queen you want to be, how are you different from all the other tyrants that came before you?") and perspective ("Children are not their fathers, luckily for all of us").[12]

A very small man *can* cast a very large shadow. Martin's transformation of Tyrion comes full circle by the seventh season of *Game of Thrones*. Tyrion is able to bring Jon Snow—now the King in the North—together with Daenerys, forge alliances with the Starks and Greyjoys, and negotiate a ceasefire with the Lannisters. Even as the White Walkers descend on the Seven Kingdoms, his relatively quiet, humble influence guides Daenerys at a crucial time for her, the Seven Kingdoms, and Westeros.

The Accidental Strategist

In *Game of Thrones* the transformation of Tyrion Lannister appears almost as happenstance, a fortunate turn of circumstance. Nothing could be further from the truth.

History is replete with examples of influential strategists; men like Machiavelli and Clausewitz serve as two prominent cases. But many others came before, and still more have come since. The lessons of Sun Tzu and Thucydides resonate from antiquity; the works of B. H. Liddell Hart and John Boyd do the same in a more contemporary sense. Modern navies owe much to Alfred Thayer Mahan and Julian Corbett, and air power might not be what it is today without the influential efforts of Giulio Douhet and Billy Mitchell. Rarely were these influential figures great captains of battle, but men and women who, when afforded the opportunity, rose to the occasion and forged a timeless legacy that shaped the knowledge and understanding of future generations.

What separates these figures from those who aspire to but never attain such influence is quite simple: intellect, opportunity, and conviction. Remarkable mental acuity and perceptiveness are the hallmarks of a strategist; only the best among them are afforded the opportunity to serve in positions of significant influence. These men and women were among a rare breed of strategists who possess the conviction to cast an enduring legacy in their wake, to capture the lessons of their vicarious learning for those who follow.

In *Game of Thrones* Tyrion's ascent is presented as happenstance, a trick of fate, an accident. But it is no accident. He is Martin's Machiavelli—the voice of reason in a sea of chaos. A trusted confidant and adviser as adept at offering sage counsel as he would be penning a scandalous limerick. The astute strategist who serves wisdom from the depths of a wineskin. At the same time both ordinary and extraordinary. Easily overlooked but impossible to ignore. At its core, *Game of Thrones* is a grand Machiavellian epic, and Martin's fantasy tale would be incomplete without his own Niccolò Machiavelli at center stage. And for that, he has Tyrion Lannister—a seasoned intellect and wily opportunist intent on preserving his place in history, as well as history itself.

There are no accidental strategists.

NOTES

1. Dave Hill, "Home," season 6, episode 2, dir. Jeremy Podeswa, *Game of Thrones*, aired May 1, 2016, on HBO.
2. Niccolò Machiavelli, *The Prince*, trans. Harvey C. Mansfield Jr. (Chicago: University of Chicago Press, 1985).

3. Machiavelli's version was a period retelling of Apuleius's "The Golden Ass." The poem uses the animals as an allegorical device to explore human characteristics such as bravery, cruelty, violence, conceit, and greed. In Greek mythology, Circe is a goddess of magic often cast as a nymph or sorceress.

4. David Benioff and D. B. Weiss, "Winter Is Coming," season 1, episode 1, dir. Tim Van Patten, *Game of Thrones*, aired April 17, 2011, on HBO.

5. David Benioff and D. B. Weiss, "Mhysa," season 3, episode 10, dir. David Nutter, *Game of Thrones*, aired June 9, 2013, on HBO; David Benioff and D. B. Weiss, "Dance of Dragons," season 5, episode 9, dir. David Nutter, *Game of Thrones*, aired June 7, 2015, on HBO.

6. David Benioff and D. B. Weiss, "A Man without Honor," season 2, episode 7, dir. David Nutter, *Game of Thrones*, aired May 13, 2012, on HBO; David Benioff and D. B. Weiss, "The Kingsroad," season 1, episode 2, dir. Tim Van Patten, *Game of Thrones*, aired April 24, 2011, on HBO.

7. Benioff and Weiss, "Kingsroad"; Benioff and Weiss, "Mhysa."

8. Bryan Cogman, "Cripples, Bastards, and Broken Things," season 1, episode 4, dir. Brian Kirk, *Game of Thrones*, aired May 8, 2011, on HBO.

9. Bryan Cogman, "What Is Dead May Never Die," season 2, episode 3, dir. Alik Sakharov, *Game of Thrones*, aired April 15, 2012, on HBO.

10. Edward Cox, *Grey Eminence: Fox Conner and the Art of Mentorship* (Stillwater OK: New Forums Press, 2011).

11. David Benioff and D. B. Weiss, "Beyond the Wall," season 7, episode 6, dir. Alan Taylor, *Game of Thrones*, aired August 20, 2017, on HBO.

12. Benioff and Weiss, "Beyond the Wall"; David Benioff and D. B. Weiss, "The Queen's Justice," season 7, episode 3, dir. Mark Mylod, *Game of Thrones*, aired August 20, 2017, on HBO.

23

Why the Westerosi Can't Win Wars

CHUCK BIES

In order to use battle to bring an enemy to heel, the losses have to matter. In Westeros the losses not only do not matter, but they do not threaten power structures. Therefore, the tactical level of war in Westeros is divorced from the strategic level of war. Dead peasants and sellswords matter little in the game of thrones. For battles to matter, they must be a part of a coherent operational and strategic approach that hits the enemy where it hurts and destroys either their will or means to continue fighting. The only leader that seemed to intuitively understand this was Tywin Lannister, and though "The Rains of Castamere" survived him, the lesson that it taught did not.

> TYRION: "Rain fire on them from above" . . . you're quoting father, aren't you?
> CERSEI: Why not? He has a good mind for strategy, doesn't he?
> TYRION: Call it tactics, not strategy, but yes, he does have a good mind for it. The best mind some would say.[1]

During the above brother-sister discussion prior to the Battle of the Blackwater, Tyrion was exactly right. In Westeros even the greatest military minds lacked an understanding of what tactics, operations, and strategy are, let alone how they must be employed in concert to achieve victory in the game of thrones. This is not just a matter of nuance or semantics; it is also the reason why warfare in Westeros is seemingly endless and endemic.

To ensure common understanding, it's worthwhile to explain what we mean by the different levels of warfare: the tactical, operational, and strategic levels of war. Executed correctly, there are linkages between the three that will all but guarantee the success of a war; one or two battles will all but guarantee success. Executed incorrectly and the balance sheet of battles won and lost loses relevance, and the conflict becomes an unproductive and costly grind.

The tactical level of war

- refers to actions on the ground, usually manifested in battles or engagements between forces;
- is doctrinally defined as "the level of war at which battles and engagements are planned and executed to achieve military objectives assigned to tactical units or task forces";[2]
- includes modern tactical unit echelons that range from squad up through division;
- covers a time horizon that ranges from seconds to days;
- is the lowest level in terms of scale and closest in terms of proximity;
- can be easily categorized as area and mobile defenses, penetrations, envelopments, frontal attacks, flank attacks, infiltrations, and turning movements.

The strategic level of war

- refers to the employment of a nation's or state's resources, including nonmilitary capabilities, to achieve national level objectives;
- is viewed in terms of ends, ways, and means at the national level;[3]
- covers a time horizon measured in months and years;
- includes three general categories referred to as strategies of attrition, exhaustion, and annihilation.[4]

In comparison, the operational level of war

- resides between tactics and strategy and defies categorization;
- is the planning of campaigns and a series of engagements (tactical actions) to achieve the strategic objective (national strategy);
- encompasses the events that lead up to, surround, and follow engagements;
- involves the sustainment and movement of formations, from battalions through armies;
- covers a time horizon that ranges from days to months.

Despite its imprecise nature, the operational level of war is essential to connecting the tactical level of war to the strategic level of war. A battle fought without the context of an overarching operational approach is just that—a battle. On its own, it will not yield the decisive results necessary to achieve the strategic objective. Similarly, a strategic framework, no matter how well constructed, will not translate to success if there is no operational approach to translate national-level means to the tactical level; the best strategy cannot assure victory on the battlefield without an operational approach to mass resources to support the tactical engagement.

History provides several examples of where commanders and leaders succeeded or failed to employ these levels of war in concert. One of the most striking examples of success is Napoleon Bonaparte's Ulm Campaign during the War of the Third Coalition from 1803–6. Over the course of the Ulm Campaign, Napoleon skillfully maneuvered his corps around the Austrian army led by General Karl Mack von Leiberich; he used small tactical engagements to fix portions of the Austrian host while he maneuvered his corps around the Austrian flanks. After a few weeks, Mack found himself isolated from allied support and was compelled to surrender his army. This knocked Austria out of the coalition as a credible opponent, enabling Bonaparte to focus his efforts against the rest of the coalition. To quote Napoleon, "I have destroyed the enemy merely by marches." A few months later, he annihilated the Russian army at Austerlitz, ending the coalition against him. This was a shining example of the operational level of war to achieve coherence between tactics and strategy.[5]

An example of where the operational level was neglected was World War I from 1914 to 1917. During this bloody four-year period, national strategies on both sides failed because the operational level of war was absent and tactics were able to trump strategy. Despite local successes, neither side possessed the strength to capitalize on those victories and achieve a breakthrough. The two sides were too evenly matched, and neither could exploit those local successes. The strategies employed by both sides—whether opening additional fronts or "bleeding France white" at Verdun, in the words of German general Erich von Falkenhayn—failed because neither side was able to expand success beyond the immediate battle, destroy the enemy or their will to continue fighting, or appreciably erode the enemy's resources.[6]

Strategy in Westeros

In Westeros few leaders and commanders truly grasp strategy. An example of this is during Tyrion Lannister's war council with Daenerys and her allies—the Martells of Sunspear, the Tyrells of Highgarden, and the rogue Greyjoy flotilla. Tyrion outlined a coherent strategy at this council: the Martells would attack the Stormlands from the south to pull Cersei's forces away from King's Landing, the Tyrells would attack King's Landing from the southwest to seize the capital, and Daenerys's army of Unsullied and Dothraki would seize Casterly Rock to neutralize the Lannister alliance's source of power.[7]

It quickly became apparent that few of the participants at the meeting were capable of thinking strategically and were focused at the tactical level of war. Yara Greyjoy focused on using dragons against King's Landing—a narrow and tactical approach that, as Daenerys pointed out, would result in her losing the support of the people and, therefore, the war. Daenerys had no intention of being the Queen of Ashes.

Lady Olenna and Lady Martell were focused on the combat between their armies and the Lannisters and failed to grasp how they fit into supporting and shaping the larger strategic and operational goals. They resented that their armies would be used for lengthy sieges while Daenerys's would not. The only two people in the room who seemed to understand the bigger picture were Tyrion and Daenerys. They not only had a clear visualization of their end, but they understood that their means could only be employed in specific ways. Though the Unsullied and dragons presented an overwhelming advantage, they could only be employed against armies in the field and away from the Seven Kingdoms' seat of power. They lacked the resources and allies to fight a war of either attrition or exhaustion. They had to dismantle Cersei's alliance piece by piece in order to stand a chance of winning, and to do so, they had to draw the Lannister armies into the field, where they could be annihilated. Though they succeeded in destroying a significant portion of the Lannister army, it was, ultimately, Daenerys's alliance that was dismantled.

What of the Lannisters? Their objective was to remain in control of the Iron Throne; their means for doing so were the Lannister army and diplomacy with key players. By season 7, the Lannisters had only two allies remaining, the Greyjoys and the Tarlies. Though they dispatched most of their enemies, they were surrounded by threats; the Starks to the north, the Martells and Tyrells to the south, and the Targaryens and the Iron Bank across the sea to the east. They managed to subdue the Tully threat from Riverrun, and the Arryns to the north remain a wild card. But most of their key allies, specifically the Boltons and the Freys, had been dispatched. By ruling the seas and holding a central position, their strategy was to use their opponents' inability to concentrate against them to take on their opponents in series. They succeeded in destroying the Tyrells, but in the process, they lost their Tarly allies, Casterly Rock, most of their army, and most importantly the gold they needed to settle their debts with the Iron Bank. True, the Martells remained uncommitted, which resulted in the Lannisters' southern flank becoming more secure, but the Lannisters now face an increased risk of the Iron Bank hiring every mercenary company in Essos against them.

This illustrates why Daenerys and Tyrion, by the end of season 7, had failed and the war remained suspended in stalemate. Instead of focusing on isolating the Lannisters from their allies and annihilating both them and their allies in the field to set conditions to attain the Iron Throne, their strategy was to defeat the Lannisters so that they could seize King's Landing. They failed to appreciate that the strategic value of King's Landing is little more than a pile of rocks. Seizing the Iron Throne itself does not equate to seizing the power of the Iron Throne; the Targaryens, Baratheons, and Lannisters were able to rule the Iron Throne because they annihilated those who challenged their rule and subsequently assumed the Iron Throne, not because they had possession of it. Even after losing Casterly Rock, the Lannisters still retained the ability to effectively prosecute the offensive, as evidenced by their capturing Sunspear's leaders and sacking Highgarden.[8] The Lannisters removed the threats to their south, and their adversaries remained unable to concentrate against them. As long as the Lannister army survived, Cersei and Jaime would continue to rule. Though Tyrion and Daenerys's strategy was coherent, it was still flawed.

In comparison, Robb Stark's (earlier) war against the Iron Throne was doomed to failure. He won multiple battles against Tywin Lannister's alliance, but in the end, these battles didn't matter. Without being able to cut out what was then the Lannisters' true source of power, their allies and their money (which, according to Littlefinger, were little more than just numbers on paper), any victory over the Lions of Casterly Rock was temporary, since the Lannisters were able to hire new hosts to replace their losses in the field.

Tactical and Operational Warfare in Westeros

The lack of appreciation for war above the tactical level appears to be common throughout Westeros. Early on in the War of the Five Kings, we see Robb Stark admonish his uncle Edmure Tully after an engagement with Ser Gregor Clegane's army. Edmure Tully was focused on his victory over Clegane at the Battle of the Stone Mill; he saw Clegane's host, engaged it in a costly battle, and won. At the tactical level, this was a success.[9]

At the operational level, this success was pyrrhic. Robb intended to lure Clegane into an area where he could be fixed, isolated, and ultimately killed or captured along with his army. Battle with Clegane was a means to an end, not an end in itself. When Edmure prematurely engaged Clegane's army and defeated him, he compelled Clegane to retreat, unraveling Robb's plan to trap Clegane and either ransom or kill him. Edmure's failure to appreciate warfare above the tactical level was a costly setback for Robb Stark.

When battles have effects that extend beyond the tactical level out to the operational and strategic levels, they are known as decisive battles. This extends far beyond a simple rout or bloody engagement; decisive battles change governments, language, and history. The quintessential historical example of a decisive battle is the Battle of Hastings. William, the Duke of Normandy, invaded England to challenge King Harold's succession to the English throne and met Harold's Anglo-Saxon army at Hastings. Harold was killed late in the day during the battle, causing the Anglo-Saxon army to break and the Norman invaders to annihilate it during the pursuit. William, later crowned as the Conqueror, subdued remaining resistance in the vicinity of London before some of Harold's surviving loyalists fully capitulated, but the true victory had already been won at Hastings. Hastings had effects so far reaching that it put a Norman on the English throne and went so far as to change the English language for centuries to come.[10] Though the term "decisive" is used frequently, in history they are in fact rare.

If decisive battles are few and far between in reality, in Westeros there are even fewer. Prior to the events of the series, the only decisive battle of note was the Battle of the Trident, wherein Rhaegar Targaryen was killed by Robert Baratheon; it resulted in Robert Baratheon becoming the king of the Seven Kingdoms but did nothing to quell the violence, rebellion, and infighting endemic to Westeros. In the series, there are only two major battles that come close to being decisive: the Battle of the Blackwater and the Battle of the Bastards. However, even in these two battles, the tactical success failed to yield strategic and operational success.

In the Battle of the Blackwater, Stannis Baratheon besieged King's Landing with his army, using the pirate Salladhor Saan's fleet to transport his host to the city walls. Tyrion Lannister employed wildfire against the encroaching fleet and succeeded in destroying many ships but not enough to stop Stannis, who succeeded in reaching and breaching the city's walls. Only the timely arrival of Tywin Lannister at the head of a Lannister-Tyrell army saved the city from being sacked. His army broken and his fleet in shambles, Stannis was sent back to Dragonstone to recover. Stannis failed to take King's Landing and would never be able to attempt the feat again; instead, he turned northward to answer Jon Snow's call for aid. A Lannister king remained on the Iron Throne.[11]

On its surface, this seems decisive, but in truth it was not. Cersei Lannister and her progeny remained set upon by enemies, and the Seven Kingdoms remained engulfed in war. The Lannister alliance, though still strong, was eventually weakened as they were abandoned by Highgarden and Sunspear, the Vale under Petyr Baelish threw its support behind Jon Snow to destroy the Boltons, and Walder Frey was assassinated. Winning at King's Landing did nothing to secure peace for the Lannisters. An analog to a more modern conflict would be the Brusilov Offensive during the First World War—a catastrophic success for the Russians that ended a German onslaught and broke the Austro-Hungarian Army's back. Ultimately, Russia could not recover from its losses, and the cost of success set conditions for the Bolshevik Revolution.

Similarly, the Battle of the Bastards, fought between Jon Snow (born Aegon Targaryen) and Ramsay Bolton (born Ramsay Snow), did not do much to alter the strategic prospects of either Jon Snow or Westeros as a whole. True, the defeat of Ramsay Bolton effectively destroyed the Dreadfort as a power in the North and returned the Starks to Winterfell. But little changed to enhance Winterfell's strategic outlook; the North was unable to project its power southward against the Lannisters, more so than when Robb Stark remained alive. Instead of leading a campaign to avenge Eddard Stark and the North, even with the support of House Arryn, the best that Jon Snow could do is forge an alliance with Daenerys Targaryen to combat the undead hordes north of the Wall. The North remained at war with the Lannisters and no viable prospects of securing victory over them.[12]

Why Are There No Decisive Battles in Westeros?

In review, strategy is combining ends, ways, and means to achieve an objective. Throughout the War of the Five Kings, all of the combatants have employed similar strategies: create divisions within enemy alliances to weaken the main adversary and then use an army to fight the enemy's army in order to seize the enemy's castle. Assassination and arranged marriages are often used as tools to shape the diplomatic landscape to facilitate these military ways, and these tools are often creative. But ultimately, there is not much variety beyond sex, murder, and war.

This is important. A key element of a strategy to achieve a specific end is the way the means are used. In other words, when you change what you target with your means (the "ways"), then you are changing your strategy. In almost every case, the feuding lords use their armies to target other armies and military apparatus (fortresses, castles, etc.).

This begs the question of who or what was being targeted during the War of the Five Kings. What was the connection between Westerosi soldiers and their lord? This is the core problem of why, in Westeros, there were neither decisive battles nor lasting victories, because at its core there was no real allegiance at any level. The great nobles constantly shifted their alliances for their own benefit, and the houses themselves enjoyed no loyalty from the peoples who fell under their dominion. Targeting lords produced no effect on their people, and vice versa.

Much like in medieval Europe, Westerosi "soldiers," in most cases, just happened to live on the land owned by the lord. They fought because their feudal lord called them to fight. They fought for the false promises of adventure and glory. They fought for coin. They fought because they had no other prospects. Make no mistake, none of the "soldiers" who fought in this war were citizen-soldiers with a vested interest in their lord's success. One lord is the same as another; victory or defeat, their lot in life remained constant with the change of one banner to another. Modified to fit the screen and presented in season 6 by Brother Ray, the "Broken Man" speech from the books best explains the lack of connection between the soldiers, their lords, and their wars as a whole.[13]

Unlike the knights they served under, Westerosi "soldiers" lacked training. Training does more than just teach a soldier how to wield a weapon; it teaches them how to steel their resolve in the face of death. Training teaches soldiers to bury their fear to perform effectively, especially when they are so scared that their hands are shaking. Training teaches soldiers to stand their ground, especially when it means protecting their friend next to them. Westerosi soldiers had none of these things. The reward for success in battle and surviving and staying with the army was fighting in more battles. These soldiers had more incentives to desert and loot corpses for valuables than to pursue a defeated enemy.

This was the nature of battle in Westeros. The fighting continued until one side's morale broke and they fled, and the "winning" side was too exhausted and content to pursue their enemy's destruction. As a result, battles fought between Westerosi armies could not be decisive. Few armies were annihilated outright, the lords prosecuting the war did not lose their stomach for war, and there were always more men willing to fight.

None of this is to say that the lords of Westeros would have been better off targeting civilians as an element of their strategy. The people of Westeros suffered enough already, and no one wants to be the king or queen of ashes. Rather, the key point is that the leaders of Westeros generally failed to think beyond individual battles, and even Westeros's most brilliant military minds failed to grasp alternative strategies beyond simply engaging the enemy's power in combat. For battles to be decisive, they have to be nested within a larger campaign, and the ways and means must be appropriate for achieving the end. Operational art was either beyond understanding or too impractical to execute given the shortcomings of subordinate commanders.

There was no sense of citizenship, and both peer and peasant alike knew that loyalty would be mercurial. In comparison, in the modern era, wars are fought and peace is won with soldiers who are also citizens.[14] Originally articulated by Machiavelli in *The Art of War* as "civic virtu," when soldiers are intrinsically motivated rather than extrinsically, the state can expect them to fight harder and without as draconian measures of control. In return, the state must not waste their sacrifices and must offer them a measure of franchise during peacetime. Strategies that target these soldiers and seek decisive battle hold the potential for victory in the modern era because these soldiers are part of the state.

The key reason that strategies failed and combats meant little in Westeros is the soldiers employed to fight in them. War, as a tool of politics, was focused on killing people who did not matter to those prosecuting the wars. As Tyrion reminded Daenerys, "Killing and politics aren't always the same things."[15]

NOTES

1. David Benioff and D. B. Weiss, "A Man without Honor," season 2, episode 7, dir. David Nutter, *Game of Thrones*, aired May 13, 2012, on HBO.

2. Headquarters, Department of the Army, *Terms and Military Symbols*, Army Doctrine Reference Publication 1-02 (Washington DC: Government Printing Office, November 16, 2016).

3. Here, "ends" refers to the objective—the desired outcome, or the "what" of the strategy. "Ways" refers to the "how" of the strategy and how the strategy will achieve the desired ends. "Means" correlates to "with what" and refers to specific things, like armies, navies, and diplomatic and economic resources.

4. A strategy of attrition aims to erode the enemy's means to continue resistance until those means are reduced to the point that the enemy must capitulate. An exhaustion strategy, also referred to as a Fabian strategy, aims to reduce the enemy's resolve to continue fighting over time; whereas an attrition strategy targets means and resources, exhaustion seeks to sap will and morale. Strategies of annihilation seek to neutralize an enemy's means and will to resist in a short time frame, generally over the course of a single battle or campaign.

5. For a study of Napoleon Bonaparte and how he made war, there is simply no finer English study, or history book in general, than David Chandler's *The Campaigns of Napoleon* (New York: MacMillan Company, 1966). It went out of print many decades ago, so if you have the means to acquire it, this author recommends you do so immediately.

6. Erich von Falkenhayn, *General Headquarters, 1914–1916, and Its Critical Decisions* (London: Hutchinson, 1919), 286, https://archive.org/details/generalheadquart00falk.

7. Bryan Cogman, "Stormborn," season 7, episode 2, dir. Mark Mylod, *Game of Thrones*, aired July 23, 2017, on HBO.

8. In this sequence, even Jaime Lannister himself tells the soon-to-be-dead Lady Olenna Tyrell that "Casterly Rock isn't worth much anymore." David Benioff and D. B. Weiss, "The Queen's Justice," season 7, episode 3, dir. Mark Mylod, *Game of Thrones*, aired July 30, 2017, on HBO.

9. For the discussion between Robb Stark and Edmure Tully, see David Benioff and D. B. Weiss, "Walk of Punishment," season 3, episode 3, dir. David Benioff, *Game of Thrones*, aired April 14, 2013, on HBO.

10. The linguistic aftereffects of Hastings and the Norman rule of England are evident today in the culinary world. Livestock is so named after the English words: chicken, cow, pig, lamb. However, the food products from those animals take on their French origins: poultry (*poulet* is "chicken" in French), veal (*veau* is French for "calf"), pork (*porc* is "pig" in French), and mutton (*mouton* is French for "sheep"). The English took care of the animals, while their Norman lords enjoyed the culinary by-products of said animals.

11. This battle served as the centerpiece of George R. R. Martin, "Blackwater," season 2, episode 9, dir. Neil Marshall, *Game of Thrones*, aired May 27, 2012, on HBO.

12. This battle is the focus of David Benioff and D. B. Weiss, "Battle of the Bastards," season 6, episode 9, dir. Miguel Sapochnik, *Game of Thrones*, aired June 19, 2016, on HBO.

13. This speech can be found in George R. R. Martin, *A Feast for Crows* (New York: Bantam, 2005), 533. "They've heard the songs and stories, so they go off with eager hearts, dreaming of the wonders they will see, of the wealth and glory they will win. War seems a fine adventure, the greatest most of them will ever know. Then they get a taste of battle. For some, that one taste is enough to break them. Others go on for years, until they lose count of all the battles they have fought in, but even a man who has survived a hundred fights can break in his hundred-and-first. Brothers watch their brothers die, fathers lose their sons, friends see their friends trying to hold their entrails in after they've been gutted by an axe. They see the lord who led them there cut down, and some other lord shouts that they are his now. They take a wound, and when that's still half-healed they take another. There is never enough to eat, their shoes fall to pieces from the marching, their clothes are torn and rotting, and half of them are shitting in their breeches from drinking bad water. If they want new boots or a warmer cloak or maybe a rusted iron halfhelm, they need to take them from a corpse, and before long they are stealing from the living too, from the smallfolk whose lands they're fighting in, men very like the men they used to be. They slaughter their sheep and steal their chickens, and from there it's just a short step to carrying off their daughters too. And one day they look around and realize all their friends and kin are gone, that they are fighting beside strangers beneath a banner that they hardly recognize. They don't know where they are or how to get back home and the lord they're fighting for does not know their names."

14. I am purposely avoiding use of the term "citizen-soldier," because that term implies a lack of professionalism either in leadership or in soldiers. What is critical is that whether professional or amateur, soldiers bear a responsibility to the welfare of their regime.

15. David Benioff and D. B. Weiss, "Hardhome," season 5, episode 8, dir. Miguel Sapochnik, *Game of Thrones*, aired May 31, 2015, on HBO.

24

Strategic Storytelling in *Game of Thrones*

JAYM GATES

"I want YOU for U.S. Army / Enlist now!" the iconic poster declares, and just over one hundred years later, we still feel that atavistic pull, a straightening of spine, a surge of patriotic pride under those hawkish eyes and that bony finger. It's a visual we all know, one spread throughout media, history, and culture. It's propaganda. It's narrative. Sparse, lean, punched with color and a sharp message, it spares no frivolity in spreading its message.

The 1940s saw the rise of powerful propaganda in the United States. In 1941 Frank Capra began making films for the war effort. He was up against a masterpiece of the genre, Leni Riefenstahl's *Triumph of the Will*. "It scared the hell out of me," he said later, regarding the film. "It fired no gun ... but as a psychological weapon aimed at destroying the will to resist, it was just as lethal."[1]

Propaganda is a common concept, a powerful political tool in civilian and military spaces alike. But it is the result of a strategy, one that makes use of the human predilection for story, a framework to fit complex and often alienating ideas into a cohesive form, the power of narrative. If you Google the phrase "the power of narrative," thousands of results turn up, from courses offered by Harvard Business School to the use of antibiotics. Humankind has always used stories to relate to the world and to better understand it. It is, perhaps, no surprise that it is such a powerful tool for strategic use as well, as it is a form understood by every culture across history.[2]

What, then, is the difference between narrative, narrative strategy, and propaganda? Put simply, narrative is the big story. Narrative strategy is how that story may best be implemented for use. Propaganda is the specific communication and interpretation of that strategy.

According to the *Harvard Business Review*, "A strategic narrative is a special kind of story. It says who you are as a company. Where you've been, where you are, and where you are going. How you believe value is created and what you value in relationships. It explains why you exist and what makes you unique."[3] It goes on to discuss the importance of personalized interaction, a cohesive interpretation of the company's role and goals, and consistency.

Narrative is one of the oldest, and strongest, human strategies. The Egyptians spent incredible wealth on their narrative, building their greatness over generations.[4] The fear of Sparta was as potent a weapon as their swords, a mythology that has lasted to this day, despite the nation's size and short-lived supremacy. The Romans used narrative to bolster their expansions, and the story of the Huns spread terror farther than they ever rode, softening the enemy and changing military strategy even in their absence.[5]

Narrative strategy has many applications. It can be invisible, sowing fear and chaos within the enemy. It can give courage to an army or incite a rebellion. It can swing politics, culture, and academia. It creates a plot that can be followed even in times of high stress. Similar to physical training, it calls to the basic narratives that might as well be encoded in our DNA: honor, dignity, courage, responsibility, sacrifice, justice. If you look at stories like *Star Wars*, *Lord of the Rings*, *Captain America*, or *Game of Thrones*, they aren't new plots; they are stories told on an existing framework that has been reskinned over thousands of years. We've used those stories to illustrate important points of civil discourse, military strategy, government, morality, and the understanding of law.

It is easy, though, to look at something like *Game of Thrones* and ask how dragons, incest, and eunuchs can teach us anything about strategy. Based on the War of the Roses, *Game of Thrones* is a brilliant study of communication, loyalty, and propaganda in fictionalized form. We see conflicted loyalties, shifting moralities, dynamic battlefields, evolving technology (dragons are not so different from our own missiles, as another piece in this collection demonstrates), and narrative influence. Specifically, this piece illustrates how we see in *Game of Thrones* the power of myth and evolving narrative, particularly in the person of Daenerys Targaryen, a very young woman who finds herself mythologized to her known world and also thrust into the role of saving that world. Compared to all of that, being mother to a few dragons probably seemed simple.

Her saving grace was her status as a mythological being born of flame, the Mother of Dragons, liberator of slaves, defender of the people. It was a built-in narrative just waiting for proper usage, and she was the woman for the job.

Daenerys is one of the most adept users of narrative in *Game of Thrones*. From her early interactions with the Dothraki to the hatching of the dragons and, finally, to her great entrance to the meeting in season 7, she understands the power of visual propaganda. No matter how powerful you are, a woman on a fire-breathing, flying monster is going to at least make you pause so that she can get a word in edgewise.

Her development and deployment of the Unsullied is yet another brilliant use of narrative. She has rescued these hopeless slaves and given them a purpose. She is their mother, their hero, their guiding star.[6] If this sounds familiar, it is not unlike the mother and bride symbolism in classic Russian mythology, as well as more modern Communist symbolism.[7] They are fanatically loyal to her, and their faith in the narrative is what makes them powerful.

Looking back at modern military strategy, there are plenty of overlaps. The military of the United States is an army of choice. Soldiers are no longer drafted; they choose to join, often after years of knowing what path they wanted to take. Military lineages run in families, communities, and across cultural divides. Why? Because recruiters tell a story of heroism just around the corner. Grandpa tells a story of brotherhood and the bonds of war. The media tells a story of adventure and glory.

A narrative that can reach across cultural, lingual, generational, and geographic distances must be iconic, clear, and coherent. The tricky part is that the narrative needs to serve multiple purposes, including the offensive purpose of pressuring the enemy.

The American Historical Association sums it up clearly: "Today's war is four-dimensional. It is a combination of military, economic, political, and propaganda pressure against the enemy. An appeal to force alone is not regarded as enough, in the twentieth century, to win final and lasting victory. War is fought on all four fronts at once—the military front, the economic front, the political front, and the propaganda front."[8]

In a global battlefield, propaganda must be instantly understood by those who do not speak your language or share your cultural viewpoint, and so the development of a simple, iconic language becomes necessary. Most of us understand the visuals of Soviet iconography and the distinct style of Russian propaganda and can identify it as such. U.S. propaganda is no less distinctive but less foreign to the American mind, clearly—much of it carried through to World War II and Vietnam and has become a central component of our visual cultural identity. With the rise of social media and meme culture, military visual communication is more widespread and related to than ever, for better or for worse.

That saturation of narrative isn't confined to visuals. Movies, music, video games, science fiction, thrillers, TV, even clothing, the American obsession with all things military is filling the pockets of corporations and creators everywhere. After Iraq and the intensely nationalistic movement following 9/11, there is an almost mythical narrative surrounding soldiers and the military. The narrative of valor, honor, and duty has borne fruit across many levels of society. More than ever, we have a clear example of the evolution of a society that has been steeped in a narrative strategy over an extended period of time.

But the military is a little unique, because it's not a company or brand. It's a juggernaut on the American landscape, and its story is one that has been *lived* by millions in a way that no other story can be. That lived, shared experience gives it a cultural power that is unmatched on American soil by any other narrative. It's binding, a connection that weaves hundreds of thousands of disparate minds into a deadly force, one that feeds the narrative and is, in turn, fed *on* it.

But as mentioned earlier, it is all too easy for such a powerful tool to be used to destroy the cohesion and strength of its users. Miscommunication, misunderstanding, and lack of context can be deadly. For example, Greg Miller and Scott Higham described how some have "bridled at what they considered the unseemly spectacle of a U.S. government entity behaving like a social-media punk." They recorded counterterrorism consultant and former CIA case officer Patrick M. Skinner as saying, "They're trying to reach these kids, but it's backfiring. . . . It's like the grandparents yelling to the children, 'Get off my lawn.'"[9]

As our society becomes more digitized, we face a problem with more miscommunication through lack of context. Email, social media, and even visual and vocal communication programs do not give the nuance and connection of a face-to-face meeting. We are seeing a staggering rise in interpersonal conflicts across the internet, between religious and social groups, and within professional groups. It is far too easy to fire off a quick email, an angry tweet, or other communication that lacks nuance and forgets the audience that will be viewing it and the permanence of the form.

In *Game of Thrones* the endless miscommunications and conflicting narratives come to a head when Daenerys calls the houses together. You finally start seeing what they believe, what they have in conflict with each other, what they have in common with each other, and the misunderstandings. But for the first time, they see it too. It still isn't enough. It's been too long with the miscommunications of the past, with too many hereditary and cultural differences, and the communication breaks down quickly.

That narrative takes a sharp turn when one of the wights is released from its cage. Suddenly, there's no more misunderstanding; there's no "Maybe this is an intrigue," "Maybe this is another lie told by the Lannisters," "Maybe this is another lie told by the Targaryens." Suddenly, it's hard, cold reality.

The dragons and wights in *Game of Thrones* can easily map to superior air power and terrorist insurgents. Dragons present a foe that cannot really be planned for or defended against. Bringing one down will come at terrible cost, and the enemy not only has more where that came from but is likely to be *really unhappy about the loss*, which traditionally ends poorly for those who brought down the powerful weapon. But the dragons don't actually need to be present to destabilize and spread fear. The mere fact that they could show up is enough to leech courage from even a stouthearted force—again, story wielded as weapon.

The wights are a more complex example. Relentless, faceless, unstoppable, they are not unlike the shifting dangers our soldiers face as terrorism becomes less conveniently *other* and erupts more frequently at home. They are people we know, but they are unknown to us now.

The wights are also a convenient Other in another way. The most common tactic of military narrative is to paint the enemy as an alien force. The Japanese and Nazis were caricatures and jokes, the Romans fought tribes rumored to practice the blackest arts, science fiction portrays relentless waves of bug-like aliens. They speak a different language and call their god by another name, and to fight them effectively, the other side must believe that they are monstrous and heartless.

A common villain in a story where no one is really a hero, the wights make a convenient enemy to draw the houses together. But the fear and mysticism surrounding them prevents the living soldiers from understanding how to fight, and it is only when Daenerys and her allies bring fire that a new narrative is born.

It is a narrative we would be wise to heed. The battlefield is changing. The enemy is not what it once was. Technology is advancing faster than we can comprehend, climate change is stressing the human race at an unprecedented level, and Americans are being radicalized at a growing rate. Our dragons may be powerful, but as Daenerys learned, the enemy can get dragons too.

With the rise of globalization, the spread of "fake news," the power of social media, and the rise of new powers, war is no longer just armies clashing on a distant battlefield or terrorist attacks or even house-to-house guerrilla fighting. War is around us every day, from the memes we spread to the way we vote. We have more ability than ever to understand the powerful currents that move armies, but if we do not learn how those currents move, war will become part of our lives in a much less abstract way. As British general Gerald Templer said in February 1952, victory in war "lies not in pouring more soldiers into the jungle, but in the hearts and minds of the people."

In an era of cyberattacks, climate shifts, pandemics, homegrown terrorism, rapid technological advancement, cultural upheaval, war between nationalism and globalism, and strained resources, understanding the narrative strategies around us gives us a clearer understanding of what the world has become and will help us to forge a new strategy to face the future.

NOTES

1. Steve Rose, "The ISIS Propaganda War: A Hi-Tech Media Jihad," *Guardian*, October 7, 2014, https://www.theguardian.com/world/2014/oct/07/isis-media-machine-propaganda-war.

2. Aminatta Forna, "Selective Empathy: Stories and the Power of Narrative," *World Literature Today*, November 2017, https://www.worldliteraturetoday.org/2017/november/selective -empathy-stories-and-power-narrative-aminatta-forna.

3. Mark Bonchek, "How to Build a Strategic Narrative," *Harvard Business Review*, March 25, 2016, https://hbr.org/2016/03/how-to-build-a-strategic-narrative.

4. William Kelly Simpson, "Egyptian Sculpture and Two-Dimensional Representation as Propaganda," *Journal of Egyptian Archaeology* 68 (1982). "Messages emanating from the royal palace were intended to communicate well-defined statements about royal power and allegiance to the crown, while those from private individuals were meant to demonstrate high social status"; Ronald J. Leprohon, "Ideology and Propaganda," in *A Companion to Ancient Egyptian Art*, ed. Melinda K. Hartwig (Hoboken NJ: Wiley Blackwell, 2015), 309.

5. Nic Fields, *The Hun, Scourge of God AD 375–565* (Oxford, UK: Osprey Press, 2006).

6. Annie Shapiro, "Connections: Mother Symbolism in Russian Culture," in *The Motherland Calls*, accessed November 3, 2018, http://omeka.macalester.edu/courses/russ151/exhibits /show/love-thy-mother--symbolic-moth/connection.

7. Joanna Hubbs, *Mother Russia: The Feminine Myth in Russian Culture* (Bloomington: Indiana University Press, 1993), 302; Ellen Rutten, *Unattainable Bride Russia: Gendering Nation, State, and Intelligentsia in Russian Intellectual Culture* (Evanston IL: Northwestern University Press, 2010).

8. Ralph D. Casey, "War Propaganda," in *What Is Propaganda*, educational manual (EM-)2 (Arlington VA: War Department, 1944), available online at American Historical Society, accessed November 3, 2018, https://www.historians.org/about-aha-and-membership/aha -history-and-archives/gi-roundtable-series/pamphlets/em-2-what-is-propaganda-(1944) /war-propaganda.

9. Greg Miller and Scott Higham, "In a Propaganda War, the U.S. Tried to Play by the Enemy's Rules," *Washington Post*, May 8, 2015, https://www.washingtonpost.com/world/national -security/in-a-propaganda-war-us-tried-to-play-by-the-enemys-rules/2015/05/08/6eb6b732 -e52f-11e4-81ea-0649268f729e_story.html?utm_term=.0b7676453665.

25

Resources, War, and the Night King's Deadly Arithmetic

ANDREW A. HILL

"Strike hard who cares—shoot straight who can / The odds are on the cheaper man."[1]

Thus runs a verse of Rudyard Kipling's "Arithmetic on the Frontier," a poem that beautifully and starkly conveys an enduring characteristic of war—namely, that the ability to create military forces more rapidly and cheaply than one's adversaries is itself a powerful strategic advantage. Kipling's poem brutally concludes,

> With home-bred hordes the hillsides teem.
> The troopships bring us one by one,
> At vast expense of time and steam,
> To slay Afridis where they run.
> The "captives of our bow and spear"
> Are cheap, alas! as we are dear.

In this stanza, Kipling brilliantly captures the huge disadvantage in military force generation of the British, relative to their local opposition—in this case, Afridis of the Pashtun, but it could just as easily be the Taliban,

ISIS, Boko Haram, or even Chinese antiship missiles. Precious British troops arrive "one by one" and at "vast expense," while the Afridis literally sprout from the hills, endlessly supplying a resistance that can afford to lose men.

The painful consequences of a disadvantage in military force production is vividly illustrated in *Game of Thrones*, which features the "home-bred horde" to beat all hordes: the White Walkers' Army of the Dead (or wights), reanimated corpses under the command of the Night King, a spectral, blue-hued demon who was once a man. One of the series's most memorable scenes clearly demonstrates the cheapness of the wights. Near the conclusion of season 5, Jon Snow travels north of the Wall to visit Hardhome, the haven of the Free Folk, who have long been enemies of the Night's Watch, which Snow commands.[2] Seeking to form an alliance with the Free Folk and bring them to the safer side of the Wall in preparation for the zombie war Snow knows is coming, Snow convinces a minority of the Free Folk to trust him and follow him on the ships he brought. While the refugees are boarding the boats that will take them south, the Night King attacks Hardhome with a massive horde of wights. Hardhome's defenses are quickly overwhelmed. Only those already in the boats escape slaughter at the hands (or teeth) of the wights. Standing in the last boat to depart, Snow watches as the wights kill everyone left behind. Then the Night King emerges, striding through the mayhem and walking to the dock. Looking at Snow, the Night King raises his arms. Snow watches in appalled horror as thousands of dead Free Folk begin to jerk to life, rising from the earth as new members of the Night King's awful army.

Jon Snow understands the significance of the Night King's demonstration of the power to mobilize a population simply by willing it. Snow commands the Night's Watch, a professional military force. In fighting, an individual, ordinary wight does not rival a good ranger of the Night's Watch. But that sort of misses the point. Rangers are recruited—either by force or by choice—"one by one," to echo Kipling's phrase, from the various cities of Westeros, and their effectiveness is the result of years of discipline, training, and fighting. The Night King can create a wight in seconds. All he needs is the will to do it and a dead body. He has an abundance of the former, and the war against humanity will provide plenty of the latter. Collectively, the wights' sheer numbers and their mindless commitment to fight and kill pose a terrible threat to even the best-trained military force, and the Night King can produce them by the thousands simply by wishing it. Not only that, but every dead enemy of the Night King (even a dragon) is a potential recruit to his Army of the Dead. The "cheaper man" indeed.

Of course, zombie hordes are a fiction, as is all of *Game of Thrones*. It is, as yet, impossible to reanimate the dead and transform them into single-minded killing machines utterly obedient to the whims of some blue monster with a vendetta against humanity. Yet the mobilizing power of the Night King underscores an important aspect of strategy in war that has become all too obscure in American military thought—the ability of a society to produce military forces cheaper and faster than its adversaries. This is a pity, because in many respects the quick production of military force (usually infantry of some kind) is the oldest, simplest, and most reliable of all military strategies—"Git thar fustest with the mostest," in Nathan Bedford Forrest's (almost certainly apocryphal) words.

This problem is not new. For the military theorist Antoine-Henry Jomini, force generation was a minor detail of strategy. He wrote, "Strategy decides where to act; logistics brings troops to this point."[3] John Shy commented that for Jomini, armies appeared as "faceless masses, armed and fed in mysterious ways."[4] The historian Michael Howard lamented the effect of Clausewitz in leading military strategic thinkers to ignore logistical considerations.[5] Strategy, he argued, has operational, logistical, social, and technological dimensions.[6] Modern military strategic thought has tended to emphasize the first and last of these, with little attention to the middle two. Yet as Howard wrote, "No campaign can be understood, and no valid conclusions drawn from it, unless its logistical problems are studied as thoroughly as the course of operations."[7]

The Roman and Mongol Empires were largely built through innovations in force development, and the United States developed and exploited an advantage in force generation to its benefit in the three crucial wars of American history. Indeed, concerning the victory of the U.S. Civil War, for example, Michael Howard observed, "Fundamentally, the victory of the North was due not to the operational capabilities of its generals, but to its capacity to mobilize its superior industrial strength and manpower into armies which such leaders as Grant were able . . . to deploy in such strength as the operational skills of their adversaries were rendered almost irrelevant."[8] Put differently, in Clausewitz's arbitrarily precise formulation, "The skill of the greatest commanders may be counterbalanced by a two-to-one ratio in fighting forces."[9] This is a key point. The generation of force is not just a support to strategy; it *is* strategy. And we in the developed world ought to give it more thought.

Rome's rise was aided by the ability to produce military forces faster than they were consumed. Rome defeated Carthage in the First Punic War in large part because it could build and rebuild a navy. In the first five years of the war, Rome painstakingly learning how to build warships and conduct naval warfare against the much more experienced Carthaginians. Then, Rome lost three-quarters of its fleet—over 280 ships—in a storm in 255 BCE. Rebuilding its fleet, Rome suffered a similar disaster two years later.[10] Rebuilding its fleet yet again, in 249 BCE Rome suffered a significant naval defeat, shortly followed by the loss of over one hundred ships in another storm.[11]

More than a century later, the Roman consul Gaius Marius changed the course of Roman history by introducing what came to be known as the Marian military reforms. Prior to his innovations, in times of war, Roman citizens joining the army had to equip themselves at great expense. Furthermore, the majority of the Roman public was restricted to serving as unarmored skirmishers. Marius changed this, supplying conscripts with weapons and armor provided through the state. He also reorganized the legions to standardize and professionalize them. Although Marius turned service in the Roman legions into a career (as opposed to a wartime calling), he drastically lowered the barriers to entry into the military, "throwing open the legions to proletarians on terms of voluntary enlistment," in the words of historians M. Cary and H. H. Scullard.[12] With the system of force production designed by Marius, Rome conquered the Mediterranean world.

The Mongol example is even more instructive, for the Mongols came closer than any people in recorded history of mimicking the Night King's power of the spontaneous generation of military forces. If you imagine a Venn diagram in which two circles represent "qualities of an ordinary, adult male" and "qualities of a warrior," in Mongol society these circles overlapped almost completely. Other people have attempted to build effective military forces through the normal activities of citizens, from the longbowmen trained in the forests and marshes of Britain to the "embattled farmers," in the words of Ralph Waldo Emerson's "Concord Hymn" inscribed on the base of the Minute Man Statue at the site of the Battle of Concord.[13]

Yet the Mongols seem to have exceeded all in matching civilian life to the development of military capability. Mongols began training for military service early in life, and many of the skills they acquired in learning to be effective hunters on the Asian steppe were equally useful in preparing for war. As the historian Denis Sinor writes, "For the men of Inner Asia military service was a natural occupation. . . . Fighting was a precondition of survival."[14] Sinor continues, "The combination of inborn courage and discipline acquired through constant training accounts for the excellence of the Inner Asian warrior."[15]

The crucial war machine of the Mongols was the horse, which was also fully integrated into Mongol life and "the most formidable single factor of Inner Asian military power."[16] Sinor quotes the poet Sidonius Apollinaris, speaking of the Huns but equally applicable to the Mongols: "Scarce has the infant learned to stand without his mother's aid when a horse takes him on his back. You would think the man and beast were borne together, so firmly does the rider always stick to the horse."[17]

In the middle of the thirteenth century, the Franciscan John of Plano Carpini went on a mission to visit the Great Khan of the Mongols. John observed that Mongol men "hunt and practice archery, for they are all, big and little, excellent archers, and their children begin as soon as they are two or three years old to ride and manage horses and to gallop on them, and they are given bows to suit their stature and are taught to shoot."[18] Thus, Mongol man and Mongol warrior were almost synonymous, enabling the Mongols to generate military forces extremely rapidly. Furthermore, sustaining these forces required little of the mass of impedimenta that characterizes most other armies. Mongol warriors were astonishingly self-sustaining while on military campaign, living on a diet of dried meat and mare's milk.[19] The Mongols of the thirteenth century are the White Walkers of authentic history, for whom readiness for war and readiness for life were the same.

Building forces through rapid military expansion makes sense for the United States, a technologically advanced nation with tremendous natural, scientific, and industrial resources and geographic depth provided by two oceans and two friendly neighbors. Furthermore, with a population exceeding 300 million, few nations have a deeper reservoir of manpower. Given sufficient time, the United States can produce a military of immense size and capability.

Today, however, by both desire and design, the U.S. military generally focuses on maintaining a relatively small but highly effective force and ignores the significance and potential of rapid force generation. General Raymond Odierno, the former chief of staff of the U.S. Army, said in congressional testimony, "It takes approximately 30 months to generate a fully manned and trained Regular Army [Brigade Combat Team] once the Army decides to expand the force."[20] Thus, the modern U.S. Army needs two and a half *years* to create (in the case of an infantry brigade combat team) three infantry battalions and their support elements—about four thousand soldiers total. Why does it take so long? General Odierno cited the complex requirements of "policy decisions, dollars, Soldiers, infrastructure," and the nature of "today's highly technological, All-Volunteer Force" that is "much different than the industrial age armies of the past."[21]

In a nutshell, the U.S. Army's argument is that war is much more complex today, that it requires much more technological expertise, and that building this expertise requires a lot of time. This is highly suspect as both history and analysis. It oversimplifies the past and ignores an important characteristic of modern technology. Consider for a moment the thirty months the U.S. Army currently requires to build a brigade combat team. The United States was attacked at Pearl Harbor on December 7, 1941, drawing it into the Second

World War. Almost thirty months *to the day* later, on June 6, 1944, the U.S. Army and Navy led the largest amphibious invasion in history, employing almost seven thousand ships to land around 156,000 allied troops on the first day alone. One would have to be a tremendous egotist to think that such an operation was not extraordinarily complex and technological in the mere conception. Yet we are to believe that the U.S. Army today needs the same amount of time to create an infantry unit of four thousand soldiers.

Granted, from a global economic perspective, modern military service is fairly unique. Few occupational fields *outside* the military develop the human capital necessary to thrive in a combat environment. Militaries use unique technologies, and the work environment for combat units, with its requirements for physically courageous high-risk decision-making, high levels of mutual trust, willingness to sacrifice, deference to orders, and extremes of endurance in depraved conditions, is even more exceptional than the technology used in that environment. The U.S. Army, therefore, invests heavily in developing the ability of personnel to function in an environment that cannot be replicated outside the military. How can the U.S. Army reduce the required investment without lowering standards?

We can use technology to enhance the capabilities of the average person. This consists of investing in technologies that reduce the time it takes for new entrants to reach an effective level of military preparedness. Military modernization can be used to explain why creating civilian-soldiers is much harder than it used to be. A Sherman tank from the Second World War had more in common with heavy vehicles in the civilian world than an M1 Abrams tank does today. Fair enough. Yet other military technologies reduce the difficulty for an inexperienced, semi-intelligent trainee to achieve higher levels of competence. A well-designed rifle is just such a technology.

Game of Thrones also demonstrates another facet of the power of rapid force generation—winning the allegiance of opposing or neutral forces. The Night King's most capable opponent, Queen Daenerys Targaryen, conquers the cities of Slaver's Bay and builds the foundation of her invading army not through the power of her dragons but by converting the forces of her adversaries, be they the erstwhile masters of Slaver's Bay or the chiefs of Dothraki (George R. R. Martin's version of the Mongols). In fact, the *real* Mongols were similarly masters of transforming opposing forces into useful units under Mongol command. According to Jack Weatherford, the Mongols turned captive peasants into "an extension of their decimal organization of the military."[22] Captives performed menial but labor-intensive tasks such as getting food and water for the animals and soldiers and moving and operating siege engines. The Mongols also acquired highly capable engineering units by bringing defeated enemies under their banner. Weatherford explains, "More than merely using [siege] weapons, Genghis Khan acquired the engineering intelligence needed to create them. The Mongols eagerly rewarded engineers who defected to them and, after each battle, carefully selected engineers from among the captives and impressed them into Mongol service. . . . With each new battle and each conquest, [Genghis Khan's] war machinery grew in complexity and efficiency."[23]

The two greatest armies in George R. R. Martin's fantasy world are built by experts in force generation. The modern U.S. military should take a cue from this and focus on innovative approaches to building military forces.

The development of technologies that rapidly increase the lethality and military decision-making ability of relatively fit, intelligent Americans should be a major theme for U.S. Army modernization in the coming years. But it probably will be ignored, because modern, professional militaries want to preserve military competence as a special category of training and conduct. The more military effectiveness seems like the product of years of investment, the less likely the nation is to reduce standing military resources. The U.S. Army's lack of imagination in force generation is therefore predictable and lamentable.

Alas, the subtleties of government resource allocation give an army in peacetime little incentive to become good at building forces rapidly. Standing military forces are expensive, and unused military capacity is highly inefficient. Civilian leaders will therefore tend to demand constant justification for peacetime military forces. A military that is capable of swift expansion will tempt civilian leaders to give it fewer resources when it is not needed. Given these dynamics, it is hardly surprising that the U.S. Army is so lacking in creativity and innovation when it comes to expansion.

However, an explanation is not an excuse, and we need to do better. In a military expansion, the army is engaged in the production of soldiers. The raw material in this production process is the pool of manpower. The army takes human capital from this pool and invests time and energy into developing it into something fit for service in an operational unit. For the Mongols, the investment required was relatively modest. The modern U.S. Army, in contrast, sees the investment required as vast. Another writer on this topic asserts that all of that time is "essential for [soldiers] to develop reasonable expertise in increasingly difficult military skill sets" and that it is "required to develop even a modicum of expertise on the complex battlefield systems and network modalities of the 21st century."[24]

This emphasis on technology as a barrier to the rapid creation of military force ignores a crucial point—the pattern of technological innovation globally is to *reduce* barriers to entry for normal people to do sophisticated things that used to be the domain of professionals and experts. Software allows business owners to manage financial accounting without the aid of an accountant. We have technology today that can help an untutored person make smart tactical choices on a complex battlefield. On a more mundane level, modern military rifles can turn a slightly overweight, middle-aged, nonlethal academic into a much more lethal version of himself.[25]

The ability to build military forces quickly also makes other things in war less important. The Night King does not need to be a tactical genius to win a battle. In the same way, the United States did not rely on tactical brilliance or individual (i.e., platform-to-platform or soldier-to-soldier) superiority for its victories in the Civil War and World War II. In Greek mythology, Cadmus, the founder of Thebes, slays a dragon and then, following Athena's instructions, sows the dragon's teeth in the ground. To his astonishment, warriors began to grow from the teeth, rising out of the ground like so many stalks of corn.[26] In the Second World War, the United States reaped its own astonishing harvest from dragon's teeth. The military's total strength grew from 458,365 (all services) in 1940 to over 12 million in 1945, a twenty-six-fold increase.[27]

Conflict may not be the natural state of humanity, but it is a common occurrence and one that often surprises us, defying the expectations of even the most forward looking of military thinkers. An old adage asserts that "quantity has a quality all its own." It provides resilience against the shocks that are an inevitable part of war. A society with the power to create military forces faster and more cheaply than its adversaries has a significant advantage in war.

Which brings us back to the where we began. White Walkers (or Mongol warriors or ISIS fighters) are produced cheaply and quickly, while the Night's Watch (or the U.S. military) carries on building its forces, echoing Kipling, "one by one" and "at vast expense." We should be careful about that, because the "odds are on the cheaper man."

The U.S. military has lost one of its core strategic competencies—rapidly generating enormous numbers of soldiers, sailors, marines, and pilots through mobilization on a grand scale. This is not an argument for a peacetime draft. It is a call for innovation in how a nation builds military forces when those forces are needed. Unfortunately, instead of exploring how to prepare people and build equipment more rapidly in war, modern U.S. military leaders persist in a dubious, self-serving argument for maintaining the gold-plated military that the nation seems to need at all times, regardless of circumstances. This needs to change.

NOTES

1. Rudyard Kipling, "Arithmetic on the Frontier," in *Departmental Ditties and Other Verses* (London: Methuen, 1922), 95.
2. David Benioff and D. B. Weiss, "Hardhome," season 5, episode 8, dir. Miguel Sapochnik, *Game of Thrones*, aired May 31, 2015, on HBO.
3. Baron de Jomini, *The Art of War*, trans. G. H. Mendell and W. P. Craighill (Philadelphia PA: Lippincott, 1862), 69.
4. John Shy, "Jomini," in *Makers of Modern Strategy*, ed. Pater Paret (Princeton NJ: Princeton University Press, 1986), 160.
5. Michael Howard, "The Forgotten Dimensions of Strategy," *Foreign Affairs* 57, no. 5 (1979): 976.
6. Howard, "Forgotten Dimensions of Strategy," 978.

7. Howard, "Forgotten Dimensions of Strategy," 976.

8. Howard, "Forgotten Dimensions of Strategy," 977.

9. Carl von Clausewitz, *On War*, trans. Michael Howard and Peter Paret (Princeton NJ: Princeton University Press, 1976), 195, quoted in Lawrence Freedman, *Strategy: A History* (Oxford: Oxford University Press, 2013), 89.

10. Richard Miles, *Carthage Must Be Destroyed: The Rise and Fall of an Ancient Civilization* (New York: Viking, 2010), 189.

11. Miles, *Carthage Must Be Destroyed*, 192.

12. M. Cary and H. H. Scullard, *A History of Rome Down to the Reign of Constantine*, 3rd ed. (London: Palgrave, 1975), 219.

13. Clifford J. Rogers, "The Military Revolutions of the Hundred Years' War," *Journal of Military History* 57, no. 2 (1993): 241–78. According to Rogers, "England developed a pool of strong yeomen archers over decades of more-or-less constant warfare against the Scots and the Welsh—it is no coincidence that Cheshire archers, considered the best in England, came from the Welsh marches."

14. Denis Sinor, "The Inner Asian Warriors," *Journal of the American Oriental Society* 101, no. 2 (1981): 135.

15. Sinor, "Inner Asian Warriors," 137.

16. Sinor, "Inner Asian Warriors," 137.

17. Sinor, "Inner Asian Warriors," 139.

18. John of Plano Carpini, *The Mongol Mission*, ed. Christopher Dawson (London: Sheed and Ward, 1955), 18.

19. Jack Weatherford, *Genghis Khan and the Making of the Modern World* (New York: Crown, 2004), 86–88.

20. General Raymond Odierno, "Department of Defense Appropriations for Fiscal Year 2016," *U.S. Senate, Subcommittee of the Committee on Appropriations* (Washington DC: U.S. Government Publishing Office, March 11, 2015), 9.

21. Odierno, "Fiscal Year 2016," 9.

22. Weatherford, *Genghis Khan and the Making of the Modern World*, 92.

23. Weatherford, *Genghis Khan and the Making of the Modern World*, 94.

24. John Evans, *Getting It Right: Determining the Optimal Active Component End Strength of the All-Volunteer Army to Meet the Demands of the 21st Century* (Washington DC: Center for 21st Century Security and Intelligence, Brookings Institution, 2015), 21.

25. The author of this essay once had the opportunity to shoot a modified variant of the U.S. Marine Corps' M40 sniper rifle. With no instruction or practice, I bull's-eyed a target two inches wide at one hundred yards. After achieving this feat, I remarked (only half in jest), "Even a monkey could do that," and monkeys are cheap.

26. See Ovid, *Metamorphoses*, bk. 3.

27. Data from "Research Starters: US Military by the Numbers," National World War II Museum, accessed February 27, 2019, https://www.nationalww2museum.org/students-teachers/student-resources/research-starters/research-starters-us-military-numbers.

26

The Red Wedding and the
Power of Norms

THERESA HITCHENS

Even for nonaficionados, the Red Wedding episode in book 3, *A Storm of Swords*, in George R. R. Martin's *Song of Fire and Ice* saga, and episode 9, "The Rains of Castelmere," in season 3 of the televised *Game of Thrones*, has become a notorious example of deadly political and military deception. The events that flow from that horrific, and extremely bloody, betrayal also elucidate how violations of norms can exact economic, political, and strategic costs.

The Red Wedding episode begins with Robb Stark, heir of House Stark and Winterfell and self-proclaimed King in the North, entering into a marriage pact with one of Lord Walder Frey's daughters in exchange for the allegiance of House Frey against the Iron Throne held by House Lannister in the War of the Five Kings. But Robb subsequently falls in love with another girl and reneges on that promise. In revenge for the marriage pact's breach, Lord Walder implements a plot (backed up by Lord Tywin Lannister and Lord Roose Bolton) to assassinate Robb. He invites Robb; Robb's mother, Catelyn; and Robb's loyal men-at-arms to the wedding of Robb's uncle Edmure Tully to Roslin Frey as a gesture of reconciliation. As the wedding feast winds down, Frey unleashes his own forces, who slaughter Robb, Catelyn, and most of the visiting Winterfell party.

The Red Wedding is an example of a violation of a societal "norm of behavior" writ large—in this case, the norm of hospitality that sets boundaries on the behavior of hosts and guests. Norms of behavior—both actions that are prescribed and those that are proscribed—not only are the underpinnings of civilizations dating back as far as known history but also serve as an important foundation for international relations and the development of international law in today's world. Norms not only can be implemented via "customary international law" or "soft law," but they can also be eventually translated into legally binding accords via international law and bilateral or multilateral treaties.[1]

The concept that hosts owe guests certain rights (and vice versa), including a guarantee of safety, dates back at least to the ancient Greeks, where the rules were known as *xenia* (guest-friendship) and were protected by the father of the gods himself, Zeus. Indeed, the Trojan War was a direct result of a violation of *xenia* by the Trojan prince, Paris, in abducting Menelaus's wife, thus ensuring Zeus's wrath and his championship of the Greek side.[2] In the pre-Viking Anglo-Saxon world, the rules of hospitality were widespread in custom at all levels of society, and in some cases, they were written into local laws,[3] showing how customs can be, and often are, eventually translated into legal instruments (although it should be said that "laws" in the fifth and sixth centuries were rather more fluid than today's Western concept of "legal" instruments). George R. R. Martin has noted that the Red Wedding concept was based on history, including the infamous 1692 Glencoe Massacre in Scotland—where Clan MacDonald was slaughtered by an army of Clan Campbell after the Campbell Captain asked for shelter from the winter weather on the pretense that the nearby fort was full.[4] The massacre was a violation of King James VI's 1587 edict, "Slaughter under Trust,"[5] designed to reduce wars among the Scottish clans by punishing those who tricked their clan enemies into a massacre by offering peaceful terms, and to this day the Claichag Inn in Glencoe sports a sign above the door denying entry to members of Clan Campbell.

While the concept of host-guest rights has lost much of its meaning in the modern Western world, the long-standing normative prohibitions against deception as a means of military strategy for killing or capturing enemies remain in place today—both via customary international law and via treaties. In particular, the Geneva Conventions define this sort of deception as "perfidy." Perfidy is defined in Additional Protocol I, Article 37(1) and Article 85(3)(f) as an act where one gains the enemy's confidence by promising protection under the laws of war, for the purposes of intending to kill, wound, or capture them.[6] In the Rome Statute of the International Criminal Court, perfidy is also a crime, though it is not as precisely formulated as it is in Additional Protocol I. The definition of perfidy in the Rome Statute, Article 8(2)(e)(ix), only criminalizes killing or wounding, not capturing.[7] In addition, the International Committee of the Red Cross has put together a website that examines perfidy in law and in customary international law by surveying national military manuals and laws, international practice, and legal opinion. For example, pretending to be Red Cross representatives to gain access to adversaries is considered perfidy and a crime.[8]

Treaties and laws can be enforced by various means—although international law requires states to provide enforcement—and generally spell out both consequences and enforcement measures within their terms. Norms, which are politically but not legally binding and thus by their nature "soft law," have neither prescribed enforcement terms nor specific methodologies to do so. Even when norms have been deemed "customary international law," enforcement of violations often does not occur, because states are generally unwilling to act unless their national interests are directly impugned.

In the *Game of Thrones* universe, the conspirators at first seem to only reap benefits from the violation of the "bread and salt" norm of hospitality.[9] House Lannister gets rid of its only real rival for the Iron Throne. Lord Tywin Lannister grants pardons, bestows titles to the houses of the perpetrators, and enacts marriages tying those houses to House Lannister for protection.

However, negative consequences of the Red Wedding ripple out across the rest of the saga, so much so that it totally undermines the stability of Westeros and the belief of the common people in the feudal system of the

Iron Throne and the great houses. It also underpins plotlines in each of books 3, 4, and 5. The distrust and disgust sowed by the Red Wedding is a foundational reason of a number of downfalls not just for House Frey but also for House Lannister that are portrayed in seasons 5 and 6 and in the books *A Feast for Crows* and *A Dance with Dragons*. Neither house can keep allies because of the Red Wedding, and indeed the incident fires the unending rebellion against the Iron Throne. While the Red Wedding ends the immediate threat to House Lannister's grip on the Iron Throne from House Stark, it shortly thereafter spurs several other lords and houses into broadening and deepening their military attacks. First, the collapse of Winterfell lures House Greyjoy to try to take over the North and further its bid for independence. It also piques Brynden Tully, Catelyn Stark's uncle also known as the Blackfish, to attack the Freys and take back his family seat of Riverrun. In *A Feast for Crows* (and episode 6 of season 6, "Blood of My Blood"), Jaime Lannister, one of the three siblings of House Lannister, is sent to help the Freys oust Tully. Jaime wants to end the standoff by offering the Blackfish a peace treaty but is warned by his aunt (who is married to one of the Freys) that this "won't work." She says, "Terms require trust. The Freys murdered guests beneath their roof." In the same book, Lord Rodrik Greyjoy sums up the overall situation in the Seven Kingdoms: "Crows will fight over a dead man's flesh and kill each other for his eyes. We had one king, then five. Now all I see are crows, squabbling over the corpse of Westeros."[10]

Specifically, it is the catalyst for the gruesome incident of the "Frey pies" in *A Dance of Dragons*, which suggests that Ser Wyman Manderly (a Stark loyalist from the North whose son was killed at the Red Wedding) serves Lord Walder three of his sons in a pie, and for the resurrection of Catelyn Stark in *A Storm of Swords* as Lady Stoneheart (who doesn't appear in the show) and her subsequent immortal quest for vengeance.[11] Finally, it is also part of the reason that the Sparrows religious sect are suspicious of Cersei Lannister (Tywin's daughter, whose son ends up on the Iron Throne) and an underpinning to her later arrest by the leader of the order, the High Septon, in *A Sword of Stones*.

Likewise, today, violation of norms also can, and has, come with costs—political, economic, and strategic. States often comply with norms precisely to avoid such potential costs, including political shaming and isolation or economic sanctions. Some violations, particularly those related to gross violations of human rights, also have seen state action to use military force to punish perpetrators.

In one example of the power of norms, in order to avoid political shaming, many states who are not parties to the 1997 Convention on the Prohibition of the Use, Stockpiling, Production and Transfer of Anti-Personnel Mines and on Their Destruction (known as the Ottawa Convention and stemming from norm setting by the International Campaign to Ban Landmines championed by Diana, Princess of Wales) have since decided to comply with the norms set by the treaty, refusing to use landmines and committing to voluntary efforts at destruction. Indeed, the United States (along with China and Russia, a nonsignatory of the Ottawa Convention) now bans the production and acquisition of antipersonnel landmines, as well as their use outside the Korean Peninsula.[12]

China's antisatellite (ASAT) weapons test of January 2007 is an example of how norms violation can lead to political censure and force a change of behavior. China's ASAT test violated not one but two standing norms agreed on by the international community. The first was the long-standing norm against explicit tests of ASATs. Prior to 2007 the last ASAT tests were conducted by the United States and the Soviet Union in the mid-1980s, which subsequently led to a gentleman's agreement between the two superpowers to discontinue such tests, due to concerns about their destabilizing effect on the nuclear balance and the negative effects for the space environment, because of the creation of debris, which poses risks to operational satellites due to possible collisions. That gentleman's agreement, in essence, created a norm that had not been violated by other countries up until the Chinese test. The second norm that the test violated was related to the issue of debris creation on orbit. Space debris—that is, pieces of junk emanating from launch, such as spent booster rockets; failure of satellites on orbit; or collisions with other on-orbit objects—has been internationally recognized since the 1990s as a threat to the space environment and the functioning of satellites. The Chinese ASAT test created nearly one thousand pieces of debris in a highly used orbit that could destroy active satellites.[13] Further, the test came in the midst of UN negotiations to develop a set of voluntary best practices for reducing the creation of space debris—negotiations in which China was a participant. To make matters worse, China had been chosen as the site of an April 2007 technical meeting supporting those negotiations. International outrage was immediate, and China was forced to back out of its plans to host the April meeting. Since that time, China has not conducted another debris-creating, or an explicit, ASAT test.

The 2013 use by Syria of chemical weapons against cities and civilians in its civil war is an example of when the threat of military force was brought to bear to uphold norms. The attacks were considered particularly egregious because they involved deliberate targeting of civilians in a noninternational conflict, something that is considered prohibited under customary international law. Furthermore, they violated the norm against the use of chemical weapons—despite the fact that Syria was, at the time, not a signatory of the 1993 Chemical Weapons Convention (CWC), which requires signatories to declare and destroy all chemical weapons stockpiles and production facilities. A UN investigation concluded in December 2013 that there were "reasonable grounds" to prove the use of sarin gas from Syrian Armed Forces stockpiles at several locations.[14] This resulted in enormous pressure—including economic sanctions—on Syrian leader Bashar al-Assad to adhere to the CWC and disarm. It also resulted in a threat by the Obama administration to respond with military force—a threat that was not, however, acted on after Russia proposed a diplomatic plan to dismantle Syrian weapons.[15] Following negotiations in late 2013, Syria adhered to the CWC, and inspectors from the Organization for the Prohibition of Chemical Weapons (OPCW) found that Syria had destroyed all weapons at its "declared" facilities. However, the investigators also stressed that they could not determine whether all Syria's chemical weapons were destroyed, due to suspicions that Assad hid the existence of some stockpiles. In 2014 and again in 2016, the Syrian government used chlorine gas in attacks on rebels in several cities—although the use of chlorine is banned by the CWC, its production is not.[16] However, it wasn't until April 2017, under the Trump administration, that a chemical weapons attack by the government on Khan Sheikhoun resulted in a missile strike by the United States.[17] In April 2018, as a result of three chlorine gas attacks in February, the United States, France, and the United Kingdom joined forces to launch yet more missile strikes on three weapons storage and research centers owned by the Syrian Armed Forces.[18]

Norms are a foundational element of international relations, as well as military practices. While norms are not always strictly upheld by the international community, violations often do come with negative political, economic, or strategic consequences. Even in the *Game of Thrones* universe, where seemingly "no good deed goes unpunished," the ramifications of the gross violation of societal norms exemplified by the Red Wedding came at costs over time to the perpetrators and to the stability of Westeros as a kingdom. Thus, states (whether fictional or real) should think twice before judging norms of behavior as easily discarded in pursuit of short-term aims, and they should beware of strategic thinking in which the ends justify the means.

NOTES

1. Customary international law is defined as international obligations arising from state practice. According to Article 38(1)(b) of the Statute of the International Court of Justice, customary law is one of the sources of international law. It can be shown by citing state practice, or *opinio juris*. An example is the prohibition on civilian attacks in noninternational armed conflicts (i.e., civil wars). See "Customary International Law," Legal Information Institute, accessed December 4, 2018, https://www.law.cornell.edu/wex/customary_international_law. Soft law is defined as rules that are neither strictly binding nor completely lacking legal significance. In international law, soft law refers to guidelines, policy declarations, or codes of conduct, but they are not directly enforceable. United Nations resolutions are a primary example of soft law. See "Soft Law and Legal Definition," U.S. Legal, accessed December 4, 2018, https://definitions.uslegal.com/s/soft-law/.

2. See "Hospitium," *A Dictionary of Greek and Roman Antiquities 1890*, ed. William Smith, William Wayte, and G. E. Marindin (London: John Murray, 1890), online at Perseus, http://www.perseus.tufts.edu/hopper/text?doc=Perseus:text:1999.04.0063:entry=hospitium-cn.

3. Tom Lambert, "Hospitality, Protection and Refuge in English Law," *Journal of Refugee Studies* 30, no. 2 (2017): 243–60, https://doi.org/10.1093/jrs/fev035.

4. Stacy Conradt, "The Real-Life Events That Inspired *Game of Thrones*' Red Wedding," *Week*, June 5, 2013, https://theweek.com/articles/463588/reallife-events-that-inspired-game-thrones-red-wedding.

5. "Slaughter under Trust," Clan Donald Heritage, accessed December 4, 2018, http://clandonald-heritage.com/slaughter-under-trust/.

6. Jonas Alastair Juhlin, "Rules of Deception" (research paper, Royal Danish Defence College, May 2015), http://www.fak.dk/publikationer/Documents/Rules%20of%20Deception.pdf ?pdfdl=RulesofDeception. See also *Protocols Additional to the Geneva Conventions of 12 August 1949* (Geneva, Switzerland: International Committee of the Red Cross, May 2010), 30, 61, https://www.icrc.org/en/doc/assets/files/other/icrc_002_0321.pdf.

7. Juhlin, "Rules of Deception."

8. "Rule 65. Perfidy," International Committee of the Red Cross, Customary IHL Database, accessed December 4, 2018, https://ihl-databases.icrc.org/customary-ihl/eng/docs/v1_rul_rule65.

9. The "bread and salt" norm is mentioned by Robb Stark's mother, Catelyn, in *A Storm of Swords* just before the start of the Red Wedding; it stipulates that once a guest has eaten of "bread and salt" within a host's home, the host is bound to "do no harm." To this day, the concept of "breaking bread" with an enemy is a metaphor for a peaceful encounter. George R. R. Martin, *A Storm of Swords* (New York: Bantam Books, 2011), 671.

10. George R. R. Martin, *A Feast for Crows* (New York: Bantam Books, 2011), 714, 237.

11. George R. R. Martin, *A Dance with Dragons* (London: HarperCollins, 2011), 437. In the television series, it is Arya Stark who bakes the pies for Lord Walder; David Benioff and D. B. Weiss, "The Winds of Winter," season 6, episode 10, dir. Miguel Sapochnik, *Game of Thrones*, aired June 26, 2016, on HBO. In the novels so far, Lord Walder remains alive.

12. Daryl Kimball, "The Ottawa Convention at a Glance," Arms Control Association, January 2018, https://www.armscontrol.org/factsheets/ottawa.

13. Leonard David, "China's Anti-Satellite Test: A Worrisome Debris Cloud Circles Earth," Space.com, February 2, 2007, https://www.space.com/3415-china-anti-satellite-test-worrisome-debris-cloud-circles-earth.html.

14. UN Security Council, *United Nations Mission to Investigate Allegations of the Use of Chemical Weapons in the Syrian Arab Republic: Final Report*, A/68/663–S/2013/735, December 13, 2013, http://undocs.org/A/68/663.

15. "The Obama Administration on Syria, 2009–2017," Ballotpedia, accessed December 4, 2018, https://ballotpedia.org/The_Obama_administration_on_Syria,_2009-2017.

16. Colum Lynch, "To Assuage Russia, Obama Administration Backed Off Syria Chemical Weapons Plan," *Foreign Policy*, May 19, 2017, http://foreignpolicy.com/2017/05/19/to-assuage-russia-obama-administration-backed-off-syria-chemical-weapons-plan/.

17. Ashish Kumar Sen, "A Brief History of Chemical Weapons in Syria," Atlantic Council, April 9, 2108, http://www.atlanticcouncil.org/blogs/new-atlanticist/a-brief-history-of-chemical-weapons-in-syria.

18. Helen Cooper, Thomas Gibbons-Neff, and Ben Hubbard, "U.S., Britain and France Strike Syria over Suspected Chemical Weapons Attack," *New York Times*, April 13, 2018, https://www.nytimes.com/2018/04/13/world/middleeast/trump-strikes-syria-attack.html.

27

Daenerys Targaryen's Coalitions for War

MICK RYAN

At the beginning of season 7 of *Game of Thrones*, Daenerys Targaryen lands at Dragonstone island, as her dragons weave lazy circles in the air above. Daenerys drops to her knees in the wet beach sand and feels the solid earth of her native Westeros for the first time. Accompanied by her entourage of advisors, she enters and explores the deserted Dragonstone castle. Daenerys continues to the empty throne room, seeing the volcanic rock throne of House Targaryen. After pausing a moment, Daenerys strides past the throne and enters the Chamber of the Painted Table. She does so as a queen, khaleesi, Mother of Dragons, strategic commander, and coalition leader.

By this stage of the *Game of Thrones* story, she oversees powerful land, sea, and air (with her fire-breathing dragons) forces. She occupies a powerful and isolated fortress of Valyrian design. And she now possesses the only source of one of the only substances known to kill White Walkers—Dragonstone. These combined provide powerful incentives for other houses on Westeros to ally with her. As Daenerys looks at the Painted Table, she turns to her advisor Tyrion and states, "Shall we begin?" It has been quite a journey for the young queen.

A key story arc across all the seasons of the *Game of Thrones* saga has been the exiled descendant of the realm's deposed ruling dynasty, Daenerys, and her exploits in seeking a return to the Iron Throne. In the earliest days of this epic series, this was the crusade of her brother, Viserys. He had claimed the Iron Throne as King Viserys III in the wake of his father being killed in Robert's Rebellion. But he never sat on the Iron Throne. After Viserys is murdered by Khal Drago (by having molten gold poured over his head, no less), Daenerys makes the fateful decision to continue her brother's quest to seize back the Iron Throne for the Targaryen family.

The exploits of Daenerys cover multiple trials, relationships, coalitions, and continents, all to support her triumphant return to Westeros and accession to the Iron Throne. Her journey sees Daenerys assume new titles—khaleesi, queen, and Mother of Dragons—and results in her development as a commander, leader, and strategist. Above all, Daenerys develops a profound understanding of the requirement for coalition partners. By the conclusion of the seventh season, she possesses a superbly honed capacity to seek out potential allies, build mutually beneficial relationships, and apply the art of compromise in the quest of her strategic objective.

Before progressing in this examination of Daenerys's coalition-building skills, it is worth examining the difference between alliances and coalitions. These are not terms that are interchangeable. From a military perspective, alliances are formal arrangements for broad, long-term objectives and are often underpinned by formal treaties. A coalition, however, is a less formal agreement for common action between two or more entities (mainly nations but, for our purposes here, also houses, tribes, and ethnic groups).[1] For Daenerys Targaryen the majority of her security partnerships are coalitions—temporary relationships that sometimes come undone and sometimes provide significant advances in her pursuit of the Iron Throne. She has few true allies. Over the seven seasons of *Game of Thrones* it is only the Unsullied who could truly be defined as allies. This distinction between allies and coalition partners is important to remember.

This chapter examines the development of Daenerys Targaryen as a coalition builder. The narrative covers key steps in her development as a coalition builder, while examining the rationale for her seeking allies. This chapter also reviews her personal style and methods in soliciting and building these relationships. Finally, it examines lessons for coalition building that we might take away from the experiences of Daenerys Targaryen.

The recent U.S. National Defense Strategy noted that alliances and partnerships are *crucial to strategy, providing a durable, asymmetric strategic advantage that no competitor or rival can match.*[2] While Queen Daenerys, khaleesi and Mother of Dragons, may not have used these precise words, she was a fast learner when it came to seeking out and nurturing coalition partners. When we first meet her at the start of *Game of Thrones*, Daenerys is the subject of a trade between her brother (seeking an army) and Khal Drogo (seeking a wife). Despite this repugnant treatment by her brother and Drogo, she rapidly learns the ways of the Dothraki, through observation, empathy, and the advice of characters such as Jorah Mormont. She eventually gains the trust of the Dothraki by learning and respecting their ways, including wearing their clothes, learning their language, and even at one point eating a stallion's heart. She has learned the art of influence (a strategic skill in itself) and the value of gaining partners in achieving larger goals.

Her influence sees Khal Drogo eventually agreeing to move his forces, by ship, to Westeros to fight for the Iron Throne. But we soon observe that Daenerys's influence in sustaining this partnership with the Dothraki has its limits. With the death of Drogo following ritual combat and the stillbirth of their child, she is ostracized by the Dothraki. Her capacity to sustain influence with the Dothraki was based on her marriage to Drogo. She learns from this. It is a limitation that she will not allow to compromise her future efforts in alliance building to achieve her seizure of the Iron Throne.

At the end of the first season of *Game of Thrones*, we see Daenerys evolve her approach to leadership through a mix of personal inspiration and mysticism. The majority of the Dothraki have deserted her, leaving behind a small band of her supporters. She appeals to the remaining khalasar that they are free to go or follow her. And she appropriates the mysticism of fire and dragons (soon to be more than old myths) in demonstrating to this small band of followers that she is destined to ascend the Iron Throne.

It is her arrival in Astapor, in the Bay of Dragons, where Daenerys reveals a growing sophistication in coalition building. Accepting the advice of Jorah that she will need to build a greater source of strength to provide a foundation to eventually enlist the Dothraki in her cause, she trades a dragon for a small army of eight thousand Unsullied warriors. Using her new warriors, she captures Astapor. Demonstrating her growth as a leader, she then frees the Unsullied, who all elect to remain in her service. She then uses her new army, and a newly formed partnership with Daario, to capture the second key city in the Bay of Dragons, Yunkai, and eventually the largest city of Meereen.

Later, in season 6, we see Daenerys apply all she has learned to grow the size of her army through a new alliance with the Dothraki. While negotiations start poorly, she turned the tables on an assemblage of Dothraki leaders and burned them all alive. The remaining Dothraki pledge their allegiance to the Mother of Dragons, and she leads them back to Meereen. There she is challenged by the slave masters. Using dragons to burn the slave masters' ships, she negates the threat of the old masters of Meereen.

Not long after, Daenerys is approached by Yara and Theon Greyjoy to form a partnership. They offer to provide one hundred ships to Daenerys if she helps them defeat their uncle Euron Greyjoy. Dany accepts Yara's offer but demands that the Ironborn end all pillaging. The Ironborn agree to her terms; Daenerys and Yara Greyjoy make a pact to work together.

Daenerys Targaryen now commands a coalition that comprises mounted and dismounted land forces (the Dothraki and the Unsullied), an aerial support element (her dragons), and the means to transport her coalition force across the Narrow Sea to Westeros (the Greyjoy fleet). This represents the results of a multiyear effort on her behalf to bring together disparate forces from across Essos and, through compromise and guile, build a force that will enable her to fight for the Iron Throne in Westeros. The final episode of season 6 sees this coalition force led by Daenerys commence its move across the Narrow Sea to Westeros.

Her return to Westeros sees further expansion of her coalition. First, she forms a partnership with Ellaria Sand, who agrees to provide an army from House Martell for the conquest of Westeros. She also possesses a nascent relationship with House Tyrell, forged by Olenna Tyrell after the deaths of her son and grandchildren at King's Landing. The coalition is further expanded when Jon Snow is swayed to join Daenerys in the wake of her assistance to his mission north of the wall. This time, however, coalition partnerships are not secured with threats or armed force but with her personal negotiations with the principals: Jon Snow, Ellaria Sand, and Olenna Tyrell. While her maritime forces suffer a defeat at the hands of Euron Greyjoy and Ellaria is captured, the forces of the khaleesi's coalition are poised and ready for the conquest of the Iron Throne.

But as we depart season 7, for the first time in her quest for the Iron Throne, Daenerys must place this goal on hold. While the perfidious Cersei is the most obvious obstacle to her assuming the Iron Throne, the threat of White Walkers moving south of the Wall is a more compelling and existential threat to her goals—and to Westeros. The Army of the Dead represents the most dangerous obstacle to everything she has strived for. To defeat it will demand that she apply everything she has learned in strategy, command, and coalition management.

The Daenerys Method of Coalition Building

Over the seven seasons of *Game of Thrones*, the Mother of Dragons builds a deep appreciation of the need for coalitions to achieve her goals. Applying her own experiences and the advice of trusted advisers such as Jorah and Tyrion, she develops a sophisticated view of coalitions as a key "ways" in achieving her strategic "ends" of gaining the Iron Throne. The first part of this chapter has reviewed her dawning appreciation of the importance of building and sustaining alliances. As this narrative describes, it was a learning process built on failure and success over many years. Using her experiences, the khaleesi develops her own method of building and sustaining coalitions. This "Daenerys method" has several components.

First, Daenerys always retains a focus on her overall strategic objective of regaining the Iron Throne. She never deviates from this end state. This provides her with a unifying purpose for coalition formation and sustainment.

It also allows her to offer incentives to the leaders of different groups should their endeavor be successful and should she be able to claim leadership of Westeros and its spoils.

Second, Daenerys learns to apply various approaches to coalition building. There is no "one size fits all" to building an effective coalition army. She uses compassion with the Unsullied and with the slaves of Meereen. She exploits marriage to partner with the noble families of Meereen and avoid a conflict that would distract her from preparing for the conquest of Westeros. She applies other inducements with the Dothraki, the Greyjoys, House Tyrell, and Jon Snow in the conquest of Westeros in later seasons. This demonstrates a growing shrewdness in how she differentiates incentives for different coalition partners.

Finally, she demonstrates a streak of ruthlessness in forming coalitions. As she matures in her strategic decision-making, Daenerys essentially embraces a "join me or die" approach. This was used against Dothraki leaders at the Khalifa Vezhven and against the slave masters at Meereen during their revolt against her rule. In both instances, it was a choice between alliance and fire; both resulted in the incineration of her adversaries. Toward the end of season 7, we once again witness this approach when Daenerys has the dragon Drogon roast Randyll and Dickon Tarly when they refuse to ally with her after the Battle of the Goldroad. While this ruthlessness is somewhat ameliorated through the advice of Tyrion Lannister, it remains an instinctive stance for Daenerys and something we are likely to witness in future.

Lessons from Khaleesi's Coalitions

While *Game of Thrones* exists in the fantasy world, it nonetheless offers the contemporary strategic leader useful lessons on coalition formation and sustainment. The building of coalitions is almost as old as warfare itself. The twentieth and early twenty-first centuries have seen multiple occasions where the benefits of building coalitions can be demonstrated. The First and Second World Wars, the Cold War, and first Gulf War are good examples.[3] What might be the lessons from *Game of Thrones* and the coalition building of Queen Daenerys?

First, coalitions allow for the achievement of strategic objectives that individual actors or nations may not otherwise possess the means to achieve. When national resources from multiple nations can be pooled toward an individually unachievable goal, collective action is highly desirable. When we first meet Daenerys at the start of *Game of Thrones*, she possesses little more than her name and an aspiration to return to Westeros with her brother. She learns that as her aspirations grow, so too must she grow the means to achieve these aspirations. Only through coalition building, and the maintenance of increasingly larger coalitions, can she do this.

Second, friction within coalitions may be as significant as that between the coalition and its adversaries. There is deep historical evidence of coalitions and alliances being notoriously difficult balancing acts. Whether it was frictions within the Delian League during the Peloponnesian War generated by Athenian use of its navy or the "caveat management" of NATO leaders for the fifty countries engaged in Afghanistan operations in the twenty-first century, coalition management is a tricky business.[4] This is mirrored in Daenerys's experiences and the challenges of the changing affiliations of the Dothraki and the slave masters and will potentially manifest in the future in her relationship with the conniving and vicious Cersei Lannister.

Third, practical necessity and shared goals dictate the formation of most coalitions. Once they are formed, coalitions need coordination of effort to achieve their agreed common objectives.[5] For Daenerys, her all-consuming goal is gaining the Iron Throne. While achieving this often requires subsidiary efforts, she never veers away from this single goal. It provides the clear and unifying vision for how she views coalition formation and provides the rationale for her relationship building and maintenance for coalition formation.

Fourth, coalitions must be underpinned by cultural awareness. In seeking to build and sustain a consensus around strategic objectives, it is critical that coalition members demonstrate understanding of the cultural norms and sensitivities of their partners. During the Peloponnesian War, the Athenians were not always the masters of this, even though they managed to keep the Delian League together until their eventual defeat. The khaleesi displays an early appreciation for this aspect of coalition building and leadership.

She learns and mimics Dothraki habits and traditions and develops a deep empathy for partners such as the Unsullied, freed slaves, and Jon Snow's forces. As such, she increasingly establishes the capacity to balance her own objectives with the different cultural mindsets and approaches of the members of the collation she leads.

Finally, coalitions are built on personalities. Whether it is the modern example of General Dwight D. Eisenhower's masterful orchestration of partners for the liberation of Europe or the ancient example of Philip II of Macedonia and his League of Corinth, personal relationships matter in building and sustaining coalitions.[6] History's most outstanding coalition builders and leaders deeply appreciate how their personal leadership approach complements the national imperatives of each nation for joining the coalition. Tolerance, cultural awareness, empathy, good leadership, and courage (physical and moral) have defined the great coalition leaders of history. So too is this the case with Daenerys. While these qualities are not evident early in the series, she develops and hones these qualities over multiple years to eventually lead a powerful invasion force to Westeros. These personal qualities put her very close to achieving her goal of the Iron Throne at the end of season 7, before the intervention of the Army of the Dead.

Conclusion

The growing maturity of Daenerys's strategic decision-making manifests most clearly in the coalition that she has assembled by the end of season 7. From innocent young princess at the start of the series, she progresses through a broad range of experiences that hone her ability to build coalitions of different groups in order to ascend the Iron Throne. This demanded a significant level of personal resilience but also enhancing a variety of interpersonal skills that underpin her management of the key leaders in her coalition force that is now lodged in Westeros.

Daenerys demonstrates a growing sophistication in her approach to coalition building and leadership. Maintaining her ruthless focus on the goal of gaining the Iron Throne and applying different methods for different coalition partners, her actions offer a range of insights for contemporary strategic leaders and thinkers. And while the eventual outcome of her campaign to regain the Iron Throne is yet to be revealed, Daenerys Targaryen, khaleesi and Mother of Dragons, offers us an outstanding exemplar of a coalition builder and commander.

NOTES

1. Wayne A. Silkett, "Alliance and Coalition Warfare," *Parameters* 23, no. 2 (Summer 1993): 74–85.
2. Jim Mattis, *Summary of the 2018 National Defense Strategy* (Washington DC: U.S. Department of Defense, 2018), 8, https://www.defense.gov/Portals/1/Documents/pubs/2018-National-Defense-Strategy-Summary.pdf.
3. One useful history that cover this aspect of the Cold War is John Lewis Gaddis, *The Cold War: A New History* (New York: Penguin Press, 2005). See also Frank N. Schubert and Theresa L. Kraus, eds., *The Whirlwind War: The United States in Operations Desert Shield and Desert Storm* (Washington DC: Center for Military History, 1995).
4. For more, see Robert B. Strassler, ed., *The Landmark Thucydides: A Comprehensive Guide to the Peloponnesian War* (New York: Free Press, 1998). Details of the fifty coalition members can be found at "NATO and Afghanistan," North Atlantic Treaty Organization, last updated November 27, 2018, https://www.nato.int/cps/en/natohq/topics_8189.htm.
5. Silkett, "Alliance and Coalition Warfare."
6. Among the references of Eisenhower's coalition building, see Louis Galambos, *Eisenhower* (Baltimore MD: Johns Hopkins University Press, 2018); Carlo D'Este, *Eisenhower: A Soldier's Life* (New York: Henry Holt, 2002); Dwight D. Eisenhower, *Crusade in Europe* (New York: Permabooks, 1952). For a useful examination of Philip II and the League of Corinth, see Nicholas Hammond, *Philip of Macedon* (London: Bristol Classical Press, 1998).

28

Arya Stark's Targeted Killing and Strategic Decision-Making

CRAIG WHITESIDE

House Stark's fall from grace in *Game of Thrones* is a shocking and tragic event for a family whose lineage as the Kings (and more recently Warden) of the North dates back eight millennia. Following the execution of Eddard (Ned) Stark by the Lannisters and the massacre of Robb and Catelyn Stark at the Red Wedding, the bleak prospects of the splintered family, made worse by mistaken reports of the demise of several of the Stark siblings, serve as a foundation for a powerful subplot of redemption and triumph as they eventually reunite and regain their lost inheritance and authority over the North.

Arya Stark plays a significant role in this restoration, even though her journey back to Winterfell, the ancestral home of the Starks, is strange and dark. Her one-woman war, waged behind the lines against unsuspecting Stark enemies, peaks with her murder of Walder Frey, the architect of the Red Wedding, as well as the males of his line—serving as a poignant warning to potential challengers of Stark suzerainty in the future. The irony here is great; while the men of the Stark family serially fail to achieve success by arms and honor, Arya—an unlikely warrior to be sure—used deception and the heart of a cold-blooded killer to achieve some important results on behalf of her family. What should we make of this contrast in approach? Has Arya discovered a new way of war for her house, one that might prove more successful in a changing Westeros?

While it is necessary and fair to judge leaders like Arya on outcomes, this doesn't help us understand basic strategy. Instead, it is more instructive for us to deconstruct decisions in order to learn leader intention, preparation, and execution of strategy. Did her decisions lead to the restoration of her house, or did it happen in spite of her efforts? And what was the cost of her decisions, both long-term and short? I found Arya's personal journey to be a cautionary tale, with a distinct disconnect between her actions and a renewal of political power for her family. Arya Stark's choice to start a solitary campaign of revenge against her family's enemies, over other more conventional options, has disastrous consequences for her personally—and for her family's political future—that should not be overlooked despite the successful restoration of one of the great houses of Westeros.

Emotions and Strategy

The crafting of strategy, at its heart, is often perceived as a rational process. Leaders match ideas on how to achieve a realistic goal with the minimum resources to achieve it. This process, although intuitive, is sometimes criticized for its formulaic nature.[1] For political leaders like the Starks, these goals are linked to aggregating more power relative to internal rivals and external foes. While leaders are influenced by nonrational elements in their goal selection and willingness to expend resources, an appropriate balance between rationality and emotional influences is ideal. In contrast, Thucydides highlighted the dangers of a military strategy driven by popular passions when he described the disastrous Sicilian Expedition in his history of the Peloponnesian War.[2]

The remnants of the Stark family, while not specifically trained in any of this strategic calculus, nonetheless benefited from what could be described as a strategic family culture.[3] Ned Stark, the family patriarch, worked tirelessly before his demise to impart to his children a series of general strategy lessons rooted in family lore, stressing preparation for hardship ("Winter is coming" is the house motto) and the need to work together in times of crisis. This canon is overcome by events when the family crisis hits unexpectedly and overwhelmingly, atomizing the group and precluding much collaboration between key members. The loss of successive Stark family leaders in quick order forced the remainder of the siblings to act independently and prioritize survival over family goals. Each chose different paths to adapt to the new reality. Jon Snow chose political sequestration in the Night's Watch before returning to the family, and Sansa Stark chose to submit to adversary families in the hope of creating new opportunities. Arya's unexpected choice to seek revenge for what was done to her and her family makes for compelling drama, but using it as the basis for a strategy is a terrible idea.[4]

Arya as a Strategic Leader

In some ways, Arya's youthful insistence to her father to be treated as an important member of the Stark's political-military unit is vindicated when she is thrust in the critical role as a Stark survivor, with the legacy of the family to uphold. Of the three able-bodied siblings, she alone sought out training and dedicated mentorship from the likes of master swordsman Syrio Forel and Jaqen H'ghar, one of the Faceless Men of Braazos. This training is directly correlated to the path she chooses to follow and in this sense is a pretty reasonable series of acts.

Selection of an attainable goal while balancing other factors like resources, time, and acceptable risk is the most crucial aspect of strategy making. Considering Arya's decisions after the fall of House Stark, discerning any political or military goal that advances the interests of the Stark family is difficult, if one exists at all. What passes for an overarching vision guiding her actions is a virtual list of individuals who played a part in the misfortunes of the Starks and need to be tracked down and killed. Worse from a strategic perspective, the list grows with the addition of insignificant actors, like the random Lannister soldier whom Arya watches mocking the Stark slaughter at the Red Wedding. This event triggers Arya's decision to give up reuniting with her family and become a professional assassin, with the young soldier as her first victim. Her path back to her family suffers a willful and lengthy detour at this point that tests her mettle and teaches her valuable skills for a fighter who cannot rely on brawn. At this critical juncture, Arya recovers good sense and rejects the false objective of becoming an assassin, renewing her desire to return to her family.

Another key aspect to strategy formulation is the development of a shared faith in a series of actions that in concert should produce concrete results in the attainment of the objective. These steps answer *how* the goal will be accomplished. While Arya never wavers in her conviction of what must be done to her enemies, as demonstrated regularly in her bedtime death-list recitation, she has no idea how any of it will be done. Instead, she adds new people to the list as quickly as others are removed. Nor is there any priority for this list, which even her companion the Hound makes fun of. The events happen randomly, as she careens from city to city with little appreciation for her own agency or her own input into what she will do the next day. Her departure from Westeros to train with the Faceless Man is symbolic of her desertion from the field at a critical time for the Stark family. Lost in the pursuit of her private ambition, she has become what she originally hated in others, like the Hound—an unfeeling, unthinking killing machine.

Inexplicably, she is rescued from an unenviable fate as a life-term member of an assassins' guild by her belated recognition of her true identity as a Stark and the responsibility that comes with it. Finally reunited with her family, she is able to use some of her newfound skills to defend against Petyr Baelish's intrigues and help her sister Sansa's regency of House Stark while Jon Snow is away dealing with the White Walker threat. The family reunion of three tried and tested siblings, assisted by a fourth sibling with incredible powers of sight and knowledge of the past, makes the house a formidable player once again in the Westeros political landscape. It is hard to argue that this happened by design instead of by chance, and Arya is fortunate that her siblings are so happy to see her that they inexplicably fail to ask the hard questions about her choices.

Arya's Game of Many Faces

Arya's list of enemies and her decision to target them individually have some fairly obvious parallels to conflict today. Targeted killing is used by both the strong and the weak in what scholar Tom Greer calls "mirror images [of] terrorist campaigns." Both sides in this asymmetric battle use clandestine methods to strike the other, in the hope that the relentless fear of an unexpected death will terrorize the other side, causing them to quit the fight. These actions could take the form of suicide bombings, drone strikes, or small-scale raids targeting individuals. This would be in contrast to the large-scale bombing campaigns of World War II, whose goals were more linked to psychological warfare than an effective means of hitting military targets. Targeted-killing tactics can be part of a larger strategy of attrition of an enemy force or exhaustion of the enemy's will to fight, and a viable option for actors of any size.[5]

There are valid criticisms regarding how well these strategies work, or if they are even counterproductive in other ways.[6] Nonetheless, they are used extensively, even predominantly by some countries and groups, so Arya's choice to engage in a campaign of targeted killing has some merit. To use this tactic as part of a larger strategy, however, the decision maker must have some idea of whether the end state is achievable and the costs are bearable, as well as the additional risks that might develop from the use of these tactics. These risks can come in the forms of failing to achieve the end state, experiencing excessive casualties to the friendly force or to civilian populations, losing public support, and increasing moral injury among those executing these missions. Slow, deliberate campaigns of attrition or exhaustion are notoriously hard to measure, with seemingly little correlation between individual deaths and the termination of the campaign. How does this one death secure a better peace?[7] More importantly, when is killing in war justified, and when is it murder or assassination?[8]

Critiquing Arya's focus on securing vengeance for her family, often described in dismissive terms as irrational, seems reasonable until one considers the U.S. decisions to use force in the past two decades. The official wording in the congressional Authorization for Use of Military Force passed in the wake of the 9/11 terrorist attacks is brief, and today it is still used as the legal justification for military action on multiple continents. Devoid of many qualifications, it authorizes "the use of United States Armed Forces against those responsible for the recent attacks launched against the United States."[9] Of note, there is no strategic guidance in this document, and the only restriction presented by its authors refers to the existing requirements of the War Powers Resolution, which are too frequently ignored by presidents anyways.

This American policy to use force—constrained by congressional spending limits and the occasional threat to produce a new, more limited authorization—is often justified as an effort to protect the country from attack by external enemies that have demonstrated ill will and a real capability to reach the homeland. Yet it can also, more honestly, be described as revenge for the original attacks and a demonstration of will to deter future acts of terrorism. Security studies scholar Thomas Waldman calls one subsequent campaign—the 2003 invasion of Iraq—"an ideologically driven war of revenge that was only possible in the unique political conditions of the immediate, emotionally charged aftermath of 9/11."[10] In this light, our judgment of Arya's various diversions needs to be tempered by an acknowledgment that she made the necessary course correction in a reasonable amount of time. In contrast, the war against global jihadists continues, with no end in sight.

All strategies have opportunity costs. Arya lost time in her journey that could have been used for better purposes. The current U.S.-led campaigns against global jihadists, as terrorism experts Daniel Byman and Will McCants argue, are too expansive, unjustifiable, and unsustainable. A new strategy that prioritizes efforts to disrupt foreign operations cells, deny militant control of major population centers, and prevent genocidal campaigns would be a better use of time and resources, while keeping the United States and its partners safe.[11] The need to regulate this limited campaign against a dispersed foe is stronger than ever as more important threats to U.S. interests arise.

Much like Arya's misadventures in Braavos, the current fixation with global jihadi movements has possibly obscured the rise of credible threats to the liberal global order as understood by policy makers. Although the rise of China has inspired U.S. strategic shifts toward the Pacific in previous administrations, these efforts have been frustrated by continued diversions to stamp out fires in the Middle East. Efforts to engage China have largely failed, requiring additional thought, an alternative approach, and a laser-like focus.[12]

Our Own Game of Thrones

As a character, Arya never seems interested in the game of thrones, even after becoming an important role player in the struggle. Loyal, smart, and willing to kill for her family without remorse, she has become an ideal functionary for a traditional power family that is desperate to reassert itself. She has learned a great deal and has become a better decision maker through experimentation and experience—the gift of combat, if you will, for those who survive. On the other hand, like her siblings and many others in Westeros, she has survived horrific encounters and seen unforgettable events in her journey. There is a chance that she has suffered what is called moral injury, with consequences yet to be seen.[13] There is also the possibility that her past as an assassin will reflect poorly on the reputation of her house, which has a culture that has stressed honor and integrity. Finally, her connection with figures like the Faceless Man will most likely return at the worst possible moment, with requirements that will conflict with her duty to her family.

Judging Arya for her detour into the heart of darkness is easy for us when we examine her decisions from the basis of normative strategic models. It is well understood that basing strategy on emotions can lead to bad results. And yet a comparison of Arya's decisions with our own struggles to craft a limited and efficient strategy to fight al-Qaeda and ISIS found many more similarities than one would think. While we can take little solace in this revelation, it is possible to use this critique of a young woman and her evolution into a political and military strategist to honestly assess and adjust the conduct of our own efforts to keep the peace in our version of Westeros.

NOTES

1. Jeffrey W. Meiser, "Are Our Strategic Models Flawed? Ends + Ways + Means = (Bad) Strategy," *Parameters* 46, no. 4 (Winter 2016–17): 81–91.

2. Thucydides, *History of the Peloponnesian War*, trans. Rex Warner (London: Penguin Classics, 1974), 414–26, 536–37.

3. Colin S. Gray writes about strategic culture as context in *Modern Strategy* (New York: Oxford University Press, 1999), 129–51.

4. While it might seem unfair to critique Arya's choice here, Arya believes she is the sole remaining Stark not in enemy hands or in the Night's Watch, making her the de facto political leader of House Stark. The merits of her choice to wage a solitary, irregular warfare campaign against her enemies are worth examining here. Revenge as a motive for strategy could be justified, but often the logic of strategy is lost.

5. Tom Greer's book review of Antulio Echevarria's *Military Strategy: A Very Short Introduction* argues that targeted killings are not a strategy but that they fit better under larger categories like attrition and exhaustion; see Tom Greer, "Book Notes—Military Strategy: A Very Short Introduction," *Scholar's Stage*, May 1, 2018, http://scholars-stage.blogspot.com/2018/05/book-notes-military-strategy-very-short.html.

6. Recent scholarship differs on the efficacy and long-term impacts of removing leaders. See Jenna Jordan, "Attacking the Leader, Missing the Mark," *International Security* 38, no. 4 (Spring 2014): 7–38; Jenna Jordan, "When Heads Roll: Assessing the Effectiveness of Leadership Decapitation," *Security Studies* 18 (2009): 719–755; Byran Price, "Targeting Top Terrorists: How Leadership Decapitation Contributes to Counterterrorism," *International Security* 36, no. 4 (Spring 2012): 9–46; Michael Freeman, "A Theory of Terrorist Leadership and Its Consequences for Leadership Targeting," *Terrorism and Political Violence* 26, no. 4 (2014); and Patrick Johnston, "Does Decapitation Work? Assessing the Effectiveness of Leadership Targeting in Counterinsurgency Campaigns," *International Security* 36, no. 4 (Spring 2012): 47–79.

7. James Igoe Walsh, "The Rise of Targeted Killings," *Journal of Strategic Studies* 41, nos. 1–2 (2017).

8. Tom Junod, "The Six-Letter Word That Changes Everything," *Esquire*, June 11, 2008.

9. 107th Congress, Pub. L. No. 107-40, Joint Resolution, 115 Stat. 225 (September 18, 2001).

10. Thomas Waldman, "Vicarious Warfare: The Counterproductive Consequences of Modern American Military Practice," *Contemporary Security Policy* 39, no. 2 (2018): 181–205.

11. Dan Byman and Will McCants, "Fight or Flight: How to Avoid a Forever War against Jihadists," *Washington Quarterly* 40, no. 2 (Summer 2017): 67–77.

12. Aaron L. Friedberg, "Competing with China," *Survival: Global Politics and Strategy* 60, no. 3 (2018): 7–64.

13. Nancy Sherman, *Afterwar: Healing the Moral Wounds of Our Soldiers* (New York: Oxford University Press, May 2015).

29

Ned Stark, Hero of the Seven Kingdoms, and Why the Good Guys Win (in the End)

ML CAVANAUGH

"Heroes do things and they die," Daenerys explained to Tyrion, because they compete to see "who can do the stupidest, bravest thing."[1]

To many fans, Ned Stark, Lord of Winterfell, was just such a fool—more heroic in his convictions than strategic at his core. At least one critic has pointed out that Ned was apt to "confuse nobility with stupidity," while another has assembled a list of Ned Stark's "political missteps" during the first season of *Game of Thrones*.[2] The way this telling goes, in step with Cersei's assessment, Ned was "just a soldier, following orders," and marched to the beat of his own mindlessly moralistic drum—right up to the gallows and his own beheading.[3]

But while some see Ned as naive, others find in him the "show's moral compass," the "one character who's truly unforgettable" and an "undeniable hero."[4] The actor Sean Bean, who played Ned Stark, has said in an interview that Ned was an "anchor" to many fans due to his "principles and morals and values" in contrast to so many of the other "poisonous" characters that populated the show.[5]

So which is it? Was Ned a moralizing moron or a hardened hero? Or is it a little bit of both? Just what can the case of Ned Stark—Lord of Winterfell, the Hand of the King to Robert Baratheon, husband to Catelyn, and father to Robb, Sansa, Arya, Brandon, and Rikkon—teach us about heroes, good guys, and victory at war?

It turns out the answer is "a lot," because even in a digital age full of advanced drones and artificial droids, thinking about heroes still matters. As one political scientist has pointed out, we "can't understand any number of wars and conflicts without paying attention to duty and honor and other romantic notions."[6]

That's because when humans go to war, heroes rise. Heroes inspire others through myths and unify disparate allies. And these two characteristics— willpower and allies—often mean the difference between victory and defeat at war.

Heroes without Capes

The word the ancient Greeks used for "hero" translates, in English, to "protector."[7] The mythologist Joseph Campbell has described the hero as "someone who has given his or her life to something bigger than oneself" and sometimes even "performs a courageous act in battle or saves a life."[8]

So a hero is someone who serves and sacrifices for the protection and betterment of others. This is, biologically speaking, a little strange. Charles Darwin's theories about natural selection ran counter to such an instinct, and he wrote, "He who was ready to sacrifice his life, as many a savage has been, rather than betray his comrades would often leave no offspring to inherit his noble nature."[9] Or more bluntly, as the writer Chris McDougall put it, "Selfish Bastard's kids would thrive and multiply, while Hero Dad's kids would eventually follow their father's example and sacrifice themselves into extinction," and so "if natural selection eliminates natural heroism, why does it still exist?"[10]

Think of the Lannisters' self-interested behavior. Tywin Lannister fret- ted constantly about the good of the family. Darwin's theory might predict that his offspring would do very well in a harsh world. But it's not quite so simple—in many ways, Ned Stark's children had more wind in their sails.

That's because it appears that humanity's social instinct has won out over our individual, selfish needs. We are, after all, the "most helpful species that's ever existed," and at war "we unite in fantastic numbers."[11] And while natural selection remains generally predominant, humanity's social development does favor traits that "introduce highly cooperative behavior into the physiology and behavior of group members," according to Harvard biologist E. O. Wilson's theory of eusocial evolution.[12] That's why two species have essentially conquered our planet—the ants and us.

Society's designated warriors developed codes, or ethos, to push back against the instinctual desire for self-preservation.[13] And looking back over the long sweep of history, Amy Chua has pointed out that each and every world power that has "achieved global hegemony" and dominance was relatively tolerant and able to achieve some degree of loyalty and unity out of very diverse coalitions.[14]

There's a deep tension, then, between the self-inclined, selfish individual and the self-abnegating, self-sacrificial person willing to give all for their society. So there are two ways of looking at the hero. Viewed narrowly through a focused, individualistic lens, Ned's choices may appear foolish, naive, even stupid. But by looking more broadly, at the value of his behavior to a society and group (i.e., the Starks, Winterfell, the North, and the Seven Kingdoms), we might see Ned's choices in a different light.

And this is what heroes do. The Greeks saw that the empathetic drive and urgency to protect others gave heroes their greatest strength.[15] The same idea runs through G. K. Chesterton's well-worn aphorism that the "true soldier fights not because he hates what is in front of him, but because he loves what is behind him."[16]

Ned Stark, Hero of Winterfell and the Seven Kingdoms

Ned Stark was a hero because he served causes greater than himself—his family, his house, and the Seven Kingdoms—and he was willing to sacrifice for them.

Right from the beginning, Ned's actions were consistent with his values, as when he taught his children that the one "who passes the sentence should swing the sword" or the moment he told Arya, "The long winter is coming," and, "We must look after each other, protect each other."[17]

Perhaps Ned's service to others was most evident when his friend and king, Robert Baratheon, asked Ned to be the Hand of the King, the individual responsible for security and defense of the Seven Kingdoms. Ned did not want the job but could not turn it down, because he had sworn an oath to serve the sovereign. He told his wife, Catelyn, that he didn't "have a choice." Catelyn argued, resisted, and said that she could not run Winterfell without him, and yet Ned left anyways to take the job—even though it clearly came at a painful cost to both him and his family.[18]

Ned's service as Hand of the King was sorely tested when King Robert wanted to take an action that violated Ned's ethical code. King Robert learned that Daenerys Targaryen was pregnant with a child that might grow to threaten his throne, and so King Robert wanted Ned, as Hand of the King, to endorse and oversee the killing of the rival house's mother and child.

Ned pointed out that this assassination would have been dishonorable and made the case that it would also be unwise because the two young Targaryens were not a strategic threat, as the Dothraki horde they were allied with would never be able or willing to cross the Narrow Sea and attack into Westeros.

Still, though they acknowledged Ned's point, the Small Council unanimously decided to authorize the killing. Ned resigned as Hand of the King, removed his symbolic fist pin, and then gave King Robert some final, direct, unvarnished criticism: "I thought you were a better man."[19]

Ned was willing to serve, but within moral boundaries. Moral frameworks are important as guideposts that signal to others stable behavior that builds trust and confidence. The deed—to kill a young mother and unborn child—was wrong in itself but also a poor strategic choice. While it may have had some near-term upside (removal of threat), that would have been overwhelmed by a significant long-term downside in the likely blowback as well as in the fear of coalition partners, who would look to hedge their loyalty out of concern for who might be next.

Perhaps most importantly, Ned showed that he was willing to give up his powerful position, and prestige, for principle.

Later, after King Robert's death, when Ned was wrongly chain-bound because he knew the throne claimed by Joffrey (and Cersei) was Stannis Baratheon's by right, Lord Varys went to the dungeon to visit and convince Ned to falsely confess to treason, plea for his life, and "bend the knee" to Joffrey.[20]

Ned refused and responded, "You think my life is some precious thing to me? That I would trade my honor for a few more years of what—the Wall? You grew up with actors, you learned their craft, you learnt it well. But I grew up with soldiers. I learned how to die a long time ago."

At this point, Ned appeared resigned to his fate. Unbowed "in the face of death," Ned showed a type of courage that, Steven Pressfield has written, "must be considered the foremost warrior virtue."[21] Ned was willing to stand on principle all the way to his death. But Varys made one last argument as he left the dungeon: "What of your daughter's life? Is that a precious thing to you?"

This was the comment that convinced Ned to change his mind, to abandon his own hard-edged rejection of the lying, deceitful conduct of Cersei and Joffrey and the Lannisters. Ned was willing to confess to a crime he did not commit and to lie in order to protect his daughters.[22] Ned was an ethical pragmatist, willing to die for his beliefs but willing to be persuaded by the exigencies of life to abandon those beliefs, when necessary, not for personal gain but to protect others.

Why Heroes Never Really Die (and Usually Win)

Heroes inspire others to carry on and unify around certain ideals. Sean Bean once pointed out that Ned was the heart of the show long after his death and that Ned "posthumously guid[ed] the Stark children throughout their own journeys."[23]

The psychological damage caused by Ned's death was truly traumatic— Bran and Rikkon Stark saw, in their dreams, a supernatural Ned moving about the family crypt. Catelyn and Robb could not contain their grief, and both experienced extreme, spontaneous outbursts.[24]

But it was less in the initial moments of grief, which are to be expected, than in the longer shadow of his example that Ned impacted his children. Robb said that Ned was the "best man" he ever knew and that he taught Robb about leadership and fear and how to conduct himself as the King in the North.[25]

Arya and Sansa reminisced about their father's manner and how Ned would secretly watch Arya practice her skills with the bow.[26] Ned's memory, his ideals, impacted them deeply.

Through Jon Snow, of course, we find the greatest remembrance and connection to Ned Stark. From Ned, Jon learned a sense of duty, a sense of law, a sense of justice. Jon repeatedly references Ned in his journey to leadership, from offhand comments in which he cites Ned's aphorism that "true friends" are found "on the battlefield" to Jon's visit to Ned's crypt at Winterfell to Jon's stirring speech in defense of blunt honesty with allies: "I'm not going to swear an oath I can't uphold. Talk about my father if you want; tell me that's the attitude that got him killed. But when enough people make false promises, words stop meaning anything. Then there are no more answers, only better and better lies. And lies won't help us in this fight."[27]

To Jon especially, who called Ned "the most honorable man I ever met" and who acknowledged that he felt Ned was a part of him, Ned's impact drove Jon's life in many important ways.[28]

Jon's leadership is a direct continuation of Ned's tutelage and ideals. That's because Ned inspired Jon and he taught Jon the right way to live, focused on a purpose (and a "Why?") as opposed to narrow considerations centered on short-term gains and tactical considerations (i.e., "What's in it for me?"). Simon Sinek, a writer on modern leadership, refers to this distinction as the playing of finite versus infinite life-games.[29]

Ned Stark and his direct extension, Jon Snow, practice leadership that lives on because they put principles first. And people are loyal to them for that reason.

The Lannisters—Tywin, Jamie, and Cersei in particular—provide a useful contrast. They seek cheap victories through indirect methods, which, in some ways, Sun Tzu would likely appreciate. When Tywin struck a deal with Walder Frey to put down the Stark threat in the infamous Red Wedding; when Jamie used leverage and trickery to break the Blackfish's grip on the castle at Riverrun; when Cersei wielded wildfire to blow up a significant part of King's Landing to wipe out her rivals—these were short-term gains with long-term consequences. And that long-term consequence is clear— nearly nobody wants to ally with the devil.

As Cersei put it, "When you play the game of thrones, you win or you die. . . . There is no middle ground."[30] This is the Lannister fallacy—that leadership is zero sum, all or nothing, and focused on limited gains.

The reality, which Ned Stark shows us, is that heroes unify others through their good will and principled leadership. King Robert once tried to teach this principle to Cersei, who apparently did not learn it, when he asked her whether five or one was the "greater number." That's when he held up a hand, with the five fingers splayed, and then balled them together into a fist—a perfect representation of the military principle of unity of command.[31]

That's what heroes do. They unify.

And they inspire myths. We live by myths, much more than we know, and myths go on to inspire new heroes.

Yuval Noah Harari's influential book *Sapiens* noted that humanity's rise is "rooted in common myths."[32] According to Joseph Campbell, myths are "stories about the wisdom of life" that have a sociological function in that they often validate a "certain social order."[33] They also can serve a pedagogical purpose—to teach us to live better lives. Historian William McNeill once argued that such myths are at the "basis of human society."[34]

Ned Stark was a hero who served and sacrificed. He did not win, in the classic sense, in his lifetime.

But because he unified others through his conduct and principles and inspired others through his life and the mythmaking that extended his life's example, he gave rise to others who took up and carried on with the cause after he fell.

That's the lesson we can take from Ned Stark, hero of the Seven Kingdoms—especially if Jon Snow and the Starks' partners are successful in gaining the Iron Throne. The good guys usually do win in the end; it just takes a little longer.

NOTES

1. David Benioff and D. B. Weiss, "Beyond the Wall," season 7, episode 6, dir. Alan Taylor, *Game of Thrones*, aired August 20, 2017, on HBO.

2. Paul, "My New Favorite Thing, Stupid Ned Stark," *Unreality Magazine*, 2011, http://unrealitymag .com/television/my-new-favorite-thing-stupid-ned-stark/; Dan Selcke, "And the Dead Game of Thrones Characters Fans Miss the Most Is . . . ," *Winter Is Coming*, February 3, 2016, https:// winteriscoming.net/2016/02/03/and-the-dead-game-of-thrones-characters-fans-miss-the -most-is/.

3. Bryan Cogman, "Cripples, Bastards, and Broken Things," season 1, episode 4, dir. Brian Kirk, *Game of Thrones*, aired May 8, 2011, on HBO.

4. Cicero Estrella, "'Game of Thrones': Is Ned Stark Being Resurrected for the Final Season?" *San Jose (CA) Mercury News*, March 14, 2018, https://www.mercurynews.com/2018/03/14 /game-of-thrones-is-ned-stark-being-resurrected-for-the-final-season/; Leigh Blickley and Bill Bradley, "Sean Bean's Role in 'Game of Thrones' Was Much Bigger Than You Thought," *Huffington Post*, March 17, 2018, https://www.huffingtonpost.com/entry/sean-bean-game-of -thrones_us_5aa6b621e4b087e5aaeca1fc; Rod Lurie, "Rod Lurie (*Straw Dogs*) Talks David Benioff and D. B. Weiss' *Game of Thrones*," *Talkhouse*, May 23, 2014, https://www.talkhouse .com/rod-lurie-straw-dogs-talks-david-benioffs-game-of-thrones/.

5. Blickley and Bradley, "Sean Bean's Role."

6. Brian Rathbun, "Ned Is Dead, Baby. Ned Is Dead," *Duck of Minerva*, June 14, 2011, http:// duckofminerva.com/2011/06/ned-is-dead-baby-ned-is-dead.html.

7. Christopher McDougall, *Natural Born Heroes: How a Daring Band of Misfits Mastered the Lost Secrets of Strength and Endurance* (New York: Alfred A. Knopf, 2015), 26.

8. Joseph Campbell, *The Power of Myth*, with Bill Moyers (New York: Anchor Books, 1991), 151–52.

9. Charles Darwin, quoted in McDougall, *Natural Born Heroes*, 26.

10. McDougall, *Natural Born Heroes*, 26.

11. McDougall, *Natural Born Heroes*, 205.

12. See E. O. Wilson, *The Social Conquest of Earth* (New York: Liveright, 2012).

13. Steven Pressfield, *The Warrior Ethos* (New York: Black Irish Entertainment, 2011), 12–13.

14. Amy Chua, *Day of Empire: How Hyperpowers Rise to Global Dominance—And Why They Fall* (New York: Doubleday, 2007), xxi, xxiv, 330, 336.

15. McDougall, *Natural Born Heroes*, 204.

16. G. K. Chesterton, *Illustrated London News*, January 14, 1911, available at "Quotations of G. K. Chesterton," American Chesterton Society, https://www.chesterton.org/quotations-of-g-k -chesterton/#War%20and%20politics.

17. David Benioff and D. B. Weiss, "Winter Is Coming," season 1, episode 1, dir. Tim Van Patten, *Game of Thrones*, aired April 17, 2011, on HBO; David Benioff and D. B. Weiss, "Lord Snow," season 1, episode 3, dir. Brian Kirk, *Game of Thrones*, aired May 1, 2011, on HBO.

18. Benioff and Weiss, "Winter Is Coming"; David Benioff and D. B. Weiss, "The Kingsroad," season 1, episode 2, dir. Tim Van Patten, *Game of Thrones*, aired April 24, 2011, on HBO.

19. David Benioff and D. B. Weiss, "The Wolf and the Lion," season 1, episode 5, dir. Brian Kirk, *Game of Thrones*, aired May 15, 2011, on HBO.

20. David Benioff and D. B. Weiss, "Baelor," season 1, episode 9, dir. Alan Taylor, *Game of Thrones*, aired June 12, 2011, on HBO.

21. See Pressfield, *Warrior Ethos*, 13.

22. To forestall his execution, Ned Stark confessed to a crime he did not commit to save his family during season 1, episode 9. He said, "I am Eddard Stark, Lord of Winterfell and Hand of the King. I come before you to confess my treason, in the sight of gods and men. I betrayed the faith of my king and the trust of my friend Robert. I swore to defend and protect his children, but before his blood was cold, I plotted to murder his son and seize the throne for myself. Let the High Septon and Baelor the Blessed bear witness to what I say. Joffrey Baratheon is the one true heir to the Iron Throne, by the grace of all the gods, Lord of the Seven Kingdoms and Protector of the Realm."

23. Blickley and Bradley, "Sean Bean's Role."

24. Robb Stark repeatedly hits a tree with his sword and says: "I'll kill them all. Every one of them"; David Benioff and D. B. Weiss, "Fire and Blood," season 1, episode 10, dir. Alan Taylor, *Game of Thrones*, aired June 19, 2011, on HBO.

25. David Benioff and D. B. Weiss, "Prince of Winterfell," season 2, episode 8, dir. Alan Taylor, *Game of Thrones*, aired May 20, 2012, on HBO.

26. Benioff and Weiss, "Beyond the Wall."

27. David Benioff and D. B. Weiss, "The Winds of Winter," season 6, episode 10, dir. Miquel Sapochnik, *Game of Thrones*, aired June 26, 2016, on HBO; David Benioff and D. B. Weiss, "Dragonstone," season 7, episode 1, dir. Jeremy Podeswa, *Game of Thrones*, aired July 16, 2017, on HBO; David Benioff and D. B. Weiss, "The Dragon and the Wolf," season 7, episode 7, dir. Jeremy Podeswa, *Game of Thrones*, aired August 27, 2017, on HBO.

28. Benioff and Weiss, "Beyond the Wall"; Benioff and Weiss, "Dragon and the Wolf."

29. By focusing on "why," you acknowledge principles and ideals that essentially have no end. But by overemphasizing short-term, narrow objectives, like money or power, you focus on finite issues that are ultimately unsatisfactory. Simon Sinek, "Simon Sinek with Arthur Brooks: 92Y Talks Episode 131," *92Y Talks*, podcast, MP3 audio, 1:20:32, February 22, 2018, http://92yondemand.org/simon-sinek-arthur-brooks-92y-talks-episode-131.

30. David Benioff and D. B. Weiss, "You Win or You Die," season 1, episode 7, dir. Daniel Minahan, *Game of Thrones*, aired May 29, 2011, on HBO.

31. Benioff and Weiss, "Wolf and the Lion."

32. See Yuval Noah Harari, *Sapiens: A Brief History of Humankind* (New York: Harper Collins, 2015), 30.

33. Campbell, *Power of Myth*, 39.

34. William H. McNeill, "The Care and Repair of Public Myth," *Foreign Affairs* 61, no. 1 (Fall 1982), https://www.foreignaffairs.com/articles/1982-09-01/care-and-repair-public-myth.

White Walkers and the Nature of War

PAUL SCHARRE

When Jon Snow comes face-to-face with the Night King and his army at Hardhome, it's clear they are an enemy like nothing he has seen before. Defeating the White Walkers will require new weapons, such as dragonglass, and new tactics, like using fire against the wights, the White Walkers' army of undead foot soldiers. But even more than that, the enemy's inhumanity means that the fundamental nature of the conflict Jon Snow is engaged in is different from other wars against humans. The wights show no fatigue or fear, and at least at the start of season 8, the White Walkers' aims are unknown. They seem uninterested in negotiation and immune to the political intrigue, subterfuge, and shifting alliances that are so common among the human wars of Westeros. The war Jon Snow and his allies are fighting against the White Walkers is unlike any other war they have fought in the past, if it is a war at all.

The Character of Warfare and the Nature of War

In Western military circles, it is common to speak of the ever-changing character of warfare and the immutable and unchanging nature of war.[1] *Warfare* refers to the means and methods of fighting and is constantly in flux as militaries develop new tactics, technologies, and strategies. The essential nature of *war*, however, is timeless. War is a violent struggle among competing groups of people for political power.[2] Or as the Prussian strategist Carl von Clausewitz wrote, "War therefore is an act of violence to compel our opponent to fulfil our will."[3] Even while the means and methods of fighting (the character of warfare) change over time, all wars have common characteristics that stem from its unchanging, underlying nature. One of the U.S. Marine Corps' fundamental doctrine publications, *Warfighting*, states in its chapter on the nature of war, "The essence of war is a violent struggle between two hostile, independent, and irreconcilable wills, each trying to impose itself on the other. War is fundamentally an interactive social process."[4]

It may seem strange to describe war as an "interactive social process," but as practitioners and observers know, war is a human endeavor.[5] It is a struggle between people, even if the tools they use evolve over time. Because of the human nature of war, some elements of war are constant. Wars are motivated by, as Thucydides wrote some 2,400 years ago, some combination of "fear, honor, and interest."[6] Once underway, violence, uncertainty, and chance rule the battlefield. The life of the warfighter across all ages has been marked by danger, physical exertion, exhaustion, and suffering. And battlefields are home to what Clausewitz described as friction, which is best summed up in his statement, "Everything is very simple in War, but the simplest thing is difficult."[7] Friction is the message that didn't make it through to a unit, the supply train that got lost in the night, the vehicle that got stuck in the mud, and the battle that was lost as a result.

Could the Nature of War Change?

There is great value in differentiating between continuity and change in war. War is the most extreme of human endeavors, taxing individuals and even entire nations to their maximum limit with the gravest of consequences on the line. Yet militaries, in truth, rarely fight wars, or at least not big ones. Most of the time—thankfully—nations are at peace and militaries occupy their time with training and preparing for war. Knowing how best to prepare, however, is an immense intellectual challenge, akin to training a professional sports team for a game that is played only once a generation, where the rules are unknown and constantly changing and where losing a play could mean death. Military scholars have quite reasonably sought to distill from the millennia-long history of war some lessons to guide their planning.

There is danger, however, in leaping from the well-founded observation that wars in the past have always had certain commonalities to a future-looking statement that the nature of war can *never* change. If the nature of war is to mean anything, it should be possible to define conditions under which it might change, even if those conditions seem unlikely. To assert simply that it cannot change, no matter what, is not a scientific statement—it's a faith-based statement. Then military thinkers are no longer studying war, but war becomes a religion and Clausewitz a prophet. If scholars of war want to truly understand it, then they must open their minds to the possibility that the nature of war might change.

James Mattis, retired general of the U.S. Marines and secretary of defense under President Donald Trump, has raised precisely this intriguing possibility. During a conversation with reporters about artificial intelligence, he remarked, "I'm certainly questioning my original premise that the fundamental nature of war will not change. You've got to question that now. I just don't have the answers yet."[8] Mattis's statement is a bold proposition in Western military circles and one that challenges a tightly held dogma about the unchanging nature of war. Yet there are a number of disruptive technologies, including artificial intelligence and synthetic biology, that are certain to change the character of warfare and quite possibly raise intriguing questions about the nature of war. It's a bold assertion, but one worth considering. What would it mean for the nature of war to change?

The War against the White Walkers

Game of Thrones gives us a good vehicle to consider this question. We can examine a conflict—albeit a fictional and fantastical one—in which the nature of war might be different. So what is the nature of the conflict Jon Snow is fighting against the White Walkers?

There are many elements of the fight against the White Walkers that illustrate the changing character of warfare. The wights are already dead, and so they are unbothered by wounds that would kill a human, like an arrow to the head. Wights move with an unnatural speed. White Walkers' weapons will shatter a traditional sword. And the White Walkers can be harmed only with dragonglass or Valyrian steel (and possibly dragon fire). Jon Snow takes these lessons learned at Hardhome and other battles to refine his army's tactics and weapons. These are examples of the changing character of warfare in action.

But the White Walkers and their wight soldiers present a much deeper and more fundamental challenge to the nature of war—they are no longer human. Again, war—at least war as we conceive of it now—is a human endeavor. This is not merely a minor definitional issue, arguing that all wars have in the past been between humans. The fact that war is fought by humans against other humans is foundational to its nature. War is political—"a continuation of policy by other means," as Clausewitz described it.[9] But what are the White Walkers' aims? Are they also motivated by some combination of "fear, honor, and interest"? Do they seek power in a sense that the Westerosi lords would understand? At the outset of season 8, we simply do not know. It is possible that they have humanlike aims and motivations. It is also possible that they have no more desires than a virus has.

Even if their motivations could be understood in human terms, the inhuman nature of the White Walkers and the wights means that many commonalities in wars against people do not apply. Strategy often involves anticipating an enemy's move and using deception to trick an enemy. The ancient Chinese strategist Sun Tzu stated, "All warfare is based on deception."[10] Anticipation and deception require a working theory of mind in order to predict how an enemy thinks. While White Walkers are clearly sentient, it isn't clear how similar their thought processes are to humans. Some fan theories speculate that they can even see the future, which would fundamentally change essential elements of warfare, like deception.

In battle, the undead wights are immune to many of the challenges that human warfighters face. The U.S. Marine Corps' *Warfighting* manual observes that "individual conscience, emotion, fear, courage, morale, leadership, or esprit" are important, intangible "moral forces" in war that exert an even greater influence on the outcome of war than physical forces.[11] On fear in particular, the manual states, "Since war is a human phenomenon, fear, the human reaction to danger, has a significant impact on the conduct of war. Everybody feels fear. Fear contributes to the corrosion of will. Leaders must foster the courage to overcome fear, both individually and within the unit. Courage is not the absence of fear; rather, it is the strength to overcome fear."[12]

The wights do not feel fear, fatigue, conscience, or emotion. Their morale cannot be sapped; their esprit de corps cannot be broken. They are an unthinking and unfeeling wave of partially decayed flesh, more like a natural force than a human opponent. When Jon and his band of raiders are trapped beyond the Wall, there is never a sense that the wights might tire of their siege or succumb to fatigue or exhaustion. The Marine Corps manual points out that (for humans) "it is physically impossible to sustain a high tempo of activity indefinitely. . . . The tempo of war will fluctuate from periods of intense combat to periods in which activity is limited to information gathering, replenishment, or redeployment."[13] The wights do not need to rest, however. They are unburdened from supply lines or the need to tend to their wounded and bury their dead. They are already dead. These moral forces of war still weigh on Jon and his comrades and are an aspect of war for them, but not for their enemy. The nature of *this* war is different.

The war against the White Walkers is a kind of war, but it is different than any of the wars among the humans of Westeros. The inhuman nature of the enemy means that some elements of the nature of war have changed. Definitionally, this presents something of a challenge. If it does not meet all the criteria that define war, then what is it? The most sensible approach would be to define it as another kind of war, broadening the horizon for what war is into two categories—human wars and wars against nonhumans.

Prospects for Changes in the Nature of War

Short of a White Walker invasion, it is possible to envision scenarios in the real world where evolutions in technology do indeed truly lead to changes in the nature of war itself. Five possibilities are outlined below. None of these possibilities are necessarily likely, either in the short term or the long term. They are most certainly not predictions. Rather, they are merely thought experiments to help conceive of developments that might require a rethinking of the nature of war.

War against a Nonhuman Adversary

The most obvious candidate for a nonhuman adversary in war would be advances in artificial intelligence that could lead to the creation of an artificial entity that would pursue its own aims in a conflict. These aims need not be aligned with human desires or even appear sensible from a human standpoint. In science fiction, AI is often depicted as "waking up" and turning against humans, but that need not be the case. AI threats could come from nonsentient but intelligent AI systems, like an adaptive cyberweapon that is capable of resource acquisition, planning, and causing harm and is pursuing its own aims. While such an AI system would originally be designed by humans, it could slip out of control due to an accident. In fact, designing goal-driven intelligent systems that stay within the bounds of intended human design is an unsolved problem in machine learning and artificial intelligence.[14]

Changes in Human Nature

Synthetic biology offers the potential to alter humans directly, leading to the prospect of wars in the future that are still fought by humans, but humans who are unlike those who fought wars in the past. While still science fiction today, it is possible to imagine a world in which biological advances empower humans to fight without fatigue, exhaustion, conscience, fear, or mental weakness. Such a development would change the nature of war, humanity's relationship with it, and even humanity itself.

Changes in Human Organization

War is not merely violence. It is organized violence among competing groups for political aims. Social media is a new tool of organizing humans, and its introduction is as profound as that of the printing press. Already, social media has demonstrated a radically democratized information landscape where ideas and memes can spread virally without any hierarchical human organization to promote them. This has, among other things, led to a transformation in the nature of terrorist threats. The Islamic State is both an organization and a decentralized global movement that can inspire people around the globe through social media to carry out lone-wolf attacks on their own. The organization can be destroyed. Defeating the ideas is much harder. In the space of ideas (but not yet violence), competing ideologies and memes spread and evolve on social media in cycles of reaction and counterreaction. While organizations and groups may participate in these cycles of ideas, generating hashtags and arguments, they do not control the spread of ideas. No one does.

Changes in the nature of war are unlikely at the current state of social media, but we are only at the beginning of a new age of human communication. It would be unwise to anticipate that social media in its current incarnation will remain static. As digital technology evolves, the depth and breadth of human communication will continue to evolve as well. It is possible to conceive of future forms of democratized human communication that could lead to viral outbreaks of violence by individuals radicalized by social media. If this violence caused reactions and counterreactions, it is conceivable that it might occur on the scale of what we think of as war, particularly if other advances in future technology increase the destructive potential of individuals (for example, if advances in synthetic biology made it possible for individuals to create virulent pathogens in a garage that could target certain racial or ethnic groups). Such an activity would have many characteristics of war—violence, uncertainty, suffering, friction, political motivations, and human aims—but not the organization that has characterized wars in the past. This could make it uniquely difficult to control or end such wars, since it would not be a war among any groups or entities as they have traditionally been conceived—such as nation-states, tribes, religions, or paramilitary organizations. Rather, it would be a violent struggle for political supremacy among competing ideas. Individual humans would be both the authors and agents of those ideas, but there would be no organizations to sit at a negotiating table or declare an end to the war. The nature of such a war would be different than that of wars in the past, driven by an unprecedented change in human organization and communication.

Weapons Whose Destructiveness Renders Politics Irrelevant

The twentieth century saw the advent of nuclear weapons whose destructive power eclipsed human understanding, and the twenty-first century has the potential for even more transformative weapons in artificial intelligence and synthetic biology. It is possible to imagine weapons so destructive that they render politics irrelevant, since everyone would be dead. A hypothesized doomsday device that destroyed humanity would be such a weapon. There could be no rational policy aims for actually using such a weapon, since there would be no political outcome to achieve after its use. There might be reasons to threaten to use such a weapon and even to brandish one, as a threat of mutual suicide, but none for its use. Many wars have been fought in which both sides came out worse than before, but a war that was certain to obliterate both sides would be a war unlike any other. It would shift conflict to coercion and brinkmanship beforehand, a contest not in violence but in risk-taking. The nature of this contest would have some similarities to war but would be different in other ways. And if such a war were actually fought, it would be unprecedented—a war without any purpose.

Nuclear weapons flirt with this threshold of destructiveness, with some defense intellectuals arguing that the only purpose of nuclear weapons is to prevent the other side from using them.[15] Certainly, no rational policy aims could be achieved in a mass exchange of nuclear weapons among superpowers. Even more destructive weapons are conceivable. During the Cold War one conceptualized weapon was a salted nuke, which would leave radioactive fallout that could render an area uninhabitable for generations and an arsenal of which could extinguish humanity. Other potential dooms-day devices include bioengineered plagues or AI weapons.

War without Political Aims

Another conceivable development in weapons could be automation that led to automatic war without political aims—that is to say, a set of machine-enabled reactions and counterreactions that led to a war without human intent. Humans would have designed the system, but once in place, the system would spring into action of its own accord. If everything works according to plan, then the automation would be the embodiment of human intent. But if things were to go awry—if this automated network of reactions were to interact with the enemy or the real world in some unexpected way leading to a reaction that was *not* intended by humans—then the result would be something else entirely: a war without political aims.

While mishaps from malfunctioning machines are a part of everyday life in the form of software bugs and frozen computer screens and occasionally lead to fatal accidents, such as from self-driving cars, large-scale mishaps are rare. Few domains are so automated that humans cannot step in and correct errors. Stock trading is a rare exception, and machine-driven accidents like flash crashes have come hand in hand with the rise of algorithmic trading.[16] Should militaries automate their forces to a similar degree, perhaps driven by an arms race in speed as was the case in financial markets, then a com-parable accident could result—a flash war.

Once underway, humans may be able to regain control of their systems and shut them down, but the damage could already be too great. An oppo-nent may not be willing to ignore an incident simply because "the machines did it." With passions and tensions inflamed, machine-generated war could give way to a more traditional human war. Or a machine-initiated war could simply subside, a spasm of apolitical violence. Such a concept is not entirely new. In his escalation ladder of levels of war, nuclear strategist Herman Kahn put at the top a "spasm or insensate war," a nuclear strike delivered by virtue of automatic protocols put in place ahead of time by leadership but devoid of considered intent or political purpose. Kahn described such a war as "blind and irrational."[17] War without political purpose is not war as it is traditionally understood, and an insensate war would be of a fundamentally different nature than wars in the past.

Humility in Our Vision of the Future of War

None of these five visions presented above is necessarily likely, but defense thinkers should keep their minds open to the possibility that future technological developments *might* change the nature of war. To believe otherwise is to willfully blind oneself to possible risks. The future is, as always, uncertain. In his essay "War—Continuity in Change, and Change in Continuity," the strategist Colin Gray remarked, "We know everything there is to know about war, unsurprisingly, since we have variable access to at least 2,500 years of bloody history. But we know nothing, literally zero, for certain about the wars of the future, even in the near-term."[18]

Ironically, Gray goes on in his essay to reiterate the claim that the nature of war is immutable. But we cannot know that. Scholars would be well served to keep in mind Gray's observation of our profound uncertainty about the future. For thousands of years, the nature of war—a violent clash of wills between opposing groups of people for political power—has not changed. Might it change in the future? It is possible. Jon Snow's war against the White Walkers is a vivid illustration of the possibility of a war of a fundamentally different nature than wars in the past.

NOTES

1. For example, see Colin S. Gray, "War—Continuity in Change, and Change in Continuity," *Parameters* 40, no. 2 (Summer 2010): 5–13; U.S. Marine Corps, *Warfighting*, Marine Corps Doctrinal Publication 1 (Washington DC: U.S. Government Printing Office, 1997); and Christopher Mewitt, "Understanding War's Enduring Nature alongside Its Changing Character," *War on the Rocks*, January 21, 2014, https://warontherocks.com/2014/01/understanding -wars-enduring-nature-alongside-its-changing-character/.

2. While the political nature of war is taken as an unquestioned assumption in contemporary Western defense circles, it is worth noting that there are dissenting points of view. Historian John Keegan opens his sweeping tome *A History of Warfare* by stating, "War is not the continuation of policy by other means. The world would be a simpler place to understand if this dictum of Clausewitz's were true. . . . War embraces much more than politics: . . . it is

always an expression of culture, often a determinant of cultural forms, in some societies the culture itself." John Keegan, *A History of Warfare* (New York: Alfred A. Knopf, 1993), 3, 12.

3. Carl von Clausewitz, *On War*, trans. James John Graham (London: N. Trübner, 1873), bk. 1, chap. 1, available online at the Clausewitz Homepage, https://www.clausewitz.com/readings /OnWar1873/BK1ch01.html#a.

4. U.S. Marine Corps, *Warfighting*, 3.

5. For example, see H. R. McMaster, "The Pipe Dream of Easy War," *New York Times*, July 20, 2013, https://www.nytimes.com/2013/07/21/opinion/sunday/the-pipe-dream-of-easy-war.html.

6. Thucydides, *The Peloponnesian War*, trans. Richard Crawley (London: J. M. Dent; New York: E. P. Dutton, 1910), bk. 1, chap. 76, online at Perseus, http://www.perseus.tufts.edu/hopper/text?doc= Perseus%3Atext%3A1999.01.0200%3Abook%3D1%3Achapter%3D76%3Asection%3D2.

7. Clausewitz, *On War*, bk. 1, chap. 7.

8. Aaron Mehta, "AI Makes Mattis Question 'Fundamental' Beliefs about War," *C4ISRNET*, February 17, 2018, https://www.c4isrnet.com/intel-geoint/2018/02/17/ai-makes-mattis -question-fundamental-beliefs-about-war/.

9. Clausewitz, *On War*, bk. 1, chap. 1.

10. Sun Tzu, *The Art of War*, trans. Lionel Giles, chap. 1, online at http://classics.mit.edu/Tzu /artwar.html.

11. U.S. Marine Corps, *Warfighting*, 16.

12. U.S. Marine Corps, *Warfighting*, 15.

13. U.S. Marine Corps, *Warfighting*, 10.

14. Dario Amodei et al., "Concrete Problems in AI Safety," preprint, submitted July 25, 2016, 4, https://arxiv.org/pdf/1606.06565.pdf; Stephen M. Omohundro, "The Basic AI Drives," *Self-Aware Systems*, 9, https://selfawaresystems.files.wordpress.com/2008/01/ai_drives _final.pdf; Stuart Russell, "Of Myths and Moonshine," *Edge*, November 14, 2014, https:// www.edge.org/conversation/the-myth-of-ai#26015; and Nick Bostrom, *Superintelligence: Paths, Dangers, Strategies* (Oxford: Oxford University Press, 2014).

15. Associated Press, "McNamara Calls on NATO to Renounce Nuclear Arms," *New York Times*, September 15, 1983, https://www.nytimes.com/1983/09/15/world/mcnamara-calls-on -nato-to-renounce-nuclear-arms.html.

16. U.S. Commodity Futures Trading Commission and U.S. Securities and Exchange Commission, *Findings Regarding the Market Events of May 6, 2010* (Washington DC, September 30, 2010), 2, http://www.sec.gov/news/studies/2010/marketevents-report.pdf; Maureen Farrell, "Mini Flash Crashes: A Dozen a Day," CNNMoney, March 20, 2013, http://money.cnn.com/2013 /03/20/investing/mini-flash-crash/index.html; Matt Egan, "Trading Was Halted 1,200 Times Monday," CNNMoney, August 24, 2015, http://money.cnn.com/2015/08/24/investing /stocks-markets-selloff-circuit-breakers-1200-times/index.html; Todd C. Frankel, "Mini Flash Crash? Trading Anomalies on Manic Monday Hit Small Investors," *Washington Post*, August 26, 2015, https://www.washingtonpost.com/business/economy/mini-flash-crash -trading-anomalies-on-manic-monday-hit-small-investors/2015/08/26/6bdc57b0-4c22 -11e5-bfb9-9736d04fc8e4_story.html?utm_term=.c12bdb13b4e2.

17. Herman Kahn, *On Escalation: Metaphors and Scenarios* (London: Pall Mall, 1965), 194.

18. Gray, "War—Continuity in Change, and Change in Continuity," 5.

Epilogue

Down from the Citadel, Off the Wall

ML CAVANAUGH

What happens when a society is cut off from its wisest and bravest members?

Game of Thrones addresses this very question. When the end-of-the-world threat arrived, those in critical professions were either too self-interested or so far removed that they couldn't connect when it counted.

As the White Walker army continued its ceaseless march south, the amiable Samwell Tarly tried to convince the archmaesters at the Citadel (the unequal-parts Westerosi blend of Harvard, Oxford, and Hogwarts) to wield their considerable intellectual powers to defeat the threat from the undead.[1] Yet instead of helping, a committee of maesters laughed off Tarly's call to academic arms, went back to their dusty books, and essentially decided to leave Westeros without its sharpest minds in the war to come.

Tarly learned of the White Walker threat while in service with the Night's Watch on the Wall. The Night's Watch are the sworn defenders of the realm, stationed on the remote, icy barrier that separates the Seven Kingdoms from the Free Folk (and whatever else threatens from the frigid far north). The Night's Watch was neglected for decades and generations by the rest of Westeros, and over time what began as a legitimate frontier force devolved into a small slice of unfortunates who were involuntarily split off from society and summarily shipped off to serve. And when frightful threats emerged, the Night's Watch sent ravens to warn the rest of Westeros. Nearly nobody listened.

We see some of the same in the real world. Too often, academic experts are unavailable when society needs them the most.[2] Instead of "the Citadel," however, the derisive term we typically use for the place highfalutin academics occupy is "the ivory tower." Or today, expertise itself is questioned.[3] And the military is becoming smaller and smaller and more separated from the rest of society.[4] Here, instead of a "Wall," though, when we describe the distance between civilians and soldiers, academics prefer a term like "the gap."[5]

If anything, *Game of Thrones* can teach us that we must find better ways to come together. In an age when deadly technologies become less expensive and more destructive—insanely cheap and ridiculously powerful—scholars and soldiers must collaborate with society to inform the body politic and help them decide on critical issues of national defense and even, in extreme cases, national survival. And if pop culture is where these groups intersect—where we can find common ground to talk about modern war—then perhaps series like this are indeed more useful than they might otherwise appear.

Of course, the look of a book can deceive. Retired general Stanley McChrystal, former commander of all forces in Afghanistan, wrote recently, "Wisdom is where you find it. Don't be afraid to look in unexpected places."[6] Sometimes, popular fiction, like *Game of Thrones*, can reveal hard truths.

That's because we can use art to teach a thing or three about modern conflict and strategy. When the distinguished Cold War historian John Lewis Gaddis wrote his end-of-career, long-view book on grand strategy, he made heavy use of film and fiction to describe the concept.[7]

Why? Because as authors and screenwriters well know, fiction can make us *feel* in a way that raw data simply cannot. Writer Tim O'Brien has said that he uses stories to tell others about the Vietnam War because fiction can help us experience war as close as possible, to the degree that the reader feels partly in it.[8] This bestows a sense of empathy, says author Dave Eggers, as it "allows us to look through someone else's eyes and know their strivings and struggles."[9]

More than that, art can convey complex ideas about war to democratic societies that must make difficult decisions on dangerous threats. For example, at the dawn of the nuclear age, the famed doomsday clock, which portrayed the impending likelihood of nuclear war as a clock approaching midnight, debuted in 1947 on the first cover of the *Bulletin of the Atomic Scientists*. The clock was designed by the oil painter spouse of one of the magazine's scientist members.[10] That potent, artful image has served the public interest ever since by providing a concise, easy-to-understand mental image of the estimated proximity of nuclear war.

Film and fiction can also predict what's to come and inspire us to meet that future. Novelist and science-fiction writer Ray Bradbury's books *Fahrenheit 451* and *The Martian Chronicles* were well ahead of their time and stimulated his readers to confront the consequences of where those roads might lead.[11]

When it comes to war and strategy, art, film, and fiction can teach us, make us feel, reach others, contemplate what may pass, and even propel us to prepare for the upsides and the downsides to come. That's because war fiction is "not an escape from reality"; as the philosopher Christopher Coker has said, "it animates reality."[12]

And *Game of Thrones* is the series that launched a thousand lessons. A quick query online suggests that the show and books can teach us about subjects as diverse as debt, the workplace, flexible learning, digital marketing, game theory, the Magna Carta, parenting, the "perfect" wedding, and, yes, even the meaning of life.[13]

Of course, whatever the series might offer in the way of helpful hints for matrimonial bliss or rat racing, the truth is that *Game of Thrones*, at its core, is about human conflict. We can see this in the show's incredible scripts, which contain a seemingly endless source of quotations that provoke thought and stimulate debate.

Take the slippery Petyr Baelish, who said, "If war were arithmetic, mathematicians would rule the world."[14]

Other, less important characters also provide quotable wisdom. Braavosi swordsman Syrio Forel, Arya Stark's combat instructor, dispensed this gem:

"Watching is not seeing. That is the heart of true swordplay," an observation as useful for strategy as it is for swordplay.[15]

Maester Aemon Targaryen, learned advisor to the Night's Watch, pointed out that "love is the death of duty," a comment that would likely sting the ear of every warrior who has left home for war.[16]

In a more lighthearted way, every soldier turned parent would nod at Ned Stark's comment that "war was easier than daughters."[17] And even the show's combat sounds and visuals can teach us a bit of always useful trivia, like how many arrows it takes to put down a giant. (The answer is thirty-six, plus a spear.)[18]

Who could forget Tyrion Lannister's mighty wisdom? When he said, "I drink, and I know things," it was funny, but we also took seriously his lifelong commitment to sharpening his truest weapon when he said that "a mind needs books like a sword needs a whetstone."[19]

Likewise, Tyrion's sister, Cersei Lannister, observed that "when you play the game of thrones, you win or you die. There is no middle ground."[20] (One must acknowledge that there are, in fact, exceptions to Cersei's theorem—in pursuit of titles and lands, poor Theon Greyjoy seems to have lived an excruciating nightmare in which he has claimed neither victory nor death . . . yet.) But Cersei's comment is undoubtedly right in at least one way—at war the stakes are high. Indeed, they are the highest, both in our world and in the *Game of Thrones* universe. This fact alone should keep us glued to the lessons of modern war embedded in the strategic storytelling in *Game of Thrones*.

First, we should remember that all war is relative. Strategy is always practiced against some competitive enemy or within a cruel environment. In short, there is always some opposing force, and so there is no such thing as "good" or "bad" strategy.[21] There is only "superior" or "inferior" strategy, because we're constantly made to measure our relative performance against our opposition. Translated into *Game of Thrones* speak, it is of no use to look at Daenerys Targaryen or Jon Snow in isolation—you've always got to measure their performance against their opponent(s).

Second, mind the map.[22] Geostrategy is the relationship between force and space—or as the scholar James Kurth has put it, where history, geography, and culture intersect, the "realities and mentalities of the localities."[23]

The importance of geostrategy has been hammered into viewers every time the show's opening credits fly across the map of all the contending factions and warring parties. If, as the adage goes, "where you stand depends on where you sit," then in *Game of Thrones* how you fight depends on where you're from. The Northerners do well in winter weather, while the Baratheon and Lannister (or southern) armies struggle in the frost. And the Dothraki horsemen, content to raid and ride across Essos, have never considered crossing the Narrow Sea into Westeros (that is, until they meet a certain khaleesi). Each distinct group of people thinks differently, fights differently, and thinks about fighting differently—which is why they could be said to have distinct strategic cultures.[24]

We also see the role of chance and contingency at war—the iron law of unintended consequences. These are the factors beyond one's own control. For example, it's clear that Cersei did not intend to kill Ned Stark, yet her son Joffrey's decision to execute the Stark patriarch set in motion a series of events that shook all of Westeros and ultimately resulted in Cersei's unlikely ascension to the Iron Throne.

Nobody is safe, and "once you realize that heroes die," as *Game of Thrones* showrunner David Benioff has said, "everything becomes that much more terrifying."[25] So it goes in modern war.

Distant events that matter greatly to us all are happening all the time, hidden by the limited range of our own view. Consider the average Westerosi citizen, minding her own business as a shopkeeper in King's Landing. Just think about all the far-flung occurrences that are coming together from all directions to impact her life.

From the north the White Walkers and Free Folk from beyond the Wall now head her way. From the south, in Dorne, vengeful plotters threaten to shake up the kingdom. From the east rises Daenerys and her dragons, and from the west the berserk Euron Greyjoy commands an immense fleet of Iron Islanders to accompany his sizable appetite for pillaging. All the while, at home, just up the hill at the Red Keep, Cersei considers the destruction of all those ill-intentioned comers.

For our unsuspecting shopkeeper, this multidirectional gathering storm is certain to have some sort of impact. In our world, we should take heed the shopkeeper's predicament—the farthest clouds may yet bring the most lightning, thunder, and rain to our own lives.

These principal lessons from this "reel" war, especially its visual aspects, have been molded by some true creative genius. Showrunners D. B. Weiss and David Benioff have shepherded the HBO series from a relative success to a global cultural phenomenon that demands discussion, and they ought to be commended for their efforts in so doing.

Even more credit is due to author George R. R. Martin, who originally envisioned and wrote this series. Martin said that he is "fascinated by war" and pointed out that armed struggle "brings out the best and worst in people."[26] In that same interview, Martin also said, "Literature of the past used to celebrate the glory of war; then the hippie generation in the 1970s wrote about the ugliness of it. I think there's truth in both." He's right. War can be both dark and beautiful, and he has shown both sides of the war coin.

There's an irony to Martin's success in propagating so many lessons about war. The series that has inspired millions to learn a little something about war was conceived by someone who sat out the biggest conflict of his own youth. Though he is not and never was a pacifist (he's always felt "that sometimes war is necessary"), Martin asked for and was awarded conscientious-objector status during the Vietnam War and chose alternate national public service in Chicago during that war.[27]

With *Game of Thrones*, George R. R. Martin and Weiss and Benioff have brought war and human conflict into the homes of many millions. They've used art to fuse entertainment and education in a way that has brought in multitudes of fans to watch the course of one long struggle and war. And while Martin may have chosen to sit Vietnam out, he merits some recognition for his service to the public in this creative endeavor.

He's given those of us locked away in the Citadel or stuck far atop the Wall the opportunity to come down from our high-up and far-off places, to connect with society again, to talk about the threats to come in our real world.

He's reminded us that winter always returns.

And to win in Westeros, as in our world, we'll need all the help we can get.

NOTES

1. Dave Hill, "Eastwatch," season 7, episode 5, dir. Matt Shakman, *Game of Thrones*, aired August 13, 2017, on HBO.

2. Nicholas Kristof, "Professors, We Need You!" *New York Times*, February 15, 2014, https://www.nytimes.com/2014/02/16/opinion/sunday/kristof-professors-we-need-you.html.

3. See Tom Nichols, *The Death of Expertise: The Campaign against Established Knowledge and Why It Matters* (Oxford: Oxford University Press, 2017).

4. See James Golby and Hugh Liebert, "Midlife Crisis? The All-Volunteer Force at 40," *Armed Forces and Society* 43, no. 1 (2016), 115–38; Conrad Cranes, "The Future Soldier: Alone in a Crowd," *War on the Rocks*, January 19, 2017, https://warontherocks.com/2017/01/the-future-soldier-alone-in-a-crowd/.

5. See Kori Schake and Jim Mattis, eds., *Warriors and Citizens: American Views of Our Military* (Stanford CA: Hoover Institution Press, 2016).

6. Stanley McChrystal, foreword to *Strategy Strikes Back: How Star Wars Explains Modern Military Conflict*, ed. Max Brooks, John Amble, ML Cavanaugh, and Jaym Gates (Lincoln: University of Nebraska Press, 2018), xii.

7. John Lewis Gaddis, *On Grand Strategy* (New York: Penguin Press, 2018), 17. Gaddis glowingly cites screenwriter Tony Kushner's take on strategy in Kushner's work on the script of the 2012 film *Lincoln*, when one character asks President Abraham Lincoln how Lincoln can reconcile a righteous aim with less-than-lofty methods. In Kushner's words, the character Lincoln recalls his younger days as a surveyor: "[A] compass . . . [will] point you true north from where you're standing, but it's got no advice about the swamps and deserts and chasms that you'll encounter along the way. If in pursuit of your destination, you plunge ahead, heedless of obstacles, and achieve nothing more than to sink in a swamp . . . [then] what's the use of knowing true north?"

8. Tim O'Brien, "War and Literary Fiction," Pritzker Military Library and Museum, November 3, 2017, https://www.pritzkermilitary.org/files/8915/1922/7865/2017_Symposium_Tim_OBrien_transcript.pdf.

9. Dave Eggers, "A Cultural Vacuum," *New York Times*, June 29, 2018, https://www.nytimes.com/2018/06/29/opinion/dave-eggers-culture-arts-trump.html.

10. Rachel Bronson, "Can We Turn Back the Hands of the 'Doomsday Clock'?" Commonwealth Club of California, YouTube video, 1:05:46, June 13, 2018, https://www.commonwealthclub.org/events/2018-06-13/bulletin-atomic-scientists-ceo-rachel-bronson-can-we-turn-back-hands-doomsday.

11. See Ray Bradbury, *Ray Bradbury: The Last Interview*, ed. Sam Weller (London: Melville House, 2014), 4–6. In *Fahrenheit 451*, published in 1953, Bradbury envisioned earbuds, flat-screen televisions, extreme school violence, and the fall of the American newspaper. In the same interview, Bradbury alluded to the fact that the earliest American astronauts read *The Martian Chronicles* and were inspired by his book to explore space.

12. Christopher Coker, "Men at War: What Fiction Tells Us about War," Oxford University, *Changing Character of War*, podcast, MP3 audio, 54:23, October 28, 2013, http://podcasts.ox .ac.uk/men-war-what-fiction-tells-us-about-war.

13. Using the Google search engine, the author performed web searches for *"Game of Thrones"* and each of these subjects on June 1, 2018, finding relevant content for each.

14. Vanessa Taylor, "Garden of Bones," season 2, episode 4, dir. David Petrarca, *Game of Thrones*, aired April 22, 2012, on HBO.

15. George R. R. Martin, "The Pointy End," season 1, episode 8, dir. Daniel Minahan, *Game of Thrones*, aired June 5, 2011, on HBO.

16. David Benioff and D. B. Weiss, "The Watchers on the Wall," season 4, episode 9, dir. Neil Marshall, *Game of Thrones*, aired June 8, 2014, on HBO.

17. David Benioff and D. B. Weiss, "Lord Snow," season 1, episode 3, dir. Brian Kirk, *Game of Thrones*, aired May 1, 2011, on HBO. See also ML Cavanaugh, "Sixteen Lessons on War from a Three-Year-Old," Modern War Institute, August 27, 2014, https://mwi.usma.edu/2014827sixteen -lessons-about-war-from-a-three-year-old/.

18. David Benioff and D. B. Weiss, "Battle of the Bastards," season 6, episode 9, dir. Miguel Sapochnik, *Game of Thrones*, aired June 19, 2016, on HBO. Using the highly sophisticated, advanced technological approach of freeze-framing this episode at 53:29, just after the giant has crashed through the front gate of Winterfell, one can see that the giant has twenty-five arrows embedded in his body at that moment. Ten more are then fired into the giant's massive frame, in addition to a spear that pierces his hand. That makes thirty-five arrows, and the thirty-sixth and final arrow is Ramsay Bolton's into the giant's eye.

19. George R. R. Martin, "Blackwater," season 2, episode 9, dir. Neil Marshall, *Game of Thrones*, aired May 27, 2012, on HBO; David Benioff and D. B. Weiss, "The Kingsroad," season 1, episode 2, dir. Tim Van Patten, *Game of Thrones*, aired April 24, 2011, on HBO.

20. David Benioff and D. B. Weiss, "You Win or You Die," season 1, episode 7, dir. Daniel Minahan, *Game of Thrones*, aired May 29, 2011, on HBO.

21. Steven Jermy, "Strategy for Action: Using Force Wisely in the 21st Century," Oxford University, *Ethics, Law and Armed Conflict*, podcast, MP3 audio, 41:30, October 26, 2011, http://podcasts .ox.ac.uk/strategy-action-using-force-wisely-21st-century.

22. See "The Geopolitics of Ice and Fire," *Geopolitical Futures*, April 1, 2017, https://geopoliticalfutures .com/geopolitics-ice-fire/.

23. James Kurth, quoted in Ronald J. Granieri, "What Is Geopolitics and Why Does It Matter?" Foreign Policy Research Institute, YouTube video, 1:00:51, February 25, 2015, https://www .fpri.org/multimedia/2015/02/what-is-geopolitics-and-why-does-it-matter/.

24. "Strategic culture" refers to the "beliefs and assumptions that frame" a particular country or culture's attitudes toward war. Stephen Peter Rosen, quoted in Jeffrey S. Lantis and Darryl Howlett, "Strategic Culture," in *Strategy in the Contemporary World: An Introduction to Strategic*

Studies, ed. John Baylis, James J. Wirtz, and Colin S. Gray, 4th ed. (Oxford: Oxford University Press, 2013), 80.

25. D. B. Weiss and David Benioff, "Game of Thrones Interview: DB Weiss and David Benioff," interview by Ed Cumming, *Telegraph*, April 10, 2012, https://www.telegraph.co.uk/culture /tvandradio/game-of-thrones/9195683/Game-of-Thrones-interview-db-Weiss-and-David -Benioff.html.

26. George R. R. Martin, "Game of Thrones: Interview with George RR Martin," interview by Jessica Salter, *Telegraph*, March 25, 2013, https://www.telegraph.co.uk/culture/tvandradio /game-of-thrones/9945808/Game-of-Thrones-Interview-with-George-rr-Martin.html.

27. Martin, "Interview with George RR Martin."

CONTRIBUTORS

JOHN AMBLE is the editorial director at the Modern War Institute at West Point and codirector of the Urban Warfare Project. A military intelligence officer in the U.S. Army Reserve, he is a veteran of the wars in Iraq and Afghanistan. He holds a BA from the University of Minnesota and an MA in intelligence and international security from King's College London.

J. DANIEL BATT is a writer, artist, and futurist. He serves as creative and editorial director for 100 Year Starship, creating visual engagement for 100YSS programs and activities. He also serves as a lead researcher with Deep Space Predictive, focusing on developing tools and systems to ensure success in human group dynamics on deep space missions. His books include the novel *Young Gods: A Door into Darkness* (Sacramento CA: Storyjitsu, 2015) and the children's book series *The Tales of Dreamside*. His short fiction has been published in *Bastion Science Fiction Magazine*, *Bewildering Stories*, and other periodicals. He edited the science fiction anthology *Visions of the Future*, published through Lifeboat Foundation, and is coeditor of the anthology *Strange California* (Charlotte NC: Falstaff Books, 2017).

LIONEL BEEHNER is an assistant professor at the Modern War Institute at West Point and teaches courses on military innovation and research methods. He holds a PhD in political science from Yale University and is formerly a fellow at the Truman

National Security Project; a member of the *USA Today* Board of Contributors; and a term member with the Council on Foreign Relations, where from 2005 to 2007 he worked as a senior staff writer for its award-winning website, cfr.org. He holds an MA in international affairs from Columbia University. His research examines the transnational nature of conflict and combat, civil-military relations, and limited military interventions. His writing has appeared in *Orbis*, the *Atlantic*, *Foreign Affairs*, the *New York Times*, the *Washington Post*, the *National Interest*, and the *New Republic*, among other publications.

BENEDETTA BERTI is a foreign policy and security researcher, analyst, lecturer, and author. She got her BA in Oriental studies at the University of Bologna and achieved her MA and PhD in international relations at the Fletcher School at Tufts University. She has written four books and was awarded the Order of the Star of Italy in 2015. Her work has been published in *Al-Jazeera*, *Foreign Policy*, *Foreign Affairs*, the *New York Times*, the *Daily Beast*, and the *Wall Street Journal*. While being both a TED senior fellow and an Eisenhower global fellow, Berti has also maintained positions at West Point, the Institute for National Security Studies, the Foreign Policy Research Institute, and Harvard University. She is currently a lecturer at Tel Aviv University and was appointed as a member of the Commission on the Study of Radicalization in 2016 by the Italian government.

CHUCK BIES is an armor officer in the U.S. Army. He serves as study manager for the Army Science Board and holds a BS in engineering from Duke University and an MA in diplomacy and military studies from Hawaii Pacific University. He previously served as an assistant professor in the Department of History at the U.S. Military Academy. He won the 2016 Gen. George S. Patton Award at the U.S. Army Command and General Staff School as the best tactician in his class of 1,300.

JONATHAN BOTT is special assistant to the commander in the Fourth Fighter Wing at Seymour Johnson Air Force Base in Goldsboro, North Carolina. He has five combat deployments in the F-15E Strike Eagle. Lieutenant Colonel Bott received his master's degree from the U.S. Army School of Advanced Military Studies.

MAX BROOKS is an author, public speaker, nonresident fellow at the Modern War Institute, and senior resident fellow at the Atlantic Council's Art of Future Warfare Project. He is the author of *World War Z* (New York: Three Rivers Press, 2006) and *The Harlem Hellfighters* (New York: Broadway Books, 2014).

JOE BYERLY is an armor officer and recently served as a special advisor within U.S. Special Operations Command. He received his bachelor's degree from the University of North Georgia and his master's degree from the U.S. Naval War College. He is a nonresident fellow at the Modern War Institute at West Point and the founder of From the Green Notebook, a website emphasizing military leadership and professional development. His writings have been published in *War on the Rocks*, ARMY magazine, *Strategy Bridge*, and *Small Wars Journal*.

ML CAVANAUGH is a U.S. Army strategist with global experience in assignments ranging from the Pentagon to Korea and Iraq to Army Space and Missile Defense Command. A nonresident fellow with the Modern War Institute at West Point, he has written for the *New York Times*, *Washington Post*, and *Wall Street Journal*, among other publications. For more, visit MLCavanaugh.com.

KELSEY CIPOLLA is a writer and editor who has covered topics ranging from food and fashion to nonprofits and social issues. She is currently the communications coordinator at the University of Kansas School of Business and a writer for *In Kansas City* magazine.

LIAM COLLINS is a career Special Forces officer who has served in a variety of special operations assignments and conducted numerous combat operations in Afghanistan and Iraq as well as operational deployments to Bosnia, Africa, and South America. He is a graduate of numerous military courses, including Ranger School, and his military awards and decorations include two valorous awards for actions in combat. He is the director of the Modern War Institute at West Point and previously served as the director of the Combating Terrorism Center at West Point. He has a BS in mechanical engineering from the U.S. Military Academy and an MPA and PhD from the Woodrow Wilson School at Princeton University.

MICK COOK is an Australian writer, digital content producer, and veteran of the war in Afghanistan. He hosts *The Dead Prussian* podcast and is passionate about encouraging critical thought on war among military professionals, policy makers, and the wider community.

JONATHAN E. CZARNECKI is currently a professor of joint maritime operations at the Naval War College in Monterey, California. He is a retired U.S. Army and Army National Guard colonel with more than twenty-seven years of experience in the field and on staff. He received his MA and PhD in political science and applied social statistics from the State University of New York at Buffalo and his BS in social sciences–industrial management from Clarkson University. He has published numerous articles on the topics of joint operations, organizational behavior, and operational art.

GREGORY S. DROBNY was an Airborne Infantryman at 6th Ranger Training Battalion, a private security contractor in Central America, and a psychological operations team chief during Operating Iraq Freedom; he currently works as an assistant operations manager and range marshal at Makhaira Group. He holds a BA in history and an MS in organizational psychology, has written extensively for *The Rhino Den* and *Unapologetically American*, and contributed to *War Stories: New Military Science Fiction* (Lexington KY: Apex, 2014) and *Redeployed: How Combat Veteran Can Fight the Battle Within and Win the War at Home* (Dallas TX: Frisco House, 2013). He currently blogs at *Havok Journal*.

JAYM GATES has spent a decade as a science fiction editor, game developer, and author, with over a dozen anthologies and more than fifty published short pieces of fiction and nonfiction to her credit. She is a coeditor of *War Stories: New Military Science Fiction* (Lexington KY: Apex, 2014) with Andrew Liptak, has judged writing contests for the Atlantic Council, managed media relations for Uplift Aeronautics/ Syria Airlift Project, helped develop a crisis simulation role-playing game for Harrisburg University, and is a juror for the Canopus Award for Interstellar Fiction.

ANDREA N. GOLDSTEIN is an officer in the U.S. Navy Reserve and a nonresident fellow at the Modern War Institute at West Point. A nonprofit leader, military strategist, and veterans' advocate, she has published widely, with bylines in the *New York Times*, *Task & Purpose*, *Proceedings*, the *Fletcher Forum of World Affairs*, *War Horse*, and *Business Insider*, and with reports for the Center for a New American Security, Joint Special Operations University, and the *International Feminist Journal of Politics*. Andrea is a Pat Tillman Scholar and holds a master of arts degree in law and diplomacy from the Fletcher School at Tufts University and a bachelor's degree in history and classics from the University of Chicago. She lives in upstate New York.

ANDREW A. HILL is the chair of strategic leadership at the U.S. Army War College and founder and editor-in-chief of *War Room*, the Army War College's online journal. His research focuses on strategy and innovation in organizations. He received his doctorate in management from Harvard Business School.

THERESA HITCHENS is a senior research associate for the Center for International and Security Studies at the University of Maryland, where she focuses on space security, cyber security, and governance issues surrounding disruptive technologies. From 2009 through 2014 Hitchens was the director of the United Nations Institute for Disarmament Research Geneva. A former journalist, she spent eleven years at *Defense News* covering issues ranging from U.S. Air Force programs to arms-control treaties; she served as editor from 1998 to 2000.

ERICA IVERSON is a U.S. Army strategist with a range of strategic career assignments spanning the globe in Asia, Europe, and the Middle East. An experienced speechwriter for several U.S. Army four-star commands with combat deployments to both Afghanistan and Iraq, she recently completed a year serving in the U.S. consulate in Jerusalem. She is presently assigned to the Pentagon.

MIKE JACKSON is a lieutenant colonel in the U.S. Army. He holds a master of arts degree in liberal studies, with a concentration in international affairs, from Georgetown University and a master of military arts and science degree from the U.S. Army Command and General Staff College. Lieutenant Colonel Jackson has combat experience spanning the levels of platoon, company, brigade, division, and corps, during five deployments to Afghanistan and Iraq as an infantry officer and U.S. Army strategist (FA-59). He has also served with the chief of staff of the U.S. Army's Strategic Studies Group, in an interagency fellowship as the special advisor for manufacturing policy to the U.S. secretary of commerce, and as deputy director of the Modern War Institute at West Point. His areas of academic interest are international affairs and security studies.

MICHAEL JUNGE is a surface warfare officer and served afloat in USS *Moosbrugger* (DD 980), USS *Underwood* (FFG 36), USS *Wasp* (LHD 1), and USS *The Sullivans* (DDG 68) and was the fourteenth commanding officer of USS *Whidbey Island* (LSD 41). He also served with U.S. Navy Recruiting, Assault Craft Unit Four, the Office of the Secretary of Defense, Headquarters Marine Corps, and as the deputy chief of naval operations for communication networks (N6). He is the author of numerous articles that have been published in the U.S. Naval Institute's *Proceedings* magazine, as well as a monograph on command responsibility, *Crimes of Command.*

JONATHAN P. KLUG is a U.S. Army strategist. He has extensive overseas experience, and he taught military and naval history at the U.S. Air Force Academy and at the U.S. Naval Academy. Currently, he is in the U.S. Army War College Professor Program and a PhD candidate at the University of New Brunswick.

NINA A. KOLLARS is an associate professor in the U.S. Naval War College's Strategic and Operational Research Department and a published researcher and writer with a specific concentration on cyber security and military innovation. She is currently an editorial board member for the *Special Operations Journal.* Her work has been included in various publications, such as the *Palgrave Handbook of Security* and the *Special Operations Journal.* She is also a member of the Committee for the Analysis of Military Operations and Strategy.

STEVE LEONARD is an author, a speaker, and currently the director of the graduate program in business and organizational leadership at the University of Kansas. After serving for twenty-eight years in the in the U.S. Army, he made a career in writing and speaking and is the cofounder of Divergent Options and a founding member of the Military Writers Guild. An alumnus at the School of Advanced Military Studies, he led the interagency team that authored the U.S. Army's first stability operations doctrine and penned the doctrinal principles for the army design methodology. His writings on foreign policy, strategy, and leadership have been published numerous times, and he is currently the author of four books.

BRYAN MCGRATH is the founding managing director of the FerryBridge Group, specialists who concentrate primarily on naval and national security issues, including national and military strategy, strategic planning, and executive communications. After twenty-one years of service, he is now a retired U.S. Navy officer. McGrath is the deputy director of the Hudson Institute's Center for American Seapower. He is also a published commentator in the fields of national and maritime strategy.

RICK MONTCALM is a lieutenant colonel in the U.S. Army; he most recently served as the deputy director of the Modern War Institute at West Point and is currently a PhD student at Vanderbilt University. He received a master's degree in policy management from Georgetown University and a bachelor of fine arts degree from Austin Peay State University. Before his West Point assignment, Lieutenant Colonel Montcalm served as an executive officer in the U.S. Army TRADOC Command Group, following his key developmental assignments as a squadron executive officer and an executive officer in the First Brigade of the 101st Airborne Division. He has also been on armor, Stryker, and infantry brigade combat teams with positions held in Iraq and Afghanistan.

MAGNUS F. NORDENMAN is a writer, speaker, and noted NATO and maritime affairs expert. He has served, among other positions, as the deputy director of the Brent Scowcroft Center on International Security at the Atlantic Council in Washington DC. He graduated from the Virginia Military Institute and the University of Kentucky. He is the author of *The New Battle for the Atlantic: Emerging Naval Competition with Russia in the Far North* (Annapolis MD: Naval Institute Press, 2019).

JOSHUA D. POWERS is an infantry officer in the U.S. Army and founder of *The Field Grade Leader*, a blog focused on organizational leadership in the military. Captain Powers has been in the U.S. Army for nearly fifteen years. He received a bachelor's degree in history from the Virginia Military Institute and a master's degree in military art and science through the School of Advanced Military Studies. Josh is currently assigned to the headquarters of U.S. Army Pacific in Hawaii, where he serves as an operational planner.

MICK RYAN is an Australian Army officer and currently commands the Australian Defence College in Canberra. A distinguished graduate of Johns Hopkins University, the U.S. Marine Corps Staff College, and the U.S. Marine Corps School of Advanced Warfare, he is a passionate advocate of professional education and lifelong learning.

PAUL SCHARRE is a senior fellow and the director of the Technology and National Security Program at the Center for a New American Security. He is the author of *Army of None: Autonomous Weapons and the Future of War* (New York: W. W. Norton and Company, 2018), and his articles have been published by the *New York Times*, CNN, *Time*, Fox News, *Foreign Affairs*, and various other media outlets. He is a term member of the Council on Foreign Relations. He received his MA in political economy and public policy and a BS in physics from Washington University in St. Louis.

P. W. SINGER is a strategist at the New America Foundation and professor at Arizona State University. He was recognized by the Smithsonian as one of the nation's one hundred leading innovators and by Defense News as one of the one hundred most influential people in defense issues. He has written award-winning books, including *Corporate Warriors: The Rise of the Privatized Military Industry* (Ithaca NY: Cornell University Press, 2003); *Children at War* (Berkeley: University of California Press, 2006); *Wired for War: The Robotics Revolution and Conflict in the 21st Century* (New York: Penguin, 2009); *Cybersecurity and Cyberwar: What Everyone Needs to Know* (Oxford: Oxford University Press, 2014), with Allan Friedman; *Ghost Fleet: A Novel of the Next World War* (Boston: Mariner Books, 2016), with August Cole; and *LikeWar: The Weaponization of Social Media* (Boston: Houghton Mifflin Harcourt, 2018). He has held positions at the Office of the Secretary of Defense, *Popular Science*, and Harvard University and was the founding director of the Center for 21st Century Security and Intelligence at Brookings.

JOHN SPENCER is a retired U.S. Army infantry major currently serving as the chair of urban warfare studies at the Modern War Institute at West Point. He served over twenty-five years in the U.S. Army, including two combat deployments to Iraq. An expert on urban warfare, his writing has appeared in the *New York Times*, the *Wall Street Journal*, *Politico*, *Foreign Policy*, and other publications.

ADM. (RET.) JAMES STAVRIDIS is the twelfth and current dean of the Fletcher School of Law and Diplomacy at Tufts University. He served in the U.S. Navy for more than thirty years and retired in 2013 after completing a four-year tour as supreme allied commander of NATO. He has published six books, including most recently *The Leader's Bookshelf* (Annapolis MD: Naval Institute Press, 2017) with R. Manning Ancell and *Sea Power: The History and Geopolitics of the World's Oceans* (New York: Penguin, 2017). He received his PhD from the Fletcher School. He tweets at @stavridisj.

JESS WARD is an Australian Army officer in the Royal Australian Electrical and Mechanical Engineers. She is currently serving as an instructor at the Royal Military College at Duntroon and has over ten years of military experience, both in Australia and on operations in the Middle East. Jess is the founder and chief editor of the Junior Officers' Book Shelf.

CRAIG WHITESIDE is an associate professor at the Naval War College, where he teaches national security affairs to military officers as part of their professional military education. He is a fellow at the International Centre for Counter-terrorism–The Hague. Whiteside's current research focuses on the Islamic State's grand strategy and military doctrine. A graduate of the U.S. Military Academy at West Point, he has a PhD in political science from Washington State University and is a former U.S. Army officer with combat experience in Iraq.